Pluralism by the Rules

Conflict and Cooperation in Environmental Regulation

American Governance and Public Policy

A SERIES EDITED BY

Barry Rabe and John Tierney

This series examines a broad range of public policy issues and their relationship to all levels of government in the United States. The editors welcome serious scholarly studies and seek to publish books that appeal to both academic and professional audiences. The series showcases studies that illuminate the successes, as well as the problems, of policy formulation and implementation.

Pluralism by the Rules;
Conflict and Cooperation in Environmental Regulation.

Edward P. Weber

GEORGETOWN UNIVERSITY PRESS / WASHINGTON, D.C.

Georgetown University Press, Washington, D.C. 20007
© 1998 by Georgetown University Press. All rights reserved.

10 9 8 7 6 5 4 3 2 1   1998

THIS VOLUME IS PRINTED ON ACID-FREE ⊗ OFFSET BOOK PAPER

Library of Congress Cataloging-in-Publication Data

Weber, Edward P.
    Pluralism by the rules : conflict and cooperation in environmental
regulation / by Edward P. Weber.
        p.   cm.—(American governance and public policy)
    Includes index.
    1. Environmental policy—United States. 2. Environmental
management—United States. 3. Pluralism. 4. Environmental law—
Economic aspects—United States. I. Title. II. Series.
GE180.W43   1998
363.7'00973—dc21
ISBN 0-87840-671-9 (cloth)
ISBN 0-87840-672-7 (pbk.)   97-37976

For my wife and soulmate,
Andrea Heyliger Weber,
a woman who has shaped my being, shared my life, and
taught me the meaning of unconditional love.

For my mother,
Carol Layne Weber,
wise, kind, giving, gentle, and
always willing to listen—thank you.

Contents

Contents

Preface

Part way through the research on this book, I visited the World Wide Web, in particular the website for *High Country News*. As many students of environmental and natural resource issues can attest, *High Country News* is a useful, twice-monthly compilation of information about the status of environmental issues in the Western United States. Surfing through their database, I happened upon a special issue devoted to the burgeoning use of consensus-based decision-making processes in Western natural resources policy. The combination of articles, as well as ensuing letters to the editor responding to the special issue, encapsulate the many divergent views on collaborative endeavors in the voices of the warrior–zealot, the skeptic–naysayer, and the (ex-warrior) pragmatist–optimist. The first two "voices"—the warrior–zealot and the skeptic–naysayer—weave a tale that is familiar to scholars and practitioners in the fields of political science, public policy, and public administration. The voice of the (ex-warrior) pragmatist–optimist is another matter; it is often ignored. Yet it is the voice of the pragmatist–optimist that captures the dynamic of the pluralism-by-the-rules framework that is the heart of this book, in terms of both why collaboration emerges when it does and the possibilities for successful governance arrangements flowing from collaborative endeavors.

Steve Kelly, the director of both the Friends of the Wild Swan and the Montana Ecosystems Defense Council, is the warrior–zealot who thrives on no-holds-barred combat, often in the form of litigation. To Kelly, such an approach to policy issues and decisions is the best and perhaps the only legitimate way to protect one's interests, especially in the face of what he views as a political system that is primarily responsive to profit-oriented economic elites who care little for environmental protection. In *High Country News*, the warrior–zealot focuses his ire on a collaborative effort involving the U. S. Forest Service, the timber industry, and national environmental groups. The various stakeholders are trying to hammer out an agreement for reintroducing grizzlies to Idaho's Selway–Bitterroot Wilderness in order to strengthen the area's biodiversity. The reintroduction would be managed by a citizens' committee composed of the same cross section of interests.

Kelly rejects the attempt to resolve the problem of ecosystem integrity through collaboration, calling it "the biggest sham that's ever been promoted in the northern Rockies," and claiming that when environmentalists "crawl into bed with the enemy, [they] become the enemy." Instead, the warrior–zealot does what he has done for the past two decades—initiates a lawsuit to stop the consensus-based plan from being put into action—and then boasts that "I'm filing more lawsuits than ever before . . . [because] foot-rubbing sessions with the timber industry . . . [and] seances with miners [are] . . . crap [that] doesn't work here" (Jones 1996, 3).

Michael McCloskey, chairman of the Sierra Club,[1] is the skeptic–naysayer who sounds the alarm over the dangers collaboration poses for democracy. McCloskey (1996) reviews the supposed benefits of community-level or place-based collaboration in the realm of environmental policy, but dismisses them as utopian ideals that ignore both history and current political reality. Instead of "empower[ing] . . . communities that were formerly kept in a submissive position by agency bureaucracies," collaboration is more likely to "totally disempower" those citizens not represented by organized interests (pp. 2, 3). Instead of better policy solutions that will be more sustainable, the skeptic–naysayer sees "[o]nly lowest common denominator ideas surviv[ing] the process" (p. 3). In fact, McCloskey argues that the emergence of collaboration as a substitute for conflict is nothing more than a subtle plan by industry to disenfranchise environmental advocates and "maximize the influence of those [economic elites and representatives from extractive industries] who are least attracted to the environmental cause and most alienated from it. . . . Industry thinks its odds are better in [collaborative] forums. It is ready to train its experts in mastering this process. It believes it can dominate them over time . . ." (pp. 2, 3). Further, there is the danger that environmentalists, by devoting "too much time" to consensus-based forums, may unwittingly succeed in "demobilizing and disarming our side" (p. 3), thus giving industry the clear path it needs to undo the hard-fought victories of national environmental advocates over the past several decades. The skeptic–naysayer's fear is palpable. Today's collaborative forums are reminiscent of the time when mining, logging, grazing, water development, and other economic interests controlled congressional committees, government agencies, and ultimately public policy outcomes which tended to reflect industry's own narrow, private interests, and which frequently excluded environmental protection from consideration.

A succinct summary for the first two voices might read as follows. Not only is conflict preferred and ubiquitous, given the prevalence of conflict, collaboration is unlikely to succeed. Moreover, eschewing

conflict for cooperation is un-American precisely because it is dangerous for democracy.

Stacked against these voices are the (exwarrior) pragmatist–
optimists like Daniel Kemmis, the mayor of Missoula, Montana; Dan
Daggett of Arizona; and the Applegate Partnership, an ecosystem-
based collaborative effort in southwestern Oregon. Kemmis points to
the limited capacity of centralized, federal management and the conflict-based, "us versus them" approaches adopted by ideologues on
both sides of environmental issues as nothing more than a prelude to
hard-fought, yet temporary victories (Jones 1996, 2). Daggett not only
finds hope in alternative consensus-based mechanisms, seeing them as
harbingers of progress in the battle against environmental degradation;
he decries the futility of conventional politics, lawsuits, and, by implication, traditional administrative arrangements used to manage the environment. Explains Daggett,

> [t]hat's why . . . when it's time for the biennial bloodletting we call elec-
> tions, I won't be leafleting neighborhoods, calling voters or putting up
> signs. I'll be out in the world of trees and grass and bugs and streams.
> Sleeves rolled up, I'll be with one of a number of groups of ranchers,
> vegetarians, wise-users, and Earth First!ers I've been working with for a
> couple of years now. Together, we'll be celebrating small successes that
> can be measured in green meadows, healing riparian areas and increased
> biodiversity. . . . I had been a soldier in the environmental wars for so
> long—22 years—I had forgotten how uplifting it is to be part of a group
> of people who don't paint the world in shades of guilt and look for
> someone to blame. . . . And we get better results than the politicians do
> when they try to solve our problems for us (Daggett 1995, 1–2).

Daggett then goes on to describe the successes of the Toiyabe Wetlands
and Watersheds Management Team in Nevada and the Malpai Border-
lands Group in New Mexico and Arizona. The Applegate Partnership,
in a direct response to McCloskey's skepticism, makes the case for
collaboration as a vehicle for community empowerment. Collaborative
arrangements work within the larger framework of national laws, not
in lieu of them, to prevent degradation, to provide long-term, holistic
solutions to complex local problems, and to enhance the degree of local
oversight and implementation expertise. From Applegate's perspective, collaboration is a way to customize one-size-fits-all national laws
to the particular conditions of individual ecosystems and communities
(Applegate Partnership 1996).

When it comes to the subject of collaboration among diverse, opposed interests in American politics, the voices of the warrior–zealot
and the skeptic–naysayer are mirrored in the conventional wisdom of

the political science, public policy, and public administration literature. The dominance of these two voices leaves little opportunity for the third voice, that of the pragmatist–optimist, to be heard. In fact, it is probably not an overstatement to say that the theme of ubiquitous conflict evoked by the warrior–zealot is accepted as part of the folklore of American life. The American political system is famous for its adversarial political culture, a fragmented interest-group system, and the "openness" provided by separate institutions, checks and balances, and federalism.[2] Bitter, adversarial relations between stakeholders are the norm, whether in terms of business versus environmentalists, business versus government, environmentalists versus government, federal versus state interests, Reaganite conservatives versus proenvironment Democrats, or congressional attitudes toward the bureaucracy.[3] The fragmentation of policy interests through large numbers of single-issue interest groups complicates cooperative endeavors by making it harder to include a full cross section of disparate interests in policy solutions (G. Wilson 1981). The system of separated powers, with its multiple checks and balances, then provides losers in policy battles with ample opportunity to vent their grievances elsewhere in the policy process, often to the effect of stopping policy from being implemented (Rabe 1988). The combination of fragmented, opposed interests and separated powers means that success requires the maintenance of a coalition through the entirety of the policy process. This is infinitely harder to do than mounting an opposing coalition for the purposes of blocking policies you dislike. And unlike European democracies, the U.S. political system has done little to establish institutions for the express purpose of facilitating collaboration toward common national policy goals (Badaracco 1985). Each component raises the collective action threshold, thereby leading to the conclusion that not only is collaboration unexpected, it is virtually impossible to initiate, much less sustain to a successful conclusion. Moreover, developments over the past thirty years have only made policy making more open, fragmented, and conflictual, particularly in national pollution control politics.[4]

The skeptic–naysayer is also echoed in the larger literature in political science, public policy, and public administration with the following theme: although collaboration is difficult to achieve, it can and does occur, but with negative consequences for American democracy. The first set of critics suggest that although collaborative arrangements can deliver bureaucratic effectiveness, they may not be accountable, given their propensity to produce policy outcomes benefiting the few at the expense of the many. Accordingly, collaboration is dangerous for democracy because it leads to agency capture and special-interest government, the co-optation of public policy goals, and the failure to protect fundamental rights and other policy values important to a democratic society (Amy 1987; Bernstein 1955; Ingram and Smith 1993; Lowi 1979; McConnell 1966; Selznick 1957). Past experiences in environmental policy provide considerable ammunition for this perspective, especially Maass (1951), Lord (1979), and Gottlieb and FitzSimmons (1991) in water resources, and Culhane's (1981) comprehensive investigation of the policy and politics of the Forest Service and the Bureau of Land Management.[5] The second stream of criticism is grounded firmly within traditional public administration theory as defined by the Progressive reform tradition and the classic Weberian legal–rational model of bureaucracy. Collaboration violates several of the cardinal precepts of administrative doctrine, which are designed to ensure democratic accountability. Problems arise in the areas of the inclusion of citizen participation on a par with bureaucratic experts; the breach of the sacrosanct public–private boundary; the acceptance of administration as an inherently political, rather than "neutral," decision-making process; and the dissolution of hierarchical authority relationships in favor of shared power with nongovernmental stakeholders.[6]

In these ways, the two voices of the warrior–zealot and the skeptic–naysayer represent the bias of conventional wisdom in political science against collaboration as either a realistic alternative to the general theme of "ubiquitous conflict" or a positive force in American democracy. Conventional wisdom thus discourages research into the possibilities for successful governance arrangements flowing from collaborative endeavors. By doing so, it necessarily places artificial limits on the ability of political science to assist contemporary policy makers and administrators in their struggle to cope with a system of separated powers, multiple points of access, and a fragmented interest-group universe. This book constitutes one effort to fill this gap. The evidence developed herein suggests that the collaborative phenomenon is a pragmatic attempt by participants in national pollution control politics to come up with institutional arrangements that are more effective at resolving the complex regulatory dilemmas found in a traditionally adversarial policy arena. The participants of collaborative efforts interviewed for this project are not driven by starry-eyed romanticism; rather, they are hard-nosed realists, wary of collaboration and its potential pitfalls. But relative to the high transaction costs and inefficiencies encountered under standard ways of doing business in the regulatory arena, they perceive that in some situations collaboration may be a better choice than the traditional game of no-holds-barred conflict, one that is capable of producing win–win outcomes benefiting a broad variety of interests. The stories told in this book show how erstwhile adversaries in national pollution control politics, like the pragmatist–

optimists already described, are working together to overcome the difficulties of the collective action dilemma and to sustain the collaborative game over time such that jointly constructed remedies can be implemented and transaction cost savings collected.

Underlying this research is a scholarly sense of urgency tied to the fact that the world of policy administration has changed in important ways, in terms of both the context within which policy is administered and the actual choices of administrative arrangements being made by policy makers and bureaucrats. The new world of policy implementation involves five main elements: the emergence of the global village economy, the information technology and communications revolution, fiscal scarcity, the presence of a formidable public interest lobby, and the growth in citizen demands for a larger participatory role in policy making and implementation. When combined, these elements exert a strong decentralizing effect, increase the importance of organizational and program adaptability to changing and/or varied conditions, emphasize interdependence as a prerequisite to public policy success, add complexity to public management arrangements, and provide an added measure of protection against policy outcomes designed to benefit the few at the expense of the many. For example, the widening distribution of personal computers and advanced telecommunications technologies, as well as the advent of 500-channel television and the increasing development of the information superhighway (the Internet) mean that the control of communication systems in the United States "is increasingly exercised through the horizontal extension of network alliances. . . . As networks become structurally decentralized, ever wider publics gain access to them in ways that lead to an increase in the rate and density of public exchange. This, in turn, threatens to undermine the control of information as a discreet, privatized commodity" (Keane 1991, 162, as quoted in Friedland 1996, 186). Or, as in the case of fiscal scarcity in the public sector, administrators encounter tremendous pressure to do more with less, often through the use of innovative arrangements seeking to catalyze all sectors—public, private, and voluntary—in the service of public policy goals. And public interest groups and individual citizens have benefited tremendously from the passage of numerous national environmental laws and the creation of new citizen rights that have lowered the barriers to entry to both the administrative and judicial spheres of action. As a result, and unlike the past, environmental advocates now have the skill, the power, and the tools to offset cozy coalitions of interests seeking policy outcomes benefiting economic growth at the expense of environmental quality.

As others have pointed out,[7] the overall lesson is not that the new world of policy administration determines the appropriate shape and style of regulatory arrangements, but that traditional methods of organizing and controlling bureaucracy, hence administering and shaping regulatory outcomes, are less likely to be successful. When it is considered that the pressures on government agencies to cope with adaptability, decentralization, and interdependence are only likely to increase over the next several decades, the expectation is that successful governance will more and more become associated with a robust assortment of alternative administrative arrangements.

Further, we may not like, or we may rightfully fear, the burgeoning use of alternative institutional arrangements that potentially threaten cherished ideals of liberal democracy, increase the risk of agency capture and special-interest government, or place citizen input on a seeming par with policy mandates from elected officials. But, whether we like it or not, policy makers and administrators *are not* waiting on scholars to decide whether such arrangements are appropriate or not. They are choosing alternative institutional arrangements that defy the traditional Weberian/Progressives approach to bureaucracy, whether it is in terms of including more bottom-up citizen input, sharing power with private-sector groups, adopting holistic integrated approaches to pollution control, or practicing catalytic government that ultimately blurs the line between private and public spheres of action. In short, because practice *is* running ahead of theory, the challenge to theory is real, not imagined, and we need to figure out what it means. To the extent that traditional scholarship ignores such developments, political science is hampered in its ability as a discipline to explain and assess, much less understand, significant, interesting political–institutional phenomena such as collaborative decision-making arrangements.

Yet we lack a theoretical framework for understanding collaborative efforts and for connecting collaboration to the political science literature, more generally. This is precisely because conventional wisdom assumes ubiquitous conflict as the norm, that making collaborative arrangements work is a pipe dream, and that the potential for positive policy outcomes is something short of miraculous. Moreover, as Paul Light (1995) suggests in *Thickening Government*,[8] and as this book concurs, if "the original assumptions underpinning the principles [of administration] . . . no longer hold" (p. 6), then theory leaves us stranded once again, offering little advice on how to proceed and little guidance on the positive aspects of alternative institutional arrangements, much less how these aspects might be integrated with established principles of administration to provide a more robust model of bureaucracy in a democracy. This book takes a step in the direction of establishing a theoretical framework for understanding and maintaining collaboration by taking James Q. Wilson's advice to dig into the empirical specifics of the phenomena in question (1989, *xii*, 12). Pluralism by the rules draws primarily on the new economics of organization and the literature's concern with the transaction costs of doing business in the regulatory arena. But as the three case studies demonstrate, something more than structural incentives are required to catalyze and sustain collaborative games, to convince participants in national pollution control politics to forgo conflict in favor of collaboration. Just as scholars in the positive theory of hierarchies (Miller 1992; Kreps 1992) have begun to focus on elements of organizational culture as key to overcoming the uncertainties engendered by specific transaction cost challenges, trust and reputation play a role in the regulatory arena as well. Moreover, in a world where policy makers across the board are struggling to reinvent government, the by-the-rules framework provides one example of how the exercise of government authority can transition from hierarchies to collaborative network alternatives.

These collaborative ventures are by no means always successful, nor are they being advanced in the majority of regulatory circumstances. Nonetheless, the fact that there are successes, or even partial successes, is significant, given the formidable barriers participants must overcome. The successes and partial successes recorded in the following chapters suggest that it is time for the broader literature in political science, public policy, and public administration to devote greater intellectual energy to exploring the empirical conditions under which different kinds of institutional arrangements are best utilized and why.

This book could not conceivably have been completed without the assistance of a great many people. A large number of public officials, industry representatives, and environmental advocates generously gave of their time to answer my questions, read drafts of various chapters, and clarify the dynamics of the particular collaborative games in which they participated. I am indebted to Evan Ringquist, Gary Miller, Steve Born, Barry Rabe, Cary Coglianese, Larry O'Toole, Daniel Mazmanian, Erwin Hargrove, Bruce Oppenheimer, John Geer, and the many conference participants who read portions of the manuscript and supplied extremely helpful comments. I am deeply indebted to Don Kettl, Graham Wilson, David Canon, and Bill Freudenburg, who read the manuscript in its entirety. They provided enough positive feedback to make the process of meeting their challenges enjoyable and were instrumental in strengthening the book's arguments. My greatest debt is owed to Anne Khademian, a superb scholar, teacher, and mentor. The final product would be infinitely weaker and probably would not exist without her willingness to spend innumerable hours discussing the shape of the book, challenging me to fine-tune my arguments just one more notch, and gently prodding me to continue the project to its conclusion.

I am also grateful for the generous support I received from the University of Wisconsin–Madison, the Brookings Institution, the John and Ellen Demchalk Charitable Family Trust, Bob and Beth Loftis, John Bader, and Amy DeLouise. Vanderbilt University supplied valuable financial support during the 1995–1996 academic year and provided a safe and productive haven for putting the finishing touches on the manuscript.

Finally, this book would not have been possible without the loving support and phenomenal patience of my wife, Andrea. It is a wonder, after countless hours of listening to me droning on and on about pollution control politics, collaboration, and collective action dilemmas, that she is still sane and still my best friend. Also deserving of heartfelt gratitude are our children, Nicholas, Cody, and Alexis, each of whom displayed uncommon understanding as Daddy traipsed around the country in search of data and spent interminable hours at the library, reading books and writing this manuscript. In addition, my wife's parents, George and Dorothy Heyliger, deserve a round of applause for billeting the Weber family in comfortable style during our many forays to Colorado while I was writing this book. And to my lifelong friend, Greg Thomas, sincere appreciation for helping to keep me sane through our flyfishing expeditions to the spectacular rivers of Colorado (especially in January).

Although I have benefited tremendously from countless sources of help, the views expressed in this book, as well as any shortcomings, are solely the responsibility of the author.

CHAPTER NOTES

1. The *High Country News* article is a reprint of a memo distributed to the Sierra Club Board of Directors in November 1995. McCloskey wrote it to spur discussion; it does not represent the official position of the Sierra Club.

2. Badaracco (1985); Kelman (1981); Vogel (1986, 1989); G. Wilson (1981; 1982; 1985).

3. See Gais, Peterson, and Walker (1984); Gormley (1989); Hays (1989); Hoberg (1992); Marcus (1980); Melnick (1983); Ripley and Franklin (1984); Vogel (1986).

4. Gormley (1989); Heclo (1978); Hoberg (1992); Kraft (1990); Melnick (1983); Vogel (1986); Wenner (1982).

5. See also Wilkinson (1992) for a broad historical overview of mining, water resources, forestry, and grazing policy in the American West.

6. For a recent example that raises similar concerns over the use of bureaucratic arrangements that depart from the orthodox public administration model, see the critique by Ronald Moe (1994) of the National Performance Review's efforts to reinvent the federal bureaucracy. Moe argues that devolved and

shared power arrangements violate the hierarchical chain of command necessary to ensure accountability.

  7. See, for example, Barzelay (1992); John (1994); Osborne and Gaebler
(1993); Rabe (1994).

  8. Light examines hierarchy and span of control and finds that the application of orthodox principles of administration "thickens" government and
thereby increases the distance between hierarchical authority and bureaucratic
action, thus lessening the ability of democratically elected officials to control
the bureaucracy. Michael Barzelay (1992), with the help of Babak Armanjani,
finds that government does not have to be bureaucratic, inflexible, inundated
with written rules, and focused on top-down control in order to be accountable
and effective.

1

Replacing the Old with the New

To make regulation as effective as possible, officials must base their policies on sound technology and make allowance for technological change. Rules must be cast so as to encourage (or at least not discourage) the development of alternative processes and innovative methods for dealing with industrial byproducts. . . . Such a wise regulatory framework will be almost impossible to construct unless government, industry and environmental groups abandon their . . . adversarial relationships and work together to solve their shared problems (*Scientific American*, "Managing Planet Earth," September 1989)

Traditional pluralism builds a model of politics and policy outcomes on the ideas of countervailing forces and balanced representation. Pluralism views politics as a game in which competing interests collide, find a way to compromise, and then design policies reflective of the mix of interests stirring the policy pot.[1] In certain respects, the ebb and flow of environmental politics over the past thirty years is very much in the pluralist mold. Strong bipartisan support for environmental legislation during the late 1960s and early 1970s reflected a changing balance of power in national policy circles. Environmental groups successfully surmounted the collective action problem to become a powerful countervailing force at the national level.[2] The main protagonists—industry, regulators, and environmental advocates—have battled constantly to promote competing visions of just what environmental policy should be. They have acted and reacted to check their opponents' victories in the classic invisible hand fashion of Truman (1951). Victories in the legislative arena have often been countered by losses in the courts. Executive orders issued by President Reagan have been nullified by President Clinton. Various presidents and legislators have attempted to broker coalitions of interests both in support of and in opposition to various environmental initiatives.

In other respects, the dominant brand of pluralism found in the environmental arena is quite different, adhering less to the rule of

1

compromise than to the pursuit of absolute victory through no-holds-barred conflict and an unwillingness to concede the possibility of common ground. Yet playing no-holds-barred pluralism in the environmental arena is costly for all participants and is often accompanied by minimal environmental results. Legislative victories for environmentalists and their allies in Congress impose command-and-control-based, zero-sum outcomes favoring the environment *over* the economy on industrial losers. Experienced practitioners and regulatory scholars claim that no less than 80 percent of all major rules issued by the Environmental Protection Agency (EPA) are litigated. Rulemaking and implementation delays regularly run three to four years and, on occasion, a decade or more.[3] The information EPA needs to write regulations is costly to gather and verify, as affected interests artfully conceal as well as misrepresent their "true" stakes in regulatory issues. Compliance costs continue to escalate for industrial polluters as well as for states and municipalities. Beginning in the early 1980s, congressional gridlock became the rule rather than the exception.

The consequences associated with vast and endless conflict are inducing participants in American pollution control politics to experiment with alternatives to the no-holds-barred pluralism game. The search for alternatives is quietly revolutionizing the rules governing decision-making processes and relations among players in a number of important instances. Specifically, environmental advocates, industry, and regulators at the state and federal levels, though each driven by disparate objectives, are discovering a surprising common ground, at least some of the time, in collaborative arrangements guided by a common set of rules.[4] William Reilly, EPA administrator during the Bush Administration, labels it "a new era in the history of environmental policy, an era marked by the reconciliation of interests, by imaginative solutions arrived at through cooperation and consensus, by the resolve to listen and work out our differences."[5]

When pluralism is played "by the rules" in environmental politics, collaboration is possible and stakeholders are able to restructure the regulatory game to minimize transaction costs—the costs of developing, implementing, and enforcing regulations—and to create greater assurance that political bargains, once made, actually deliver promised benefits. Traditional adversaries consult, negotiate, and build consensus in support of regulatory arrangements emphasizing the environment *and* the economy. Power is shared between the public and private sectors. Greater discretion and flexibility are granted to regulated communities in the area of compliance decision making. Moreover, participants work together to create higher quality scientific and implementation databases upon which program specification, compliance, and enforcement decisions are made. According to Allen Hershkowitz, senior scientist at the Natural Resources Defense Council (NRDC), the "willingness to cooperate rather than litigate is spreading. . . . Today I do most of my work in alliance with industry. That's fundamentally different [than in the past]" (as quoted in Gutfeld 1992, B3).

This is a story about why collaboration is occurring in American pollution control politics. It is also a story about why collaboration is being played on such a small scale—the number of cases totals no more than forty or fifty nationwide out of thousands. Yet despite its limited application, the collaborative games played under pluralism by the rules are taking place in the most combative regulatory arena in American politics.[6] Understanding why and how collaboration is possible in this policy arena takes political scientists and public managers closer to identifying and specifying the conditions under which such games are appropriate, and therefore when scarce public sector resources should be devoted to rethinking regulation. Furthermore, when it is realized that a single collaborative effort can lock in environmental results much faster than is typical, can save the regulated community hundreds of millions or even billions of dollars per year, and can create rigorous monitoring programs to prevent cheating and ensure the capture of environmental benefits, the phenomenon does not have to be widespread to have tremendous significance for how we approach pollution control regulation. The question is: given the limited scale, what does it take to play collaborative games and move them forward to successful conclusions?

One would think that, given the possibilities offered by collaborative games, it would be the game of choice in the pollution control arena. Participants know that collaboration promises significant transaction cost savings which redound to the benefit of their organizations, whether it is faster or bigger pollution reductions; cheaper compliance; or smarter, hence more implementable and enforceable, programs. Yet transaction costs have been high and apparent to the major players in pollution control politics for some time. Changes over the past twenty-five years in administrative decision-making procedures, the frequency of legislative gridlock, and the relative balance of power between competing interests have sensitized players to the high costs of no-holds-barred pluralism, with its virtually inevitable result of litigation, paralysis, and delay. Given the strong incentives to find alternative regulatory arrangements, why is collaboration played only occasionally rather than all the time?

First, and perhaps most obviously, while high transaction costs pervade American pollution control politics, they are not high for every single transaction or for every participant in every case. Under conditions of low transaction costs, players gain little by choosing collaboration and therefore have no incentive to play. Where transactions have differential effects on individual participants, different players encounter varying incentives to abandon the status quo in favor of collaboration. Major players facing low incentives tend to prefer the status quo and will direct resources toward stopping collaborative games which threaten their interests or pose uncertain outcomes.

A second reason why collaborative games are not played on a larger scale involves the tremendous uncertainty which accompanies them. The American political system is famous for its adversarial political culture, a fragmented interest-group system, and the "openness" provided by separate institutions, checks and balances, and federalism.[7] Each component raises the collective action threshold, makes compromise more difficult to achieve, and interjects a considerable degree of uncertainty into the policy process. Yet despite the high costs and uncertainty of traditional pluralism, the parameters and anticipated responses of all players are well-established. Organizations are staffed with personnel who, through dozens and often hundreds of iterations, are practiced at strategizing and reacting to opponents' responses. Actors *expect* "losers" to take advantage of the multiple decision points available in the American system and seek more favorable outcomes elsewhere. There is a certain degree of comfort in conflict and inefficiency because the dynamics of the game are known.

Choosing the new game of collaboration, on the other hand, adds another layer of uncertainty. In order to engage and sustain the kinds of collaborative games which allow participants to maximize their goals vis-à-vis alternatives, long-standing adversaries must first reveal information that would likely remain strategically hidden under traditional pluralism. Information sharing creates opportunities for the development of a more robust set of policy choices and implementation mechanisms; the added information permits participants to discover innovative solutions to environmental problems that otherwise are beyond their reach. The revelation of private information, however, makes participants vulnerable. Precisely because the realm of possible outcomes is greater, the shapes of final agreements are less predictable. There is also the chance that participants' commitment to good-faith bargaining will be tenuous. The risk is that once certain information is revealed, players may renege on their commitment, withdraw from the process, and use the information to advance their own interests at the expense of their fellow collaborators. As well, even after a consensus conclusion is reached, there is always the possibility that others will revert back to the traditional conflict game, whether through litigation, a public relations campaign, or an appeal to political officials with the power to nullify the agreement.

Notwithstanding the added risks and uncertainty, participants are cautiously testing the collaborative game's potential for improving regulatory program development, implementation, and enforcement. What does it take to put the collaborative game into play and sustain it over time such that jointly constructed remedies can be implemented and transaction cost savings collected? The short answer is a set of rules governing the game dynamic. The "rules" are a method for managing conflict, for guiding or controlling participant interaction in a unified way toward a definite goal, in this case the goal of environmental protection. The "rules" reduce the uncertainty and risks associated with the collaborative game by selectively promoting collaboration, by structuring participant behavior to minimize the likelihood of shirking[8] and *ex post* defections, and by giving each participant a meaningful stake in outcomes. By reducing uncertainty, the "rules" engender the trust necessary for collaboration to take hold, promote ownership in the outcomes instead of legal challenges, facilitate timeliness rather than delay, and create the political space within which creative compromises leading to transaction cost savings can be crafted. In short, instead of no-holds-barred pluralism, successful collaboration is a matter of playing pluralism by the rules. Significantly, traditional pluralist theory fails to consider either the kinds of policy transactions that might fit within this expanded policy space or why such transactions might occur and be sustained in the first place.

THE "OLD" GAME OF PLURALISM AND CONFLICT

The emergence of the collaborative game contradicts conventional wisdom in political science that policy making today is more open and conflictual, particularly in national pollution control politics.[9] The historical case for conflict in American pollution control politics is a credible one. During the 1970s, environmental advocacy groups rarely adopted the insider tactics like bargaining, compromise, and consultation that are so critical to collaborative games (Gais, Peterson, and Walker 1984; Gais and Walker 1991). Environmentalists were apt to portray their industrial adversaries as evil incarnate, while industry characterized environmentalists as zealots in the thrall of some romanticist notion of a preindustrial society (Esposito et al. 1970; Nader 1965; Loeb 1993). An industry veteran of more than twenty years of environmental policy wars captures the dominant sentiment.

> The 1970s and early 1980s were a time when our position on pollution control matters used to be nothing—zero or less. The position of environmentalists, on the other hand, was 100 percent or more. Whole hog or

none, both sides. No give, no nothing. Hard stake in the ground right, hard stake in the ground left, nothing in the middle (interview, 1/21/94).

EPA employees, for their part, wore "Born to Regulate" t-shirts as a symbol of their commitment to "hard-core" regulatory policies designed to punish "evil" corporate polluters.

Such descriptions of participants' attitudes and behavior are not simply an artifact of the past. Bitter, adversarial relations among stakeholders are still the norm, whether in terms of business versus environmentalists, business versus government, environmentalists versus government, federal versus state interests, Reaganite conservatives versus proenvironment Democrats, or congressional attitudes toward the bureaucracy.[10] House Republican whip Tom Delay of Texas and Representative David McIntosh (R-Ind), with strong backing from the business community, spearheaded Republican attempts "to exterminate regulations that bug business" during the 104th Congress (Noah 1995a; 1995b, A16). House Speaker Newt Gingrich criticized environmental policies for being "absurdly expensive, . . . and misallocat[ing] resources on emotional and public relations grounds without regard to either scientific, engineering or economic rationality" (Noah and Kuntz 1995, B5). Republican efforts to reform the Clean Water Act in the 1995 session of congress prompted environmental advocates to dub the proposal the Dirty Water Act, while attempts at regulatory reform were branded a "polluter's bill of rights" (Noah and Kuntz 1995, B5). The high levels of conflict are generally explained as a natural by-product of a policy arena where stakes are high and stakeholder interests diverse, often to the point of being irreconcilable.

The volatility of the situation is exacerbated by the dominant form of regulatory arrangement used to define the relationship between the regulators and the regulated: command and control. In its most formal sense, command and control is premised on a strict hierarchical authority relationship between regulators (principals) and the regulated community (agents). The federal government uses its authority to "command" compliance with mandated policy goals and to fill in the details of regulatory programs using a top-down notice-and-comment rulemaking process. States and the private sector—both agents, or subordinates—must then comply with the rules as written. The behavior of agents during program implementation is then "controlled" by limiting their discretion regarding the means by which goals are to be achieved and by enforcement actions based largely on punitive sanctions.

In practice, this means a regulatory system designed to capture all polluter variance within national uniform rules and to manage both the substance and the process of compliance decision making. Regulators adopt a detailed, source-specific, industry-by-industry strategy of control over virtually every aspect of implementation. They identify and prescribe uniform end-of-pipe pollution control standards,[11] best available control technologies (BACT)[12] that industry must use to achieve pollution reductions, and detailed decision processes that guide industry step-by-step toward compliance (e.g., permitting) (Ackerman and Stewart 1985; Vogel 1986). Compliance failures (at least in theory) are met with immediate, harsh, punitive enforcement actions that act as deterrents to future shirking. As well, states must create and operate state implementation plans according to federally mandated criteria. Similar results occur if states default on these obligations; they suffer financial sanctions (e.g., forfeited federal funding for infrastructure projects like highway construction) and risk federal takeover of their regulatory efforts.

In the zeal to correct a political system dominated by economic growth and evil industrial polluters, and in the name of a greater public good—environmental protection—the goals of economic interests are subordinated (Vogel 1986; Wildavsky 1979). State compliance with the Clean Air Act state implementation plans is not predicated on economic feasibility. Nor does the act grant exemptions to a given corporation or industry based on capacity to absorb the economic costs of adopting new control technologies. The 1973 Endangered Species Act explicitly prohibits the consideration of cost when determining whether plants or wildlife qualify for protection under its aegis (Mann and Plummer 1994).

Yet casting the game in zero-sum terms—the environment over, or instead of, the economy—imposes concentrated costs on industry and directly threatens the two overarching goals of business organizations: profit maximization and autonomy of control over organizational decision making (see Moe 1987b; Harris 1989). Imposing fixed costs for pollution control technologies and support personnel exerts a drag on firm productivity and, in general, makes it harder to maintain profit margins.[13] Similarly, giving complete control over decisions on how best to achieve pollution control goals to government regulators, by definition, strips corporate officials of decision-making latitude and makes it less likely that economic efficiency concerns will factor into regulatory decisions. Unsurprisingly, industry typically lashes back by using a strategy "of maximum feasible resistance and minimum feasible retreat" (Hays 1989, 287–88; J. Q. Wilson 1980). The late 1960s and early 1970s, a period of dramatic gains for the environmental lobby, are notable in this regard for prompting a strong countermobilization effort by industry, whose overarching purpose was a reversal of environmentalists' gains and a return to the pre-1970 status quo.[14]

Conflict arises not only as a matter of principled opposition to command-and-control regulations that industry views as coercive and intrusive, but also from command and control's reliance on centrally specified uniform standards and pollution technology controls that are likely to be unworkable or arbitrary across a wide range of industrial applications. Excluding from consideration the wide variation in states' geographic and economic–industrial conditions often prompts resistance at the state level, as officials struggle to reconcile national priorities with local political, economic, and ecological realities. From industry's perspective, the imposition of these "irrational" and suboptimal rules justifies high levels of resistance via noncompliance, obfuscation, and delay in their dealings with regulators, and litigation challenging the factual and analytical justifications for agency regulations (Stewart 1988, 156; interviews with industry 2/22/94; 2/10/94).

Resistance by industry makes EPA's job as an advocate for the environment more difficult and, when combined with what many consider the impossibly stringent nature of some statutory goals,[15] contributes to implementation delays, a growing backlog of missed congressionally mandated deadlines, and bureaucratic inaction on controversial rules. To environmentalists, it often seems that "[i]nconvenient environmental language [is] simply ignored or treated as congress's opinion. EPA programs seem to be all input and virtually no output. The promise of environmental statutes is reduced to dead letters" (McCloskey 1990, 82). As a result, and in an attempt to breathe new life into seemingly moribund statutes, environmental advocates are aggressive litigators. Groups like the Natural Resources Defense Council (NRDC), the Sierra Club, and the Environmental Defense Fund (EDF) owe much of their reputation for influence over pollution control policy to their legal prowess. Court actions seek not only to force bureaucratic action, but to produce interpretations of congressional intent favorable to the environmental side of the equation. Environmentalists' willingness to play the conflict game is further facilitated by administrative reforms designed to balance group representation, citizen suit provisions attached to pollution control laws, and liberalized judicial standing requirements (Lowi 1979; Mitchell 1991; Rosenbaum 1989).

Given this context, it is not surprising that incessant conflict in the form of lengthy and expensive court battles, legislative stalemate, and powerful resistance by industry to command-and-control regulatory rules are the stuff of legend in environmental politics.[16] A senior EPA official argues that implementation is best characterized as a process of regulatory rulemaking followed automatically by litigation.

When the law is passed, we write rules; when we write rules, the industry litigates; when the industry litigates, the environmentalists counterlitigate.

> The pattern has evolved over twenty years to the point where nothing gets accomplished. The [major stakeholders] have all learned how to stop everything (interview 1/11/94).

Nor has the political climate been conducive to alternative regulatory arrangements over the past twenty-five years. Market-based incentives that explicitly incorporate cost-effectiveness concerns into the regulatory framework are generally acceptable to some academics and some Republicans, but have simply not been a credible mainstream alternative in the eyes of most Democrats and other major stakeholders (Eads and Fix 1984; Kneese and Schultze 1976; Levin 1982). Moreover, the idea of sitting down with erstwhile adversaries to jointly explore and develop innovative solutions to regulatory problems, much less giving industry and environmentalists an active role in shaping regulations during rulemaking, is nothing short of heresy for key players on all sides of the environmental battleground. In short, if ever there was a case of policy making where common ground and collaboration do not exist, this is it.

THE NEW GAME OF COLLABORATION

In a limited but key number of cases, adversaries are opting for a collaborative game which relies on (1) consultation and negotiation; (2) flexible, power-sharing arrangements that are a stark departure from the command-and-control status quo; (3) a concerted search for better information; and (4) the generation of "win–win" outcomes. With credible stakes in regulatory outcomes, participants end up claiming ownership of game results and are thus more inclined to target resources in support of, rather than in opposition to, those results.

First, whereas the conflict game is about adversarialism, endless litigation, and letting the courts decide, collaboration is about resolving differences among affected parties through the extensive use of consultation and negotiation at different, and occasionally successive, levels of the regulatory process—lawmaking, rulemaking, and implementation. Congressional lawmaking defines the overarching substantive rules of a particular regulatory program. Rulemaking fills in program details or, as some have said, this is where the bureaucracy "fleshes out the bare-bones laws" passed by congress. Implementation is where the rubber meets the road, where the rules of the game are operationalized and enforced.

Second, instead of grabbing power through the imposition of strict command-and-control hierarchies, the collaborative game is about sharing power and choosing innovative regulatory programs that emphasize a greater degree of discretion and flexibility for both the bureaucracy and private-sector polluters. Command still exists since government retains authority to issue policy goals, allocate pollution property rights, enforce decisions, and so on. But with respect to "control," to *how* the bureaucracy decides the details of final program rules and *how* pollution control goals are achieved once regulations are operationalized, the authority relationship is relaxed and power is shared (see NAPA 1995, 70–118). Regulatory negotiations and consensus-based "roundtable" rulemakings invite environmentalists, state officials, and business interests to the bargaining table for the purpose of having them help government regulators write (fill in the details of) regulations. Public-private partnerships are at root a collaborative redefinition of existing regulatory arrangements. At the invitation of Amoco Oil, EPA spent three years studying an oil refinery to better match rules with pollution problems and to prevent pollution instead of simply regulating its release. U.S. corporations in the iron and steel industry, the electronics and computer industry, the auto industry, and the printing industry, along with federal and state regulators, national environmentalists, and locally based environmental justice groups, are attempting to rationalize the existing regulatory rules for each industrial sector and construct a "common sense" approach to environmental regulations (USEPA 1994a). In Colorado, four of the largest employers (and polluters)—Coors Brewing, Martin Marietta,[17] Hewlett Packard, and the Public Service Company of Colorado—are collaborating with EPA, the League of Women Voters, environmentalists, and the state to find innovative ways to prevent pollution (Pollution Prevention Partnership 1993).

Authority and responsibility are also shared with major stakeholders by granting the regulated community relative freedom of choice regarding how they will achieve compliance, whether in terms of the flexibility of choice afforded by market-based mechanisms, the ability to choose an alternative (equivalent or better) compliance path in lieu of existing arrangements, or the latitude to choose pollution prevention methods associated with upstream production processes rather than be limited to the proverbial government-specified end-of-pipe controls. In fact, a hallmark of regulations produced by negotiated rulemaking is more flexible compliance arrangements. As well, the reliance of integrated pollution control approaches on interpollutant trading implies that greater latitude should be given to industry decision makers.

Third, rather than a game where the rule is to conceal political stakes and technical information, negotiated rulemaking involves revealing stakes and working together to create higher quality scientific and implementation databases upon which program specification, compliance, and enforcement decisions are made. In turn, grounding regulatory decision making on better information creates opportunities for transforming the design of regulations. Restrictions so typical of the broader command-and-control-based system of regulatory control fall by the wayside. Integrated pollution control, as opposed to single-media approaches, and risk assessment reviews are more of a possibility as the extensive chemical-specific databases and whole-facility risk profiles needed to make them work are created. One-size-fits-all rules give way to solutions customized to industrial sectors or individual facilities, or are designed with "averaging-based" pollution emissions standards in place of unit-by-unit compliance requirements. Greater rigor in monitoring arrangements becomes possible, and rules focusing on real environmental results begin to replace proxy-based enforcement regimes.

Finally, instead of imposing zero-sum outcomes of benefit to only a few interests, the collaborative game focuses on producing the kinds of "win–win" solutions necessary for building and maintaining consensus among all interests. "Win–win" outcomes are achieved when each player reaps greater benefits (transaction cost savings) through the collaborative game format than they would expect to receive under a no-holds-barred pluralism scenario. Players do not have to harvest the same kinds of savings to meet the "win–win" criteria; rather, they can experience savings in the areas of most importance to them. For an environmentalist, this might mean faster environmental results, more stringent pollution control standards, or an overall cap on emissions. Industry, on the other hand, might benefit from lower compliance costs or greater flexibility leading to improved responsiveness to changing market conditions. Regulators might encounter savings through less litigation and improved rulemaking timeliness, which is likely to stem the intensity of and costs associated with congressional oversight activities. The important thing is that each interest is "winning" or garnering benefits simultaneously within the same transaction.

We can think of "win–win" outcomes in the pollution control arena as those giving explicit consideration to the environment *and* the economy. As part of this, environmental protection initiatives employing market-based incentives and promising "faster and cheaper" environmental results are being explored and implemented across the country at a dizzying pace—for acid rain, in Southern California's RECLAIM program, the Massachusetts IMPACT program, the Great Lakes region, Florida, Georgia, Texas, Illinois, North Carolina, and the Ozone Transport Commission's efforts in the Northeast and mid-Atlantic regions of the United States. Just as important, these market-based innovations are being promoted in collaborative fashion, with traditional skeptics like environmental advocates and government regulators in full support and in some cases being the leading advocates for collaboration. In another example of the new game, the Nature Conservancy brokered a pioneering effort in the Texas Hill Country involving dozens of public agencies and private interests in an attempt to help economy and ecology flourish together (Stevens 1992). In Wisconsin, local chapters of Trout Unlimited are forging innovative partnerships with the Wisconsin Department of Natural Resources, private landowners, and local communities to protect coldwater resources (e.g., fish), while at the same time recognizing agricultural and community economic needs. Across the Western United States, more than seventy coalitions of environmentalists, ranchers, county commissioners, government officials, loggers, skiers, and off-road-vehicle enthusiasts are cooperating in an attempt to improve ecosystem and public, as well as private, lands management arrangements (Jones 1996; McClellan 1996).

Nor are the participants in environmental politics alone in their search for and use of alternative means to resolve regulatory disputes. Within the framework established by the Negotiated Rulemaking Act of 1990 and under the guidelines of the (now defunct) Administrative Conference of the United States, regulatory negotiations are employed by federal agencies such as the Nuclear Regulatory Commission; the Federal Aviation Administration; the Federal Trade Commission; the departments of Education, Interior, Agriculture, and Transportation; and the Occupational Safety and Health Administration.

The emerging game dynamic is similar to "responsive regulation"; there "is not a clearly defined program or a set of prescriptions concerning the best way to regulate" (Ayres and Braithwaite 1992, 5). The underlying message is that:

> no single policy approach—whether market-based or command-and-control—can be a panacea for the diverse environmental and market resource problems we face. The real challenge is to choose the right policy for each job (Stavins et al. 1991, 13).

Although it appears to make a world of sense, it is only recently that such responsive regulation has carved a niche in American pollution control politics.[18] The hegemonic world of command and control is giving way to a smorgasbord of choices at the behest of the major stakeholders—industry, national environmental advocacy groups, state and federal regulators, and congress. Government-imposed markets, negotiated rulemaking, and public–private partnerships are products of this new world as stakeholders attempt to maximize their goals by collaborating and ultimately restructuring the regulatory game to minimize transaction costs.

TRANSACTION COSTS IN THE REGULATORY ARENA

Transaction costs were first introduced by Ronald Coase (1937) in his seminal article, "The Theory of the Firm." Coase argued that transaction costs were a critical factor in industrial organizations' institutional choices. Since that time, a growing number of scholars have developed the concept of a transaction cost to better understand the structure, development, and behavior of a wide range of political and economic institutions.[19] The transaction cost approach views organizational (or, more generally, institutional) relationships as a series of contracts. It is concerned with contract or program design as a reconciliation of the need for authority and accountability with information asymmetries, conflicts of interest among self-interested parties to an exchange, and a preference for efficiency. Transaction costs represent the costs of doing business under a particular contractual, organizational, or institutional arrangement.[20] They are the economic, or political, equivalent of friction in physical systems[21] and are an analytical tool by which we can measure (or at least identify) the uncertainty and direct costs accompanying contractual arrangements. More specifically, transaction costs represent the costs of writing, implementing, and enforcing contracts. In the regulatory arena, they are the costs associated with developing, implementing, and enforcing regulations.

Transaction costs are encountered at both the individual organizational level and the system level. At the system level, transaction costs reflect the sum total of costs experienced by participants to an exchange and the residual costs, such as rulemaking and implementation delays, stemming from participant interaction. In the movement toward collaborative games, stakeholders in pollution control politics are careful to compare not only the transaction costs, but especially the cost effectiveness of different regulatory arrangements.[22] When comparing alternatives, participants assess cost effectiveness for their own individual circumstances, not necessarily for the system as a whole. To the extent possible, each wants to reduce personal costs and maximize the ability to attain the goals of most individual importance. When a particular transaction inhibits the achievement of preferred goals, participants work to slow or halt the policy process so as to minimize the consequences (i.e., damage to their goals). The friction stemming from resistance elevates the transaction costs encountered by the system and makes it more difficult to achieve collective goals. Conversely, as more players perceive that a regulatory transaction promises to produce more of their own goals (vis-à-vis possible alternatives), participants spend less time inhibiting the regulatory process and more time actively facilitating it. As a result, regulatory arrangements experience a greater likelihood of successful implementation. Put differently, statutes and regulations are less likely in this case to face the conflict and resistance which impede and often prevent the achievement of collectively defined public policy goals.

Three categories of transaction costs are of primary importance to stakeholders engaged in regulatory games.[23]

Process costs Transaction costs include efforts devoted to information search, program specification, and program negotiation. These costs are primarily an issue for government regulators. Information search constitutes the cost of discovering what the relevant prices are (Coase 1937). Applied to regulatory politics, information search acknowledges that regulators and legislators are constrained by conditions of imperfect information and therefore must expend resources searching for information relevant to the policy or problem at issue. The search for information is complicated by the existence of information asymmetries, a situation where subordinates "know more than their principals do about the business at hand."[24] The basic problem is one of control. It matters whether the legislators and regulators have control over, access to, or the ability to confirm the quality of necessary information.[25] Program specification and negotiation, on the other hand, focus on the costs of negotiating, writing, and concluding an agreement among interested parties. Uncertainties associated with information asymmetries, the resolution of future contingencies, the open nature of the American political system, and concern over the possibility that adversaries will shirk or defect after a transaction has been finalized affect not only an organization's level of resource expenditures and the timeliness of the decision-making process, but also the character of regulatory arrangements as interested parties strive to lower uncertainty by locking in benefits for the long term (Moe 1989).[26]

The written program establishes the rules of the regulatory game. It communicates to stakeholders how implementation is to be achieved, the level and distribution of compliance costs, the basis upon which compliance is determined, and ultimately whether an organization's interests are reflected in the final compact. As such, these rules directly affect transaction costs in the other two categories: implementation costs and costs tied to participant behavior.

Implementation costs Government regulators expend resources on monitoring and enforcement activities in an attempt to ensure compliance (minimize shirking) with program goals.[27] The regulated community—states and the private sector—confronts a variety of compliance costs required to meet program mandates. Leading examples include resources devoted to pollution control and monitoring technologies, specialized pollution control personnel, and general administrative expenses. There are also program adaptability costs. Program adaptability measures the response capacity of regulatory arrangements to changes in exogenous conditions such as technological advances, market developments, and the scientific knowledge base. It is concerned with the strategic utilization of compliance-related assets in response to changing conditions and, in particular, the costs of redeploying or developing compliance assets in response to these changes. In empirical terms, program adaptability reflects the degree to which regulations foster or constrain the rate of technology innovation for environmental purposes[28] and the capacity of regulated firms to respond to changing market conditions. The rate of technology innovation is important for environmental advocates and their allies because it affects the range of policy options available to policy makers and the probability of environmental program success over the long term (Dudek and Palmisano 1988; NACEPT 1991, 5). On the other hand, industry's response capacity can be critical for maintaining a firm or industry's competitive edge in the rapidly changing conditions associated with a globalized economy.

Costs associated with participant behavior There can be considerable transaction costs tied to participant behavior, either in anticipation of a particular outcome or in response to statutes and regulations as written. Participants whose interests are not included or who anticipate losing often react adversely in the hope that others' gains will be thwarted or that bargains will be reconstructed more to their liking (Weingast and Marshall 1988; Williamson 1985; J. Q. Wilson 1980). Transaction costs arise in several areas. "Losers" may rally their allies in congress to block legislation contrary to their interests. Or they might take the policy dispute to the next level via litigation and let the courts decide. Losers often exploit information asymmetries by refusing to share information; by offering only partial, biased information supportive of their position; by withholding information until the last minute; or by overwhelming the bureaucratic rulemaking process with data in an attempt to obfuscate the issues needing resolution. Bureaucratic decision makers may obfuscate and delay decisions on controversial policies or in areas where congress is trying to compel an outcome counter to agency or executive branch interests.

There is also the matter of the "wheel-spinning" phenomenon. Wheel-spinning involves the relationship of implementation costs to environmental benefits and occurs when regulators and the regulated spend organizational resources, yet perceive themselves as producing few environmental results or even deleterious environmental effects.

In other words, investments are yielding little or no progress toward intended policy results. It is viewed as a cost since the perception of ineffectiveness often translates into an adverse reaction which may prevent or delay policy from being implemented.

In each case, the friction created by conflict impedes goal achievement by "winners" and forces them to incur additional transaction costs as they battle to push through policies consonant with their preferences and fight to protect initial gains. On the positive side, policies taking more explicit account of regulated communities' concerns, or enforcement strategies designed to induce greater rates of voluntary compliance, can reap significant benefits through higher rates of compliance for the same or lower agency expenditures on enforcement activities.[29]

WHY COLLABORATION?

Given the considerable opportunities to affect policy outcomes afforded by the open American system of government, the technical complexity of the policies being decided, and the conflicting orientations motivating a series of powerful players, it is easy to see how and why transaction costs often escalate to the point at which policy ineffectiveness and disgruntled stakeholders become the rule rather than the exception. It is also easy to see why collaboration and common ground are in scarce supply in national pollution control politics. Why reveal valuable information and expend effort collaborating with erstwhile adversaries when chances are the outcome will prove ephemeral? Yet collaboration is occurring, and it is occurring where we would least expect it—in the most combative of all regulatory arenas—pollution control politics. The question is why? How do we explain collaboration?

Conventional wisdom proffered by the political science and regulatory politics literature is of little help. It predicts that when powerful groups collide, one of four things happens: (1) The groups coalesce and dominate policy making while leaving broader public interests unserved;[30] (2) no one set of interests scores a decisive victory; rather, ineffective bureaucracy results;[31] (3) there is constant adversarialism without the promise of compromise, particularly between government and business (Vogel 1986, 25, 142–96), or (4) there is partisan mutual adjustment leading to incremental changes in existing policy (Lindblom 1959, 1979; Hayes 1992, 13–26).

But the new game of collaboration among powerful, competing interests suggests that bureaucrats and environmentalists *are* interested in pursuing the public good of a cleaner environment, instead of simply settling for tough-sounding rhetoric and symbolic policy victories that do more to secure their own organizations' futures than to provide a cleaner environment. Collaborative arrangements also demonstrate the willingness of regulators and politicians to devolve authority (share power) over the details of compliance decision making to the private sector. This is contrary to the conventional portrayal of these stakeholders as jealous guardians of the many prerogatives accruing to them within a command-and-control system. Industry, on the other hand, defies expectations by opting for arrangements that minimize barriers to entry as much as possible.[32] Further, collaboration suggests that politics, while still distributional in nature,[33] is capable of generating more efficient regulatory arrangements.

As well, the new collaborative game operating under pluralism by the rules, while it involves partisan mutual adjustment, is a distinct departure from the more traditional concept of pluralism and partisan mutual adjustment offered by Lindblom (Table 1.1). Instead of consultation and negotiation to discover the lowest common denominator around which everyone can unite, and instead of constructing a minimum winning coalition, the by-the-rules framework focuses on maximizing participants' preferences and practicing inclusion. Rather than negotiations marked by information deficits and limited consideration of policy alternatives, there is shared information, a concerted search for more reliable information, and a more robust search for policy innovations and alternatives. Moreover, partisan mutual adjustment under pluralism by the rules is premised not only on an "organic" decision-making process in which leadership is crucial, but on belief in the possibility of both trust and consensus. Differences in process translate into differences in policy outcomes as well (see Table 1.1). Furthermore, since pluralism by the rules can be played during either the lawmaking or administrative phase of the policy process, administrators can use the rules to maximize participants' preferences and improve the efficiency of legislative outcomes produced under traditional pluralist conditions. In such a case, the "rules" attempt to transform the degenerative dynamic of litigation, obfuscation, and delay— in which even the most incremental policy changes are minimized or nullified by the resistance of policy losers—into positive-sum, win–win outcomes benefiting a broad array of stakeholders.

Given conventional wisdom, how are we to explain the willingness of participants in pollution control politics to engage in collaborative games, even if only on a limited basis? The answer is in three parts: the anticipation of lower transaction costs, the incentives posed by changes in the larger institutional context, and the presence of an assurance mechanism. The promise of transaction cost savings and the way the contextual elements reinforce players' sensitivity to the

TABLE 1.1   Two Models of Partisan Mutual Adjustment

	Pluralism	*Pluralism by the Rules*
Consultation and negotiation	To discover the lowest common denominator needed to pass policy[1]	To maximize participants' preferences
Size of coalition	Minimum winning coalition	Inclusive of all major stakeholders with ability to obstruct or otherwise hamper goal achievement
Style of decision-making process	Mechanical; policies are the political resultants of interaction among interests[2]	Organic; entrepreneurial leadership is critical to success
Role of information	Technical and political information jealously guarded (kept "private") Incomplete knowledge due to limits on human cognitive capacities and costs of acquiring reliable information Information deficit limits consideration of policy alternatives	Information is shared and political stakes revealed Accepts bounded rationality and information deficits as constraints but engages in a proactive search for more reliable information Better information allows examination of a more robust set of policy options
Agreement on ends and means	Impossible given conflicting interests and divergent values	Consensus is possible on ends, but especially means

costliness of playing no-holds-barred pluralism provide the incentives to *consider* collaborative games. But catalyzing and sustaining collaborative games and implementing their results requires an assurance mechanism that is the heart of pluralism by the rules. The "rules" take the game from the point where participants recognize the positive potential of collaboration to the end point, or outcome, in which the improved flow of benefits for each interest is achieved.

Transaction costs are high under the traditional regulatory framework. Traditional hierarchy-based, command-and-control regulatory arrangements are costly to negotiate and specify, information costly to gather and verify, and monitoring and enforcement costly and uncertain. The preference for detailed, top-down, one-size-fits-all solutions reduces program adaptability to changing conditions and forces industry to pay premium compliance rates. Participant behavior typically and quickly degenerates into vitriolic rhetoric, maximum resistance, and the use of tactics designed to quash or delay victories by one's adversaries. More often than not, the end result is a policy process characterized by conflict, litigation, and delay.

TABLE 1.1 *Continued*

	Pluralism	*Pluralism by the Rules*
Role of trust in facilitating bargains	Establishing trust among erstwhile adversaries is a utopian ideal[3]	Trust, manufactured and enforced by hierarchical rules and reputation, is possible[4]
Policy Outcomes	Incremental adjustments differing marginally from existing policies Inefficient/ineffective bureaucracy and regulations Incomplete knowledge enhances bias toward one-size-fits-all solutions Incomplete knowledge hampers government monitoring and enforcement activities	Potential exists for nonincremental policy changes Improved efficiency in bureaucratic/regulatory programs Responsive regulation—improved knowledge permits innovation and customization Improved accountability through increased rigor in monitoring programs and differentiated enforcement focusing on "bad apples"

[1] Lowest common denominator compromises provide a way for participants to insure against total defeat. Each party to the bargain gives up the chance to maximize their preferences for the certainty of an assured, if suboptimal, stream of benefits (Moe 1989; see also Ackerman and Hassler 1981; Yandle 1989).

[2] Lindblom (1979, 523); Truman (1951). See also Hayes (1992, 19). In *Who Governs?*, however, Dahl (1961) rejects the proposition that public policy is simply the end result of group pressure.

[3] Notable exceptions to this rule are Richard Fenno (1973) and Donald Matthews (1960), both of whom stress the role of trust among legislators as essential to the lawmaking process.

[4] Trust is likely to be limited to individual transactions. Iterative play and repeat successes might extend trust beyond a single transaction as players discover the benefits of regulatory interaction using a trust-based collaborative format.

At the same time, changes over the past twenty-five years in the context of the environmental policy world have heightened the relevance of these costs. Competitive, more concerted efforts by the legislative and executive branches of government to hold the EPA accountable, legislative gridlock, the enhanced openness of administrative decision making and an activist judiciary, an obvious power equilibrium between environmental and business interests, the altered relationship between federal and state governments, and the increasingly global nature of service and product markets make alternative regulatory arrangements essential to all the players.

Just as scholars in the new economics of organization posit the reduction of transaction costs as a motivating force in the choice of institutional arrangements, participants in pollution control politics are motivated to pursue alternative collaborative processes promising more workable, cost-effective regulations, more effective enforcement, fewer delays, a lesser likelihood of litigation, and ultimately greater certainty of environmental results.[34]

But the motivation to reduce costs and improve results is only a necessary and not a sufficient condition to collaborate. Under pluralism by the rules, collaboration is possible because the "rules" engender sufficient trust among participants to hurdle the collective action dilemma. Players must be convinced that others are not simply using the collaborative format to advance hidden agendas and that sharing private information, taking the time to negotiate creative compromises with the enemy, and risking *ex post* breaches in compromise agreements will not come back to haunt them. Enough trust must be established to move the collaborative game from the stage where players merely consider it as one of several alternatives to the active engagement and completion of the game such that transaction cost savings are delivered. Without assurance that agreements will be binding and that everyone's stake in policy outcomes will be protected, each player has an incentive to avoid the unknown dynamics of collaboration and stick with the known costs of the command-and-control-dominated conflict game—and likely litigation, paralysis, and delay.

Therefore, before they switch the game from conflict to collaboration, players are insisting that pluralism be played by the rules. The "rules" allow collaboration to take hold rather than conflict, give participants the assurances they need in order to reveal strategically important private information, and create the political space necessary for the discovery of creative win–win solutions. Specifically, pluralism by the rules introduces greater certainty into the collaborative effort through an assurance mechanism composed of six constituent parts, or rules for managing conflict and guiding participant interaction in a unified way toward the goal of pollution control. The institutional backbone of the assurance mechanism consists of five rules—certain transaction-specific conditions, formal binding agreements to govern negotiations and their aftermath, a reputation for commitment to collaborative processes by the public agency in charge of the regulation, the inclusion of all stakeholders in a position to block or effectively undermine outcomes, and the need for participants with long-term interests in pollution control policy. The sixth rule—entrepreneurial political leadership—is a dynamic, fluid component based on the ability of agency and game leaders to evince credible commitment toward the collaborative effort. Using their reputation, rhetoric, and authoritative action, entrepreneurial leaders champion the benefits of collaboration to game participants, while simultaneously assuring them that their interests will be protected during program negotiation, specification, and implementation. In short, when pluralism is played by the rules, participants in pollution control politics are willing to come to the regulatory table to collaborate, to stay at the table, and to bring the results to fruition through implementation and enforcement.

Table 1.2 displays the optimum conditions under which successful collaborative games are expected, the conditions under which collaboration is possible but unsustainable, and the conditions under which collaborative games are either highly unlikely or unexpected. Solving the collective action dilemma and sustaining collaboration in a high-transaction-cost world requires the presence of the full pluralism-by-the-rules framework (Box 7). When only a partial by-the-rules framework exists (two or more elements), collaboration is possible because enough trust can be engendered to carry the collaborative process forward to where transaction cost savings are discovered. But lacking

TABLE 1.2 Conditions Influencing the Emergence of Collaborative Games

		Transaction Costs		
		High and Applicable to All Players	*High for Most Players but Not All*	*Low*[1]
PLURALISM BY THE RULES	**Absent**	1. No collaboration (strong incentives and no trust)	2. No collaboration (mixed incentives and no trust)	3. No collaboration (no incentive and no trust)
	Partial	4. Collaboration possible, but not sustainable (strong incentives and partial trust)	5. Highly unlikely (mixed incentives and partial trust)	6. No collaboration (no incentive and partial trust)
	Full	7. Sustained collaboration (full trust and strong incentives)	8. Collaboration possible, but not sustainable (full trust and mixed incentives)	9. No collaboration (full trust, but no incentive)

[1]"Low" costs are interpreted in relation to costs encountered under alternative decision-making arrangements. Hence, the level of costs are interpreted in relative rather than absolute terms (Williamson 1985).

the full rules framework, sustaining the game to where savings are produced is unlikely (Box 4). Likewise, collaboration is possible in cases where transaction costs are high for most but not all major players (mixed incentives) and where a full pluralism-by-the-rules framework is in place. Sustaining the collaborative effort in such a case is another matter, however. Because one or more major players will reap minimal benefits by engaging the collaborative format, they encounter little incentive to play. Therefore, they prefer the status quo to collaboration and will most likely stand in the way of successful implementation of any final agreement (Box 8).[35] Further, collaboration will not occur in cases where either of the two major conditions are missing. With low transaction costs across the board, players gain little by choosing collaboration and therefore have no incentive to play. On the other hand, without the trust manufactured by the "rules" framework, combatants perceive the collaborative game as foolish. The mind-numbing uncertainty of collaborating with erstwhile adversaries in the regulatory arena, even when the potential gains are substantial, is enough to stop the game before it starts.

The relationship between collaboration and pluralism by the rules is examined by using empirical data from three collaborative games: (1) the *negotiated rulemaking* used to develop the reformulated gasoline rule mandated by the 1990 Clean Air Act Amendments; (2) the acid rain *government-imposed market*, also a product of the 1990 Clean Air Act; and (3) the Yorktown Project—a multiyear *joint exploratory venture* (public–private partnership) involving Amoco Oil, EPA, and Virginia's Department of Environmental Quality that examined the potential of integrated pollution prevention (water–air–solid waste) for oil refineries. Each case highlights the transaction cost savings anticipated by participants and how pluralism by the rules facilitates the collaborative game, whether during congressional decision making (government-imposed markets), bureaucratic rulemaking (negotiated rulemaking), or implementation (joint exploratory venture). Extensive open-ended interviews with major players in the pollution control policy network and archival documentation are used to explore stakeholder perceptions of transaction cost reductions for each collaborative arrangement,[36] to verify the presence and characteristics of assurance mechanisms, and to examine whether each arrangement delivers transaction cost savings as expected.

Close examination of the collaborative game in action shows that pluralism by the rules succeeds in solving the initial collective action dilemma and in producing or discovering anticipated transaction cost savings. In the one case that only discovers instead of delivers transaction cost reductions, the Yorktown Project, we find that the omission of key elements of the assurance mechanism illuminates their importance to eventual success. Yet even the presence of the full pluralism-by-the-rules framework does not automatically ensure success. The three outcomes confirm that the daunting uncertainty associated with collaborative bargaining arrangements can be reduced but never entirely eliminated. The impossibility of eradicating uncertainty guarantees that developing and managing collaborative games in the regulatory arena will continue to be an extremely difficult task, rules or no. In short, the game's applicability is clearly limited.

Yet a point of arguably more importance is that despite the collaborative game's selective nature and despite the inevitability of uncertainty, the contextual changes that have made pluralism by the rules possible still exist. Because the context continually reminds participants of the damaging relationship between high transaction costs and their own organizational goals, participants continue to encounter strong incentives to play collaborative games generating more regulatory bang for the regulatory buck.

Chapter 2 develops the changes in the larger institutional context that have sensitized pollution control stakeholders to the high costs of no-holds-barred pluralism. Chapter 3 reviews transaction cost theory and outlines the particular transaction costs motivating participants to embrace the new game of collaboration. Chapter 4 sets out the assurance mechanism framework that is the heart of pluralism by the rules, and chapters 5 through 7 analyze the three collaborative games described here.

Chapter 8 develops the implications of collaborative games for our studies of public policy and policy making by addressing such questions as the following. Do collaborative games, by emphasizing efficiency and effectiveness, compromise our ability to hold public sector decision makers accountable? How can we keep entrepreneurial public sector managers focused on the larger issues of the public interest when performance is driven by results? How stable are the "win–win" outcomes produced under the pluralism-by-the-rules framework? Does everyone who needs to be at the bargaining table have a chance to participate or, at a minimum, have the opportunity to influence collaborative outcomes? Or are collaborative games simply a replay of the "heavenly chorus" pluralist dynamic described by E. E. Schattschneider (1960), except that major national environmental groups are now part of the elite circle of interests invited to play?

The questions are important because participants in national pollution control politics continue to encounter incentives to devise alternatives to the traditional game of no-holds-barred pluralism and, of even greater significance, participants continue to choose collaboration at the national, state, and local levels of governance. A final chapter briefly explores the latter point, while also suggesting some ways to exploit the natural limits of collaborative games and to further research in this area.

CHAPTER NOTES

1. Truman's (1951) group theory holds that powerful competing interests collide and interact much like billiard balls in a three-dimensional political space. Public policy is the net result of the struggle. In this approach, freedom of association rather than voting is of paramount importance, and policy outputs are conditioned more by group action and reaction in the periods between elections. Robert Dahl (1961) offers a more sophisticated version of pluralism than group theory. Issue areas contain distinctive coalitions of interests brokered by elected political leaders, and democratic accountability flows from the fact that elected officials are responsive to the demands of the electoral arena. Lindblom (1959; 1979) makes the case for incrementalism and mutual partisan adjustment as the expected derivatives of a political system based on separate institutions sharing power and on numerous competing groups with conflicting interests and divergent values.

2. J. Q. Wilson (1973). While Wilson's extension of Olson's (1965) incentives argument is right on the mark, the rise and sustenance of the environmental lobby is much more than a story of incentives. The ability and willingness of federal government "patrons" to set the framework for action by relaxing laws on nonprofit group lobbying and channeling considerable financial help toward major environmental organizations are a key part of the story as well (Mitchell 1991, 102–04; Walker 1983).

3. For the estimated 80 percent litigation rate figure, see Bryner (1987, 117); Council on Environmental Quality (1985, 3); Ruckelshaus (1985, 463). However, see Coglianese (1997) for an empirical assessment of this claim. He finds that the actual rate of litigation in the area of EPA rulemaking is substantially less, falling somewhere in between approximately 19 and 44 percent, depending on the method of counting rules and the pollution control statute in question. For rulemaking delays at EPA as well as other regulatory agencies, see Mashaw and Harfst (1990); McGarity (1992); Thomas (1987).

4. A number of scholars have noted similar changes. What they offer, however, are primarily descriptions of the phenomenon that do not explain either why collaboration is taking hold or why we are getting the particular outcomes that we do. McFarland (1990; 1993) asks whether the interest group cycle, which alternately favors business and reform-minded interests, is "flattening" such that both sides are more willing to accommodate opposing interests than in the past. Berry (1984), Bosso (1987), and Browne (1986; 1988) find a growing willingness among traditional adversaries to sit down and negotiate their differences in the policy areas of food, pesticides, and agriculture, respectively. Harris (1989) argues that the 1970s social regulatory explosion forced a heightened degree of regularized contact between major stakeholders such

that much of corporate America now shares a common objective with social regulators (government and environmentalists): "to increase certainty in the regulatory environment" (p. 275). Meidinger (1985; 1987) argues that the changes, at least within the sphere of air pollution control, are the product of an emergent regulatory culture based on "new" environmental professionals. Other scholars find collaboration to be a natural outgrowth of a policy-making process dominated by corporate America and a pragmatic, conservative, even co-opted, national environmental lobby (Faber and O'Conner 1989; Gottlieb and Ingram 1988).

5. As quoted in Shabecoff (1989, A14).

6. See Lazarus (1991b). Coglianese (1997) disputes the conventional wisdom in this area, arguing that "the frequency of adversarial conflict in administrative rulemaking has more often been asserted than documented" (p. 39). In the pollution control arena, in particular EPA hazardous waste rulemakings under the Resource Conservation and Recovery Act (years 1988–1991), Coglianese finds it "striking that less than half of EPA's most significant rules [in the hazardous waste area] actually exhibit . . . conflict. And this is among the very rules where conflict is most likely" (p. 40). But the purported lack of conflict in a world of finite time, money, and personnel resources may be nothing more than a strategic calculation on the part of actors to devote their resources to the issues where they are most likely to win, or are most strongly affected. Adversaries may engage in conflict as much as they can reasonably afford to do so. Unless one is willing to accept that all rulemakings affect a set of interests equally, or that the chances of winning the day (and, conversely, the level of risk encountered) are equal across disputes, it is difficult to see why a conflict level involving half of all rules proves a lack of ubiquitous conflict. Moreover, not all legal language found in regulatory rules offers the same opportunities for dispute. Even the most hardened skeptic of congress's ability to write clear laws must agree that, on occasion, laws are grounded with a legal certainty that make court challenges unwise, opportunity costs being what they are in a world of scarce resources.

7. Badarracco (1985); Kelman (1981); Vogel (1986; 1989); G. Wilson (1981; 1982; 1985).

8. Shirking is defined as evading the performance of an obligation, legal or otherwise.

9. See Badaracco (1985); Berry (1989); Gais, Peterson, and Walker (1984); Heclo (1978); Hoberg (1992); Jones (1979); Kraft (1990); Marcus (1980); Melnick (1983); Vogel (1986); Wenner (1982); G. Wilson (1981; 1982; 1985); J. Q. Wilson (1980).

10. See Gais, Peterson, and Walker (1984); Gormley (1989); Hays (1989); Hoberg (1992); Marcus (1980); Melnick (1983); Ripley and Franklin (1984); Vogel (1986).

11. Dr. Thomas Hauser (1993), executive director of the American Institute of Pollution Prevention, notes that since its inception in 1970 over 90 percent of EPA resources have been spent targeting command-and-control-based end-of-pipe solutions (p. 19).

12. Other manifestations of the same phenomena are maximum available control technology and lowest achievable emissions rate. These are all

technology standards. See Chapter 3 for a discussion of a second type of technology standard: the rate-basis standard.

13. The exception is a case of monopoly where competition is nonexistent, or when regulations raise the barriers to entry enough to preserve the competitive positions of existing producers to the disadvantage of potential new producers. However, see the discussion on international competition and economic deregulation in Chapter 2 for reasons why the barriers-to-entry argument is less compelling today than in the past.

14. Allardice, Mattoon, and Testa (1993, p. 10); McFarland (1990); Vogel (1989); interviews with environmentalists (1/7/94; 1/13/94; 3/31/94), industry (1/21/94; 1/12/94; 2/10/94), and regulators (EPA, 1/11/94; 1/13/94). Of course, the countermobilization of the business community was in response to social regulations writ large, and not just environmental regulations (e.g., consumer protection, occupational safety and health, highway traffic safety). Further, despite widespread resistance to stringent environmental controls, some industrial sectors, or firms within sectors, doubtlessly benefited from a command-and-control system because it created a costly barrier to entry for potential competitors. To the extent that environmental regulations were successful in dampening competition, existing industry could earn extra economic rents and thus had little incentive to seek relief. See Greve and Smith (1992); Pashigian (1984); Yandle (1989).

15. For example, the zero-discharge goal of the 1972 Clean Water Act.

16. Bardach and Kagan (1982); Cohen (1992); Kraft (1990); Melnick (1983); Stewart (1988); Wenner (1982).

17. Now known as Lockheed Martin.

18. This observation supports another body of literature, small but growing, that discusses the increased effectiveness of regulatory systems favoring induced cooperation instead of deterrence-based enforcement, and an adaptable, discriminating system of regulation (e.g., Bardach and Kagan 1982; Braithwaite 1985; Hawkins and Thomas 1984; Kagan and Scholz 1984; Scholz 1984; 1991).

19. Moe (1984; 1990); Miller and Moe (1986); Hammond and Miller (1985); Hammond (1984); Horn (1995); Joskow (1991); North (1990); Weingast and Marshall (1988); Williamson (1975; 1985).

20. See Arrow (1969).

21. Williamson (1985, 19).

22. Much of the transaction cost literature focuses on the role of transaction costs as the primary explanatory variable for institutional choices. Decision makers gravitate to those organizational or contractual forms promising low transaction costs vis-à-vis possible alternatives. Implicit within this literature, however, is the idea of *cost effectiveness*. A singular focus on transaction costs at the expense of the benefits those transaction costs produce may lead to arrangements where transaction costs are indeed lower than before, yet participants to an exchange are no better off or are worse off than before. For example, a certain agreement delivers forty units of benefits for eighty transaction costs. An alternative arrangement promises to reduce transaction costs to forty and, in fact, succeeds in doing so. But if participants do not keep in mind the benefits being produced by the alternative forty transaction cost arrangement, the new deal may leave you with twenty or fewer units of benefits. In cost-effectiveness terms, this leaves you with either the same 2:1 ratio of costs to benefits or less than 2:1. In effect, the transaction cost savings are illusory in this hypothetical case since the level of benefits has dropped as well. In terms of a rational decision-making calculus, participants are not likely to embrace new programs or organizational arrangements without placing transaction costs in the broader context of overall cost effectiveness.

23. The conceptual separation of costs into three distinctive categories clearly oversimplifies the interrelationship of costs encountered in practice. For example, the level of information search and program negotiation costs, both "process" costs, are a function of the objective difficulty of the relevant policy problem and the behavior or reaction of participants to the final program design. See also the discussion in Chapter 3 regarding the relationship of public sector enforcement costs to levels of industry resistance.

24. DiIulio, Garvey, and Kettl (1993, 26).

25. Stephen Breyer (1982) writes, "Obtaining accurate, relevant information constitutes the central problem for agenc[ies] engaged in standard setting. [They] have difficulty finding knowledgeable, trustworthy sources" (p. 103).

26. Uncertainty affects the level of transaction costs in two main ways. First, it forces players to focus resources on an entire array of possibilities, from negative reactions to proposed policies by adversaries to the creation of a proprietary database as protection against false or biased information from competing sources and so on. Second, uncertainty means there is less chance that chosen strategies will yield expected benefits. For example, challenging regulatory decisions in the courts does not guarantee results beneficial to your interests. Research suggests that industry and environmentalists have roughly a 50–50 chance of winning when cases are litigated. Moreover, winning often does nothing more than remand the case back to the EPA for reconsideration. In many cases EPA's response to these court orders has little or no effect on the substance of its original decision, in which case winning litigants have spent large sums of money and staff time and often years of effort for an outcome that leaves their interests no better off vis-à-vis the start of the process (see Chapter 2).

27. See Alchian and Demsetz (1972); Miller and Moe (1986); Weingast and Marshall (1988); Williamson (1975; 1985).

28. The term "technology innovation for environmental purposes" includes all types of technology innovation that have a beneficial effect on the environment—i.e., pollution prevention (such as manufacturing process changes), pollution control and remediation, information systems, and management practices. Other similar phrases, such as "innovative environmental technology," are used interchangeably (see NACEPT 1991, 5, footnote 1).

29. Malcolm Sparrow (1994) reports that the Internal Revenue Service is refocusing its tax-collection strategies toward the inducement of greater rates of voluntary compliance by "inculcat[ing] in citizens a heightened sense of responsibility toward taxes" (p. *xxiii*). Each percentage increase in voluntary compliance "produces between $7 and $8 billion in additional revenue" (p. *xxiii*). One of Sparrow's central arguments is that environmental protection, policing, and tax bureaucracies are "realiz[ing] that the best approach to

enforcement . . . is to minimize the need for it" (p. *xxiii*). As a result, each agency is undergoing profound changes in its approach to procuring compliance, from coercive, deterrent-oriented strategies, "fueled through vigorous prosecutorial efforts" (p. *x*), to more flexible, results-oriented, partnership approaches (pp. *xvii–xxiii*). See also NAPA (1995).

    30. Becker (1983); Lowi (1979); McConnell (1966); Peltzman (1976); Stigler (1971). James Buchanan and Gordon Tullock (1976), Peter Pashigian (1984; 1985), Bruce Yandle (1989), Michael Greve (1992), and others have applied the Economic Theory of Regulation (ETR) framework to American environmental politics. Buchanan and Tullock (1976) argue that industry prefers emissions standards to emissions taxes because they do a better job of raising barriers to entry for new firms, hence increasing the profits of existing firms. Likewise, the definition of a special "private" interest is extended to environmental advocacy groups. In this view, environmentalists care more about maximizing or maintaining their organizational bases of power than their reported goals of a cleaner environment (Ackerman and Hassler 1981; Greve 1992). Further, command-and-control arrangements are preferred precisely because they enhance the power of elected officials and bureaucrats by giving them control over the distribution of property rights, the specification of control technologies, and compliance decision-making processes (e.g., permitting). This arrangement ensures the delivery of special-interest benefits much more so than it does the delivery of environmental quality (Ackerman and Hassler 1981; Yandle 1989, 103, 152). As a result, environmental policy outcomes are best understood as a case where special interests—industry *and* environmentalists—pressure congress into providing inefficient solutions to environmental problems.

    31. Moe (1989) finds that the design of the American political system, including the election cycle, length of terms in office, and checks and balances, is responsible for the two main features of American politics: political uncertainty and political compromise. Political uncertainty leads winners to use structural solutions to impose outcomes on losers and to protect their interests over the long term. However, the high likelihood of political compromise in such an "open" political system makes it very difficult to shut out losers entirely, hence an ineffective bureaucratic structure results (p. 329).

    32. The most noted case is that of market-based mechanisms. Although these barriers can still be substantial, ETR scholars suggest that firm profits correlate positively with the height of the barrier to entry. Hence, it is plausible to argue that if industry was really interested in protecting itself from competition, it would opt for regulatory arrangements offering the highest barriers to entry. See Derthick and Quirk (1985) for a similar criticism, yet focused on the inability of ETR to explain deregulation in the latter half of the 1970s. See also Yandle's (1989) final chapter, where he discusses the growing importance of international competitiveness factors and how it weakens the barriers-to-entry argument.

    33. My use of "distributional" is broader than the privatized, material benefits of policy implied by ETR and others such as Olson (1965). It can also be the ability of a policy mechanism to deliver the goods—the policy goal "benefits"—important to stakeholders. For example, policy instruments that produce more of the public good of environmental quality benefit regulators and environmental advocates.

34. Moe (1984; 1990); Miller and Moe (1986); Hammond and Miller (1985); Hammond (1984); Joskow (1991); North (1990); Weingast and Marshall (1988); Williamson (1975; 1985).

35. The sustainability problem can be overcome in this case by linking transactions together to create a high-transaction-cost scenario for all major players. Successful linkage moves the dynamic over to Box 7. Each participant encounters "full" trust and a strong incentive to play, given the possibility of substantial transaction cost savings for all. Collaboration under these circumstances thus is possible but will be limited, given that linked transactions encounter greater objective difficulty in satisfying the transaction-specific conditions element of pluralism by the rules (see Chapter 4).

36. The emphasis on stakeholder perception derives from James Q. Wilson (1980). Wilson put forth the idea that policies lead to politics. Actor perceptions of the costs and benefits associated with proposed policies mobilize different actors and lead to different types of politics—majoritarian, clientele, interest group, and entrepreneurial (p. 372). My study differs in that stakeholders are responding to the perceived transaction costs associated with *existing* as well as proposed regulatory programs. The *perceived* comparative benefits (i.e., reduced transaction costs) offered by alternative regulatory arrangements are instrumental in inducing collaboration. In both cases, the perceptions of stakeholders matter precisely because perceptions lead to action.

2

When Transaction Costs Can No Longer Be Ignored

The late 1960s and early 1970s brought a new awareness of the environmental damages wrought by economic growth and industrial expansion. Among others, Rachel Carson's (1962) *Silent Spring*, Stewart Udall's (1963) *The Quiet Crisis*, and John Esposito's (1970) *Vanishing Air* publicized the plight of the environment. Other studies demonstrated that industry knew how to reduce emissions and could afford environmental protection, yet willfully chose to ignore the social "bad" of pollution (Nader 1965). The theory of market failure provided by welfare economics made explicit the connection between a deteriorating environment and the unwillingness of industry to clean up: because pollution, a waste by-product of industrial processes, is not directly linked to the incentives provided by marketplace dynamics, prices of goods and services do not reflect the negative effects of pollution on public health or, more generally, the overall quality of life. The failure of markets to incorporate such a negative externality into product prices means that industry has no incentive to clean up on its own. The authority of government was therefore needed to coerce industry into a more socially responsible decision-making framework aimed at ensuring acceptable levels of environmental quality.

The perception of environmental crisis stemmed as much from the limited successes of earlier national attempts to manage pollution as from the unwillingness of government to use its authority to correct for market failure. Air and water pollution control policies designed during the 1950s and 1960s[1] delegated considerable implementation authority to the states. Policy success was stymied by the fact that many states did not share the federal government's commitment to environmental protection, while others lacked the resources required to administer the programs.

Whatever the cause, the American public responded to the perceived crisis by making concern for the environment a top priority. In 1965 only 35 percent of the American public thought the problem of water pollution was very or somewhat serious, but by 1968 this fraction had increased to 58 percent. In the area of air pollution there was a similar jump: from only 28 percent in 1965 to 55 percent by 1968.[2] By 1970, concern for environmental protection placed in the upper echelon of national policy concerns, ranking third behind national defense and the health of the economy (Dunlap 1990). Further evidence of the public's commitment to a cleaner environment came when millions joined the first Earth Day demonstrations in 1970.

Environmental advocates, dismayed by what they saw as the clear failure of earlier attempts to manage pollution and seeking to tap the power of public concern, lobbied congress for new policies giving the federal government enhanced authority over the nation's pollution problems. Politicians, seeing the rapid growth and tremendous size of the new environmental constituency, sought ways to satisfy the apparent consensus that pollution was out of control and that a more prominent federal role was needed to rectify the situation. Yet, given the general nature of the demands, it was not entirely clear just what the constituent components of a stronger and better federal pollution control policy were supposed to be. It was, as Charles O. Jones (1975) said, "a majority in search of a policy" (p. 175). The initial lack of a clearly defined framework for dealing with pollution control issues did not deter legislators from acting. In the ensuing decade, congress enacted pollution control legislation at a pace and scale unprecedented for the environmental arena, with levels of bipartisan support verging on unanimity.

By the latter half of the 1970s, however, there were signs that citizens' and politicians' eagerness to support an ever-expanding environmental revolution had limits. Declining public support, the resurgence of conservative Republicans led by Ronald Reagan, and a general sense that ineffective implementation was the rule rather than the exception significantly slowed and even stalled the environmental juggernaut. EPA went from an agency enjoying widespread support to an agency under siege, struggling to survive under the weight of continual court challenges, expanding responsibilities, and massive budget cuts. Environmental legislation in congress no longer enjoyed near-consensus margins of victory. Instead, gridlock became the rule. Greater citizen access to environmental decision making through open administrative processes and liberalized rules of standing, and an activist judiciary less willing to defer to EPA experts, allowed more voices and values to be heard. But they also contributed to the paralysis and delay so common to bureaucratic decision making in the environmental arena. The ascendancy of the environmental lobby gave way to an offsetting balance of power in which both industry and environmentalists possessed the power to derail or seriously compromise each others' initiatives. The growing exposure of the American economy to global economic forces created new imperatives for industry to find cost-effective regulatory methods. In their quest for cost effectiveness, the business community was joined by growing numbers of regulators and environmentalists. State governments, accustomed to federal largesse in the area of environmental protection, began to chafe more and more under the combined weight of federally imposed environmental priorities and a declining willingness on the part of federal authorities to finance mandated pollution control initiatives.

Together, these institutional and economic developments have done much to sensitize stakeholders in pollution control politics to the high transaction costs accompanying the no-holds-barred game of pluralism. The changed context is one in which major stakeholders are now more willing to entertain alternative, collaborative games promising to reduce transaction costs.

THE POLITICAL–BUREAUCRATIC NEXUS

Regulatory actions in environmental politics during the late 1960s and early 1970s reflected the dominant fears of the day: policy decisions were less the product of democratic deliberation than of special-interest manipulation and bureaucratic dominance.[3] In response, strategies were devised to ensure greater political accountability, the EPA being no exception to the rule.[4] Yet the vigorous and competing attempts by congress and the executive branch to hold EPA accountable during the 1970s and 1980s created considerable uncertainty for agency decision makers, while the demands for improved regulatory performance beginning in the late 1970s increased agency decision-making costs. The added uncertainty and higher costs gave regulators additional incentive to seek out alternative collaborative arrangements.

EPA's enabling legislation rejected the independent commission model of regulation and opted for direct control by the president through the principle of executive integration.[5] The EPA was dedicated to pollution control, was independent of established cabinet-level departments, and was headed by an administrator chosen by the president. The scope of EPA's jurisdiction—multi-industry—was also significantly different than previous regulatory agencies (Hawkins and Thomas 1984). Further, the Nixon administration's original plan for EPA's organizational structure was predicated on an integrated, or cross-media, approach (there were no media-based offices at all). The integrated approach accepted that, because the chemical constituents in pollution readily transcended the mediums of air, water, and land, the agency's organizational design should treat pollution problems in the same holistic fashion. But the integrated vision quickly succumbed to the more particularized demands of congressional committees and the single-media design of major pollution control statutes. The result was an organization that mixed cross-media-based functions, such as research, monitoring, standard setting, and enforcement writ large, with single-media-based programmatic offices (air and water) and categorical offices (pesticides, radiation, and solid waste). From the beginning, however, "the media-oriented offices have been the dominant power. The laws, the congressional committee system, public opinion, and the training and loyalties of EPA employees . . . all lean in the direction of media-oriented approaches. Thus, even some of the nominally functional offices are, in reality, subordinate parts of the air, water, and other media offices" (Davies 1990, 53).

Congress, for its part, concentrated on reducing the authority and degree of discretion afforded the bureaucracy (Gormley 1989). A more frequent and consistent pattern of oversight created strong incentives for the EPA to enforce regulatory rules "by the book" in order to demonstrate fairness and to demonstrate that legislative intentions were having the desired effect (Bardach and Kagan 1982; Lazarus 1991a, 212–13). Likewise, congress controlled the EPA by statutes "that defined with some precision the role and responsibility of the regulators" (Marcus 1980, 20). Chief examples include the imposition of scientific and technological norms on bureaucratic decision-making processes,[6] clear law with action-forcing mechanisms such as compliance deadlines and procedural timetables, statutory language designed to ensure oversight by environmentally friendly committees, and statutes requiring agencies to develop large amounts of factual material before issuing a rule (Lowi 1979; McGarity 1992; Rosenbaum 1989, 214).

Despite incessant congressional demands for agency responsiveness during the 1970s, EPA was not yet an agency under siege. Strong bipartisan support in congress and high levels of public support for pollution control meant that agency resources grew steadily throughout most of the 1970s.[7]

Congress, of course, was not the only player in the regulatory game. The executive branch competed to influence pollution control outcomes. Beginning in the late 1970s amid growing concerns about regulatory excessiveness, the effects of *all kinds* of regulation on economic productivity and overall macroeconomic health,[8] and growing demands for improved agency performance, the EPA's political and fiscal bases came under sustained attack. Presidents vigorously attempted to control decision-making through agency budget allocations, political appointments, and recentralized executive branch control (Moe 1985).

In the last two years (1979–1980) of Jimmy Carter's presidency, EPA's budget authority suffered a 33 percent decline (see Figure 2.1). The trend continued with Ronald Reagan. President Reagan reduced the federal government's role in environmental regulation by slashing EPA budgets and personnel even farther and devolving regulatory authority to the states. From 1980 to 1983, pollution control and compliance spending at the EPA was cut by 40 percent in real dollars. Personnel expenditures declined from $636.9 million in 1980 to $557.8 million three years later. From 1978 to 1983, the EPA's research and development budget was cut by 75 percent, and the total agency budget by 56 percent. By 1992 the EPA budget had regained some ground, being 21 percent higher in real dollar terms than 1983.

Yet even this degree of improvement left EPA's buying power at only 53 percent of 1978 levels. The steady growth in federal budget deficits make it unlikely that EPA will recover these funding cuts in full anytime soon, even given the advent of the more environmentally friendly Clinton presidency.[9] Of greater significance, these figures do not take into account the growth in EPA's regulatory responsibilities, especially in the area of Superfund (reauthorized and expanded in 1986) and the Clean Air Act Amendments of 1990.[10] The "general pattern [is one] of geometrically expanding responsibilities accompanied by arithmetically decreasing or stagnant resources once inflation is factored in" (interview with EPA 1/7/94).

Other facets of the Reagan Administration's attempt to improve EPA's responsiveness to its agenda of deregulation and regulatory relief included the appointment of prodevelopment EPA officials and the recentralization of executive branch control by using the Office of Management and Budget (OMB) and executive orders.[11] McGarity (1992) reported the "chilling" effect of OMB review on agency decision making.

> Because OMB officials feel free to substitute their views for the policy judgments of the agencies to which Congress had delegated regulatory authority, OMB review *interjects substantial uncertainties into the rulemaking process*. There is uncertainty at the very outset, as agency officials cannot know whether internally generated solutions to problems that arise in the early development of a rule will withstand OMB review (p. 1433, emphasis added).

The uncertainty was especially acute for EPA. In 1989, 2,200 rules were submitted to OMB for review from all government agencies. OMB found 1,638 rules (73.8 percent) consistent with its requirements and ordered no changes. For EPA, however, only 97 of 201 rules (48.3

percent) were approved without change (Executive Office of the President 1990, 636, 638). Between 1984 and 1989, on average, OMB found that only 61 percent of all EPA rules required no changes (Percival 1991, 163). According to agency officials, the steady pattern of OMB intervention has two main effects on the rulemaking process. It creates a powerful disincentive to write regulations imposing additional regulatory burdens and it is "a pain in the ass because it takes a long, long time to get anything through."[12]

Reagan-era operatives also reorganized the EPA. A new, politicized level of management halfway between career professionals and top-level political appointees was added, the Office for Enforcement was dismantled, and decision making was centralized by removing discretionary authority from regional offices (Cohen 1986). Systematic efforts designed to change the balance of professionals inside EPA constituted a second facet of reorganization. The role of economists in agency decision making (as opposed to lawyers and scientists) grew significantly with the integration of economic criteria into internal policy processes (Cook 1988; Eisner 1993, 177; Marcus 1980). Further, Reagan continued the practice initiated by President Carter of using a special council to review the benefits and costs of proposed regulations, as well as their compatibility with the rest of a president's policy program (e.g., Carter's Regulatory Analysis Review Group; Reagan's Regulatory Relief Task Force). For the remainder of the 1980s and then into the 1990s with the Quayle Competitiveness Council, these councils earned a reputation as the primary forum where industry could petition for regulatory relief. The added opportunity for industry to make a "late hit" in rulemaking processes through either the White House-based councils or OMB limited EPA discretion even more, forced additional resources to be devoted toward establishment of a full decision-making record, and increased the likelihood that EPA's rules would be watered down, completely dismantled, or significantly delayed.[13]

Finally, congressional demand for oversight of EPA activities intensified, starting in the late 1970s. Richard Lazarus (1991a) testified that a typical year of congressional supervision includes "lengthy and rigorous appropriation hearings on the agency's budget, numerous appearances by EPA officials at hearings, between 100 and 150 congressionally commanded reports to congress, approximately 5,000 congressional inquiries to the agency, and doubtless even more frequent, less formal agency contacts" (p. 211). The General Accounting Office also requested up to forty reports annually from EPA. The period 1980 through 1988 averaged twenty-five reports per year, fully 47 percent more than the 1970 to 1978 time period. Likewise, during the initial year of EPA Administrator Anne Gorsuch-Burford's tumultuous tenure, and in part

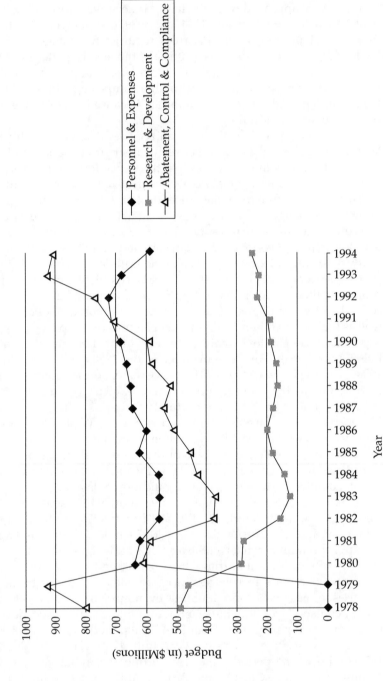

Figure 2.1 EPA Budget Authority 1978–1996 (Constant 1982–1984 $Million)

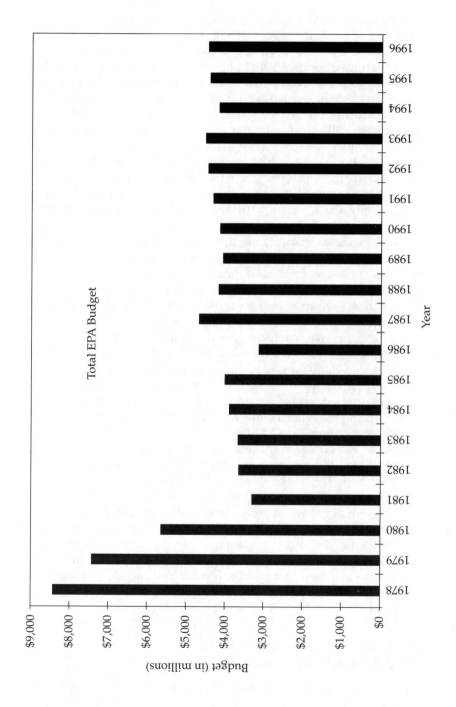

Total EPA Budget

as a response to OMB's enhanced review authority over environmental regulations, the chairs of six different committees initiated investigations of the EPA.[14] Moreover, appearances by EPA officials in congressional hearings during the 96th Congress (1979–1980) jumped to 212, an increase of 68 percent compared to the average number of appearances during the four previous sessions of congress. The intensity of this particular form of oversight stayed high throughout the 1980s, with EPA officials called to testify at a rate 43 percent higher than during the 1970s.[15] Joel Aberbach (1990) describes a corresponding rise of police-patrol oversight of EPA during the 1980s, in which committee staff regularly monitor agency activities looking for possible problems, rather than simply waiting for an aggrieved constituency group to trigger a "fire alarm" (pp. 98–101; see McCubbins and Schwartz 1984). The added intensity of congressional oversight activities was only compounded by the consistently negative nature of the oversight. As EPA Administrator Lee Thomas reported, EPA bashing adds to the "chilling effect oversight has on decision making in the agency. You need to make reasonable decisions with the understanding that you're accountable for them, you may well hear about them, but that it's not going to end up as some kind of posturing [or] personal attack."[16]

Such aggressive, competing, and often conflicting demands on EPA's time and resources by the legislative and executive branches contributes to the paralysis in environmental protection so common over the past twenty-five years. With much of the agency's limited resources directed toward "defending its decisions in court, negotiating with OMB and the White House, and justifying its decisions to multiple congressional committees" rather than toward environmental protection per se, EPA decision makers have ample incentives, if not a great deal of latitude, to seek a way out of this restrictive box (Lazarus 1991b, 313; *New York Times*, 11/30/84, A30). Moreover, the integration of economic analysis into everyday agency decision-making processes and the gradual growth of professional staff trained in economics predisposes more and more agency decision makers to favor alternatives to command-and-control regulation.[17] In recent years this is exactly what EPA officials have been doing: seeking collaborative alternatives designed to improve agency effectiveness and placate a broad array of interests in the hope that improved clientele satisfaction will result in less intervention by hierarchical political principals.

LEGISLATIVE GRIDLOCK AND UNCONVENTIONAL LAWMAKING

A sizable contingent of legislators in congress, including more than a few Republicans, were not content to stand idly by and watch President

Reagan dismantle the environmental policy gains of the preceding decade. Environmentalists and their congressional allies successfully defeated attempts to emasculate the Clean Air Act in 1982. The Democratic leadership in the U.S. House of Representatives refused to bring other laws needing reauthorization to the floor, fearing that to do so only risked weakening the statutes. The result was legislative gridlock (Bryner 1993; Kraft 1990 1994; Moe 1989, 320). According to Senator Max Baucus (D-MT) (1993), a key member of the Senate Environment and Public Works Committee,

> [b]itter divisions between the Executive branch and Congress, and between industry and environmental groups, made advances impossible. Legal and political battles, not scientific analysis and cooperation, dominated the environmental landscape. The result, of course, was that for a full decade, from the early 1980s to the early 1990s, environmental progress halted, and at times was reversed (pp. 139–40).

The 97th Congress (1981–1982), for example, was virtually devoid of proposals for new environmental policies. While eight major pieces of environmental legislation were up for reauthorization, only two passed, both in 1982 (Endangered Species Act and Toxic Substances Control Act). Action was deferred in the areas of clean water, clean air, hazardous wastes, pesticides, safe drinking water, and noise abatement (Cook and Davidson 1985; Kraft 1990, 109). Throughout the 1980s Henry Waxman (D-Ca), Gerry Sikorski (D-Minn), and George Mitchell (D-Maine), among others, introduced dozens of acid rain bills to no avail. Furthermore, while gridlock eased during the latter half of the 1980s, the perception of a deadlocked congress left a lasting impression on environmentalists and regulators charged with promoting and ensuring environmental progress.[18]

> Gridlock [was] expensive, both in terms of the usual definition of expense, namely dollars, but also in terms of public and environmental health. If we do not do anything about a problem because we cannot decide what to do about it, whatever health threat or environmental threat exists is certainly not going to be mitigated or alleviated. . . .[19]

Similarly, from industry's perspective, gridlock and delay on legislation up for reauthorization prevented the rationalization of the inefficient, high-cost regulatory superstructure (see Chapter 3).

Gridlock also posed a problem for legislators concerned with environmental progress because it left them with nothing tangible for which they could claim credit. In addition, Democratic (majority) party leaders were hampered in the achievement of their two main goals: helping to formulate and pass the party's policy agenda and to maintain their party majority in congress (Canon 1992, 9). As a result, both individual legislators and party leaders had more of an interest in innovative regulatory programs that bridged gaps among adversaries and therefore helped to facilitate the coalition building necessary to move the environmental agenda forward.

Devising a legislative contract capable of bridging the *substantive* gaps among opposing interests is, however, but one part of the puzzle in today's congress. A newer, and arguably more difficult, challenge for legislators and party leaders is finding a way to *procedurally* shepherd agreements through the uncertainty of postreform congressional lawmaking. Observers report that the ability of the committee system to structure the legislative process and produce policy outcomes in predictable fashion is in decline (Canon 1992; Khademian 1993; Shepsle 1989). Under a strong committee system, members select committee assignments according to their electoral needs, are granted almost exclusive control over proposals within their committee's jurisdiction, and are able to use their agenda-setting powers to impose outcomes they prefer (see Moe 1987a; Polsby 1968; Shepsle 1989). Formal rules of procedure and institutional norms of reciprocity, deference, and seniority facilitate the operation of the system and provide the certainty required to forge consensus among members with diverse constituent needs and priorities (Weingast and Marshall 1988). But decision making in the postreform congress is much more open and unpredictable than Weingast and Marshall and others allow. The proliferation of subcommittees with overlapping jurisdictions, the growing independence of individual lawmakers, and the weakened powers of committee chairs have so significantly decentralized authority that the existing rules for collective decision making no longer produce timely legislative action (Khademian 1993; Shepsle 1989; Cohen 1992). Individual members now pursue a wide range of policy concerns with extensive staff and subcommittee resources, limiting the control any one committee has over jurisdiction (Salisbury and Shepsle 1981). As well, changes in the rules governing floor voting increase uncertainty at the floor stage of lawmaking (Smith 1989). The result is a postreform congress where uncertainties encountered during the legislative decision process effectively limit the ability of the traditional committee system to manage lawmaking.

The uncertainties associated with an unpredictable lawmaking process create strong incentives for legislators, party leaders, and interested stakeholders to seek assurances that their primary interests will be protected for the duration of the policy process. Barring such guarantees, it is unlikely that even collaborative deals like acid rain (see

Chapter 6) will go forward. The conundrum becomes: how do you legislate together under such conditions? What will reintroduce enough certainty into the legislative equation to allow the deal to move forward?

One way to reduce the uncertainty of legislating in the postreform congress is by relying on unconventional lawmaking. The inability of the traditional committee system to manage the legislative process creates a void increasingly filled by activist majority party leadership (Canon 1992). Examples include recent leadership summits with presidents on matters of the budget,[20] appropriations without authorizing legislation, legislation that bypasses committees and floor debate entirely,[21] more closed and restrictive rules, compressed debate, leaders playing power broker between deadlocked committees, and greater use of ad hoc institutions like task forces, backroom negotiations, and joint committees (Canon 1992; Cohen 1992; Collie and Cooper 1989; Khademian 1993; Kettl 1993; Rohde 1991; Sinclair 1992).

Paradoxically, the unconventional institutions that party leaders use to reduce the uncertainty of legislating are responsible for increasing the uncertainty of legislative outcomes in another way. Given that unconventional lawmaking is based on ad hoc interpretations of the circumstances surrounding individual pieces of legislation, the timing and nature of the rules of the game are subject to broad variation (see also Canon 1992; Khademian 1993). The variation in the decision-making dynamic heightens uncertainty by making it harder for legislators to know what to expect in each case. The implication for the collective decision-making dynamic is the same as before. Legislators have strong incentives to devise institutions capable of overcoming the uncertainty.

Legislators minimize the uncertainty of unconventional lawmaking by "craft[ing] legislation in explicit terms. Bargains or winning positions [are] set in concise terms so each member involved in the negotiations has some certainty about the ultimate legislative product" (Khademian 1993, 12). The operating principle is "trust, but verify" (congressional staff interview 1/18/94). The point is significant precisely because it suggests that the cause of statutory specificity is something more than conventional wisdom admits. Instead of explicit language being the product of interest group conflict or conflict between executive and congressional branches of government, *specificity is a response to an internally generated collective action problem of congress itself.*[22] In the past, under conditions of strong committee government, formal rules of procedure and institutional norms created enough certainty that explicit language was not needed (Weingast and Marshall 1988). Yet the rules of the game in congress have changed dramatically. Simply put, the high transaction costs of postreform congressional decision making induce majority party leaders to use unconventional lawmaking institutions to solve the transaction cost problem. In turn, expanded use of unconventional lawmaking, while solving the first problem, creates a new kind of uncertainty which leads legislators to insist on explicit language as added protection for agreements. In other words, legislators have their own reasons for adopting explicit statutory language.

Legislators and stakeholders in national pollution control politics seek alternative, unconventional means of legislating because legislating in the environmental arena has become particularly costly. With gridlock as the rule, individual legislators and party leaders alike achieve fewer of their primary goals, whether they are rooted in electoral, party, or policy considerations. Environmental advocates are unable to address new problems of degradation as they arise, much less amend the flaws and loopholes in existing statutes. Industry is stuck with the rigidity and high costs of compliance imposed by existing laws. Each has an incentive to consider innovative regulatory arrangements and unconventional lawmaking methods precisely because, taken together, they facilitate legislative decision making and help to create credible stakes in outcomes for participants, thus helping each participant to maximize distinctive primary goals.

OPENING UP THE ADMINISTRATIVE PROCESS AND JUDICIAL ACTIVISM

The shape of the regulatory regime in environmental politics drew on the prevailing wisdom of the 1960s and 1970s in another way. Critics of interest-group liberalism claimed that bureaucratic decision making too often favored special interests at the expense of the broader public interest (Gormley 1989, 44; Lowi 1979). In a widely cited example of a closed policy-making system, or "iron triangle," Grant McConnell (1966, 211–30) showed that water resources policy was narrowly responsive to three sets of interests: Western congressmen in control of key committees, the federal Bureau of Reclamation, and local developers in the western United States. Water resources policy favored economic growth and structural solutions like dams designed for the production of electricity, flood control, and agricultural irrigation. Excluded from consideration were environmental values favoring the preservation of natural beauty, the sanctity of wildlife habitat, ecosystem integrity, and wetlands.

Interest representation reforms opened the administrative decision-making process. They were designed, first and foremost, to increase government's responsiveness to a broader public interest by forcing the inclusion of values representing other than economic interests. A variety of institutional means were used. Watchdogs for the public interest—inspectors general offices—were created inside government agencies. The right of direct participation in rulemaking was expanded through mandatory public hearings, statutory citizen suit provisions,[23] and scientific review requirements under the 1976 Federal Advisory Committee Act (FACA) (Melnick 1983; Rosenbaum 1989, 216).[24] With respect to FACA requirements, Sheila Jasanoff (1990) found that adding outside scientific review procedures to the rulemaking process delayed rule promulgation even further, given scientists' need for long research times and the logistics of selecting an advisory committee, among other things.

The EPA and other government agencies also faced an increased number of judicial challenges resulting from liberalized rules of legal standing and an increased willingness on the part of judges to second-guess agency expertise (Mitchell 1991; Melnick 1983). In the former case, prevailing legal doctrine prior to the mid-1960s "required an environmental group to prove that an agency's action injured it or some of its members in a direct economic or physical way before the group's standing to raise [an] issue in court would be recognized. This test effectively ruled out most environmental litigation, because many environmental issues involve intangibles such as threats to scenic beauty or to wildlife or to [ecosystems] generally" (Mitchell 1991, 101). Three landmark court decisions—*Scenic Hudson Preservation Conference v. Federal Power Commission* (1966), *United Church of Christ v. FCC* (1966), and *Sierra Club v. Morton* (1972)—significantly redefined standing. The class of interests entitled to seek judicial review was broadened, making it possible for environmental advocacy groups to represent their members in court for alleged harms done to them. Indirect injuries—those injuries other than economic or direct physical harm—were recognized as grounds for standing. When combined with citizen suit provisions, which gave individuals and groups the standing to sue government agencies for nonperformance (e.g., a delayed rule, a decision contrary to the intent of congress), liberalized standing forced EPA decision making to be responsive to an ever broader and more diffuse clientele (Glicksman and Schroeder 1991, 267–68).

In the latter case, courts increasingly opted for a more stringent standard of judicial review known as the "hard look" doctrine. Prior to 1970, U.S. courts typically applied a rational-basis test to agency decisions. Under the rational-basis standard, courts upheld rules unless they were "demonstrably irrational" or arbitrary and capricious. Under the "hard look" doctrine, however, courts required agencies like EPA to explain their reasoning in greater detail[25] and to develop extensive factual information to support rules.[26] They "began to conduct careful and searching reviews of the data agencies developed to support a rule and the methodology used to progress from the data to the rule" (Harter 1982, 11). In such a legal environment, rules are tested and remanded for their arbitrariness and capriciousness, irrationality, and the (in)completeness of their record. The message to agencies "is that its explanations must be exceedingly thoroughgoing in every regard, or else its rulemaking initiatives may be sent back to the drawing board. . . . The key to successful rulemaking therefore is to make every effort to render the rule capable of withstanding the most strenuous possible judicial scrutiny the first time around. . . . [Because] agencies perceive that reviewing courts are inconsistent in the degree to which they are deferential, they are constrained to prepare for the worst-case scenario on judicial review—. . . [an] *extremely resource-intensive and time-consuming* [exercise]."[27] Given that four out of every five major rules promulgated by EPA are contested in court, EPA "spend[s] as much time designing . . . rules to withstand court attack as [they] do getting the rules right and out in the first place."[28]

Moreover, powerful participants have made it harder to get the rules written and promulgated at all by insisting on additional procedural, structural, and analytical constraints as a way of keeping the "other" side from winning. Notice-and-comment rulemaking has simply become another vehicle for advancing or protecting a particular agenda, whether in the form of economic growth[29] or a social agenda designed to promote environmental protection or to stop the licensing of potentially dangerous nuclear technologies.[30]

Expanding the scope of conflict as a method of balancing representation—making sure that all "voices" are heard—and using the courts to achieve environmental victories have other limits as well. First, although the evidence is inconclusive, public hearings are generally criticized as being nothing more than symbolic forums that, except for a few minor details, end up endorsing administrative decisions.[31] An EPA official explains that

> hearings aren't really that helpful because there are usually so many people testifying on controversial rules. People are limited to ten minutes and they end up giving a summary of their main points. You don't get a whole lot of substance from a summary that will help you actually write the rule (interview 3/17/94).

Second, citizen participation in public hearings and public programs is generally limited to organized interests (including other agencies) and comes from only a limited range of those likely to be affected by the program in question (Nagel 1987; Rosenbaum 1976). Third, the limited resources of most advocacy groups means that even though liberalized standing increases opportunities to protect the environment, few groups can afford to challenge any more than a bare minimum of administrative decisions. They must be very selective not only in terms of cases but also in terms of the court chosen to hear the case, given the differentiation among the federal courts in their treatment of environmental issues (Melnick 1983). The regularized exchange of information among the "Group of 10" national environmental groups is partly designed to divide labor into niches of expertise such that limited resources could be focused more effectively. Groups then typically agree to follow the lead of the acknowledged expert in a particular policy area precisely because they cannot afford to contest all the issues they think are important to the cause of a cleaner environment (McCloskey 1990).

Fourth, even after strategically dividing labor to maximize their influence, environmentalists complain of being outgunned and outmaneuvered by industry during rulemaking and implementation.[32] The problem exists outside the EPA as well. In a study tracking the use of $500 million in funds targeted for environmental studies, Freudenburg and Gramling (1994) found that the additional opportunities for input stemming from an open decision-making process did not prevent industry domination of decision making. As a result, "bureaucratic slippage" occurred and the broad policy goals of environmental quality were "altered by successive reinterpretation, such that implementation [bore] little resemblance to the stated policies" (p. i).

Fifth, the strategic targeting of litigation resources so as to maximize the potential for gain does not guarantee that judicial decisions will be favorable. Not only do environmental advocacy organizations tend to win about as often as business interests, the Supreme Court tends to favor economic interests (Levy and Glicksman 1989; Ingram and Mann 1989; Wenner 1982).

At the same time, the openness of administrative decision making created a backlash effect which has increased the uncertainty of litigated outcomes for environmental advocates. In particular, the development of a more conservative federal judiciary during the Reagan and Bush presidencies has led to less receptiveness to the environmentalist side of the debate.[33] Although, as Lettie Wenner (1990) points out, prior court precedents and congressional action designed to restrict the application of cost–benefit analysis to environmental issues limit how far conservative courts can erode environmentalists' gains, there are some clear effects in the areas of standing and the deference of courts to government agency decisions. In *Lujan v. Defenders of Wildlife* (1992), the Supreme Court amplified a recent trend restricting the ability of environmental groups to challenge government decisions. Instead of the "generalized" claims of injury prevalent from the 1960s through the 1980s, *Lujan* ruled that environmental advocates must demonstrate that government actions will be the source of individual, concrete injury or will place them in a position where harm is imminent. Justice Scalia, writing for the majority, extended the restriction of standing to citizen suit provisions, saying that citizens suing the government must meet the new "harm" test. He also warned lawmakers that simply expanding citizen suit provisions by defining general environmental concerns as direct injuries would not be accepted by the court (Barrett 1992; Marcus 1992).

In the case of judicial deference to agency decisions, the pendulum appears to be swinging back in favor of greater deference to the expertise employed by the EPA as well as other agencies. *Sierra Club v. Costle* (1981) was one of the inaugural steps in this direction as the D. C. Circuit court supported EPA's imposition of technology-based new source performance standards under the Clean Air Act. The landmark case in this respect, however, is *Chevron U.S.A. v. NRDC* in 1984 (Starr 1986).[34] *Chevron* established a two-step test requiring courts to initially inquire "whether Congress has directly spoken to the precise question at issue."[35] If congress has addressed it, then the courts are obligated to actualize that intent, despite an agency's reasoning to the contrary. If congress has not spoken on the issue before the court or has sent conflicting signals, then the court must ask whether an agency's interpretation of the statute is reasonable. If it is, the court must defer to the agency rather than "simply impose its own construction on the statute."[36] The post-Chevron era in environmental law has seen the deferential approach of *Chevron* adopted in a growing number of cases, with "Congressional silence . . . deemed an implicit delegation of power to an agency to make policy choices."[37] The net effect of the trend toward greater deference to bureaucratic expertise, however, has been the exacerbation of uncertainty for participants in pollution control politics, since a number of federal courts still adhere to the less deferential "hard look" doctrine.

INTEREST-GROUP POWER EQUILIBRIUM

The overall message conveyed by the new regulatory order to industry was clear. Environmental progress was unlikely without a significant transfer of authority from business managers to government officials[38] and direct intrusion on managerial prerogatives through rules that "democratized the decision process and put something other than profit into the equation."[39] Nor were the costs of cleanup to be a factor in the choice of pollution control arrangements. Such an approach directly challenged the two overarching goals of business organizations—profit maximization and autonomy of control over organizational decision making (see Moe 1987b; Harris 1989). Unsurprisingly, it spurred a strong countermobilization effort by industry, whose purpose was a reversal of environmentalists' gains and a return to the pre-1970 status quo through a strategy "of maximum feasible resistance and minimum feasible retreat."[40] The adoption of such a high-cost, confrontational strategy was predicated in part on corporate America's perception that the battle to roll back environmentalism would be both successful and short.

Although the business community obviously understood the significance of the environmental movement's political successes, it was not clear that they (or anyone else for that matter) *perceived* these successes in anything other than ephemeral terms (Hays 1989, 308). Conventional wisdom among the vast majority of social scientists, political pundits, and the general public at the time treated social movements and their accompanying issues as short-lived phenomena, soon to be eclipsed by other similarly fleeting issues (Downs 1972).

Within the realm of environmental politics, the available information "consistently indicates a significant decline in environmental awareness and concern among the public in the early Seventies" (Dunlap 1990, 10). For all practical purposes, the environment as an issue was halfway through Downs' (1972) issue-attention cycle by 1972, and by the mid-1970s "his prediction that it would shortly move into the fourth stage—the decline of intense public interest—seemed very plausible."[41] Moreover, although there was evidence of a resurgence in political commitment to much of the environmentalist agenda after the 1976 election of Jimmy Carter, it quickly became clear that, given his general inability to push his agenda through congress and a continuing decline in public support for environmental protection throughout the latter half of the 1970s (Dunlap 1990), revising conventional wisdom was unwarranted.

There also emerged a broader political countercurrent to command-and-control types of environmental regulation during the late 1970s. Some of the opposition stemmed from the growing concern over the excessive costs, arbitrariness, ineffectiveness, and large informational requirements associated with social regulations in general.[42] To others it became a matter of recognizing that environmental interests were themselves a new type of "special" interest rather than a legitimate claimant on the broader public interest (Greve 1992; see Greve and

Smith [eds.] 1992). These criticisms found their strongest voice in the resurgent right wing of the American political spectrum under Ronald Reagan and became a part of the broader shift in the ideological climate toward deregulation during the late 1970s and early 1980s.[43] When combined with the growing prospect of a Republican president in 1980, these developments signaled to business that the chance for significant regulatory relief and a reversal of the environmental gains of the 1970s were right around the corner (Meidinger 1985, 460; interview with environmentalist 1/13/94).

It was not until after the first few years of the Reagan Administration and, in particular, after the embattled tenures and forced departures of Ann Gorsuch-Burford at EPA and James Watt at the Department of the Interior, that most in the business world came to a full understanding of the enduring nature of the changes wrought by the environmental revolution. Although President Reagan moved quickly to exploit the growing discontentment with government regulation, the aggressive pursuit of his regulatory relief agenda failed to elicit strong support from the general public and congress, even among Republican legislators (Kenski and Ingram 1986).

Public sentiment for environmental protection, which peaked around Earth Day 1970, nevertheless has retained a substantial level of support among the general public over the years (Dunlap 1990; Ringquist 1993, 27–29). Table 2.1 shows the strength of public concern regarding the environment in response to a variety of questions. The three questions measuring the strength of the opposition to government efforts to improve environmental quality show opposition as strongest during the early 1980s, yet declining sharply to quite low levels by 1990. Similarly, measures indicating positive public support for environmental protection show some decline during the late 1970s. But the public's willingness to sacrifice economic growth for environmental quality and the perception that environmental laws have not gone far enough, or that government is spending too little on protecting the environment, experienced a steady resurgence throughout the 1980s such that by 1990 public opinion registered levels of support that were significantly higher than were seen in the early 1970s. Significantly, this support cuts across all age groups, regions, and demographic and political groups (Kenski and Ingram 1986, 286–87).

During the 1970s, the environmental lobby capitalized on the strong base of public support by successfully establishing itself as a permanent fixture in national policy-making circles.[44] Yet the Reagan years are generally credited with transforming the green lobby into the "green giant"—a sophisticated and effective superlobby in the same league as the National Rifle Association and the national right-to-life movement

TABLE 2.1 Public Opinion on Environmental Protection: Percentage Responding Affirmatively, Selected Years

	1974	1976	1978	1980	1982	1984	1988	1989	1990
Environmental Protection Laws *Have Not* Gone Far Enough[1]	25	32	29[a]	33	37	48[b]	na	55	54
Environmental Protection Laws *Have Gone Too Far*[1]	17	15	24[a]	25	16	14[b]	na	11	11
Government is Spending *Too Little* on Protecting the Environment[2]	63	57	55	51	53	61	68	70	71
Government is Spending *Too Much* on Protecting the Environment[2]	8	10	10	16	12	5	5	4	4
Willing to Sacrifice Economic Growth for Environmental Quality[3]	na	38	37	41[c]	41	42	52	52	64
Willing to Sacrifice Environmental Quality for Economic Growth[3]	na	21	23	26[c]	31	27	19	21	15
Too Little Government Regulation in Environmental Protection[3]	na	na	na	na	35	56	53	58	62
Too Much Government Regulation in Environmental Protection[3]	na	na	na	na	11	8	12	9	16

[1] Roper Organization; [2] NORC General Social Survey; [3] Cambridge Reports, Inc.; [a] Response for 1979; [b] Response for 1983; [c] Response for 1981.
Source: Ringquist (1993, 28).

(Symonds 1982). Memberships of several major environmental advocacy organizations soared in response to perceived threats from the quintessential antienvironmental president (Hays 1989; Ingram and Mann 1989). From 1980 to 1983, the Sierra Club almost doubled in size from 182,000 to 346,000, the National Audubon Society increased by more than 150,000 members, and the Wilderness Society expanded their member base from 50,000 to 100,000. The membership rolls of national environmental groups only continued to grow throughout the 1980s and into the 1990s. By the early 1990s the Natural Resources Defense Council and the Environmental Defense Fund were each more than 150,000 strong, while the World Wildlife Fund counted over 250,000 members, the Sierra Club 550,000 members, the Wilderness Society 330,000 members, and the Nature Conservancy over 700,000 members. In fact, by 1990 the core of the national environmental lobby encompassed over ten million individual members and 4,300 professional staff, while operating on annual revenues exceeding one-half billion dollars (*Economist* 1990; Weber 1993; Baumgartner and Jones 1993, 184–89).

The failure of the Reagan Administration to register a series of quick successes in the battle against environmentalism led many in industry to fear a political backlash from environmentalists and their congressional allies that would only add to their regulatory burden, introduce additional uncertainty into their planning and decision-making processes, and further constrain their ability to maximize organizational goals. As a result, a growing number of industry leaders began to favor a more conciliatory posture toward their environmentalist adversaries and environmental concerns more generally.[45] Leaders of the national environmental community agree. It was not until the early 1980s and especially after "the Reagan clean air initiative failed in 1982, . . . that people in leadership posts in industry began to say, 'This looks like it's here for the long term and we had better start thinking about how to live with it, rather than hoping that we can get rid of it'" (interviews, 1/7/94; 1/13/94; 3/31/94).

The confluence of these factors forced the Reagan Administration to abandon full-scale attempts at regulatory relief by 1983.[46] As Samuel Hays (1989) concluded: "In challenging the environmental movement, Reagan tested its strength and vitality and thereby demonstrated the degree to which it had become a broad and fundamental aspect of American public life."[47]

INTERNATIONAL MARKETS AND DEREGULATION

Industry and regulators have been driven toward alternatives not only by changes in the broader political climate, but also by developments in the domestic and international economies.[48] Part of this dynamic is simply an extension of the earlier concerns that gave rise to the general demands for regulatory reform during the 1970s (see Eads and Fix 1984). As outlined in Chapter 3, aggregate and per unit (of pollution) compliance costs continue to escalate, while environmental regulations have put more of a drag on domestic productivity in recent years.

Placed in the context of the increasingly important dynamic of competition between American firms and their counterparts around the world, industry stakeholders face a powerful incentive to alter the traditional way that America regulates pollution (Allardice, Mattoon, and Testa 1993). International competition makes it more difficult for business to "pass through" regulatory costs to consumers. Thus, industry strategies that pursue regulations as protective barriers to entry by domestic firms have necessarily lost much of their appeal. More importantly, accelerating rates of technological change, relatively unrestricted flows of international capital, and the growing differentiation of international product markets are redefining requirements for success (Piore and Sabel 1984; see Bulkeley 1994). Success now requires high rates of innovation across the entire range of matters affecting firm productivity—including environmental compliance (Porter 1993). It also requires an ability to respond quickly to changing conditions. The competitive edge often goes to those firms that penetrate markets first. These changes in the competitive dynamic led David Allardice (1993) of the Federal Reserve to conclude that policy makers must pay closer attention to the structure of regulatory arrangements today than ever before.

> [The] stakes today are particularly high [given] the speed of global change. Lean and flexible firms do not operate with fat margins and dominant market positions. For them to prosper and succeed in [the global marketplace], public policy cannot waste or misallocate resources. It cannot be so rigid as to hamstring those firms that must themselves become highly flexible and responsive to [rapidly changing] markets (p. *ii*).[49]

By definition, regulatory programs that offer industry a high degree of production flexibility to meet these international challenges are preferred by industry (industry interview 3/10/94). A former EPA official explains the change as follows:

> smart companies . . . [are] trad[ing] extra emissions reductions for increased production flexibility. They care less about what level of control is placed on them so long as they can switch production right away without having to go through a nine-month or fourteen-month permit process controlled by bureaucrats. That's much more valuable [to a company] because they can budget pollution control costs. In fact, they can budget

them down to almost zero emissions if they have to. But [companies] can't budget for the inability to penetrate markets that they need to penetrate within a two-month time span before their product becomes obsolete (interview 1/7/94).

Heightened sensitivity to the value of production flexibility also extends to the large number of industries that have been deregulated over the past twenty years. The primary industry affected by the acid rain program—the U.S. public utility industry—is illustrative. A key concern of policy makers in the debate over acid rain was how well the heavily regulated, monopolistic utility industry would respond to the allowance trading market in SO_2 emissions. The traditional rules of the game in the utility industry have long been defined by federal and state regulators and as such have typically left utility decision makers little room or reason to innovate. As well, there was little incentive for utilities to concern themselves with the costs of government-mandated technologies, whatever the policy area, since public utility commissions (PUCs) virtually always approved rate-base increases in such cases. Given the overall incentive structure, a senior industry official explains that "the best thing you could do if you were a utility was get the thing put in the rate base. Whatever it was, get the cost put in the rate base and you'd get that plus whatever the return was and all was right with the world" (interview 1/21/94). The rules of the game rewarded rigidity rather than innovation and gave limited concern to the cost effectiveness of control technologies.

However, the passage of the 1992 Energy Policy Act effectively deregulated much of the public utility industry and, in combination with the acid rain emissions trading program, transformed the incentive structure facing industry decision makers (industry interview 2/22/94). The part of the law most responsible for the change is "third-party wheeling"—power producers outside of a public utility's power grid can now access a utility's transmission lines to deliver electricity, often to the utility's own customers. The new system places a premium on low-cost delivery of power since utilities no longer have exclusive rights to their established customer bases. This creates opportunities not only for power producers to "cherry pick" the best customers from weak utilities, but also for increased market shares by nonutility power generators, mainly independent power producers (IPPs) and alternative fuel-based power producers (APPs). The problem for established (aging) public utilities is that most IPPs and APPs, because they operate newer facilities, benefit from more efficient pollution control technologies, hence experience significantly lower compliance costs. Thus, "potentially, the worst thing you can do [if you are a public utility] is have the costs of mandated environmental technologies put into the rate base because then you have to charge your customer for it, and if some guy can make power for 6.7 cents per kilowatt hour and you make it for 6.9 cents and they can get on your transmission line and force you to wheel it to customers, you're going to lose your customers" (industry interview 1/21/94).

Whereas the "old" monopolistic game of rigid regulations and high-cost technologies meant additional profits and higher rates of return to investors, the "new" competitive game transforms these same factors into liabilities. The introduction of competition forces industry decision makers to pay closer attention to costs, the relationship between innovation and cost savings, and their ability to respond to changing market conditions. In short, the contemporary incentive structure facing public utility decision makers values regulatory arrangements offering a high degree of production flexibility much the same as firms engaged in international competition.

Regulators are also increasingly sensitive to the competitiveness concerns of industry, especially when it is clear that private-sector compliance costs are going to be particularly burdensome. Some view it as the moral obligation of public sector officials to help industry find the most cost-effective way to reach environmental goals in such a competitive global business environment (interview with EPA 1/11/94). Others, such as Mary Gade, director of the Illinois EPA (IEPA), and Dr. Anupom Ganguli, senior manager in charge of the South Coast Air Quality Management District's Regional Clean Air Market program (RECLAIM), see little choice in the matter.[50] Given that the 1990 Clean Air Act Amendments set increasingly stringent emissions-reduction goals for industry[51] and that the marginal costs per unit of required reductions are higher than in the past (orders of magnitude higher in some cases), getting industry to comply requires that regulators collaborate with industry in program design and use market-based mechanisms more frequently (interview with EPA 12/10/93).[52]

CHANGES IN THE STATE–FEDERAL RELATIONSHIP

During the 1960s and 1970s, the national centralization of authority in pollution control matters found as its justification the fact that state governments were not only ill-equipped administratively for such a task, but lacked the political will to enact pollution control statutes of their own. In the intervening years, however, key elements of the federal–state relationship have changed, in some cases quite dramatically. States have been handed greater responsibility, both administratively and financially, and have greatly strengthened their administrative decision-making machinery. At the same time, there has not been a commensurate shift in decision-making control over either the substance (the "what") or means (the "how") of achieving environmental policy goals. These developments are prompting states to seek greater flexibility and discretion in program management, as well as a greater voice in the writing of federal regulatory programs.

Fiscally, states have encountered a serious and growing resource gap—the difference between funds required to execute a federally mandated program and the funds available—in pollution control. These gaps or shortfalls make the achievement of federally prescribed pollution control goals less likely. A prominent example of a resource gap is found in the Safe Drinking Water program. EPA estimates that the states needed $304 million in 1993 for the program, yet only $142 million was available from state and federal sources, leaving a shortfall of approximately $162 million (GAO 1995, 24). Another example is the Clean Water Act's National Pollutant Discharge Elimination System (NPDES) program. USEPA (1993c) projected that state programs would need $387 million to fund NPDES requirements in fiscal year 1995 but that they would receive only $233 million, leaving a gap of $154 million. Further, the report estimated that the funding shortfall facing the states would remain in the neighborhood of $166 million annually through fiscal year 2004.[53] Moreover, state officials' concerns over the adverse effects of resource shortages increased sharply between 1980 and 1993. Forty-six percent of state environmental program managers interviewed by GAO in 1980 said that an inadequate level of federal funding adversely affected their programs to a 'great' or 'very great' extent, while 86 percent of program managers interviewed in 1993 expressed these views (GAO 1995, 23–24).

The resource gaps facing state-level decision makers are growing for four main reasons. First, environmental programs and program requirements have expanded over the years, often through administrative initiatives. Second, the costs of administering environmental protection programs is increasing, apart from added programs and added responsibilities. EPA estimates that simple maintenance of 1987 levels of environmental protection will require state governments to spend an extra $1.2 billion annually by the year 2000, or approximately 46 percent more than they did in 1986.[54] Third, scarce state revenues and increasing competition for available funds from other policy areas make it harder to find the additional moneys at the state and local level needed to finance growing pollution control responsibilities. The passage of antitax and antispending initiatives in a number of states, including Florida, Colorado, and Minnesota, only compound these difficulties (GAO 1995, 11; NAPA 1995, 72; U.S. Congress. Senate Taking Stock Hearings 1993, 190–200).

Fourth, the federal government is gradually shifting responsibility for financing pollution control programs to state and local governments, largely as the result of federal deficit politics (DiIulio, Garvey, and Kettl 1993; GAO 1991, 37–39; Kettl 1992). Federal grants for environmental programs—the traditional method of encouraging states to adopt federal environmental mandates—declined by 67 percent in real 1988 dollars between 1979 and 1989, falling from $6.8 billion to $2.3 billion.[55] Moreover, federal budgeting problems have not deterred congress from passing unfunded mandates—programs or requirements imposed on states that are not accompanied by the funding needed to implement them (Municipality of Anchorage 1992; Rees 1993). A Price Waterhouse report issued in October 1993 estimated that unfunded federal mandates would cost localities $90 billion in the five-year period 1994–1998 (Suskind 1993). The Association of State and Interstate Water Pollution Control Administrators (ASIWPCA) estimates that 1987 amendments to the Clean Water Act more than doubled states' compliance workload while simultaneously decreasing the amount of federal money given to the states for implementing the act. ASIWPCA claims to have documented more than $215 million in unfunded mandates in this bill alone (GAO 1995, 28). Local government officials, who often face additional state-sponsored unfunded mandates when federal mandates fail to fund state-level programs, find unfunded mandates a particularly "bitter pill" to swallow. It often places them between the proverbial rock and a hard place, especially when crossover sanctions are involved. They either must comply with the environmental mandate—and raise their constituents' taxes or use rates for utilities like water—or risk losing program funds in other, unrelated policy areas. The cleanup of Boston Harbor pollution problems, which figured so prominently in the 1988 presidential election campaign, has resulted in a 600 percent rate increase since 1986 for water users in the Boston area. As Douglas MacDonald, executive director of the Massachusetts Water Resources Authority, explains, "[Boston] residents have the privilege of paying $3 billion to clean up Boston Harbor, an important national priority we get to handle without any real national support."[56]

Compounding the adverse effects of fiscal issues is a system of pollution control predicated on central national control. The lack of balance in the relationship between the federal and state levels of government is evident in the areas of priority setting and the federal government's preference for controlling the means by which environmental protection goals are reached (NAPA 1995).

In area after area, the identification and scope of pollution control problems are determined by national officials. Not only are states often "preclude[d] ... from spending funds in what they consider to be the most cost-effective [manner],"[57] "state and local pollution control officials suspect that they're wasting precious time and resources—while jeopardizing precarious public support—because federal mandates based on inconclusive or inaccurate studies force them to focus on the wrong environmental problems" (Arrandale 1992, 82). According to local officials, the combination of growing unfunded mandates, the escalating costs of government, and a lack of discretion over how to target public sector resources is making budgeting and long-range planning all but impossible (U.S. Congress. Senate. Taking Stock Hearings 1993, 195). In a widely cited example, the city of Columbus, Ohio determined that meeting federal environmental standards from 1991 through the year 2000 would cost anywhere from $1.3 to $1.6 billion, depending on the inflation rate used. The portion of the budget devoted to environmental protection was expected to balloon from 11 percent, or $62 million in 1991 ($160 per household), to roughly 27 percent, or $218 million for the year 2000. Further, the expected $856 per household cost of pollution control at the turn of the century would exceed projected costs of fire and police protection for the same year (see U.S. Congress. Senate. Taking Stock Hearings 1993, 122–23).

The devolution of responsibility under the auspices of Nixonian–Reagan New Federalism triggered an era of institution building at the state level, often resulting in dramatic expansions of administrative capacity, especially in the area of environmental protection (DiIulio, Garvey, and Kettl 1993; NAPA 1995). Yet despite the states' growing abilities to administer environmental programs, EPA routinely second-guesses state decisions, dictates program activities, and determines the types of personnel required to staff particular programs.[58] Federal intrusiveness is a source of considerable tension between federal and state officials in the environmental arena. A substantial majority of state program managers interviewed by GAO in both 1980 and 1993 view "excessive EPA controls [as] a major obstacle to effective program management" (1995, 41–42). As a result, more and more states are pressuring the federal government to allow them to deploy their substantial bureaucratic expertise according to state-level criteria for program effectiveness and state-level assessments of cost effectiveness. The drama is but a microcosm of the larger policy debate involving the proper balance of authority in the U.S. federal system. Should federal assistance for fighting crime consist of additional police officers (the Clinton Administration's proposal) or should states have the latitude to determine how best to spend federal grant money (the GOP congressional proposal)? Should a welfare program such as Aid to Families with Dependent Children retain entitlement status and be predicated on automatic cash disbursements to qualified recipients? Or, as congress voted in 1995, should states be given the authority to develop their own welfare programs in this area (Toner 1995, A1)?

States are also insisting that their bureaucratic expertise be applied in another way. They want a seat at the table when federal regulations are written (interviews with state regulators 1/12/94; 3/21/94; 11/7/94a; 11/7/94b). Thomas Udall, Attorney General of New Mexico, argues that "States must be considered a special party. States are coregulators when it comes to federal environmental protection. We end up being the ones who have to live with them. We have to enforce them. We believe that at a very early stage, well before regulations are proposed, the states should be brought into [the federal regulatory] process" (U.S. Congress. Senate. Taking Stock Hearings 1993, 137).

CONCLUSION

The revelation of the deep social and political strength of the environmental movement occupies a critical watershed in the evolving regulatory strategies of corporate management. The limits of a conflict-oriented, reactionary strategy were painfully evident. Given the best political conditions in years—a Republican president and a Republican senate—the environmental opposition was unable to inflict anything other than short-term damage to an increasingly institutionalized regulatory regime.[59] The lack of success in rolling back pollution control policy legacies and gridlock in congress meant that industry still had to cope with the high transaction costs stemming from the command-and-control-based regulatory superstructure. When combined with the growing importance of global services and product markets and their concomitant competitive pressures, industry faced a powerful incentive to seek regulatory alternatives allowing them to rationalize those rules already in place and thereby to reduce the costs of their compliance activities. The changing dynamics of the marketplace also gave industry a strong interest in regulatory arrangements that transferred a greater degree of compliance decision-making autonomy back to them as a way of improving their response capacity to changing conditions. Further, conflict during the rulemaking and implementation phases of the policy process, such as litigation by environmentalists or the exponential rise in the use of citizen suits against polluters during the 1980s,[60] negatively impacted corporate planning and investment activities by increasing the uncertainty associated with final outcomes. The incentive was to find methods of managing the conflict so as to reduce the probability of these *ex post* challenges (Harris 1989). But the offsetting power of the environmental lobby and the cumulative weight of existing environmental statutes signaled that rationalization, as well as any transfer of decision-making authority from the public to the private sector, if they were to occur at all, would have to include consultation and collaboration with regulators as well as environmental advocates. Likewise, and by definition, managing conflict implied the inclusion of those members of the pollution control policy network with a stake in the outcome and the power to affect the level of *ex post* uncertainty.

Environmental advocacy organizations, meanwhile, learned a different lesson from changes in the larger institutional context. While the environmental lobby was stronger, the opposing strength of business was sufficient to block most environmental initiatives. The legislative stalemate that has dominated the past fifteen years of pollution control meant that no, or at best limited, environmental gains were being made. Yet with each passing day the evidence mounted that the environment could not wait for political solutions. New, more technically complex, and arguably more urgent types of pollution control problems remained to be solved, such as global warming, nonpoint sources of water pollution, and solid and hazardous waste disposal (Kraft 1990; Mazmanian and Morell 1992; Vig and Kraft 1990). As well, existing problems that had been targeted during the first wave of the contemporary environmental movement still remained as problems almost twenty years later (Chappie et al. 1990). For example, while there have been notable successes in cleaning up particular *sources* of air pollution (e.g., the automobile tailpipe emissions story in Chapter 3 is perhaps the most widely cited example), the larger story is one of limited success in making the kinds of reductions in air pollution that protect human health.[61] In 1988 EPA estimated that 112 million people in the United States were living in nonattainment areas—those areas that had been unable to meet the national ambient air quality standards (USEPA 1991e, 1–3). Moreover, it is not clear how much of the success in pollution reduction can be directly attributed to regulatory efforts themselves, as opposed to other factors such as industrial modernization or the ongoing shift from a manufacturing-based economy to a service-oriented one.[62] Environmentalists and regulators thus had considerable incentive to search for alternatives to command and control that might prove capable not only of bridging the impasse in congress, thereby expanding the scope and scale of environmental protection measures, but also of improving the effectiveness of existing cleanup efforts.[63]

Adding to environmentalists' incentive to seek alternative regulatory mechanisms is the growing uncertainty regarding access to the courts (standing) and the results of a litigation-based strategy due to an increasingly conservative judiciary, the inordinate delays encountered during rulemaking and policy implementation, and the mind-numbing prospect of sending ever more pollution control programs through the bureaucratic gauntlet only to see them emerge as "dead letters" years later. This does not mean that they discard litigation as a strategy, since the threat of litigation and the attendant uncertainty and transaction costs for industry is still a valuable way to bring industry to the negotiating table. But it does mean that collaborative alternatives able to move beyond symbolism (e.g., public hearings), able to avoid the uncertainty of the courts, and able to increase the certainty of bureaucratic performance by, for example, giving environmentalists greater direct control during rulemaking become more appealing to environmental advocates (interviews with environmentalists 3/17/94; 3/30/94).

In the case of the EPA, although there is evidence that high transaction costs led "pockets" of the EPA to search for innovative alternatives to command and control beginning in the mid-1970s (Meidinger 1985), the vast majority of the agency remained committed to traditional modes of regulation—and conflict, litigation, and delay. However, events during the late 1970s and the decade of the 1980s imperiled the agency's reputation as an effective advocate for the environment, if not its very survival, and forced additional agency expenditures in response to constant uncertainty and questioning by others. Thus it is not surprising that EPA has been more inclined in recent years to seek out innovative collaborative arrangements that promise to reduce both agency costs and the uncertainty surrounding the achievement of agency goals.

The persistent attempts by agency leaders to infuse the EPA with collaborative value are the most visible manifestation of EPA's desire to break the old regulatory mold and engage in decision making directed at what Philip Selznick (1957) calls institutional preservation. Starting with EPA Administrator William Ruckelshaus in 1983, agency leaders have searched in earnest for collaborative alternatives to traditional regulation. Ruckelshaus had the unenviable task of rebuilding EPA's reputation as an advocate for the environment in the aftermath of Anne Gorsuch-Burford's controversial reign. As part of this he unabashedly admitted that the early Reagan attempts to emasculate the EPA were wrong and he vowed to get tough with polluters, especially through stepped-up enforcement activities (Stanfield 1984). The other facet to his reputation-building strategy, but less reported in the popular press, was his unstinting search for collaborative alternatives to command and control. Ruckelshaus felt that command and control had gone about as far as it could go as a tool in the battle against pollution and was convinced that further environmental progress—stronger standards and faster implementation—required agency collaboration with industry (Main 1988). For Ruckelshaus, consensus-based regulatory methods like environmental dispute resolution "ha[ve] almost transcendent importance in the future of our country's dealing with problems like the protection of the environment" (as quoted in Amy

1990, 211–12). Lee Thomas, Ruckelshaus' immediate successor, was a strong advocate for the increased agency use of negotiated rulemakings as a way to save the EPA time and money, while simultaneously ensuring stringent environmental protection (Thomas 1987). William Reilly, President Bush's EPA administrator, had long been an advocate of consensus-based policy-making mechanisms as the president of the Conservation Foundation. His efforts during the 1970s and 1980s to find common ground among business, environmentalists, and government regulators earned him the sobriquet of "the great includer" (Weisskopf 1988). In confirmation hearing testimony before the Senate Environment and Public Works Committee, he explained that "strong environmental protection and strong economic development [are] fully compatible" (Shabecoff 1989). Toward this end, according to Reilly, EPA needs to be in the business of promoting sustainable economic growth by

> usher[ing] in a new era in the history of environmental policy, an era marked by the reconciliation of interests, by imaginative solutions arrived at through cooperation and consensus, by the resolve to listen and work out our differences (as quoted in Shabecoff 1989, A14).

Carol Browner, Bill Clinton's EPA administrator, has continued the trend of EPA leaders who are seeking collaboration instead of conflict with the major stakeholders in pollution control politics. She carries the reputation as a "new type of environmentalist who views economic development and environmental protection as compatible goals"[64] and whose strength as an administrator rests on "her ability to steer all parties toward agreement by balancing competing interests and avoiding ideological combat."[65]

Contextual developments are also an important part of the explanation for why state-level actors are more willing to play a collaborative, as opposed to a conflict-oriented, game. Fiscal scarcity, vast improvements in bureaucratic expertise devoted to environmental matters, and a system tilted predominantly toward federal control have led a growing number of states to seek a fundamental rebalancing of the federal–state relationship when it comes to pollution control. Because they pay more of the tab compared to the past and because many now have the institutional capacity to combat pollution effectively, states want greater control over cleanup priorities and the means by which environmental protection goals will be achieved. In short, a changed context is pushing states to seek the kinds of flexible, power-sharing arrangements found in collaborative games, which promise a greater bang for the regulatory buck.

Clearly, the larger contextual environment within which decisions are embedded is of critical importance to understanding stakeholder preferences in national pollution control politics. It helps us understand the first part of the "why collaboration" puzzle. Yet context is limited in helping us understand actual policy choices precisely because stakeholders are rational actors; they focus organizational resources where they will make a difference. From the perspective of pollution control stakeholders, these larger contextual variables appear either as immovable objects or as issues that can only be affected at the margins. Thus, stakeholders work within the constraints and opportunities provided by these larger contextual variables and channel their efforts toward institutional arrangements that are within their grasp—the regulatory programs themselves (Moe 1987b).

Increasingly, participants in pollution control politics are concluding that hierarchy—or command and control, the dominant form of regulation in the environmental arena—is an inefficient means for achieving many environmental goals. Because hierarchical arrangements are loaded with transaction costs and produce suboptimal results, from both a collective and an individual perspective, frustrated stakeholders are now seeking alternatives promising transaction cost savings. Chapter 3 describes transaction cost theory and investigates the high costs of writing, implementing, and enforcing hierarchy-based pollution control programs and how the high costs interfere with stakeholder attempts to maximize their own, often conflicting, goals.

CHAPTER NOTES

1. The Water Pollution Control Act of 1956, the Water Quality Act of 1965, the Clean Air Act of 1963, and the Air Quality Act of 1967.

2. Erskine (1969, 121–23); Waterman (1989, 107–08).

3. There was widespread concern that special-interest government, as typified by "iron triangles," was more the norm than the exception and that regulatory agencies were susceptible to capture by the industries they were designed to regulate (McConnell 1966). Other accounts feared that congressional control of the bureaucracy was weak, given ambiguous statutes (Lowi 1979); the exercise of uncoordinated, fragmented, and ad hoc oversight (Fiorina 1981); and the asymmetrical information advantage enjoyed by bureaucrats (Niskanen 1971).

4. See Moe (1989) for a dissenting view. He argued that, given the different and conflicting incentive structures facing political institutions and the interest groups most directly affected by EPA's mission, the EPA's organizational structure was bound to be ineffective and largely unaccountable to any unified notion of a national public interest. As well, Moe found that the presence of explicit statutes offering little discretionary latitude to the bureaucracy was

a product of the conflicting interests of congress and the executive branch, rather than a response to Lowi's call for clear, unambiguous law. See also Katzmann (1990) for why congress finds it extremely difficult to give clear signals to the bureaucracy regarding its legislative intent (pp. 291–97).

5. Marcus (1980). EPA was not the only agency designed for using the principle of executive integration. Others included the Occupational Safety and Health Administration (OSHA) and the National Highway Traffic Safety Administration (NHTSA) (Harter 1982, 13; Mashaw and Harfst 1990; G. Wilson 1985).

6. For example, the National Environmental Protection Act of 1969, environmental impact statements, and best available control technology requirements.

7. As Francis Rourke (1984) would say, the EPA was able to protect its power and jurisdiction within the competitive public agency environment. Examples of strong bipartisan support include, but are not limited to, the Clean Air Act (CAA) of 1970 and the National Environmental Policy Act (NEPA) of 1969. The CAA passed by a 374–1 margin in the house and 73–0 in the senate, while NEPA passed 372–15 in the house and 71–6 in the senate.

8. The late 1960s and early 1970s saw an explosion of regulatory activity along with the creation of federal agencies to carry out various regulatory mandates issued by congress. The most prominent among these were EPA, the Occupational Safety and Health Administration (OSHA), the National Highway Transportation and Safety Administration (NHTSA), and the Consumer Product Safety Commission (CPSC). The economic stagflation (low economic growth and high inflation) of the 1970s is cited by Eisner (1993) as a key reason why Presidents Nixon, Ford, Carter, and Reagan pushed ahead with their deregulation and reform agendas (pp. 176–77).

9. For a good recounting of the factual and political dynamic behind federal deficit politics, see Kettl (1992).

10. On this general point of how the lack of agency resources negatively affects the ability of EPA to implement environmental laws, see General Accounting Office (1991). See also the testimony of J. Dexter Peach, Assistant Comptroller General for Resources, Community, and Economic Development Division of the General Accounting Office, before the Committee on Energy and Commerce, Subcommittee on Oversight and Investigations, House, "Oversight of Implementation of the Clean Air Act Amendments of 1990," 102nd Cong., 1st Session (Nov. 12, 1991). He discussed the 1990 CAAA, with particular emphasis on Title III (Air Toxics).

11. Eisner (1993, 172–76); Moe (1985). For example, Executive Order #12291 required benefit–cost regulatory impact assessments on all new regulations estimated to have economic impacts in excess of $100 million. The executive order declared that "regulatory action shall not be taken unless the potential benefits to society for the regulation outweigh the potential costs to society." Even given this executive order, cost–benefit analysis is not always legal for regulatory agency decision making because specific legislative language to the contrary may nullify its effect. Or, as in the case of OSHA, the charter legislation "empowered OSHA to promote making the workplace as safe as was feasible." Feasibility is the only factor limiting the agency's regulatory authority. In

Industrial Union Department v. Hodgson 499 F.2d 467 (D. C. Circuit 1974), the court ruling "stressed that regulation might be considered feasible even if its compliance costs could affect profitability and even put some employers out of business. However, the regulation's feasibility would come into question as 'the effect becomes more widespread within an industry'" (as quoted in Eisner 1993, 160–61).

12. See McGarity (1992, 1433–34). McGarity conducted dozens of interviews with agency officials in EPA, OSHA, NHTSA, and USDA. "The officials are almost unanimous in their view that the prospect of OMB review operates as a disincentive to promulgate new rules that increase regulatory burdens" (see footnote 245, p. 1434). The quote on rulemaking delays is by former EPA Administrator Lee Thomas in the *Environment Reporter* (12/9/88). Even though OMB review causes only about a four-week delay on average, OMB can and does 'sit' on rules for months and, on occasion, years. See for example, *Inside OMB* (7/16/82, 8), *Inside EPA* (3/22/85, 12), and *Inside EPA* (4/20/84, 4) (McGarity 1992, p. 1434, see footnote 246).

13. Costle (1993, 59); interviews with state regulator (3/21/94); EPA (3/17/94); environmentalist (3/17/94).

14. Senator Stafford of the Senate Committee on the Environment and Public Works, Rep. Dingell of the Subcommittee on Oversight and Investigations of the House Committee on Energy and Commerce, Rep. Florio of the Subcommittee on Commerce, Transportation, and Tourism of the House Committee on Energy and Commerce, Rep. Levitas of the Subcommittee on Investigations and Oversight of the House Committee on Public Works and Transportation, Rep. Synar of the Subcommittee on Environment, Energy, and Natural Resources of the House Government Operations Committee, and Rep. Scheuer of the Subcommittee on Natural Resources, Agricultural Research, and Environment of the House Science and Technology Committee (see Lazarus 1991a, 216, footnote 61).

15. Included within the 1980s figure are the 96th Congress (1979–1980) through the 100th Congress (1987–1988). The average number of appearances was 180.2 per session. For the 1970s, figures for the 92nd Congress (1971–1972) through the 95th Congress (1977–1978) are used. The average for this period was 126 appearances (see Lazarus 1991a, 212, footnote 41). Figures are derived from reports done by the EPA's Office of Legislation, Legislative Division, and a computer search of the Congressional Index Service.

16. National Academy of Public Administration (1988, 27). See also Lazarus (1991a, 214, 229); Melnick (1983, 322).

17. Eisner (1993, 177). Eisner and Meier (1990) consider these two intra-agency factors as perhaps the most significant of the Reagan era changes because they institutionalize a predisposition toward markets and deregulation.

18. Interviews with environmentalists (1/7/94; 1/13/94); EPA (1/11/94).

19. William Ruckelshaus, former EPA administrator (1988), as quoted in Kraft (1990, 103).

20. Senator Phil Gramm (R) of Texas, in the aftermath of the 1990 budget summit, summarized the problem succinctly, "If the committee system worked in the first place, there never would have been a summit" (as quoted in Khademian 1993, 12).

21. Oleszek (1989, 12–14) offers two illustrative examples of this. One case was a tax increase of nearly $100 billion in 1982 and the other was the Gramm–Rudman–Hollings deficit reduction amendment. In both cases the house chose to go directly to conference with the senate, thus bypassing committees and floor debate (except for debate on the conference report).

22. Part of the conflict between branches of government is attributed by some to the growing public distrust of bureaucratic decision making and by others to divided government, where Republicans control one branch and Democrats another (Chubb and Peterson 1989; Gormley 1989; Moe 1989).

23. Citizen suits, also known as private enforcement actions, allow environmental groups "to pursue directly their disagreements with . . . industry . . . when the agencies responsible for enforcing environmental and conservation laws are unwilling to play their proenvironmental role" (Wenner 1990, 199).

24. The Sunshine Act of 1976 [Sec 557(d)] and sunset laws were also aimed at increasing agency accountability.

25. *Portland Cement Association v. Ruckelshaus*, 486 F2d 375 (DC Circuit 1973).

26. *International Harvester v. Ruckelshaus*, 478 F2d 615 (DC Circuit 1973). *Kennecott Copper Corp. v. EPA*, 462 F2d 846 (DC Circuit 1972). *Vermont Yankee Nuclear Power Corp. v. Natural Resources Defense Council*, 435 U. S. 519 (1978) put a halt to the ability of lower courts to add procedures beyond those called for in APA and substantive law at issue.

27. McGarity (1992, 1400, 1419) (emphasis added). McGarity (1992) notes that a "comprehensive study of EPA's rulemaking process for promulgating National Ambient Air Quality Standards [Berry 1984, 221] concluded in 1984 that: 'Litigation and the prospect for court review are the dominant factors that influence the NAAQS process throughout all its phases. Fear of litigation and how the courts might judge the process tends to delay decisions. Actual litigation, however, tends to force decisions to be made. The Agency shows the highest respect and response to the courts over any form of influence. Every phase of the process is designed to withstand and pass judicial review. Much of the process's attempt to do the 'right thing' is motivated by strong desire that the courts be able to find 'no errors' in the way the Agency conducts its business. It is the cautious attention given to producing 'no errors' that tends to slow the process down." James Q. Wilson (1989) notes: "Management of the EPA often has been dominated by lawyers, much to the disgust of many engineers and scientists, because the output of that agency, a regulation, is framed in a political environment that makes it more important to withstand legal attack than to withstand scientific scrutiny" (p. 284).

28. William Reilly, EPA administrator for President Bush, as quoted in Wald (1991). The virtual certainty of court battles extends to other regulatory arenas. As Graham Wilson (1985) explains: "OSHA must always anticipate Court battles when it frames standards. Indeed, the framing of standards within the agency usually involves a constant quarrel between the expert advocates of a proposed standard, anxious to tackle a health problem quickly, and the lawyers of the agency, anxious to prepare the strongest possible case for the Court battles which almost certainly lie ahead" (p. 105).

29. See, e.g., *Portland Cement Association v. Ruckelshaus* (1973, 394) (agency must respond to public comments that pass a "threshold requirement of materiality"), *cert. denied*, 417 U. S. 921 (1974); *Kennecott Copper Corp. v. EPA*, (1972) (remanding for further explanation due to "nagging problems" with the agency's explanation for its rule).

30. McGarity (1992, 1397). See, e.g., *Vermont Yankee Nuclear Power Corp. v. Natural Resources Defense Council*, 435 U.S. 519 (1978) (environmental group seeking greater procedural protections in informal rulemaking); *Kleppe v. Sierra Club*, 427 U. S. 390 (1976) (environmental group seeking greater analytical protections under the National Environmental Policy Act); *Warm Springs Dam Task Force v. Gribble*, 621 F2d 1017 (9th Circuit 1980) (environmental group seeking EPA comment on environmental impact statement prepared by development-oriented agency).

31. See Gormley (1989) for an opposing view.

32. *Environment Reporter* (10/25/91), hereinafter cited as *ER*; Hays (1989, 315).

33. Wenner (1990). Close to 60 percent of all federal judges were appointed by Reagan and Bush. Some examples of appointments to the bench who tend to favor economy over environment, or are advocates of less regulation, are Clarence Thomas and Antonin Scalia of the Supreme Court, Alex Kozinski of the Ninth Circuit Court of Appeals in California, and Frank H. Easterbrook of the Seventh Circuit Court of Appeals in Illinois (Schneider 1992c).

34. The following discussion on the *Chevron* case is indebted to Glicksman and Schroeder (1991, 286–91).

35. *Chevron U.S.A., Inc. v. NRDC* (467 US 837) (Supreme Court 1984, 842).

36. Ibid., p. 843.

37. *Chemical Manufacturers' Association v. EPA*, 859 F2d 977 (DC Circuit 1988, 984). See, for example, *Ohio v. Department of Interior*, 880 F2d 432 (DC Circuit 1989, 441); *Hazardous Waste Treatment Council v. EPA*, 861 F2d 270 (DC Circuit 1988, 291); *Mobil Oil Co. v. EPA*, 871 F2d 149 (DC Circuit 1989). Of course, there are always exceptions to the rule. See *NRDC v. EPA* (DC Circuit 1990) and *EDF v. EPA* (DC Circuit 1990). A classic application of the "hard look" doctrine can be found in the 1991 5th Circuit Court ruling on *Corrosion Proof Fittings v. EPA*. The court ruled that EPA had not considered "some less burdensome options short of doing nothing." The court went on to explain the analytic technique (cost–benefit) that EPA could use to determine if a middle-ground solution was appropriate, and went so far as to recommend that agency decision makers read an article from *The Economist* which discussed the use of discount rates for nonmonetary goods (McGarity 1992, 1422–23).

38. Weidenbaum (1978).

39. Joan Claybrook, president of Public Citizen, as quoted in Harris (1989, 264).

40. Hays (1989, 287–88); Allardice, Mattoon, and Testa (1993, 10); McFarland (1990); Vogel (1989); interviews with environmentalists (1/7/94; 1/13/94; 3/31/94), industry (1/21/94; 1/12/94; 2/10/94), and regulators (EPA, 1/11/94; 1/13/94). Of course, the countermobilization of the business community was in response to social regulations writ large, not just environmental regulations (e.g., consumer protection, occupational safety and health, highway traffic safety). Further, despite widespread resistance to stringent environmental controls, some industrial sectors, or firms within sectors, doubtlessly benefited from a command-and-control system because it created a costly barrier to entry for potential competitors. To the extent that environmental regulations were successful in dampening competition, existing industry could earn extra economic rents and thus had little incentive to seek relief. See Greve and Smith (1992); Pashigian (1984); Yandle (1989).

41. Ibid., p. 10.

42. Bardach and Kagan (1982); Eads and Fix (1984, 88–95).

43. Derthick and Quirk (1985); Litan and Nordhaus (1983); Noll and Owen (1983).

44. Ingram and Mann (1989); Mitchell (1991); Symonds (1982); Weisskopf (1990b). For example, from 1969 to 1980 memberships increased from 83,000 to 182,000 for the Sierra Club, from 465,000 to 859,000 for the National Wildlife Federation, from 12,000 to 63,000 for Defenders of Wildlife, and from 6,000 (in 1972) to 45,000 for the Natural Resources Defense Council.

45. Gilbreath (ed.) (1984); Kenski and Ingram (1986); Mosher (1981); Pasztor (1983, 15); Sheets and Taylor (1983, 26).

46. Eads and Fix (1984); Kenski and Ingram (1986); *Business Week* (1983, January 24, 85–86).

47. Hays (1989, 493). Interviews with environmentalists (1/7/94; 1/13/94), and industry (1/21/94; 4/14/94).

48. As one would expect, the concern over the competitiveness of U.S. industries in global markets is not limited to industry (interviews with Congress 3/18/94; EPA 1/7/94; EPA 12/10/93; GAO 2/25/94; and state regulator 3/1/94).

49. As the interactive (feedback) effects of global interdependence grow, so too does the need for continual policy adjustment (see Stewart 1983, 28–29).

50. Comments at Great Lakes Regional Emissions Trading Conference, Chicago, Illinois (January 27–28, 1994), hereinafter cited as Great Lakes RETC (1994).

51. See Waxman (1991) and Calcagni (1993) for empirical specifics.

52. For example, recent evidence from the Lake Michigan Ozone Study (1994) indicates that the real culprits in the formation of ground-level ozone (urban smog) are volatile organic compounds (VOCs) instead of nitrogen oxides (NO_x). In fact, the study suggests that reducing NO_x in urban areas like Chicago, Milwaukee, and Northern Indiana only makes the ozone pollution problem worse. These findings effectively eliminate NO_x reduction as a basic part of state attainment strategies in this region and place a disproportionate share of the emissions-reduction burden on VOCs. Gade of the Illinois EPA views this development as a "further rationale to develop pollution control strategies that are cost effective and that place more reliance on market-based mechanisms as a means of meeting our clean air goals under the 1990 Clean Air Act Amendments primarily because controlling VOCs is extremely expensive. . . . There is no way that a command-and-control tell-them-how-they're-going-to-do-it approach is going to work, given the expected high costs of reducing VOCs. . . . [Instead, regulators] must build on our experiences in the NO_x

emissions trading efforts in Illinois, RECLAIM, and acid rain and move forward into VOCs" (Great Lakes RETC 1994). The Illinois EPA began just such a collaborative, market-based problem-solving effort in February 1994 that includes environmentalists, business, and government at the federal, state, and local levels. According to Gade and others, they did so precisely because the juxtaposition of stringent environmental goals, high compliance costs borne by industry, and an increasingly competitive global marketplace make such "innovative and collaborative strategies in pollution control" a more attractive option for all stakeholders (interview with state regulator, 3/1/94). (The four-state region—Indiana, Illinois, Michigan, and Wisconsin—formally asked EPA for an exemption from 1990 Clean Air Act NO_x reduction requirements in February 1994.)

53. See GAO (1995, 26). The costs cited are those needed to fully implement the 1987 Clean Water Act requirements. All costs in the EPA report are presented in constant fiscal year 1995 dollars.

54. GAO (1995, 23). The estimate is from USEPA's *The Cost of a Clean Environment* report (1990c). All cost estimates used in this document are in 1986 dollars, while the level of environmental protection used in the estimate is assumed to be the level that existed in 1987. The costs are annualized at 3 percent.

55. National Governor's Association (1989). This calculation includes grants for state operating budgets and the construction of wastewater treatment plants but does not include Superfund and grants for leaking underground storage tanks.

56. Suskind (1993, A16). The Boston Harbor story is not entirely a product of unfunded mandates. It's also a story about how state-level officials targeted federal funds toward pollution control priorities other than Boston-area sewage and water treatment issues and failed to tap available federal matching grants designed to avert the pollution crisis facing Boston Harbor in the 1980s (see the testimony of Thomas Jorling, Commissioner of the New York State Department of Environmental Conservation, U.S. Congress. Senate. Taking Stock Hearings 1993, 177).

57. "For example, Wisconsin drinking water officials told GAO that EPA requires them to monitor for certain radioactive contaminants even though the state has years of data showing that such contaminants do not exist in the state's water supply" (GAO 1995, 5). Ohio, New York, and a great number of other states have experienced similar problems (Rees 1993; NAPA 1995, 61–65; U.S. Congress. Senate. Taking Stock Hearings 1993).

58. GAO (1995, 42); Jorling testimony, U.S. Congress. Senate. Taking Stock Hearings (1993, 172–77).

59. Attempts by business to effect dramatic changes in environmental statutes have met with limited success time and time again. See Melnick (1983) in the area of the Clean Air Act and Brownstein (1980) for the Resource Conservation and Recovery Act (RCRA) of 1976. RCRA was revised and strengthened in 1984. See Mazmanian and Morell (1992) for a recap of the strengthening of Superfund legislation in 1986. And while certain changes favoring business and development interests were made in the Endangered Species Act (ESA) in 1978, environmentalists were able to protect the basic integrity of the statute

(Hays 1989, 466–67). The 104th Republican Congress is meeting with similar results. Sweeping regulatory reform proposals were pronounced "dead" in July 1995 when the senate could not muster the votes needed to invoke cloture. Similarly, aggressive efforts by house Republicans to attach appropriation riders stripping enforcement funds from seventeen different EPA programs were reinstated by the Republican senate.

60. Glicksman and Schroeder (1991, 254); Wenner (1990, 199, 209). See also *Council on Environmental Quality* (1989). *Environmental Quality: Twentieth Annual Report.* Washington, D. C.: U. S. Government Printing Office, pp. 210–11.

61. USEPA (1990c). Pursuant to the 1970 Clean Air Act, National Ambient Air Quality Standards (NAAQS) were established for six pollutants—particulates, sulfur oxides, carbon monoxide, nitrogen oxides, volatile organic compounds, and lead. From 1970 to 1990 dramatic success was achieved for lead pollution, almost a 95 percent reduction that was largely due to the phasing out of lead in gasoline. Good progress was made for particulates pollution, as well as for carbon monoxide. The total amount of CO pollution was reduced from approximately 100 million metric tons per year to about 65 million metric tons. But the success in reducing sulfur oxides and volatile organic compounds has been far less than originally predicted, while nitrogen oxides pollution actually increased from 1970 to 1990 (USEPA 1991d, 7–13). Using EPA data on national emissions estimates, Portney (1990) shows the following percentage changes for each of the six NAAQS pollutants for the period 1970–1987: particulate matter, 62 percent decline; sulfur oxides, 28 percent decline; nitrogen oxides, 7 percent increase; reactive volatile organic compounds, 25 percent decline; carbon monoxide, 39 percent decline; lead, 96 percent decline (p. 48). Further, the lead success story was partly illusory, as oil companies compensated for the octane (power) losses caused by the removal of lead by increasing the use of aromatic compounds, primarily the toxic chemicals benzene, toluene, and xylene (known collectively as BTX). Gasoline was "dirtier" in 1989 than at the time of the 1970 CAA in another respect as well. The 1977 CAAA mandated that hydrocarbons (VOCs) and carbon monoxide automobile tailpipe emissions be reduced by 90 percent. The use of higher levels of butane by oil companies, however, increased fuel volatility (the tendency of fuel to evaporate) to the extent that actual tailpipe reductions in these two pollutants amounted to less than 75 percent. See GAO (1987, 29–30); OTA (1989b, figure 3); Waxman, Wetstone, and Barnett (1991, p. 1973). The net result was more air toxics pollution, a different but still serious health risk, especially for people in urban areas (Lyman 1990; Rothschild 1990).

62. USEPA (1990c). David Vogel (1986), drawing on data collected by the EPA and on Robert Crandall's (1983) *Controlling Industrial Pollution*, finds that "[w]hile the regulation of automobile emissions by the federal government since 1967 has contributed to improved air quality in many metropolitan areas, the actual impact of the controls established by the Clean Air Act Amendments of 1970 over stationary sources is somewhat less clear. . . . [S]ulfur dioxide concentrations actually declined more each year between 1964 and 1971 than they have done since 1971. During the second part of the 1960s they fell 11.3 percent per year, while during the 1970s they declined by only 4.6 percent per year. Similarly, particulate concentration levels declined 2.3 percent per year between 1960 and 1971 but only by 0.6 percent per year between 1972 and 1981. Robert Crandall [1983, 19] argues that 'these data suggest that pollution reduction was more effective in the 1960s before there was a serious federal policy dealing with stationary sources, than since the 1970 Clean Air Act Amendments'" (p. 157).

63. The story for water is much the same. According to Robert Adler (1994), a senior attorney for the Natural Resources Defense Council, EPA's National Water Quality Inventory for 1991 "demonstrates that even the interim goals of the 1972 Clean Water Act have not been met: Roughly 40 percent of our assessed rivers and lakes and roughly a third of our assessed estuaries are not meeting or fully supporting designated uses (e.g., fishing, boating, swimming, drinking water supply). Other reports . . . suggest that these numbers are seriously understated. . . . [Nor have we] eliminated the release of toxic pollutants in toxic amounts, [a key goal of the 1972 CWA]. . . . While investments in pollution control technology mandated by the Clean Water Act have reaped large dividends in total pollution reductions . . . industrial water pollution is far from contained. In 1990, for example, U. S. industries reported the release of almost 200 million pounds of toxics into surface waters, and another 450 million pounds into public sewers" (Adler 1994, 11). See also Chappie et al. (1990).

64. Schneider (1992a, B20).

65. *New York Times* (12/12/92, A22). Browner developed her initial administrative reputation as a consensus builder during her two-year stint in charge of the Florida Department of Environmental Regulation. The NAPA (1995) report *Setting Priorities, Getting Results* offers details on how Browner has attempted to transform the culture of EPA and put her philosophy of regulatory management into practice.

3

The High Costs of Doing Business in Pollution Control Politics

[There is a] stark difference between the 'ideal' regulatory world posited by environmental defenders and the real one. In that ideal world, states had comprehensive emissions inventories; prompt compliance with state-imposed requirements based on those inventories and backed by EPA would produce clean air by fixed national deadlines; and state plans offered clear guidelines citizen groups could enforce. In the real world, inventories were grossly inadequate; all requirements were subject to negotiation; no one knew how to control many emission points; 'compliance' was largely determined through unaudited self-certifications by regulated firms; states simply imposed requirements on industries that could bear the cost; the air quality effects of genuine compliance were uncertain; and a state plan could be ten file cabinets that no one had fully read. [By 1978] [i]ndustry and state agencies were already beginning to argue to Congress that the system was overloaded with expensive, unnecessary requirements that produced little real environmental benefit (Michael H. Levin, chief, regulatory reform staff, U.S. EPA 1982).[1]

During the late 1960s and early 1970s, the cause of environmental protection rose to the top of the national policy agenda. In response, national policy makers and environmentalists sought to lock in environmental gains through a federally based command-and-control system of regulation. Congressional initiatives like the Clean Air Act of 1970, the Clean Water Act of 1972, and the Resource Conservation and Recovery Act of 1976 imposed stringent national uniform emissions standards, specified action-forcing deadlines for bureaucratic compliance, and, along with the Environmental Protection Agency, mandated specific end-of-pipe pollution control technologies for industrial polluters. Proponents argued that such a hierarchical approach reduced the transaction costs associated with implementing and enforcing pollution control statutes by providing clear emissions and technology standards against which compliance could be judged (Lowi 1979). Senator Edmund Muskie, principal sponsor of both the 1970 and 1977 versions of the Clean Air Act, claimed that "specific legislation . . . would eliminate uncertainty and delay, reduce the role of the courts in policy making, and avoid having legislation by regulation" (as quoted in Melnick 1983, 103).

The EPA, created in 1970, put the philosophy of top-down regulatory management into practice through notice-and-comment rulemaking procedures. This traditional form of rulemaking gave EPA managers primary responsibility for collecting and validating the information needed to translate legislation into regulation. EPA was also charged with protecting the public interest and commanding private-sector compliance with rulemaking outcomes. Little concern was shown at the time for how much such a system of regulatory control might cost the industries and individuals responsible for pollution (Eisner 1993, 134–69). Similarly, few questions were asked about whether resistance to top-down control by industry, bureaucratic avoidance of decisions on controversial matters, or multiple interpretations of regulatory rules by interested stakeholders might effectively delay environmental protection for years and even decades (Marcus 1980, 268).

Fast forward to June 9, 1993. Standing before the Business Roundtable, EPA Administrator Carol Browner called for an end to the adversarialism which dominates pollution control politics. Linking the adversarial dynamic directly to the dominant command-and-control method of regulation, she proclaimed that the failure to "de-adversarialize" relationships among major stakeholders placed environmental progress at risk: "Many of the command-and-control policies of the past 23 years have not worked, making it obvious that conflict between industry and government will not help the agency meet its goal of protecting the environment." Browner went on to pledge that EPA would shift the focus of regulatory efforts away from command and control to a more productive approach based on consensus-based collaborative mechanisms and other ways of interacting that lessen distrust among traditional adversaries (*Environment Reporter* 6/18/93, 322).[2]

Browner's rhetoric stands in sharp contrast to the early years of the environmental regulatory revolution, when regulators and environmentalists alike built their reputations on their willingness to engage in no-holds-barred confrontation with their industrial adversaries. Yet Browner's testimony is remarkable for another reason as well: the suggestion that command and control, and its concomitant dynamic of conflict, is so transaction-cost intensive that it is often counterproductive to the collective goal of a cleaner environment.

Over twenty-five years of experience suggests that Carol Browner is right. The transaction costs—the costs of developing, implementing, and enforcing regulations—accompanying a hierarchical approach to pollution control are high, and implementation is something other than automatic. Major participants spend significant time and resources gathering technical information; preparing for and fighting court battles; anticipating and countering the other side's next strategic move; and mobilizing human, political, and economic resources to prevent adversaries from gaining advantage. State and federal regulators engage in continuous bargaining games with the regulated community in their efforts to apply command-and-control regulations to real-world situations. The constant battling for advantage delays implementation. It also limits the amount of resources available to regulators for monitoring and enforcement activities, increases the costs of such activities, and decreases the certainty that programs will deliver promised environmental results.[3] Industry struggles to remain competitive against international competition as the aggregate costs of compliance continue to balloon[4] and the lack of discretion over regulatory matters limits responsiveness. Furthermore, while the hierarchical system of regulatory control is generally credited with improving environmental quality in a number of areas, sometimes dramatically, key sections of major environmental laws remain unimplemented, many pollution problems continue to worsen, and pollution abatement costs on a per unit basis continue to escalate.[5] The high levels of friction impede the achievement of collective goals and the ability of stakeholders—environmental advocates, industry, the Environmental Protection Agency, and state-level regulators—to achieve their own organizational goals. Participants in pollution control politics thus encounter strong incentives to devise institutions or to write regulatory programs minimizing these costs precisely because reduced costs translate into greater maximization of their own goals (Coase 1937; Weingast and Marshall 1988; Williamson 1985).

This chapter explores the transaction costs associated with the traditional hierarchical approach to pollution control regulation. It starts with a generalized overview of transaction cost theory. Particular attention is paid to the often-ignored problems of control and inefficiency accompanying hierarchical arrangements. Focus then shifts to the empirical manifestations of transaction costs in the pollution control arena. Information search, program specification, and negotiation costs are examined first, followed by the problems and costs associated with program adaptability, monitoring and enforcement issues, and rules disconnected from environmental results.

TRANSACTION COST THEORY

Contracts can be written, organizations designed, or institutional relationships structured any number of ways to achieve a particular goal. From the transaction cost perspective, there are two chief areas of concern: What are the costs of choosing one arrangement over another[6] and how effectively does the arrangement convert costs into goal attainment? Theoretical inquiry focuses on four main sets of transaction costs: information search, contract specification and negotiation, monitoring and enforcement, and contract adaptability. The chief conclusion is that transaction costs bear directly on the preferences of individuals and organizations for contractual arrangements, whether it is a hierarchy, a market, or something in between hierarchy and markets. Given that high levels of "friction" impede and, on occasion, block attainment of organizations' goals, stakeholding organizations critically assess the consequences of any given arrangement and seek arrangements designed to improve cost effectiveness vis-à-vis available alternatives.[7] In the optimum case, the new contractual arrangement will reduce transaction costs and increase goal attainment, while simultaneously decreasing uncertainty.[8]

New economics of organization scholars apply transaction cost theory to relationships among political actors located in congress, the presidency, and the bureaucracy, particularly to the need of political principals to control bureaucratic agents. The problematic nature of getting bureaucrats to do what policy makers want in the uncertain environment of American politics is solved, theoretically at least, through a reliance on the hierarchical positioning of political principals and their ability to anticipate shirking[9] by bureaucratic agents.[10] According to the principal–agent formulation of the contracting problem, agent preferences and the transaction cost problems they raise through shirking are never so onerous that principals cannot overcome their damaging effects on policy outcomes. The effects of shirking can be virtually eliminated by using a variety of enforcement methods, including bureaucratic design (Moe 1989), statutory specificity (Moe 1989), congressional oversight activities (Calvert, McCubbins, and Weingast 1989; McCubbins and Schwartz 1984; Weingast 1984), a president's political appointments, and the recentralization of executive branch power (Wood 1990; Moe 1985).

The new economics of organization neatly confines the dilemma of institutional choice to a matter of which form of hierarchy is appropriate. There is no sense of exchange among members of the hierarchy, with its concomitant realization that agents possess residual power resources regardless of how strictly specified and enforced contracts are. Property rights of principals are presumed sufficient to divest agents of their own property rights, at least to the extent that they have no independent effect on policy outcomes. Thus, principal–agent theory seconds the industrial organization literature of Coase (1937), Alchian and Demsetz (1972), Jensen and Meckling (1976), and Williamson (1975)—hierarchies personify efficiency since they ease the problems of information search, program negotiation and specification, and monitoring and enforcement found in decentralized, market-oriented contractual arrangements.[11] Applied to politics, we are left with the unavoidable conclusion that hierarchy is the most efficacious way to reduce transaction costs and ensure accountability (if not the only way).[12]

In recent years, a significant and more sophisticated body of literature has developed which questions the transaction-cost-savings claims of authority-based hierarchical arrangements and, by doing so, takes us closer to modeling the empirical complexities of the contemporary regulatory arena.[13] These scholars make it clear that hierarchies[14] are subject to the same kinds of control problems and inefficiencies as arrangements based on decentralized "expert" and market-based institutions. In particular, there are costs associated with writing, executing, and enforcing contracts *inside* hierarchies due to the pervasiveness of incomplete contracts (Hammond and Miller 1985), information asymmetries (Miller and Moe 1986, 195), multiple propertied stakeholders with conflicting interests (Hammond and Knott 1993; Miller 1992; Moe 1989), and adversaries willing to act opportunistically to either thwart others' gains or reconstruct contracts more to their liking (Weingast and Marshall 1988; Williamson 1985).

Incomplete contracts   Advocates of hierarchy within the new economics of organization approach tend to assume that complete contracts are the norm; if incomplete contracts occur, enforcement is treated as a relatively costless exercise. Yet the "hierarchy as social choice" literature offers a series of formidable theoretical proofs in support of the following proposition: it is impossible to design contracts able simultaneously to maximize the multiple values and standards governing principle–agent relationships in any venue, political or otherwise (Hammond and Miller 1985; Miller and Moe 1986). As a result, *democratic* principals cannot possibly anticipate or provide a contractual or programmatic structure eliminating bureaucratic shirking *even if they are omniscient.* Regulatory programs are inevitably incomplete,[15] and whenever programs are incomplete, the uncertainty surrounding their execution increases, as does the cost of enforcement activities (Kreps 1992, 93–94; Weingast and Marshall 1988, 135; Williamson 1985, 28–29).

Information asymmetries The prevalence of complex organizations, complex transactions requiring a wide variety of expertise, and multiple values governing decision making suggest a high incidence of information asymmetries internal to hierarchies.[16] Asymmetric information occurs when subordinate agents in an organization or, more generally, those actors responsible for implementation, "know more than principals do about the business at hand" (DiIulio, Garvey, and Kettl 1993, 27). Political and regulatory principals, therefore, are likely to incur substantial information search and program specification costs as they attempt not only to gather information, but to verify its usefulness for mandated policy objectives. The clearest examples of information asymmetries within the hierarchy of regulatory politics are the bureaucratic advantage in expertise as opposed to congress (Khademian 1992; Ringquist et al. 1994), the information advantages enjoyed by private industry vis-à-vis government regulators, and the information asymmetry favoring state regulators as opposed to federal regulators regarding implementation issues.

Multiple propertied stakeholders Contrary to principal–agent approaches to policy making, formal political authority is not the only source of property rights (power) in political relationships.[17] Instead, policy making involves multiple stakeholders, each with an individual set of property rights capable of exerting an independent effect on outcomes. Elected officials have an automatic, permanent set of formal property rights granted by the constitution. Other stakeholders such as regulators accrue property rights through varying combinations of resources, legal rights, information asymmetries, and congressional delegations of authority. There are also third parties who may or may not enjoy a significant informational advantage over others, but whose group resources in terms of membership, financial strength, and access to elected officials give them substantial influence over the design and execution stages of the policy process.[18]

Conflicting interests "Propertied" or major stakeholders[19] respond to varying incentive structures and pursue conflicting goals. For example, members of congress respond to the particularistic requirements of the electoral connection, and party leaders in congress seek to pass the party's agenda and to maintain their control of congress. Meanwhile, industry seeks profit and the autonomy to pursue internally defined organizational goals. Single-issue interest groups take a narrower focus. Labor unions, for example, are charged with protecting the financial, health, and safety interests of workers, rather than the corporate bottom line per se.

Ex post opportunism   To paraphrase Miller and Moe (1986), because stakeholders have their own interests at heart, they will pursue the objectives of regulation only to the extent that the incentive structure imposed by a program renders such behavior advantageous (p. 175). To the extent that they choose to resist, we say that they are acting opportunistically. Given a hierarchy where conflicting interests give participants incentives to defect, incomplete programs create ample opportunity for shirking, and major players have the resources to resist top-down solutions, the costs to principals of enforcing program performance are high.

In sum, the new economics of organization literature offers some basic lessons for our study of politics and regulation. First, hierarchies, whether a single organization or a politically generated arrangement involving a multiplicity of interdependent, yet separate, organizations within the confines of the policy process, are treated as a series of special contractual relationships between superiors and subordinates. Effecting desired policy outcomes (i.e., maintaining accountability) requires that congress control the regulators and that regulators control agents inside their own organizations as well as within the regulated community. Second, transaction costs are key to understanding the motivation behind the selection of various institutional arrangements. Recall the expectations associated with the Clean Air Act of 1970—clear commands and hierarchical control would create a governance structure able to reduce transaction costs, hence facilitate the collective goal of clean air. Third, political relationships within the hierarchy of the policy process are as much about incentives and incentive alignment as they are about authority. Multiple propertied stakeholders pursuing self-interested, often-conflicting goals suggest that agents will not do something of their own accord; rather, you have to make the policy problem *their* policy problem. The key is to give agents a stake in the outcome, to persuade them that what is in the organization's or political principal's best interest also matches their own self-interest (or at a minimum incorporates key concerns they may have into the governing structure of the regulatory contract itself).[20] Fourth, the new economics of organization framework gives purchase on the consequences and costs of markets, hierarchies, and other arrangements simultaneously trying to achieve accountability to superiors and effective policy outcomes. It helps us to see that developing, implementing, and enforcing programs in the contemporary regulatory arena is a high-cost affair, even when regulatory transactions rely on a command-and-control hierarchy.

TRANSACTION COSTS, REGULATION, AND POLLUTION CONTROL POLITICS

The experience of the past twenty-five years in American pollution control politics suggests that new economics of organization theorists are correct; using hierarchy to command compliance in an arena replete with information asymmetries, incomplete programs, and powerful adversaries driven by conflicting incentives translates into a high-transaction-cost environment. The high levels of friction impede the achievement of collective goals and stakeholder attempts to maximize their individual organizational goals, thereby creating incentives to explore alternatives to the no-holds-barred pluralistic game. What are the costs of doing business under the traditional hierarchical approach to pollution control regulation?

INFORMATION SEARCH, PROGRAM SPECIFICATION, AND NEGOTIATION

Command-and-control arrangements experience high information search, program specification, and program negotiation costs[21] because they attempt to capture all polluter variance within national uniform rules and to manage both the substance and the process of compliance decision making. Regulators adopt a detailed, source-specific, industry-by-industry strategy of control over virtually every aspect of implementation. They identify and prescribe uniform emissions standards, best available control technologies (BACT)[22] that industry must use to achieve pollution reductions, and detailed decision processes that guide industry step-by-step toward compliance (e.g., permitting) (Ackerman and Stewart 1985; Vogel 1986). Successful specification of a command-and-control transaction requires that regulators have sufficient "expert" and organizational resources to generate and assess technical and scientific information pertinent to regulatory problems, and to translate that information into a written program capable of producing the results of environmental protection.

First, "[t]he unprecedented dependence [of social and environmental regulations] on expert analysis [make] policy highly dependent on the quality of the scientific assumptions and research used in the policy process" (Eisner 1993, 130). Information search costs therefore are bound to be high, given the high degree of scientific uncertainty accompanying such regulatory efforts. The hierarchical game of command and control, however, concentrates information search costs in the hands of government regulators, as they struggle to write rules consonant with legislative intentions (U.S. Congress. Senate Report Card 1993, 90). Regulators must maintain substantial technical and scientific resources for the purpose of discovering and testing best available control technologies, lowest achievable emission rates, maximum available control technology, and the like. Regulators must also have the capacity to evaluate effectively industry claims that a proposed technology qualifies as a viable substitute for any of these officially sanctioned approaches. As a leading EPA official attests:

> It takes regulators a long time trying to test some individual technology and see whether that technology really works, and what is the appropriate reduction target to associate with that technology. Then you tell everybody, "Well, we found that if you use this technology here, you can get a 70 percent reduction and we are going to require everybody to get 70 percent." That takes enormous amounts of resources to do that . . . testing to be able to figure out what the right number is. Besides, we always get challenged on [what the right number is] anyway. . . . It is just not clear that having us focus on a particular technology, analyze it to death, and then try to make some assumptions about the extent to which that particular technology is usable by all the industries in a sector is the best way to expend agency resources (interview with EPA 1/13/94).

Second, the search and program specification tasks of rulemaking are made more difficult by information asymmetries (Breyer 1982, 109–12). Stakeholders in pollution control, including the EPA itself, share concern over the capacity of EPA experts to cope with the daunting uncertainties associated with the technical complexities found in environmental policies. There are two areas where technical information asymmetries are of primary concern: the scientific soundness of a rule and the workability or implementability of a rule. In the former case, stakeholders fear that congress and EPA will make their decisions based on outdated science or an insufficient scientific database (Arrandale 1992; Oren 1991; Ray 1990; Wildavsky 1994). Prominent examples of pollution control regulations or salient environmental issues based on debatable or highly uncertain scientific foundations are acid rain,[23] the centralized inspection and maintenance program for motor vehicles,[24] Title VII of the 1990 Clean Air Act Amendments which attempts to staunch the deterioration of the ozone layer by eliminating the use of chlorofluorocarbons (CFCs), and the links between global warming and human activities (e.g., industrial development) as well as the severity of the global warming trend.[25] With respect to rule workability,

EPA decision making may be based on outdated industry standards or lack sufficient knowledge regarding either the complexities of industrial operations or the enforcement and implementation realities faced by state regulators. In both cases of information asymmetry, the experts closest to the compliance decision who have the most information regarding possible alternatives (i.e., in terms of cost, technical feasibility, environmental effectiveness, etc.) must rely on the judgment of federal decision makers who, by definition, have less information. Regulatory arrangements reflecting such information deficits are likely to provide "textbook" solutions to real-world problems, meaning that EPA is more likely to produce a suboptimal fit between rules and pollution problems. The uncertainty stemming from "suboptimal fits" is reflected by an often "unfortunate result"—industry must expend resources complying with rules providing uncertain or even negligible environmental results (interviews with EPA 12/10/93; 1/13/94; 3/17/94; industry 3/10/94).

Nor does industry have an incentive to help EPA by voluntarily divulging its "expert" information on industrial equipment, processes, or distribution systems. Sharing information with regulators under an adversarially based system of command and control not only risks the possibility of stricter emissions standards and the imposition of costlier control technologies,[26] it discards an important industry bargaining weapon: the control of information (Breyer 1982, 110). Breyer (1982) gives the example of a National Highway Traffic Safety Administration (NHTSA) rulemaking for automobile tire standards aimed at giving consumers more information regarding a particular tire's performance characteristics (e.g., temperature resistance, endurance, traction). Lacking industry cooperation,[27] NHTSA had to make regulatory proposals on its own. Yet each time it did, industry experts found it "relatively easy . . . to point to serious flaws in each . . . proposal" (p. 110).[28] Agency decision makers had "to satisfy industry's technical experts" if they were going to produce a workable proposal. Breyer points out that industry claims of confidentiality for its technical information makes "its bargaining position still stronger, for the agency either must work out a method to keep the information secret or do without it—and risk the industry's later technical criticisms of the agency's proposals" (p. 110). Further, industry is likely to be narrowly responsive to questions related to proposed regulatory standards. Such proposals will, by definition, offer little or no information on possible alternatives. Thus, if the original standard proves to be a bad or unworkable one, the responsible agency must repeat the information search process for each plausible alternative, a process that "take[s] forever" (p. 111).[29] Industry's unwillingness to share information often leaves the agency no recourse but to fight for access to information through the courts. In each case, regulators' low level of control over necessary technical information engenders high transaction costs for regulators.

Third, uniform BACT-based regulations governing industry operations are typically adapted to the specific and varying conditions of different plants throughout the country (Ackerman and Stewart 1985; Levin 1982; Pederson 1981).

> If you look at a command-and-control program, . . . you will find in the regulations all kinds of odd curlicues. They are supposedly imposing BACT, well, BACT is a very flexible concept. . . . So, if you go to [city X], you would probably find that what applies to [a large corporation] requires far more reduction than what applies to somebody else, and so on all around the state. There will be all kinds of differences. Well, those differences really represent human beings in the form of regulators responding to the different costs of cleanup. When an industry can come in and say, "If we do that it's going to cost $15 million." . . . If that's around $30,000 per ton, regulators know the industry is going to be able to beat them around the head and the shoulders in the legislature, so they adjust BACT to fit particular situations (interview with environmentalist 1/13/94).

Adjusting uniform regulations case-by-case entails higher costs in the areas of implementation timeliness, bargaining, and program specification.[30] The irony is that this is exactly what congress hoped to avoid with command and control. Congress imposed uniform technology-based standards "in order to avoid the transaction costs and implementation problems involved in policing environmental quality standards. [For example,] [i]n order to simplify decision making, the 1972 [Clean Water] Act ignored variations in water quality uses and goals. In implementing the Act, however, the EPA felt compelled to consider cost and other variables indirectly in setting BACT standards. This indirect approach caused the EPA to set separate standards for over 500 different industry and sub-industry standards, a majority of which were challenged in court. Long delays in implementing the statutory scheme resulted."[31] Shep Melnick (1983) reports a similar story in the case of air pollution regulations pursuant to both the 1970 Clean Air Act and 1977 amendments to the Act. National air quality standards were ultimately adjusted to differing local and regional circumstances, but only after EPA incurred significant costs in bargaining with polluters to escape what EPA perceived to be an "extremely risky and burdensome" game of litigation (pp. 193–204). Furthermore, given that "the technical information that goes into a typical permit application is mind-boggling," customizing permits inevitably adds to the public sector's already burdensome task of permit writing.[32]

Another element of the BACT system contributing to higher transaction costs for regulators is the way it incorporates scientific and technological change. Command and control tries to ensure that the best available pollution control technology is continually upgraded to the state of the art. Yet requiring *regulators* to continually update the technological component of regulatory arrangements forces the allocation of scarce administrative resources to the writing stage of the regulatory process, leaving fewer resources for monitoring and enforcement activities (Ackerman and Stewart 1985).

In short, the rhetoric of uniformity is often not matched by reality. Command and control engenders high information search, program specification, and program negotiation costs for regulators. It requires a resource-intensive information search process; yet regulators, by definition, lack access to the information needed to write regulatory rules. Therefore, regulators must not only expend agency resources fighting to get necessary information (since no one is generally willing to share it voluntarily); they typically end up with suboptimally specified regulations, given poor quality and/or incomplete information in the scientific and implementation realms. In addition, attempts at uniformity are fine in theory, but in practice command and control often requires regulators to adopt a continuous writing and negotiation mode due to the intense politicking and massive variations in the conditions—industrial, ecological, and otherwise—which inevitably shape the rules of the game during implementation.

PROGRAM ADAPTABILITY

Regulatory program design has important effects on the application of dispersed and changing information to policy problems (Allardice 1993; Breyer 1982; Goffman 1993b; NACEPT 1991; NAPA 1995). Program adaptability measures the response capacity of a regulatory arrangement to changes in exogenous conditions such as technological advances, market developments, and the scientific knowledge base. It is concerned with the strategic utilization of compliance-related assets in response to changing conditions and, in particular, to the costs of redeploying or developing compliance assets in response to these changes.

In empirical terms, program adaptability reflects the degree to which regulatory programs foster or constrain (1) the rate of technology innovation for environmental purposes[33] and (2) the response capacity of regulated firms to changing market conditions. The rate of technology innovation is important for environmental advocates and their allies because it affects the range of policy options available to policy makers and the probability of environmental program success over the long term (Dudek and Palmisano 1988; NACEPT 1991, 5). On the other hand, industry's response capacity can be critical for maintaining a firm or industry's competitive edge in the rapidly changing conditions associated with a globalized economy (see Chapter 2).

Rigid command-and-control-based programs require industry to seek authorization for changes in the configuration of their compliance assets from government regulators. They "lock in" compliance assets through the use of source-specific, technology-forcing "design standards" (Breyer 1982) and detailed permitting processes, thereby preventing or, at a minimum, making more costly participants' adaptation to changing conditions. As a result, command and control negatively affects both the rate of technology innovation and the response capacity of industry to changing market conditions.[34] At the other end of the continuum are flexible arrangements which equate with low adaptability costs. They relax the authority relationship and give industry greater freedom to choose how they wish to deploy their compliance assets. This tends to foster development of innovative environmental technologies and enhance the response capabilities of industry.

Under command and control, the regulated community has little incentive to develop new, improved control technologies. Much of this has to do with the "best available technology syndrome . . . woven into many statutes. This syndrome leads to risk aversion on the part of permit writers and companies that could potentially face severe penalties if they try something innovative that does not work" or is not accepted by EPA as "best available technology" once developed (Harper, USEPA 1993b, 160). A successful innovation might also add to a firm's regulatory burden and ultimately lead to higher aggregate compliance costs. For example, a new control technology designed to fit a particular facility or industrial process may have limited application at other facilities owned by a firm. Yet in a decision-making arena driven by uniform standards and technology applications, development of such technology not only encounters the high costs of a new permitting process, but also the likely forced application of the technology across facilities, even where its application is highly cost-ineffective. Given the lack of incentive, the regulatory game becomes one where "industry hides what they can do because if the regulators find out they will make me do it" (interview with environmentalist 1/13/94). This accentuates the "critical mass" problem—there are fewer people searching for more effective environmental technologies and, most importantly, fewer of the industry experts closest to pollution problems.

The politicization of technology specification processes under command and control also creates high uncertainty in control technology markets, hence lagging rates of investment and ultimately lower rates of innovation.[35] Because government regulators "make the market" through their control of BACT certification, investment bankers are subject to the "what is BACT today may not be BACT tomorrow" syndrome. The inherent uncertainty of the investment climate makes it harder for investors to discern market risk, given that the success of a particular technology will likely be more the result of the seemingly arbitrary decisions of regulators than more traditional technical efficiency and cost-effectiveness factors. In addition, because the demand for innovation is closely connected to the passage of new laws, market demand for control technologies is extremely volatile, taking the form of punctuated equilibriums—narrow windows of opportunities targeted on legally mandated deadlines and precipitous falloff in demand once deadlines are passed. Investor risk is heightened since they have short time frames in which to recapture investment returns on specialized plant and machinery equipment, human resource training, and so on. The high level of uncertainty encountered in both cases is a key contributor to lagging rates of investment, hence low rates of innovation in environmental technologies over the past decade. In cases where investment does occur, the relative increases in financial risk tend to push lending rates up and contribute to higher cost of compliance technologies (NACEPT 1991; *New York Times* 1989; Nikkila, South Coast Air Quality Management District, USEPA 1993b, 162; Harper, USEPA 1993b, 160).

A command-and-control system requires regulators to be a clearinghouse for permitting decisions made by industry. Traditional permitting procedures under the Clean Air Act require industry to submit detailed applications laying out almost a month-by-month schedule of compliance implementation, including interim steps between the time of the application and the time that pollution control has to be achieved. Examples of interim steps include filing requisite compliance paperwork on time, signing a contract with a pollution control technology manufacturer by a specified date, and providing detailed documentation of each and every step of the manufacturing process or product in question (interview with industry 3/10/94). Each step is enforceable as if it were a permit condition. Such detailed applications make "the compliance planning process very transaction cost intensive and inflexible."[36] Not only must regulators devote substantial agency resources to verifying and approving industry compliance decisions, industry decision makers who, by virtue of better information, changing market conditions, or the like, perceive the need for revised compliance strategies must go back to the agency and get approval for permitting changes. Yet applying for permit revisions often entails substantial bargaining costs and is accompanied by uncertainty over whether government regulators will even approve requested changes. In this way, the structure of the command-and-control-based permitting process places industry in the position of having to choose between a compliance strategy that is known to be suboptimal (because conditions have changed) and a permit revision process that is both resource-intensive and highly uncertain as to the final outcome.

Further, command and control gives industry-based compliance planners low levels of discretion, hence a firm's responsiveness to changing market conditions is closely tied to the speed at which government makes decisions. Yet, given the slow pace of government decision making, industry's response capability is inevitably constrained and its ability to compete internationally is negatively affected (see discussion on international markets in Chapter 2).

Finally, the source-specific nature of the compliance regime has implications for the organizational structure and technological sophistication of regulatory personnel (interviews with state regulator 3/1/94; EPA 1/11/94). The administrative task requires regulators to care about the microdetail of day-to-day industry operations. As noted in the case of permitting, regulators want industry to describe in intimate detail the production process and the steps taken to ensure that environmental results are achieved at the end of the pipe or at the end of the appropriate compliance period. Richard Stewart (1988) explains:

> This requires administrators to acquire and analyze an enormous amount of information about the conduct of those being regulated and the consequences of different regulatory decisions (p. 156).

As a practical matter, this is an extremely resource-intensive exercise. It require regulators "slogging through and going after pollution control problems on an industry-by-industry basis" (interview with EPA 1/13/94). It also means that regulators need virtually as much specialized expertise about industrial processes and business operating procedures as industry itself.

Staffing bureaucracies under such a system requires a large number of pollution control specialists. Much like dedicated industrial machines which specialize in a limited set of tasks, pollution control specialists' expertise is narrowly confined to a specific industry or set of sources within a particular industry. The result is that bureaucratic expertise is compartmentalized into separate organizational units aligned with their industrial counterparts. For example, an entire cadre of engineers, instrumentation specialists, chemists, economists, field inspectors, and the like are dedicated to the "paints and coatings" industry, or the glass manufacturing industry, or the paper industry.

Narrowing the focus of the organizational commitment, and along with it the system of professional rewards, engenders high program adaptability costs, however. There are high "sunk costs" (i.e., a high degree of rigidity) in terms of personnel and organizational structure. In the latter case, costs are high because authority relationships are defined hierarchically within each industry-dedicated subunit. Agencies structured in this manner duplicate tasks and personnel, thus contributing to higher agency operating expenses (i.e., overhead). In the former case, industry-dedicated regulatory expertise does not transfer easily between organizational units. Pollution control specialists have little incentive to seek innovative alternatives to prescribed operating methods or organizational problems outside of their jurisdiction, even if they do possess information or expertise capable of providing alternative solutions. Pursuing alternatives takes time and resources away from projects for which there is already an organizational commitment and for which the individual bureaucrat is likely to be rewarded. Over time, trained incapacity sets in as regulators are taught to analyze certain types of situations in a specific way, and adaptation—learning a new set of premises—is made more difficult, hence the transfer of expertise is more costly (Knott and Miller 1987, 172–81).

Configuring regulatory resources in this way is not problematic so long as the demand for regulatory services is relatively constant. However, given that demand typically varies both spatially (i.e., across industries) and temporally (i.e., from year to year and season to season), the probability increases that "dedicated" regulatory resources will be either idle or overworked under a command-and-control arrangement. The sunk costs make it extremely difficult (and costly), if not impossible, for the industry-dedicated bureaucratic resources to "flex" or shift the focus of their expertise from an area of slack demand into another area where demand for rulemaking, permitting, or compliance inspection activities is high (Allison 1969; Thompson 1969).

Lagging rates of investment and innovation in control technologies, extensive permitting paperwork burdens, the time-based dependency of private-sector decision makers on a regulatory clearinghouse, and the organizational inflexibilities accompanying command and control offer transaction cost savings opportunities for regulators, environmentalists, and industry. Regulatory arrangements able to improve the rate of technological innovation give regulators and environmentalists more tools in the fight against environmental degradation. Regulations promising less inertia, less compliance paperwork, and greater private-sector discretion over final compliance decisions are attractive to industry. To the extent these characteristics are included in mandated regulatory programs—which are designed to deliver environmental quality for society, not economic benefits for industry, by forcing industry to pay for the cleanup of pollution (externalities)—they will make such programs easier for industry to swallow. Furthermore, programs that minimize organizational sunk costs are attractive to regulators because of the potential for greater responsiveness to changing political demands and improved organizational effectiveness.

MONITORING AND ENFORCEMENT TRANSACTION COSTS

Because regulatory arrangements are, by definition, incomplete,[37] and given the likelihood of *ex post* opportunism, government regulators must expend resources on monitoring and enforcement activities in order to ensure compliance (minimize shirking).[38] Much of the push to find alternatives to coercive command-and-control regulations and adversarial notice-and-comment rulemaking strategies comes from their perceived failure to adequately consider the difficulties and costs inherent in executing the program (Bardach and Kagan 1982; Burton 1988; Fiorino 1988; Stewart 1981).

The certainty associated with monitoring and data-reporting techniques used in traditional command-and-control arrangements should not be overestimated.[39] The resource intensity of information search, program specification, and negotiation activities detracts from and fundamentally limits regulators' ability to assess how often, and to what degree, polluters are in compliance. Although it is a relatively easy task to confirm that a specified control technology is, in fact, installed, considerable uncertainty arises because "[i]nspections often cover less than 1 percent of a facility's annual emissions, usually take 2 to 4 hours to perform, and are normally conducted at major stationary sources once each year" (GAO 1990b, 19; Rabe 1994).[40] Such infrequent on-site inspections are unable to guarantee that the control technology in question is *operating* in conformance with the law (interview with environmentalist 1/10/94). For example,

> when you put a scrubber on a plant, you get 90 percent or more control, but there is a bypass stack because sometimes the scrubber doesn't work and so the operation goes on without the scrubber. You're not supposed to use it, right? But who knows? The old program would only test once every three years for a week. I mean, what happened the rest of the time? You don't know what was going on at that plant. You don't know what was going on at night. You couldn't see it (interview with EPA 1/11/94).

Compounding the problem of infrequent inspections is a typical statutory requirement forcing regulators to give industry ample notice of forthcoming inspections. Advance notice creates an opportunity for industry to "game" the system by adjusting industrial equipment prior to the inspection such that emissions readings fall within allowable regulatory limits.

Given that infrequent inspections are likely to produce poor-quality databases, regulators necessarily experience added difficulty in determining whether the data produced during inspections is reliable or not (GAO 1979; interview with environmentalist 2/11/94). GAO (1979) found that:

> The EPA's data systems, designed to track the amount of pollutants into the air, are inaccurate and rarely compatible with the States' systems. ... [Further,] EPA has no reliable means of correlating emissions with compliance status and, therefore, is unable to determine the impact violating sources have on air quality. ... As a result, incorrect progress and status reports have been issued to the Congress and the public (pp. *i*, 11).

As a result, the "reality of command and control" fails to provide the "high threshold of credibility and accountability" in pollution control programs sought by regulators and environmentalists. Therefore, if the transaction cost reasoning is sound, alternative programs should include more rigorous monitoring and emissions-tracking systems designed to reduce the uncertainty of emissions-monitoring efforts.[41]

High transaction costs are also encountered in the area of agency enforcement. This is because command-and-control-based rules of the game are almost always accompanied by industry resistance. From the perspective of the regulated community, command and control translates into high compliance costs, uncertain environmental results, misdirected regulatory efforts, restricted autonomy, and a situation where the costs of compliance are de-emphasized or even excluded from consideration. As Richard Stewart (1988) duly notes, and my own interviews with private-sector elites confirm, industry believes that the coercive, irrational, and suboptimal nature of such rules justifies high levels of resistance via noncompliance, obfuscation, and delay in their dealings with regulators, and litigation challenging the factual and analytical justifications for agency regulations (p. 156; interviews on 1/12/94; 1/21/94; 2/10/94; 2/22/94; 3/17/94; 12/1/94).

Part of this dynamic is simply an extension of earlier concerns that gave rise to the general demands for regulatory reform during the 1970s (Eads and Fix 1984; Eisner 1993, 172–77). The cost of regulatory compliance is on the rise and the impact of environmental regulations on domestic productivity has grown significantly in recent years.[42] By the end of the 1980s, estimates of the direct costs of compliance with federal environmental regulations ranged between $80 billion and $140

billion annually (Levin and Elman 1990; Schneider 1993). Total estimated costs of environmental protection, which include public sector
costs and the costs of complying with state regulations, range higher
(See Table 3.1). In the period 1972 to 1995, the costs of protecting air
quality increased by 404 percent, while the costs of complying with
water quality regulations experienced close to a 500 percent increase.
Hazardous waste protection meanwhile grew from a level of zero
expenditures in the early 1980s to $1.3 billion per year in 1985 and to
$16.8 billion in 1995—an increase of 1,292 percent in ten years. Further,
the level of expenditures devoted to environmental protection in relation to the United States' gross national product (GNP) rose from 0.9
percent of GNP in 1972 to 2.4 percent in 1995 and is expected to continue
rising in the near future.

A significant portion of these costs involve the capital construction
costs of implementing and maintaining pollution control technologies.
A single, medium-sized oil refinery in Yorktown, Virginia, projected
capital costs of environmental compliance at $53.6 million during the
early 1990s. This was in addition to estimated annual compliance costs
of $17.5 million.[43] The clean fuels mandate of the 1990 Clean Air Act
Amendments saddled the oil industry with an estimated $3 to 5 billion
one-time retooling cost on existing refineries and an estimated $20 to
30 billion conversion cost for the law's reformulated gasoline provisions. The Atlantic Richfield Company (ARCO) alone estimated its share
of the conversion effort at $2 billion over a five-year period (GAO
1990a, 4–7; *New York Times* 1991a; 1991c).

The regulated community confronts significant administrative paperwork and personnel costs as well. The administrative time devoted
to paperwork is now estimated at upwards of 6.5 billion hours per
year as of 1991.[44] Personnel requirements, too, have expanded dramatically over the years. For example, Amoco Oil's Environment, Health
and Safety Division increased staffing from two people in 1970 to over
600 in the early 1990s (interview with industry 12/1/94a).[45] Besides
imposing direct costs on industry, the administrative burden of regulatory "[r]ed tape increases the capital needed to fund a new enterprise
and diminishes the potential profit. Many small businesses keep their
workforce at 49 workers because hiring another employee triggers
a variety of regulatory requirements" (McIntosh and Weidenbaum
1995, A14).

Of even more importance to many in industry are the high costs
paid to reduce each unit of pollution. The USEPA (1990a) estimates
that the minimum cost of securing additional reductions in volatile
organic compound emissions from stationary industrial sources is approximately $5,000 per ton (p. 5). Pollution control costs in the most

TABLE 3.1 Estimated Costs of Environmental Protection, Selected Years (Constant 1986 Dollars, Billions)

	1972	1975	1980	1985	1987	1990	1992	1995	2000
Total Costs									
Air	7.9	10.9	17.6	23.3	26.7	27.6	29.7	31.9	37.5
Water[a]	9.1	14.0	22.8	30.4	34.4	38.5	41.5	45.4	51.6
Land[b]	8.4	9.8	13.6	15.9	19.1	26.5	33.0	37.2	46.1
HazWaste[c]	0.0	0.0	0.0	1.3	2.4	9.3	14.2	16.8	23.8
Total	26.5	36.8	58.0	74.0	85.3	99.9	114.2	129.4	147.9
Total as % of GNP	0.9	1.2	1.6	1.8	1.9	2.1	2.3	2.4	2.6
Federally Mandated Costs	17.7	26.5	43.5	57.9	66.8	80.8	93.8	111.0	137.2
Total as % of GNP	0.6	0.9	1.2	1.4	1.5	1.7	1.9	2.1	2.4

[a]Water quality efforts only; does not include clean drinking water costs.
[b]Includes both solid and hazardous waste management.
[c]Includes RCRA, Superfund, and LUST expenditures.
Source: EPA Administrator (1990c). Calculated from tables 3–3A, 4–3A, 8–3, 8–9A.

polluted areas are much higher, however, and can range upwards of $25,000 per ton of pollution removed.[46] Prior to the market-based emissions trading program for acid rain, affected utilities were required to install scrubbers and were accustomed to paying $1,500 for every ton of sulfur dioxide removed from the atmosphere (on the margin) (Bartels testimony, U.S. Congress. Senate. Acid Rain Hearings 1993, 116). Emissions trading effectively reduced the cost per ton to under $200 (see Chapter 6). In another case, the existing regulatory structure imposed an average cost of $2,400 per ton of pollution reduced. Yet further scrutiny by industry and regulators revealed that comparable environmental protection could be achieved for $510 per ton (see Chapter 7).

Apart from the costs of complying with pollution control regulations, industry frustration and their willingness to resist regulation is fueled by the perception that their money is inefficiently targeted and buying society little in the way of tangible progress toward stated regulatory goals. From industry's perspective, suboptimally specified programs, the uncertainty associated with monitoring efforts, and the use of "junk" science are all part of an irrational and dysfunctional system of regulatory control (Carroll 1995; Clean Air Working Group 1987; Ray 1990). The Superfund law designed to clean up existing hazardous waste sites is often cited as a classic example of inefficiency. Slow progress in remediating Superfund sites[47] has provided few benefits in improved human or ecological health in comparison to the compliance and litigation expenditures incurred (well over $10 billion dollars as of 1994) (see GAO 1994c; Hird 1994; Mazmanian and Morell 1992). Others point to the case of regulations designed to protect the earth's stratospheric ozone layer. The cost of retrofitting air conditioners and refrigerators with substitute coolants to replace Freon (the chief source of CFCs) is estimated at $100 billion. Yet research conducted by Sallie Baliunas, chair of the Harvard–Smithsonian Center for Astrophysics, disputes the link between CFCs and a thinning ozone layer as well as the link between a thinner ozone layer and an increased incidence of melanoma (skin cancer). Baliunas's conclusion, that these results make "the hysteria and costly regulations . . . entirely unfounded," provides ammunition for industry's fight against what they perceive as regulatory overreach (as quoted in Melloan 1995). Moreover, the double jeopardy associated with cross-media pollution transfers affects industry and regulators alike, since each must endure the costs of cleanup twice—two rulemakings, two sets of compliance requirements, and double the monitoring and enforcement activities.

Industry also reacts adversely to what they see as misdirected regulatory efforts—a problem of prioritizing environmental and human health risks. Most regulatory priorities in the pollution control arena accord with public perceptions of risk, rather than environmental experts' assessments (USEPA 1987b; 1990e; Breyer 1993; Finkel and Golding 1994). The discrepancy is problematic in that the public generally focuses on cleanup issues with the lowest risks. Yet the issue affects more than just industry; it directly impacts resource allocations of state and federal regulators as well. Ultimately, the focus on low risks means not only that bureaucratic and industry resources are inefficiently targeted, but "if finite resources are expended on lower-priority problems at the expense of higher-priority risks, then society will face needlessly high risks."[48]

In short, industry is not convinced that they receive value for their compliance expenditures, given the uncertainty of appreciable or even measurable environmental results and the propensity to focus the bulk of compliance resources on low-risk issues.

Conflict further arises as a matter of principled opposition to regulations viewed as coercive and intrusive and which restrict industry's autonomy regarding the disposition of compliance assets. Regulatory management through centrally prescribed standards and control technologies and tight control of permitting processes not only hampers industry efforts to access new markets by making it more difficult and costly to respond to changing conditions in a timely manner, it forces industry to implement standards and controls "likely to be unworkable or arbitrary in many applications" (Stewart 1988, 156). In both cases, the lack of private-sector discretion creates a scenario wherein environmental compliance activities become a cost center—an expenditure that detracts from the bottom line (profit) and is a drag on the competitive position of losing industries because the opportunity to manipulate compliance resources is absent (interviews with industry 1/21/94; 2/22/94).

The explicit devaluation of industry's concerns over the cost effectiveness of regulation is another major factor sparking industry resistance. Major sections of federal environmental laws are replete with zero-sum language favoring the environment to the exclusion of the economy. The Clean Water Act of 1972 not only set a national goal of zero discharge into the nation's waterways by 1985; it required EPA to develop "pollutant-specific effluent standards to be applied to all industrial categories regardless of technological or economic achievability" (CEQ 1982, 81). Under the 1970 Clean Air Act, congress instructed EPA to establish a series of national ambient air quality standards (NAAQS) "allowing an adequate margin of safety requisite to protect the public health," but without consideration of the costs involved in meeting them. Likewise, Section 112 of the Clean Air Act "required the EPA to regulate particularly hazardous pollutants to zero risk with an ample margin of safety regardless of cost."[49] The Endangered Species Act of 1973 obligates the federal government to designate critical habitat for species threatened with extinction and to produce plans to spur recovery of the endangered flora and fauna. Again, the law excludes consideration of economic factors.[50] And the Resource Conservation and Recovery Act of 1976 enjoins property owners to clean up toxic waste sites to the highest possible standards but without regard to cost.

Taken together, these factors create incentives for losing players to adopt a strategy of resistance, whether through attempts to overturn regulatory rules legislatively, obfuscation during rulemaking, or litigation after rule promulgation. Since losing means losing big—if you are covered by the rules, it is typically at an 80 or 90 percent rate of reduction, while the "winners," those left uncovered by the regulation, "can belch away"[51]—potential payoffs from such a strategy are considerable: mitigation of the rule's effects through additional legislation, delays in compliance requirements, and money saved from not having to install mandated controls during the litigation period. There is also the possibility that regulators will end up granting waivers exempting sources from a particular statute's compliance mandate. In the words of a veteran EPA official, "Industry sues if they have a shred of a chance of winning because they have nothing to lose. All they have to do is pay the lawyers. If industry loses the litigation after five years, they delay pollution controls for five years" (interview with EPA 1/11/94). When smokestack scrubbers cost $100 million apiece, "[e]ven in Washington, you can buy an awful lot of lawyer time. You can go years before you have to pay for one scrubber. . . ." (interview with industry 1/21/94).

The virtual certainty of litigation on major environmental regulations, however, translates into uncertainty and resource expenditures for other stakeholders. Not only does litigation delay environmental protection, the prospect of litigation increases the costs of preparing a rule to withstand judicial scrutiny. According to ex-EPA Administrator William Reilly, "We spend as much time designing our rules to withstand court attack as we do getting the rules right and out in the first place."[52] Further, litigation places the resolution of issues in the "uncertain" hands of the judiciary. The history of court decisions in environmental law shows that courts are just as likely to favor industry as the interests of environmentalists and regulators (Wenner 1982; McGarity 1992). In addition, the adversarial setting within which courts operate is often better suited to resolving narrow, procedural issues that have little overt effect on the resolution of the substantive environmental issues driving lawsuits (Horowitz 1977; Bacow and Wheeler 1984). As part of this phenomenon, decisions remanded back to EPA by the courts often go through the rulemaking process a second time, yet with only marginal adjustments to the ultimate effect of the rule in terms of either economic costs or environmental quality (Melnick 1983; McGarity 1992, 1390).

Finally, the top-down approach implicitly assigns regulators, not polluters, sole responsibility for program performance. As a result, and much like the laws of physics, where the presence of friction creates additional energy (resource) demands, command and control gives stakeholders more decision points against which to react and hence greater opportunities for creating friction. The additional contact points create greater opportunities for friction with its concomitant transaction costs of litigation and delay (Mashaw and Harfst 1990, 228; U.S. Congress. Senate. Senate Report Card 1993, 90). Regulator control over the substance of program rules (e.g., control technologies, permitting requirements) also allows industry to point the finger of blame at agency decision makers whenever compliance strategies are suboptimal for a company's particular circumstances. A chronic problem with command and control is that

> nobody ever hears much about the low-cost compliance examples, but you always hear about the high-cost examples, and it is a tremendous advantage [for regulators] to be able to say, "You did not have to pay those high costs. You had a lot of other options. [EPA] gave you the latitude to find another way to do it, so don't say we locked you into doing something which was stupid; we didn't." That's another reason why EPA has an incentive to pursue market-based programs (interview with EPA 1/13/94).

The uncertainties associated with monitoring and enforcement efforts under command and control are problematic for both environmentalists and regulators. Both sets of actors are left without the organizational capacity to mount a credible monitoring effort, and vigorous resistance by industry and lengthy delays in meeting environmental protection goals mean that each has an interest in improved regulatory performance. As well, regulators perceive that shifting more of the responsibility for program performance onto the private sector offers benefits by lowering the incidence of bureaucratic blame. The result is a corresponding decrease in the frequency of "fire alarms"—where aggrieved constituency groups or the general public register complaints about bureaucratic performance with congress—triggered by the regulated community (see McCubbins and Schwartz 1984). In turn, fewer fire alarms are likely to decrease agency costs devoted to congressional oversight activities. The high costs of doing business encountered by industry, on the other hand, motivate private-sector decision makers to seek regulatory alternatives promising relief from the growing costs of compliance, greater rationalization of existing rules, greater flexibility in determining the means by which pollution control goals are reached, and rules incorporating economic goals alongside environmental goals.

THE DISCONNECTEDNESS OF RULES FROM RESULTS

Successful compliance with the rules does not necessarily equate with the intended policy result of a cleaner environment, a phenomenon Donald Kettl (1983) labels "token compliance" (p. 13). Command and control attempts to control pollution by specifying technology standards on a source-specific basis. Technology standards are generally expressed in terms of an emissions rate or specified technology and are targeted at single-medium emissions (e.g., air or water or land). Yet specifying the rules of the game in such a way creates a basic disconnect between the rules and environmental results. Because successful compliance is a matter of complying with government-imposed technology standards, stakeholders have an incentive to focus on the regulatory rules rather than environmental outcomes. According to Joseph Goffman, a senior attorney for the Environmental Defense Fund, the problem becomes that "in practice, sources can be 'in compliance' without achieving the actual emissions reductions expected or necessary to achieve the environmental objective" (1993b, 1). In this sense, regulatory rules are disconnected from the bigger picture of overall pollution reduction that policy is designed to achieve. Regulators and environmentalists spin their wheels investing resources in the development, implementation, and enforcement of regulatory programs yielding limited or, in some cases, negative progress toward the ultimate goal of environmental protection. There are three areas where "disconnectedness" is especially evident: the "rate basis" problem, the growth of sources problem, and the cross-media pollution shifting problem.

Technology standards defined on a rate basis tell industry how much of a particular emission must be prevented from entering the air, water, or ground. Rate-basis approaches target end-of-pipe emissions and are calculated either on a straight percentage basis or a fuel-to-energy output ratio. In the former case, a percentage reduction of, for example, 90 percent is set. As long as the pipe emitting the specified pollutant reduces pollution output by 90 percent, compliance is obtained. In the latter case, the rate basis is calculated on pounds of emissions per million Btu of heat input (energy). "The more heat you put in, the more emissions allowed. The less heat, the fewer emissions allowed" (interview with EPA 1/11/94). If one million Btu of energy is fed into an industrial process, then industry is allowed to emit X pounds of pollution; if ten million Btu of energy is added, then emissions can equal $10X$ pounds of pollution, and so on. In either case, the problem becomes that ultimate environmental results hinge on how much production there is at [each] facility and how many hours it operates over the course of a week, a month, or a year (interview with EPA 1/13/94). If an industrial facility increases production by 30 percent, as long as the basic rate-basis standard is met, then compliance requirements are satisfied. The obvious problem is that the rules designed to bring about compliance are disconnected from environmental quality because compliance ignores the fact of 30 percent more pollution. As a result, the rate-basis approach increases the uncertainty associated with agency attempts to monitor actual levels of pollution emissions for specific sources.

The second problem concerns economic expansion and growing numbers of pollution sources. Regardless of whether the technology standard is a rate-basis or end-of-pipe approach, additional sources means increased pollution. Even in a wildly optimistic future scenario where *all* possible sources of pollution are controlled, a technology standard approach only *slows* the rate of overall pollution growth (the exception being where all sources are controlled to the zero-emissions level).

Perhaps the most prominent example of how technology standards lead to goal displacement and nonattainment of goals is the case of ground-level ozone, a pollutant affected by Title I and Title II of the Clean Air Act. The original 1970 Clean Air Act set national ambient air quality standards (NAAQS) for ozone and several other pollutants. Technology standards measures were mandated for stationary sources and mobile sources. In the case of automobiles, a 90 percent reduction was required for tailpipe emissions. On both counts 1975 was selected as the compliance deadline date. However, the 1975 date was not met; therefore congress extended the ozone attainment deadlines to 1982 and 1987 when it amended the Clean Air Act in 1977. Eventually the 1987 deadline came and went, with over 100 areas in the country still holding the dubious honor of ozone nonattainment classification. In fact, widespread ozone nonattainment was an important catalyst in the enactment of the 1990 amendments to the Clean Air Act. In 1989 there were still over 100 areas of the country in nonattainment, with some areas facing severe economic sanctions for their inability to comply with ozone mandates (Calcagni 1993; Cohen 1992; U.S. Congress. Senate. Senate Report Card 1993).[53]

The point here is that, after twenty years of trying, technology standards did not lead to optimum environmental results. It is more a matter of a growing number of pollution sources, both mobile and stationary, than of noncompliance per se. "This is because economic growth among regulated sources can result in high levels of actual emissions even if the sources are operating at low emissions rates" (Goffman 1993b). In the specific case of automobile tailpipe emissions: "Despite a 95 percent decrease in tailpipe emissions from new vehicles over the past twenty years, emissions from mobile sources continue to be a major contributor to urban air pollution as the number of vehicles and vehicle miles driven have increased" (Kosobud, Testa, and Hanson 1993, *ix*).

Further, in certain regions of the country national ambient air quality standards for ozone have not been met *even under conditions of general economic decline in the manufacturing sector.*

> Over the last two decades the Great Lakes Region has seen significant economic decline in manufacturing employment with large and permanent losses occurring during the back-to-back national recessions of the early 1980s. Over one-fifth of the region's manufacturing jobs evaporated during this time (Allardice, Mattoon, and Testa 1993, *i*).

However, the Great Lakes region continues to suffer from poor air quality. The Chicago–Gary–Lake County, Illinois–Indiana, and Milwaukee–Racine, Wisconsin, areas constitute two of the six "severe" ozone nonattainment areas covered by the 1990 Clean Air Act Amendments.[54] Eleven of thirty-two areas in the "moderate" classification are from the Great Lakes region, while eight more areas qualify for nonattainment under the "marginal" category.[55]

The ground-level ozone case is a classic example of what one leader of the national environmental community calls "winning the battle and losing the war" (interview 1/13/94). Environmentalists won the battle when the ozone NAAQS were mandated under the 1970 Clean Air Act, yet the promise of the law remains unfulfilled, partly because technology standards separate regulatory rules from ultimate regulatory goals.

The third case of disconnectedness is directly related to the traditional regulatory focus on solving individual pollution problems *within a single medium*, rather than linking them in holistic multimedia fashion (air–water–land) to the rest of the environment. Regulatory programs designed in this way may actually succeed in reducing the targeted pollutant. Yet because such arrangements misspecify the interrelationships among the several media (by ignoring them), the problem of cross-media pollution shifting arises.[56] Stated differently, the successful achievement of policy goals in one media does not necessarily mean that the pollution problem is solved. Instead, it often means that the problem is merely transferred to another part of the environment. In an assessment of twenty years of single-medium approaches in advanced industrial countries, Frances Irwin (1990) finds that "[t]he very programs that successfully cleaned up local air and water problems have contributed to a waste problem on land as the air and water pollutants have been collected and dumped into landfills or ponds. . . . The incentive is to move the waste to the least protected part of the environment rather than to prevent it being generated in the first place by changing the product or process" (pp. 5–7). Again, we are talking about a scenario in which a pollution reduction program is deemed successful because the original goals are met. But because the regulation essentially misspecifies the pollution control model, the definition of program success is disconnected from actual environmental results.

Such suboptimal environmental outcomes offer incentives to the EPA and environmentalists alike to seek alternative regulatory methods because they are getting less than they bargained for; they are not getting the environmental improvement implied by the rules of the game. The reputation of EPA also suffers since it is seen as an agency unable to achieve its basic mission of environmental protection, yet it is still, by virtue of its mandate, in the business of forcing industry and the states to spend billions of dollars in pursuit of rules with uncertain environmental results.

CONCLUSION

The results of a hierarchical approach to pollution control have not measured up to original expectations. The difficulties encountered in gathering enough information, specifying complete programs, and then monitoring and enforcing command-and-control arrangements introduce substantial uncertainty into the policy-making and implementation picture. The uncertainty contributes to a situation where stakeholders are regularly forced to settle for suboptimal results, whether in terms of environmental performance, the level of compliance expenditures, lagging technology innovation, or regulations lacking the expert input of stakeholders closest to the policy problem.

The high transaction costs engendered by hierarchy can be depicted by a "car" analogy. Command-and-control regulation represents cars on their way to a specified destination—a clean environment. The problem is that the cars, once started and on their way, are prone to crashing or running into roadblocks such that they make little if any progress, incur significant delays (from either mechanical repairs or simply waiting for roadblocks to clear), or are forced to take circuitous routes that ultimately require extra fuel to reach the chosen destination. All of which means that goals are often reached, but only after both public and private sectors incur added costs with no apparent benefits from the higher costs. In addition, the drivers (regulators) of command-and-control cars often lack good maps on how best to reach the final destination. Moreover, when drivers with "bad" maps stop to ask for assistance, people are unfriendly and generally unwilling to give them the information they need, or drivers are purposely given the wrong information. In this case, the car may eventually reach the objective, but only after expending extra time and effort exploring unnecessary detours. In other cases, the mapmakers have actually misspecified the destination such that cars are continually being sent to the wrong place. Given such difficulties and costs, it is not surprising that major stakeholders in national pollution control politics are now interested in driving different cars and devising new maps to achieve the goals of pollution reduction.

Yet the chapter's opening quote by Michael Levin makes it clear that the high costs of doing business under the traditional regulatory system have been evident for a long time (see, e.g., Bardach and Kagan 1982; Eads and Fix 1984; Kneese and Schultze 1976; Pederson 1981). At the same time, participants in environmental politics have long recognized the potential of "win–win" benefits for all stakeholders achieved through collaborative mechanisms.[57] But with few exceptions, the benefits of collaborative efforts have remained theoretical conjecture. Understanding the transition from conflict to collaboration necessitates an exploration of pluralism by the rules, the third and final component of the "why collaboration" puzzle. It is to this that we turn in Chapter 4.

CHAPTER NOTES

1. Levin (1982, 73–74).

2. For more on Browner's approach to collaboration and consensus-based mechanisms, see *Environment Reporter* (12/25/92, 2099), Oliphant's (1994) discussion of how Browner's "new approach" to environmental regulation is turning the traditional approach "on its head," and her press release announcing the Common Sense Initiative in July 1994 (USEPA 1994a).

3. The EPA is often characterized as a model of bureaucratic ineffectiveness (Dunne 1992; Kettl 1993; Marcus 1980).

4. USEPA (1990c); GAO (1991).

5. See U.S. Congress. House. Clean Air Act Amendment Hearings, Part I (1989); GAO (1994a) report on the Toxic Substances Control Act; Mazmanian

and Morell (1992) on Superfund; Weisskopf (1989a; 1989b) on general regulatory failure.

6. Williamson (1985, 20). With respect to institutional comparisons, transaction costs "are difficult to quantify. The difficulty, however, is mitigated by the fact that transaction costs are always assessed in a comparative institutional way, in which one mode of contracting is compared with another. Accordingly, it is the difference between rather than the absolute magnitude of transaction costs that matters. . . . Empirical research on transaction cost matters almost never attempts to measure such costs directly. Instead, the question is whether organizational relations (contracting practices; governance structures) line up with the attributes of transactions as predicted by transaction cost reasoning or not" (Williamson 1985, 21–22).

7. In general, transaction cost theory predicts that players will seek alternative institutional arrangements when transaction costs are high. But in reality, transaction costs cannot be understood apart from their relationship to an organization's bottom line, whether that be the pursuit of profit or some other primary organizational goal like improved environmental quality. It is really cost effectiveness—the ratio of transaction costs to the level of goals attained or expected—that the transaction cost literature is most concerned about; it is cost effectiveness, not transaction costs per se, that drives the decision to seek out and construct new arrangements.

8. Uncertainty enters the picture because it creates a classic collective action dilemma. Participants who perceive that alternative institutional arrangements can reduce transaction costs while simultaneously increasing organizational goal attainment are nonetheless often hesitant to proceed with the adoption of the new arrangements. Why? Because high uncertainty leaves too many unknowns. Not enough of their questions as to the consequences of their choice are answerable, hence risks associated with projected outcomes are high. For instance, high uncertainty makes it harder to trust potential participants to an exchange, especially when they are long-time adversaries, as is often the case in regulatory politics. What is to prevent them from taking advantage of the uncertainty to advance their own interests? Uncertainty thus causes players to discount potential gains, since it may prevent expected payoffs from being collected. Hence, uncertainty lowers the likelihood of collective action by making it less attractive.

9. Shirking is defined as evading the performance of an obligation, legal or otherwise.

10. Political principals in congress and the presidency have the authority necessary to control the bureaucracy, hence outcomes, because they occupy the top of the hierarchy; they "have unique and enormously valuable property rights by virtue of their occupation of official positions" (Moe 1990, 120–21). The theoretical task is eased considerably by assuming that political principals are omniscient (perfect information) or, at a minimum, so well-informed that they can systematically shape the preferences of bureaucratic agents. See Banks and Weingast (1992); Moe (1990, 120–22); Wood and Waterman (1991).

11. Coase challenged the efficiency premise of neoclassical economics by asking the question: if markets are so efficient, then why is so much of industry

organized along hierarchical (integrated) lines? A substantial industrial organization literature then developed on the premise that hierarchy personified efficiency since it eased the problems of information search, contract negotiation and specification, and monitoring and enforcement found in competitive markets. Kenneth Arrow (1969) attributed market failures to high transaction costs. Alchian and Demsetz (1972) developed the measurement and monitoring implications for hierarchy, concluding that "team" members will choose hierarchy up to the point where the costs of monitoring equal or exceed the efficiency gains accruing from hierarchy. In economics, the New Institutional Economics was the standard bearer for the transaction cost approach, especially contributions by Eggertsson (1990), Jensen and Meckling (1976), and Williamson (1975).

12. Hammond and Knott (1993) provide an exception to this rule. Using the principal–agent genre of theory, they formally model the multiinstitutional complexity of political–bureaucratic relationships. They find that "control" of the bureaucracy varies, with bureaucracies having considerable autonomy in certain cases and little or none in others. As well, when the bureaucracy lacks autonomy, control of the bureaucracy cannot be attributed to just one institution. Rather, it is generally the joint product of interactions among the president, house, and senate.

13. According to Miller and Moe (1986, 179), public administration is more realistically conceived as a "complex bargaining process among actors, each of whom has some degree of autonomous decision authority." The "command-based" dictatorship of the firm is dismissed as a "technical impossibility."

14. The concept of hierarchy used here is more than the traditional notion of hierarchy which focuses on the organizational structure within which industrial assets or public sector responsibilities are physically integrated (e.g., firm; government agency). It also includes transaction-based "integration" resulting from authority arrangements giving political principals de facto control over a particular sphere of the agent's domain or primary organizational activity. In this way, the traditional separation of public and private-sector organizations is conceptually unified into a single hierarchy, even if only one sphere of business activity (e.g., pollution control activities) is affected, and third-party interests such as issue advocacy groups are treated as constituent units of the transaction-based hierarchy.

15. See also Anthony Downs (1967). Incomplete contracting (for Downs, decision making) is the norm, given the costs of gathering information, bounded rationality, and the fact that uncertainty can never be completely eradicated.

16. Complex divisions of labor and specialization of tasks make "the authority of expertise a fact in today's organizations. . . . [and] further compound the problem [of hierarchical control] by building an additional pluralism of values within the organization and by reinforcing the decentralized decision rules that give subordinate units the ability to determine aspects of the organization's over-all behavior" (Miller and Moe 1986, 195).

17. Williamson (1985) makes a similar point in terms of industrial organizations. It is problematic to assume that *ownership* of property rights and/or assets in economic exchanges automatically confers complete control over outcomes (p. 29).

18. Thus, although Moe (1989) is correct when he argues that the formal property rights of political officials gives them certain advantages in initiating legislation and monitoring implementation, the perceptions and behavior of stakeholders with the power to impede or alter outcomes are too important to ignore.

19. Stakeholders are people with an interest in a policy outcome. Major stakeholders are those repeat players with the largest stakes in outcomes and thus most likely to use their resources to affect outcomes either positively or negatively (e.g., facilitating program implementation; protecting program integrity by filing *amicus curiae* briefs; or blocking, delaying, or trying to reconstruct contracts via litigation or lobbying).

20. See DiIulio, Garvey, and Kettl (1993, 24–27).

21. Contract specification and negotiation focuses on the costs of negotiating, writing, and concluding an agreement among interested parties. Uncertainties encountered here affect not only an organization's level of resource expenditures, but also the timeliness of the contracting process. In addition, written contracts are important because they establish the "rules of the regulatory game" by communicating to stakeholders how implementation is to be achieved, the basis upon which compliance will be determined, and ultimately whether an organization's interests are reflected in the final agreement.

22. Other manifestations of the same phenomena are maximum available control technology (MACT) and lowest achievable emissions rate (LAER).

23. Title IV of the 1990 Clean Air Act Amendments. In 1989, Resources for the Future reported that "a firm scientific consensus on acid rain has not emerged. It seems fairly clear that the acidity in rainfall and in deposited particles is much higher than it used to be, and that the main source of the acid compounds is coal combustion. But the extent and severity of ecosystem damage resulting from acidity are uncertain, especially in terrestrial ecosystems. Also uncertain is the extent to which emission reductions will help [solve the problems posed by acid deposition]" (Harrington 1989, 11). See also the National Acid Precipitation Assessment Program (1991).

24. The Inspection and Maintenance (I & M) program is part of Title II, the CAAA of 1990, and is designed to reduce tailpipe emissions. "Researchers for RAND, in a lengthy report on emissions tests prepared . . . for the California Senate Transportation Committee, admitted how 'surprised' they were 'by the extent to which computer-based mathematical models, often based on limited data and subject to little formal verification, govern the terms of the I/M [inspection and maintenance] debate.' Moreover, no one possesses 'the appropriate empirical data to assure that the models are sufficiently accurate and unbiased to define or perhaps even to guide policy'" (from Carroll 1995, A14).

25. Sally Baliunas, chair of the Harvard–Smithsonian Center for Astrophysics, finds that while there is ample evidence of "a buildup in greenhouse gases, particularly carbon dioxide, over the last 100 years. . . . 'No evidence can be found in the temperature measurements to support the theory of catastrophic global warming caused by human activities.' " Nor is there much scientific certainty associated with the rate of global warming or the effects of such a trend (i.e., the most widely reported effect is a substantial rise in ocean levels [by several feet] around the world). Baliunas likewise argues that " 'on two counts, the hysteria and costly regulations are entirely unfounded. . . . [First,] there is no observational evidence that man-made chemicals like CFCs are dangerously thinning the ozone layer over most of the world.' [Second,] the kind of ultraviolet rays that would be let through by a thinner ozone layer, UV-B, is not the UV that causes melanoma [i.e., skin cancer]" (as quoted in Melloan 1995, A19). See also Easterbrook (1995); USEPA (1988; 1989b); Schneider (1989); White (1990).

26. See the discussion on technology innovation on pp. 82–83 of this chapter.

27. Uniroyal eventually broke ranks and suggested a tire-grading system. The cooperation helped to bring the rulemaking to a conclusion.

28. For the record, the NHTSA tire standards rule took more than twelve years to implement (from 1967 to 1979) (see Breyer 1982, 97).

29. "The adversary process is likely to help develop information only if different segments of the industry are adversary, one to another, and if each can be relied upon to test the other's information" (Breyer 1982, 111).

30. Public sector enforcement costs also increase because "with command-and-control you end up granting waivers [on a case-by-case basis] when pollution sources don't meet their mandated goals" (Roger Kanerva, Illinois Environmental Protection Agency, Great Lakes Regional Emissions Trading Conference, hereinafter cited as Great Lakes RETC 1994).

31. Ackerman and Stewart (1985, 1363–64).

32. "What a permit writer has to do in order to come up with the terms and conditions of a [single] permit is incredibly technical, complicated, and can fill volumes. Literally, there are some permits that are forty volumes in all" (interviews with GAO 11/9/94; industry 12/1/94; state regulator 11/7/94).

33. The term "technology innovation for environmental purposes" includes all types of technology innovation that have a beneficial effect on the environment, i.e., pollution prevention (such as manufacturing process changes), pollution control and remediation, information systems, and management practices. Other similar phrases, such as "innovative environmental technology," are used interchangeably (see NACEPT 1991, 5, footnote 1).

34. See Breyer (1982, 115–16, 269–70); Kneese and Schultze (1976, 59–60); Porter (1993); Stewart (1981, 1259–60, 1279–1306).

35. The command-and-control system of regulation "discourage[s] all stakeholder groups from taking the risks necessary to develop innovative technologies—whether for pollution prevention or pollution control—and to bring them into routine use to solve environmental problems [primarily because it] . . . creates high-risk, low-reward market conditions" (NACEPT 1991, 7–8).

36. Interview with environmentalist (1/7/94). In a 1985 report, the Office of Management and Budget estimated that the private sector was spending over 5 billion hours each year just to meet government paperwork demands. The figure rose to 6.5 billion hours in 1991 (McIntosh and Weidenbaum 1995).

37. See Hammond and Miller (1985); Sen (1976).

38. See Alchian and Demsetz (1972); Miller and Moe (1986); Weingast and Marshall (1988); Williamson (1975, 1985).

39. Interviews with EPA (12/10/93; 1/11/94); see GAO (1979; 1990b). Regulators "feel they are doing well if they are able to visit a site once a year" (interview with GAO 11/9/94).

40. "Some facilities may be inspected more frequently if resources allow for it and indications of problems exist" (GAO 1990b, 19).

41. Interview with EPA (1/11/94); Dudek commentary, EDF, Great Lakes RETC (1994). At a minimum, we should see regulators and environmentalists pursuing this as one of their primary goals.

42. Jorgensen and Wilcoxen (1990) estimate that "the cost of emission controls is more than 10 percent of the total cost of government purchases of goods and services" (p. 314).

43. Amoco/USEPA Yorktown Pollution Prevention Project, Executive Summary (1992).

44. McIntosh and Weidenbaum (1995). In a 1985 report, the Office of Management and Budget estimated that the private sector was spending over 5 billion hours per year just to meet government paperwork demands.

45. The figures for paperwork hours and personnel cover industry activities in response to all government regulations concerned with health, safety, and the environment (i.e., EPA, OSHA, NHTSA, and other applicable regulations and regulatory agencies).

46. The most expensive control measure in the Los Angeles basin actually costs $62,000 per ton. See South Coast Air Quality Management District (1990, Sections 4–38 to 4–39). See also Weisskopf (1989b, A8); Weisskopf (1990a); Waxman, Wetstone, and Barnett (1991, 1951–53).

47. From its inception in 1980 to September 1994, cleanup work had been fully completed for only fifty-two of the total 1,320 Superfund sites (GAO 1994c, 2).

48. USEPA (1990e, 2). See also Douglas and Wildavsky (1983).

49. Lave and Omenn (1981, 13, 18); Vogel (1986, 162–63). Section 112 of the Clean Air Act was effectively replaced by Title III (air toxics) of the 1990 CAAA.

50. Other than a rarely used appeal mechanism which permits a team of federal government officials—known as the 'god squad' because of its power of life and death—to exempt specific projects (see Mann and Plummer 1994).

51. Interview with environmentalist (1/13/94).

52. As quoted in Wald (1991, A1). See also the extended discussion on "judicial activism" in Chapter 2.

53. As of October 1993 there were still ninety-three areas of the country classified as nonattainment by EPA (USEPA 1994b, 68).

54. A "severe" rating is the second worst category. Los Angeles is the only area in the nation that carries the worst rating of "extreme."

55. USEPA (1994b, 68). The data upon which the ground-level ozone classifications of the 1990 CAAA are based is from the 1980s, a time when poor economic conditions and job losses dominated much of the Great Lakes region. However, it is important to recognize that the Great Lakes region economy has been out of recession and manufacturing has been "booming" for the past several years.

56. A fragmented single-media approach is also noteworthy for the added paperwork burdens of multiple, often overlapping and conflicting regulatory requirements by various media-based offices (e.g., air pollution requirements may interfere with water pollution requirements and vice versa). Industry perceives that such regulations require them to spend considerable sums of money on compliance for limited environmental benefits, as well as preventing them from strategically targeting (prioritizing) their compliance resources where they will have the most effect (interviews with industry 11/7/94; 12/1/94; U.S. Congress. Senate. Taking Stock hearings, Thomas Jorling testimony 1993). The perception of inefficiency is not limited to the private sector. In a 1984 report, the National Academy of Public Administration remarked on the extent to which "EPA's budget and personnel procedures . . . mirror the disjointed legal structure of the agency. At a time when the general public understands that environmental problems comprise a seamless web, the Agency is left to administer statutes that do not reflect the interrelationships between land, air, and water. . . . EPA's statutory fragmentation leads to budgeting rigidities, impedes efficient administration and causes confusion. Statutory fragmentation, moreover, costs more money than would consistency" (p. 5).

57. USEPA (1987); Harter (1982); Krupp (1986); more generally, see Leonard, Davies, and Binder (eds.) (1977) and Gilbreath (ed.) (1984).

4

Pluralism by the Rules: The Transition to Collaborative Games

Graham Wilson (1982), Steven Kelman (1981), David Vogel (1986; 1989), Joseph Badaracco (1985), Barry Rabe (1988), and others point out that collaborative games are rather odd in American politics. There are any number of things which militate against them, chief among them an adversarial political culture, a fragmented interest group system in which competition between groups or members makes "reasonable" compromise difficult to achieve, and an open political system with multiple decision points that provides "losers" with plenty of opportunities to gain more favorable outcomes elsewhere. Nevertheless, cooperation is occurring, and it is occurring where we would least expect it—in the most combative of all regulatory arenas—pollution control politics. The question is why?

Explaining why pollution control stakeholders are on occasion choosing collaboration instead of conflict requires that we conceive of the "black box" between policy inputs and policy outputs as something more than an amorphous struggle between competing interests (Truman 1951), a process brokered only by elected officials (Dahl 1961), or a meaningless struggle, given the structural dominance of privileged interests (Edelman 1964; Lindblom 1977). A third element must be added to our explanatory framework of transaction costs and a changed institutional context: the idea of an assurance mechanism which is at the heart of pluralism "by the rules." For while the combination of transaction costs and a changed political and economic context is motivating participants to seek alternatives promising transaction cost savings, choosing collaboration in American politics *is* an uncertain gamble. The incentive of transaction cost benefits is not enough to overcome the collective action dilemma associated with collaborative games. Instead, players require assurance in the form of rules which structure how the game of pluralism will be played. The "rules" turn a bona fide gamble into more of a sure bet by structuring participant behavior, by giving each participant a meaningful stake in outcomes, and by judiciously advancing collaborative games only after certain circumstances have been met. In this way, pluralism by the rules fosters the trust necessary for initiating and moving the collaborative game forward—even in the volatile, combative arena of American pollution control politics.

Putting the Collaborative Game into Play

In Chapter 2 we saw how political and economic changes in the larger institutional context make participants in national pollution control politics more likely to recognize the high costs of doing business the traditional way and to seek alternative institutional arrangements. The logic of the changed context implies that we should have seen a massive rush toward collaborative alternatives, but we have not. Rather, there has been a limited, albeit growing, movement toward acceptance of collaborative games and their potential for innovative, positive sum regulatory outcomes.[1] Participants are cautiously testing the new game in a dynamic reminiscent of the early stages of an institution-building process (see McFarland 1993).

The reason is that collaborative games are risky. Moving forward in such a policy-making environment requires an element of trust among participants. Recent work in positive political economy by Gary Miller (1992) and David Kreps (1992) suggests a method for creating the trust necessary to overcome the collective action dilemma such that durable, effective institutional arrangements—those that successfully reduce transaction costs and help stakeholders to maximize organizational goals—can be established. According to Miller and Kreps, durable, effective arrangements are most likely to result from collaborative hierarchies. Both scholars find that the efficiency and competitiveness of industrial organizations are enhanced to the extent that *ex ante* cooperation is induced *inside* hierarchies or among trading partners. Yet the problems of information asymmetries, *ex post* opportunism, and settlement of unforeseen future contingencies introduce substantial uncertainty into collaborative efforts and often prevent the level of cooperation needed to resolve the collective action problem. Without some assurance that agreements will be binding, and that their stake in decision outcomes will be protected, subordinates and trading partners alike have an incentive to act unilaterally to guard their stakes, whether through exercising control over information asymmetries in their favor, shirking after the fact, settling unforeseen contingencies to their advantage (and to the other's disadvantage), or simply refusing to engage in trades from which both sides could reap significant benefits. Potential trading partners, as well as leaders and agents inside organizations, are thus motivated to avoid the unknowns associated with collaborative hierarchies and stick with the known costs of hierarchy—and a concomitant drag on the firm's efficiency and competitiveness. Therefore, overcoming the collective action problem and establishing low-transaction-cost institutional arrangements requires the introduction of greater certainty into the collaborative effort, specifically an assurance mechanism or set of rules governing the transaction, premised on credible commitment to the collaborative game by both principals (leaders) and agents (subordinates) (Kreps 1992; Miller 1992; Weingast and Marshall 1988).

The Kreps–Miller logic of collaborative hierarchies is transferable to the regulatory arena. In the uncertain, high-transaction-cost decision-making environment of pollution control policy making, participants have ample incentive to pursue collaborative arrangements. They know full well that collaboration can produce transaction cost savings which redound to the benefit of their organizational bottom lines, whether it be faster or bigger pollution reductions, cheaper compliance, or smarter, hence more implementable and enforceable, programs. But participants also recognize the realities of collaborating in an arena best known for its bitter adversarialism among stakeholders in congress, federal and state regulatory agencies, environmental advocacy groups, and industry. Assuring the performance of others such that transaction cost savings can be realized is a highly uncertain endeavor. Will others bargain in good faith? Will adversaries defect? Will they take advantage of the American political system's openness and seek a more favorable outcome in another venue?

In light of these possibilities, and prior to engaging the collaborative game format, participants in national pollution control politics are insisting that pluralism be played by the rules. The "rules" foster the credible commitment needed to move the collaborative game forward. They reduce the uncertainty and risks associated with the collaborative game by selectively promoting collaboration and by structuring participant behavior to minimize the likelihood of *ex post* opportunism. They also spread power among the major stakeholders of the policy network by recognizing the implicit property rights (power) that information asymmetries and complex interdependence confer on each, creating credible stakes in decision-making processes and regulatory outcomes for all. In other words, the "rules" are the catalytic component which move the collaborative game from the point of active consideration (where participants perceive the benefits of collaboration) to the point where collaboration is actively engaged and sustained to a consensus agreement and beyond. Specifically, playing pluralism "by the rules" requires an assurance mechanism premised on:

- certain transaction-specific conditions,
- a credible commitment to collaboration by entrepreneurial political leaders,
- a reputation for commitment to collaborative processes by the agency in charge of the rule,
- formal binding agreements to govern negotiations and their aftermath,
- the inclusion of all stakeholders in a position to block or effectively undermine outcomes, and
- participants with long-term interests in pollution control policy (see Table 4.1).

TRANSACTION-SPECIFIC CONDITIONS

Stakeholders in national pollution control politics know that all regulatory transactions are not created equal; some transactions are necessarily more attractive than others as candidates for the collaborative game. The transaction-specific conditions listed in Table 4.1 (Column 3) help participants to determine the attractiveness of a particular transaction by highlighting key parameters of the bargaining arena in terms of issues, players, available data, deadlines, and policy implications. The conditions offer information on the manageability of the game as well as whether the game is possible (opportunity). The more conditions met, the lower the degree of objective difficulty likely to be encountered during negotiations.[2] They also spell out the kinds of transactions where rational yet resource-limited and boundedly rational stakeholders seeking transaction cost benefits are most likely to target their efforts.

The opportunity exists to develop creative compromises There should be more than one way to resolve pertinent regulatory issues. Clear, rather than ambiguous, law and detailed legislation placing severe restrictions on bureaucratic discretion leave limited (and, on occasion, no) opportunities for the creative compromises critical to bargaining success. "Opportunity" should also be assured in another way—through the blessing of political principals in congress and the executive branch. The macropolitical level needs either to be an active participant in the game, satisfied that constituent groups important to them are amply represented at the bargaining table, or to accept the operating rules[3]—pluralism by the rules—used to guide the collaborative decision-making process because they believe them able to provide sufficient protection for their primary policy concerns. Opportunity in the latter sense is the product of either direct endorsement of the game by political principals (when they play themselves) or tacit endorsement through nonintervention. One way to create opportunity is to limit games in which political principals are not directly involved to questions of "how" (implementation), rather than "what" (substance; e.g., standard setting).

There are a limited number of interdependent or related issues Limiting the scope of the problem under consideration makes the game easier to manage, not least because it serves to limit the potential pool of stakeholders.

The policy implications of the issues to be resolved are more or less limited either programmatically, geographically, or to common practices and rules affecting a specific industrial sector The problem-solving exercise will not set binding precedents beyond the scope of the pollution control program, region of the country, industrial site, or industrial sector encompassed by the negotiations. Because they violate this condition, multimedia pollution problems are likely to be extremely difficult to resolve without the prior reorganization of EPA and rationalization of the myriad federal environmental protection statutes (see Davies 1990; NAPA 1995). Ameliorating this problem somewhat are multimedia-based transactions confined to a single industrial complex or site.

Affected interests are identifiable, relatively few in number, and cohesive Interests are defined as "a grouping of parties who are likely to be affected similarly by the regulation or who appear to have similar perspectives on the subject matter of the contemplated rule" (Pritzker and Dalton 1990, 97). Past experiences with negotiated rulemaking, for example, suggest that the maximum number of parties for which a collaborative game can be kept manageable is approximately twenty-five. Once the universe of stakeholding groups has been identified, it can then be aggregated into "interests," with a single lead representative to conduct negotiations. All others within a specific interest category attend proceedings and participate, but on a more indirect basis akin to "backbenchers" in the British Parliament. Thus, "the number of negotiators actually sitting at the table is not unwieldy but all affected interests are adequately represented" (Pritzker and Dalton 1990, 100–01). The interests playing the collaborative game should also be cohesive enough and designated representatives for each interest possessive of sufficient authority so that they can be reasonably expected to deliver

TABLE 4.1   Emerging Collaborative Games: The Explanatory Model

		Pluralism by the Rules	
Why Collaboration?	*Why Now?*	*Which Transactions?*	*Catalyzing and Sustaining the Collaborative Game*
Stakeholders anticipate transaction cost savings vis-à-vis the traditional conflict-game.	Changing institutional context increases uncertainty and the importance of transaction costs as a decision variable.	Transaction-specific conditions help explain particular choices.	Reducing the uncertainty of collaborative processes.
Examples of expected transaction cost reductions:	*Key Contextual Elements:*	*Transaction Conditions:*[1]	*Key Components:*
—reduced scope and incidence of litigation —faster environmental progress through reduced legislative gridlock and implementation delays —minimization of information asymmetries favoring industry and states —greater cost effectiveness of regulatory instruments; compliance cost savings for industry	—holding the bureaucracy accountable, or EPA as an agency under siege —the postreform Congress and legislative gridlock —the openness of administrative decision making and an activist judiciary —the environmentalist-industry power equilibrium —increasing importance of international competition and deregulation	—The opportunity exists to develop creative compromises —There are a limited number of related issues —Policy implications of issues to be resolved are more or less limited either programmatically, geographically, or to common practices/rules in a specific industrial sector —Affected interests are identifiable, relatively few in number, and "cohesive"	—Entrepreneurial political leadership —Public sector organization's reputation of commitment to collaboration and fairness —Formal binding rules to govern the negotiation process and its aftermath

continued

their organizations or constituencies in support of any final consensus agreement.

Does not involve issues of fundamental values that cannot be compromised   If fundamental values are at stake, any common ground manufactured through a consensus-building process is likely to envelop the marginal components of the problem under consideration. Central issues, upon which long-term collaborative success rises and falls, re-

TABLE 4.1 *continued*

| | | *Pluralism by the Rules* | |
Why Collaboration?	*Why Now?*	*Which Transactions?*	*Catalyzing and Sustaining the Collaborative Game*
Stakeholders anticipate transaction cost savings vis-à-vis the traditional conflict-game.	Changing institutional context increases uncertainty and the importance of transaction costs as a decision variable.	Transaction-specific conditions help explain particular choices.	Reducing the uncertainty of collaborative processes.
Examples of expected transaction cost reductions:	*Key Contextual Elements:*	*Transaction Conditions:*[1]	*Key Components:*
—greater planning and investment certainty for industry and states —accelerated rates of technological innovation (more options in battle against pollution) —increased certainty of environmental results (more rigorous monitoring, game focus on "real environmental results," not rule-based proxies)	—increasing pressures for improved state-level policy performance and a rebalancing of state-federal relationship	—Does not involve issues of fundamental values that cannot be compromised —There is a well-developed factual database to frame the discussion and resolution of pertinent issues —Firm deadlines, either statutory, judicial, or programmatic	—Degree of inclusiveness —Participants' involvement in pollution control issues are long-term, iterative

[1]See "EPA Regulatory Negotiation Candidate Selection Criteria" in Pritzker and Dalton (1990, 42); USEPA (1994a) on EPA's sector-specific Common Sense Initiative launched in 1994; Amy (1987; 1990); Bacow and Wheeler (1984, 24–26); Bingham (1986); Fiorino (1988); McFarland (1993); Susskind and Cruickshank (1987).

main unresolved for the simple reason that no common ground is possible. A good example of a policy issue that fails this test is the northern spotted owl controversy in the Northwest United States. There is a considerable contingent within the environmental community which believes that all animal life is sacred and worthy of preservation through habitat protection, especially an indicator or "bellwether" species for ecosystem health such as the northern spotted owl. Saving a considerable number of owls through compromise that preserves some but not all owl habitat is unthinkable, since it risks species extinction and broad-based ecosystem decline. On the other side are loggers and community interests who have livelihoods and a generations-old culture at stake. They are not interested in just any job to make ends meet; rather, they wish to preserve the logging jobs that have been handed down from generation to generation and are an integral part of the economic as well as social fabric of the rural Northwest.

There is a well-developed factual database to frame the discussion and resolution of pertinent issues The database can exist prior to the start of the collaborative game or the gathering of such data can be a fundamental precondition for initiating the game. Examples of data instrumental to regulatory problem solving in the pollution control arena are data regarding the technological performance capabilities, cost impact, or technical feasibility of a preferred solution, the relevant bureaucracy's capacity for implementation, and the distribution of compliance costs among the parties. Other examples include information regarding alternative methods of measuring policy outcomes and/or pollution emissions and a basic understanding of cause and effect between industrial processes and levels of pollution.

Firm deadlines exist, either statutory, judicial, or programmatic
Deadlines force participants to think comparatively during negotiations by bringing the transaction costs associated with alternative outcomes into sharp relief. As such, they motivate participants by reminding them that failure of the collaborative game has a clear consequence—higher costs and a greater likelihood that organizational goals will not be maximized.

Clearly, only a small percentage of all possible regulatory transactions, perhaps 10 to 20 percent, will qualify as candidates. Yet identifying a smaller subset of transactions conducive to the collaborative game is only the first step. While it helps to clarify institutional choices for affected stakeholders and, by doing so, stacks the deck in favor of successful collaborative outcomes, it does not put the game into play. Nor does it successfully carry the game forward such that transaction cost savings are realized.

ENTREPRENEURIAL POLITICAL LEADERSHIP

In *Managerial Dilemmas*, Gary Miller addresses the leadership dilemma of bringing the efforts of self-interested individuals in line with the needs and interests of an organization. He argues that "a hierarchy that can induce the right kind of cooperation—defined as voluntary deviations from self-interested behavior—will have an important competitive edge over other firms" (pp. *xi*, 13). Through game theoretic applications, Miller demonstrates the role of an organizational leader in building a cooperative organizational culture by establishing "mutually reinforcing expectations" among members of an organizational hierarchy (pp. 217, 220–25; see also North and Weingast 1989, 1). Implementing a cooperative hierarchical culture is difficult, however, given the presence of incomplete contracts, information asymmetries, and the now-familiar problem of *ex post* opportunism. A cooperative culture "is a form of contract that provides strong *ex post* incentives for reneging by hierarchical superiors. If subordinates anticipate self-interested reneging by superiors, they have every incentive to engage in actions that will ruin the effectiveness of the managerial strategy. . . . [I]t is therefore essential that hierarchical superiors find ways to commit themselves credibly to a cooperative culture" (pp. 217–18). The challenge of establishing a credible commitment to collaborative strategies takes the entrepreneurial leader beyond mechanical, incentive-based solutions into the "realm of the 'organic'," where he or she must build trust, reduce information asymmetries by forging lines of communication, and share the organizational success in a meaningful way with employees (pp. 217–23). Firm evidence of leadership's own credible commitment to the collaborative game, a function of past performance (reputation) and their willingness to use authority to promote, protect, and enforce consensus deals, is needed as well.

Miller notes that much of the literature in organizational economics proceeds on the premise that hierarchical organizations, like markets, move toward more efficient forms through competition.[4] If this were the case, the role of an organizational leader would be minimal; a natural progression toward efficiency requires some mechanical guidance, but not leadership. But the *political* dynamics of a hierarchy, Miller argues, differ from the dynamics of a market, and the progression toward organizational cooperation requires strong leadership to overcome (or at least alternatively direct) precisely the self-interested motivations that drive a market toward efficiency.

In the regulatory arena, political and bureaucratic leaders have primary responsibility for convincing the full range of affected interests to credibly commit to collaborative arrangements. For example, in cases where stakeholding interests (offices) *inside a government agency* are forced to play the collaborative game and where they have an uncertain stake (e.g., initially undefined), or a relatively small scale of expected return, or both, leaders must be skillful enough to inspire network members to transcend the sort of self-interested behavior that can result in shirking—and the unraveling of the deal. With respect to the

Environmental Protection Agency, many of the new collaborative efforts are intent on changing the rules of the overarching regulatory game. Relevant examples include the adoption of innovative regulatory mechanisms such as integrated pollution control or market-based incentives, or the wholesale rationalization of the existing regulatory structure for specific industrial sites. Each poses a radical challenge to the dominant single-media, command-and-control worldview, as well as existing organizational arrangements at EPA. Subordinates within EPA who participate in such collaborative undertakings can encounter considerable risks to their careers, may be unconvinced that their expertise will be used in an appropriate manner (and hence be less than cooperative participants), or face the prospect of outcomes damaging to their organizational subunit. On this last count, for example, the rationalization of existing rules might conclude that a particular office's pollution control rules, in place for decades, are unduly expensive as opposed to possible alternatives, or ineffective at reducing pollution, or both. In every case, political leadership is a crucial component. Agency leaders must continually champion the benefits of collaboration to game participants, while simultaneously providing them with assurance that their interests will be protected during program negotiation, specification, and implementation.

ORGANIZATIONAL REPUTATION

Like Miller, David Kreps (1992) examines organizational "culture" as a means to enhance the efficient operation of an organization under conditions of uncertainty. For Kreps, culture is a means to reduce the transaction costs of doing business between organizations, and of integrating work within an organization. The central dilemma for Kreps concerns the consequences of incomplete contracting: because unforeseen contingencies are inevitable, "explicit and complete contracting [is] impossible" (p. 118). If potential participants are unable to point with confidence to a range of expected behaviors regarding how contingencies will be handled, the risk of default will be higher, many transactions potentially too costly, and a lower incidence of exchange the result (p. 92).[5] Therefore, organizations must identify "focal points", or contingency settlement principles that "individuals [in an organization will] use naturally to select a mode of behavior in a situation with many possible equilibrium behaviors" (p. 121). If these principles are shared throughout the organization, they provide an organization with an "identity" that communicates a reputation to its trading partners and provides "hierarchical inferiors an idea *ex ante* how the organization will react to circumstances as they arise."[6]

To the extent that a focal principle is clear and observable by affected parties, it becomes a mechanism by which others can evaluate the propensity of an organization to shirk or to otherwise engage in moral hazard-type behavior (i.e., defect from the deal or only solve unforeseen contingencies to your own advantage). In this sense, organizational "culture" not only guides the behavior of firm subordinates and leaders, but also signals an organization's trustworthiness (reputation) to others outside the firm (pp. 93–94). The reduction of transaction costs is directly related to the development of a trustworthy reputation. Organizations that are trustworthy apply their chosen principle in a consistent fashion, even to situations where "its application might not be optimal in the short run" (pp. 93, 116; see Schelling 1960).

For Miller, organizational culture is a solution to a specific leadership dilemma—getting individuals to behave in the interest of the organization. With respect to the regulatory arena, the leadership dilemma is inducing compliance with policy goals by all stakeholders, including the bureaucracy; third-party interests like environmental advocates; and the regulated community.[7] For Kreps, culture is the solution for two related, but different, types of leadership dilemmas: communicating a reputation to other organizations and coordinating communication within an organization by defining the way things are done to hierarchical subordinates. In regulatory politics, the public agency playing the game must develop a reputation for credible commitment to collaborative processes and their subsequent outcomes, as well as a reputation for fairness when disposing of unforeseen contingencies as they arise (Kreps 1992). Otherwise, affected private-sector entities, public interest groups, and state-level interests will be more likely to discount the possible gains from collaboration, hence less likely to join in, much less promote a collaborative effort, even when the expected gains are substantial. Thus the leadership's task of persuading other major stakeholding organizations to work together in good faith is eased to the extent that an organization has established such a trustworthy reputation of commitment to collaboration.[8]

FORMAL CONSTITUTIONAL RULES

Both Kreps and Miller agree that collaborative strategies based on reputation and leadership are likely to be limited to smaller organizations.[9] Leadership based on the informal institution of reputation is necessary but not sufficient in large, complex organizations (or institutional orderings) to induce subordinates to trust employers (principals) with the information that makes it possible for principals to make efficient decisions (Miller, 235). Overcoming the prisoner's dilemma and improving the likelihood that participants' good-faith bargaining efforts will not be wasted requires a set of "constitutional" rules placing

> permanent restrictions on the ability of [principals] to pursue self-interested behavior at the expense of long-term cooperation. The most effective way to build a credible commitment to cooperation in organizations is by making a permanent change in the system of property rights, a change that gives employees the confidence to invest in the economic development of the firm.[10]

Examples of permanent changes in hierarchical property rights include sharing centralized decision-making power with employee representatives (must be more than "advisory" committees) and reallocating property rights to employees through either "ownership" or autonomy of control over those aspects of the workplace deemed most important by employees (e.g., profit sharing, removal of time clocks, training programs) (p. 226).

Within the regulatory arena, the credible restraint of hierarchy (leadership) is reinforced through formal binding rules governing the negotiation process and its aftermath. Examples include:

- bargaining arrangements granting stakeholders a direct role in writing and crafting regulatory programs,
- agreements not to litigate or otherwise intervene once regulations have been finalized,
- explicit consideration of a stakeholder's interests in legislative language (e.g., rigorous monitoring and data-reporting requirements, automatic compliance penalties, the creation of a pollution property rights regime), and
- agreements establishing the right of affected interests to choose an alternative compliance pathway upon conclusion of the collaborative effort.

INCLUSIVENESS

Inclusivity is the fifth element of the assurance mechanism, for reasons of democratic legitimacy and practical considerations related to policy implementation. Miller's (1992) theory of collaborative hierarchies suggests that all stakeholders within the relevant hierarchy in a position to block or effectively undermine outcomes must be included and given a credible stake in the collaborative game (see also Fiorino and Kirtz 1985, 40). Otherwise, the coalition of participants seeking more efficient outcomes encounter added uncertainty and face a greater likelihood of failure, as those left out in the cold mobilize resources or withhold critical information in defense of their stakes.[11] Failure to practice inclusion thus lessens the probability that implementation and the establishment of the kinds of durable, effective regulatory programs able to deliver promised transaction cost benefits (successful collaboration) will occur. As noted in the previous chapter, the de facto power equilibrium between environmental advocacy groups and the business community—each has substantial resources useful for either vetoing or severely impeding positive efforts undertaken by the other—and the resurgent importance of state-level actors in federal pollution control politics signals that collaborative games excluding direct participation by any of these three actors are played at their own peril. Furthermore, the relatively recent explosion of grassroots environmental activism, particularly the largely urban-based environmental justice movement, may add yet another indispensable player to the collaborative mix.[12]

REPEAT GAMES

A final measure of credible commitment helping to reduce regulatory uncertainty is whether participants' involvement in the pollution control policy arena is of a long-term, iterative nature. From this perspective, it matters whether potential participants are ongoing entities and whether they are embedded in the relevant policy network to the extent that they interact regularly on a number of issues and have an ongoing relationship with the regulatory agency in charge of the game. As such, viable, embedded organizations are more likely to perceive the game as an iterative one rather than as a one-time opportunity to advance their self-interest.

CONCLUSION

The ultimate lesson of Kreps (1992) and Miller (1992) is that effective, durable contracting in the context of repeated games is based on shared power rather than a strict top-down system of command. From this perspective, effectiveness requires policy makers to recognize the implicit property rights that information asymmetries and complex interdependence confer on stakeholders, and to design the rules of the game accordingly. Convincing members of the policy hierarchy—from elected officials to regulators to interest groups—to collaborate in pursuit of collective goals demands that they have a credible stake in designing and maintaining the chosen collaborative strategy. Yet while Kreps and Miller agree that creating credible stakes and enforcing agreements within a collaborative hierarchy require leadership, reputation, and an iterative game dynamic, Miller takes the framework further. Not only should collaborative games practice inclusivity as a rule; enduring cooperation among stakeholders with conflicting interests is best assured by a formal rule-bound framework that leads to permanent changes in the hierarchical ordering of property rights.

The next three chapters develop empirical examples of the collaborative choices that participants in pollution control politics perceive will reduce the costs of doing business in the regulatory arena. Chapter 5 examines the negotiated rulemaking for reformulated gasoline that was part of the 1990 Clean Air Act Amendments, while Chapter 6 details the passage of the 1990 acid rain emissions trading program, and Chapter 7 tells the story of the Yorktown Pollution Prevention Project involving Amoco Oil, EPA, and the state of Virginia that took place between 1989 and 1992.

CHAPTER NOTES

1. During the 1980s "the movement promoting cooperative techniques such as environmental mediation was growing quietly but steadily" (Amy 1990, 211). See also John (1994); National Academy of Public Administration (1995); Rabe (1994).

2. The EPA Regulatory Negotiation Candidate Selection Criteria states: "An item need not meet all of these criteria to be qualified as a candidate" (Pritzker and Dalton 1990, 42). For example, Gail Bingham's (1986) landmark study covering ten years of consensus-based environmental dispute resolution (EDR) examines 161 cases. She found that successful EDR efforts were not dependent on the presence of a deadline (pp. *xxiii–xxiv*).

3. See Redford (1969, 105).

4. See, for example, Oliver Williamson and William Ouchi, "The Markets and Hierarchies Perspective: Origins, Implications, Prospects," in Vade Ven and Joyce (eds.), *Assessing Organization Design and Performance* (New York: Wiley, 1981).

5. "Note that such contingency will necessarily involve blind faith; if we cannot foresee a contingency, we cannot know in advance that we can efficiently and equitably meet it" (Kreps 1992, 92). However, past experiences help in the construction of what a rough approximation of possible unforeseen contingencies might look like. In other words, participants are not completely blind (p. 117).

6. Ibid., p. 126. Failure in the area of communication translates into a variety of competing focal principles, making it virtually impossible to establish the coherent reputation needed for efficient transactions.

7. O'Toole (1994) builds from Miller's (1992) framework as well. He argues that "network managers" are critical to the development of cooperation within public policy networks. "Network manager" is synonymous with "entrepreneurial leader" as used here.

8. Clearly, reputation is enhanced to the extent that a succession of bureaucratic leaders pay homage to the same values. The idea of a trustworthy reputation of commitment to a particular "value" such as collaboration, with its expected benefits of durable regulatory arrangements and transaction cost savings, is similar to Philip Selznick's (1957) discussion of agencies "infused with value."

9. See Miller (1992, 225). Kreps argues that "insofar as an implicit contract [derived from organizational culture] permits greater transactional efficiency, an expansion in the span of the contract will be beneficial. But weighed against this is the problem that as the span of the contract is increased, the range of contingencies that the contract must cover also must increase. Either it will then be harder for participants to determine *ex post* whether the contract was applied faithfully or the contract will be applied to contingencies for which it is not suited. . . . From this perspective the focus strategy becomes a strategy of reducing the range of contingencies with which the implicit contract must deal, in order to deal better—less ambiguously—with those that are met" (pp. 129–30).

10. Miller (1992, 225); see also North and Weingast (1989, p. 1); Milgrom and Roberts (1992) make a similar argument. As long as central decision makers reserve for themselves the right to make selective interventions, credible commitments to a collaborative game inside hierarchies are impossible (p. 81).

11. This is much like Andrew McFarland's (1993) conclusion regarding the National Coal Policy project, although the excluded stakeholder in his case was government (elected officials). The theory of collaborative hierarchies advanced here extends McFarland's argument into a more general statement concerning all major stakeholders.

12. The permanency of the environmental justice movement and whether its influence will be wielded as part of the broader environmental movement controlled by national environmental organizations or as a separate constituency is an open question at this time. Within the confines of the Common Sense Initiative—a sector-based collaborative game initiated by the EPA under Carol Browner—the environmental justice movement did not want to be subsumed under the umbrella of the environmental community. Instead, it requested and was granted official designation as a bargaining entity separate from environmentalists.

5

Urban Smog and Dirty Gasoline: Clearing the Air through Negotiation

Upon passage of the 1970 Clean Air Act (CAA), Senator Edmund Muskie (D-MN) proclaimed the arrival of a new era in pollution control. The 1970 Act, he argued, guaranteed "that all Americans in all parts of the country shall have clean air to breathe within the 1970s."[1] Fast forward to the 1980s, and there are signs of success.[2] Yet in area after area, the larger story is one of failure to clean the air as promised. By the late 1980s the "[n]on-attainment of health-based national ambient air quality standards [NAAQS] for ozone, carbon monoxide, and PM-10 [i.e., small particulate matter] represent[ed] a pervasive and intractable problem in this country."[3] "Some 150 million Americans . . . lived in cities with pollution levels that EPA and other experts considered unsafe."[4] The failure to deliver clean air to metropolitan areas increased the pressure for congressional action both from urban constituents and from state and local officials who faced stiff federal sanctions for their lack of compliance. Adding to the momentum was the confluence of the long, hot summer of 1988—the worst in a decade for urban smog—with the upcoming presidential election. Advisors for President Bush sensed that a promise of action on clean air was a certain vote-getter, especially if the proposal made urban smog a primary concern.

The single most important cause of urban smog (ground-level ozone) is mobile sources, particularly automobiles.[5] Prior Clean Air Act initiatives concentrated on controlling mobile source pollution through automobile tailpipe standards. But with regulations requiring 90 percent reductions in tailpipe pollution already in place via technologies like the catalytic converter, and given considerable evidence that oil companies compensated for the lead phase-down in gasoline during the late 1970s and early 1980s by producing "dirtier" conventional gasoline,[6] the policy debate moved quickly to enlist alternative "clean" fuels in the fight against urban smog. Bush advisors, in particular C. Boyden Gray and Bill Rosenberg, convinced Bush that requiring

120

cars in the most polluted cities to switch from conventional gasoline to alternative fuels would significantly reduce urban smog in a cost-effective manner.[7]

BATTLING OVER REFORMULATED GASOLINE

The high-stakes nature of President Bush's clean fuels initiative, involving as it did the level of environmental protection, the distribution of billions in regulatory compliance and retooling costs, and market share in the new multibillion-dollar clean fuels market, affected a wide range of interests and prompted a contentious legislative debate. The initial battle was over whether the cleaner fuel would adhere to the Bush Administration's proposed "M–100" pure methanol standard, or whether the definition of a clean fuel would include reformulated gasoline.[8] Reformulated gasoline, which is conventional gasoline treated with oxygenate additives derived from ethanol and methanol, would give oil companies as well as ethanol and methanol interests a chance to provide cleaner burning fuel. The EPA, the national environmental community, and key members of congress with jurisdiction over clean air issues embraced the M–100 standard as one of the strongest parts of the overall clean air package. Yet oil industry lobbyists and supporters of other alternative fuels complained that the standard prevented them from establishing viable market shares (Hager 1989c, 2701). The auto industry strenuously objected as well, since they would have been saddled with the responsibility and costs of building new unconventional vehicles to accommodate pure methanol.

Opponents of the M–100 standard successfully expanded the definition of a clean fuel to include ethanol, natural gas, and reformulated gasoline. The move away from M–100, codified in a legislative amendment named for its sponsors, Hall–Fields,[9] dismayed environmentalists and their congressional supporters despite claims that the Hall–Fields M–85 standard (85 percent methanol and 15 percent conventional gasoline) would preserve virtually all of the M–100 standard's environmental benefits, impose significantly lower industry retooling costs, and protect the public from safety hazards associated with the use of a pure methanol product (Hager 1989c, 2700–01). Environmentalists labeled the compromise "unacceptably weak," while others saw it as a move designed to "help the [oil industry] block nonoil alternatives," and therefore maintain control of the national fuels market.[10]

A final compromise was reached only after several assaults by environmentalists on the Hall–Fields status quo succeeded in establishing a reformulated gasoline (RFG) program with more stringent pollution control standards. The legislation promised to reduce ground-level ozone in the nation's nine smoggiest metropolitan areas, including Milwaukee, Chicago, Houston, Los Angeles, and New York City, by requiring the use of cleaner burning reformulated gasolines. RFG was to be the only gasoline sold in these cities during the summer ozone season, or any area of the country which in the future qualified for the extreme or severe ozone nonattainment rating. In addition, the RFG program had to meet general pollution reduction standards: no net increase in nitrogen oxide (NO_x) pollution and a 15 percent reduction in volatile organic compounds (VOCs) and toxic aromatic compounds by 1995 (increasing to a total of 25 percent by the year 2000) (Sec. 211(k) 3).[11] Opportunities were also provided for states and localities not subject to the program's mandates to "opt in" to the program in the future. Finally, it was up to the EPA to develop the fuel parameters, or "model" of RFG,[12] that would achieve the required pollution control goals, to determine the way in which the program would be monitored, and to develop plans for implementation. If implemented to the letter of the law, RFG pollution controls promised a significantly cleaner environment: every year 95 million pounds of volatile organic compounds (VOCs) and millions of pounds of air toxics would vanish from the atmosphere (U.S. Congress. House. CAA Implementation Hearings, Part I 1991, EPA, Reilly testimony, 14–15).

The EPA's ambitious regulatory effort brought together a number of players from the private and public sectors, each with a stake in the RFG program. The auto industry was concerned about the impact of reformulated gasoline on engine performance, and hence on the fuel economy standards (CAFE) mandated by the EPA. If car fleets could not meet the CAFE standards with reformulated gasolines, changes would have to be made in the design of car engines—an extremely costly proposition. The industry's concern about the consequences of reformulated gasoline prompted a partnership with another player in the regulatory process, the oil industry, to study different combinations of reformulated gasolines and the implications for engine performance. The Auto–Oil Study, initiated in 1989, provided a primary source of information used to eventually develop the RFG rule.

Key to the final congressional compromise on RFG was the willingness of the oil industry to accept a small loss in market share in order "to avert drastic moves towards a national conversion to alternative fuels" (Adler 1992, 120). Yet they still faced significant compliance, conversion, and distribution costs as well as the "numbing uncertainty" introduced into their planning and investment decisions by the RFG rulemaking process. Mixing and distributing reformulated gasoline would mean an estimated $3 to $5 billion one-time retooling cost on existing refineries; an estimated three to four years of planning, permitting, design, and installation for new refinery units after the regulation was promulgated; and a compliance deadline of January 1, 1995 (set in the CAAAs).[13] The oil industry thus had a clear interest in knowing the ultimate requirements of the RFG program as soon as possible. Similar concerns confronted producers of the fuel additives, such as methanol and ethanol, and in fact their stakes were arguably higher. The definition of reformulated gasoline would determine which additive would have a higher market share. In addition, the new facilities for producing the additives were estimated at $25 billion (*New York Times* 1991a; industry official interview 3/23/94; environmentalist interview 3/30/94).

Environmental advocates, on the other hand, simply wanted to get the cleanup of urban smog started as quickly as possible. Legislative promulgation of RFG provisions was a start. Because RFG could be used in existing conventional automobiles, the pace of environmental cleanup could be accelerated and the level of emissions reductions increased. But strident public criticism of the RFG program by a leading member of the oil industry, only days after the CAAA was signed, placed the promised environmental benefits in jeopardy.[14] The recalcitrant attitude by such a major player threatened delay and made it all the more important that any regulation be enforceable. A tough, enforceable regulation not only would lock in legislative gains, but would demonstrate effectiveness to their constituencies.

Three sets of government regulators rounded out the players in the process: state regulators, the Department of Energy, and the EPA. State regulators would be responsible for incorporating the RFG program into their state implementation plans (SIPs)—federally mandated blueprints for pollution reduction. On the one hand, the RFG program provided a low-cost means for the targeted states to reduce urban smog (vis-à-vis other alternatives). On the other hand, if the regulatory process was "paralyzed" by conflict and litigation, these same state regulators would have to take the politically difficult and costly step of targeting stationary sources of NO_x and VOCs (such as the smokestack industries, many of which were already heavily regulated) in order to meet CAA compliance deadlines. Failure to comply, in turn, would trigger stiff monetary penalties and the wrath of congress. Without a timely rulemaking process, it was state regulators who would bear the brunt of the "domino effect." In the words of one state regulator:

> When EPA doesn't develop their rules in time, state legislatures are loath to adopt legal authority for something that is in draft form. Air pollution officials can't adopt a regulation . . . without the legal authority. The industry can't carry out this program since the rules aren't in place. Then the

[compliance] deadline passes and congress says, "Gee, you state and local agencies are being recalcitrant," or "Industry, you're not doing your job, because the monitors are still measuring exceedances of the standards." It's not as simple as that, but it's a clear domino effect; if it's not done right from the get-go, then we all suffer (interview 1/12/94).

While the Department of Energy (DOE) did not have a mandated role to play in the RFG program, it had access to technical and industry-related data important to the RFG program and its primary constituencies would be affected by the regulatory outcome. Concerned with the cost of gasoline for the consumer and the major oil companies, DOE wanted a regulation that was both technically feasible and able to fit with minimal disruption into the existing national gasoline distribution system. A poorly crafted regulation posed the threat of higher gasoline production costs and ultimately higher costs at the pump for gasoline consumers.

Finally, the EPA was charged with developing an enforceable, effective RFG regulation in a relatively brief amount of time. Failure to do so would bring criticism to the agency by congress and diminish the agency's reputation as a regulator. Yet the 1990 CAAA imposed a crush of fifty-five major rulemakings and thirty other guidances and actions to be completed within the first two years after passage. According to then-EPA administrator William Reilly, the workload "represented about a five-fold increase over our air program regulatory activity of the past several years."[15] The combination of workload, a nominal funding increase for EPA's Office of Air and Radiation, and the fact that major EPA rules commonly take anywhere from two to four years to complete[16] created considerable doubt that the RFG rulemaking would be concluded by the congressionally mandated deadline.

CONSTRAINTS FOR THE REFORMULATED GASOLINE (RFG) RULEMAKING

Given the technical sophistication of the EPA's task, the time and resource constraints, and the number of players with high stakes on the table, conflict and delay seemed inevitable. The key problem was a lack of technical information considered reliable by all the players. EPA's experience and expertise in reformulated gasoline was limited, the science of RFG was uncertain, and large-scale research efforts designed to clarify some of these uncertainties had not even been initiated until the summer of 1989 when the automobile and oil industries launched their multiyear Auto–Oil Study.[17] For each of the major players, the concern was that the EPA would make decisions based upon outdated science or an insufficient scientific database. There was also a concern that EPA's decisions would be based on insufficient knowledge of either the complexities of industrial operations or the enforcement and implementation realities faced by state regulators.

The RFG regulation would affect the cost and availability of fuel supplies for consumers, the timing of fuel production for the oil industry, and the distribution pattern for automotive fuels. Yet the EPA, the states, and environmentalists knew very little about the oil industry's pipeline-based, national distribution system for gasoline—a system essential to implementation of any reformulated gasoline program. As such, they were unable to answer questions concerning the feasibility and economic effect of an RFG program on the existing distribution system, much less on how such a program would affect automobile and refinery production costs, or on the best way to integrate gasoline retail outlets into the program. As one EPA official noted:

> EPA does not have all the wisdom in the world, and so we need help from others when making rules. Plus, you always need a reality check when you're regulating industry. Does the rule make sense? Does this turn the marketplace on its head? It may be a good requirement, but the way we're implementing it doesn't make sense. It's always a better rule if you're touching base with all the constituencies—the environmentalists, the states, industry, the consumer groups—because more information about how it's going to work, or not work, is always valuable . . . (EPA interview 3/17/94).

The EPA's information problems were complicated by the lack of clear congressional guidance on the RFG program and the long-standing adversarial relations among the players that made any information suspect by one side or the other. In a traditional rulemaking process (known as notice and comment), the EPA gives notice of the impending regulation and asks all interested parties to comment on the regulation as a means to provide the necessary information. The result is that stakeholders maneuver for advantage in the midst of considerable uncertainty as to how the rule will affect them and what bargaining positions will be adopted by adversaries. For the EPA, the uncertainty is compounded by the games of "cat and mouse" and "partisan posturing." Stakeholders often wait until the last minute to enter their comments on the record so opponents lack the time to respond, and when they do formulate their comments, extreme positions are often taken (posturing), making it harder for the EPA to know what the players consider a reasonable regulation.

The transfer of information necessary for an effective regulation, however, is a two-way street. EPA also has to articulate the purposes and benefits of the rule to the players in the regulatory process.[18] Yet, with limited opportunities to educate in a traditional rulemaking process, the EPA often struggles to justify one of the "partisan" positions over the other or to split the difference between the two; in either case, the likely result is dissatisfied stakeholders who challenge the rule either through litigation or through an appeal to allies in congress or the executive branch (McGarity 1992, 1438).

In an attempt to meet its mandated obligations in a timely manner, to reduce the technical and political information hurdles, and to minimize the potential for conflict, the EPA chose to bypass the traditional process of notice-and-comment rulemaking, and instead to develop the RFG program through an alternative game of collaboration. The question is why? While all the participants could see the gains to be realized by minimizing information problems and producing a rule in a more timely manner, the EPA needed to demonstrate assurances to all players that the product of this collaborative effort would not be appealed to elected officials or litigated—that it would, in fact, be binding.

THE REG-NEG ALTERNATIVE

As early as 1983, following recommendations from the Administrative Conference of the United States (ACUS) on appropriate conditions for the use of negotiated rulemaking, the EPA began to recognize the benefits of collaboration in developing regulations.[19] Throughout the 1980s EPA engaged the negotiated rulemaking, or reg-neg, format a total of seven times. Congress then added its official blessing to collaboration-based administrative decision-making processes in 1990 with passage of the Negotiated Rulemaking Act (Public Law 101–648)[20] and the Administrative Dispute Resolution Act (Public Law 101–552).

Negotiated rulemaking brings together the key players affected by a given rulemaking process in a collaborative effort with EPA to hammer out a consensus-based rule. It adheres to Administrative Procedure Act guidelines for public notice and comment, but departs substantially from traditional procedures for drafting proposed rules by allowing agency and interest-group representatives to negotiate directly with each other between the initial notice and the eventual comments (Fiorino 1988, 765). The interactive bargaining format is intended to facilitate the flow of information among interested parties such that innovative bargains can be struck in a timely manner that facilitates the interests of all players.[21] Participants in the collaborative game have the opportunity to make their cases directly to EPA decision makers, and partisan posturing is minimized by forcing participants to defend their positions through multiple iterations in the rulemaking process. Further, by giving stakeholders a direct role in writing the rule, as an ex-EPA administrator explained, the likelihood is increased that players at the table "underst[and] exactly what [is] meant by the regulation and what [is] expected of them once the regulation [is] final" (Thomas 1987, 3). Through direct participation, a sense of "ownership" in the rule among participants is thought to preempt the litigation considered inevitable for most EPA rulemaking efforts.[22]

If a collaborative effort could produce a rule that better reflected the preferences of stakeholders and considered their political and economic constraints, endless litigation and implementation delays might be avoided and players might instead unite in support of an agreement. As one participant from the Department of Energy put it, the clean fuels regulation was a good example of something that "cried out for collaboration. It was very complicated, and cooperation with industry would result in better information with which the government could write the regulations" (interview 3/23/94). The general perception was that a traditional notice-and-comment rulemaking procedure would limit the flow of technical information on the reformulation process that was essential to an effective, implementable rule.[23]

Yet while all participants could see that the RFG program "cried out" for a reg-neg, so too have many other regulatory situations. It is not clear why, given the tremendous uncertainty facing potential participants in collaborative games—an uncertainty that most predictably sabotages collaboration more often than not—a collaborative framework was constructed and held together in this instance, and not in others. The sticking point for collaborative efforts is the fear among regulatory participants that rival players will not bargain in good faith and will not honor the consensus-based result. Without some type of assurance mechanism that the negotiated agreement will be binding, that participants will not end-run the process by appealing to elected officials or the courts, and that individual players' stakes in the process are credible, each player has an incentive to avoid the unknown dynamics of collaboration and stick with the known costs of notice-and-comment proceedings—and likely litigation and delay. Overcoming the uncertainty of the collective action dilemma requires an understanding of the difficult combination of factors that came together to build a community of trust among participants.

OVERCOMING UNCERTAINTY BY BUILDING TRUST

The story of the reformulated gasoline rulemaking is, at its core, a story of trust among traditional adversaries. Building the trust, or providing the certainty, required to solve the collective action dilemma and move the collaborative game forward necessitated the presence of pluralism by the rules. In particular, it necessitated an assurance mechanism composed of certain transaction-specific conditions, the inclusion of all major players with stakes on the table, the entrepreneurial efforts of a public manager with a reputation for effective and fair negotiation, the growing credibility of the EPA as a supporter of collaborative efforts, and a set of binding rules specifying the inability of participants to plead the negotiated outcome to the executive or legislative branches.

The RFG collaboration met certain preselection criteria, or transaction-specific conditions. Thirty-five affected parties were identified and grouped into seven interest categories ranging from oil interests and oxygenate producers (ethanol and methanol) to environmental advocates, the automobile industry, state-level regulators, and the Department of Energy. Cohesiveness for interest groupings was maintained throughout the process, as was evidenced most strongly in the aftermath of the actual reg-neg when ethanol interests defected and the remaining interests stood firm in support of the agreement. In particular, the well-established reputations for tough advocacy and expertise brought to the table by the two environmental interests, the Natural Resources Defense Council (NRDC) and the Sierra Club, led to broad support for the effort among grassroots environmental groups. Policy implications in terms of binding precedents were limited both programmatically to the EPA air office and geographically to nine urban areas.

Fundamental values were not at stake in the reformulated gasoline rulemaking. Rather, it was a matter of deciding how much pollution would be removed from the air, how quickly, what implementation and enforcement would look like, and what final market shares for fuel producers would be.[24] Data to frame the discussion were scarce at the beginning, but this situation was rectified in relatively short order through DOE assistance, research by the National Petroleum Council, EPA's own internal efforts, and the ongoing Auto–Oil study. Opportunity to play the collaborative game stemmed from explicit congressional (statutory) and presidential (formal protocol) blessings, the ambiguity of statutory provisions, recognition that given the complexity of the RFG program several solutions were possible, and the fact that the game was limited primarily to questions of "how" (implementation) rather than "what" (e.g., standard setting). Deadlines also played a prominent role in the RFG collaboration. A two-year congressional deadline for finalizing the rulemaking, a self-imposed EPA deadline of August 1991 for developing a consensus agreement using the reg-neg format, and a four-year statutory deadline with respect to the program's starting date continually reminded participants of the comparatively high costs of a traditional notice-and-comment rule-making.

To move the collaborative game forward, however, required something more. Bill Rosenberg was EPA's assistant administrator in charge of the Air Office and the RFG rulemaking. It was up to Rosenberg to be an entrepreneurial leader, to convince stakeholders that if they cooperated in good faith in the collaborative effort, others would do likewise. On this count, his reputation was crucial. Rosenberg had long been a proponent of alternative fuels as a key link in efforts to clean the air, and he had worked closely with White House counsel Boyden Gray to develop the original Bush Administration proposal in this area. He therefore had both an administrative and a personal stake in seeing the program succeed. In addition, during the legislative battles over clean air Rosenberg had earned a reputation as "an obsessive strategist, balancing the demands of environmentalists against the realities of a cost-conscious White House. He was . . . an entrepreneur . . . in perpetual search of clean air deals. . . . In meeting after meeting, . . . he looked for the sweet spot of compromise: what it would take to fix the problem" and bridge the gap among competing interests. Finally, Rosenberg's reputation as "the pit bull of clean air" earned him the respect of his EPA staff and key leaders of the national environmental lobby, while his business background and clear concern for cost effectiveness offered assurance to industry. This vital combination helped him to "sell" the benefits of participating in the collaborative game to the individual stakeholders, and inspired participants to transcend the sort of self-interested behavior that can result in *ex post* opportunism (Weisskopf 1990a, A21; EPA interview 1/11/94).

Rosenberg's entrepreneurial efforts were buttressed by the EPA's previous experience with the reg-neg format. EPA administrators Ruckleshaus, Thomas, and Reilly had successfully established an organizational reputation as an agency committed to greater collaboration among stakeholders. The reputation stemmed not only from their exhortation and symbolic support for collaborative efforts, but from the employment of various reg-negs as a legitimate replacement for top-down, notice-and-comment rulemaking.[25] In addition, the EPA was extremely selective in its use of the reg-neg format and assigned top-level policy makers as agency representatives to the process. When unforeseen contingencies arose, every effort was made to resolve them in a fair manner. Even in the case of "failed" reg-negs, where a full consensus and final agreement was not reached, EPA managers, environmental advocates, and industry participants found the exchange of information "valuable" and the process "worthwhile" because they were able to learn more about the "real-world" conditions relevant to the rulemaking, were able to have a direct dialogue with EPA decision makers, and were able to hear other parties' concerns as well as explain their own. The EPA's clear commitment to collaboration and its successful use (even when consensus was not reached) was essential to removing uncertainty for prospective participants in the RFG rulemaking.[26]

Further, environmental advocates and state regulators insisted that the price for their participation was a formal, written protocol guaranteeing that their good-faith bargaining efforts would not be wasted due to intervention from the Bush Administration. In the fifteen years prior to the RFG rulemaking, central administrative review (primarily by the OMB, President Carter's Regulatory Analysis Review Group, President Reagan's Regulatory Relief Task Force, and most notably, the Quayle Competitiveness Council established during the Bush Administration) became an important dynamic in environmental rulemaking. Whether emphasizing benefit–cost analysis or simply the opportunity for industry to take a "late hit," this form of intervention increased the likelihood that EPA's rules would be "watered down," "completely dismantled," or significantly delayed.[27] In short, participants in the regulatory game had ample reason to be concerned that the leadership of Rosenberg and the commitment of the EPA to the reg-neg format would not be sufficient to prevent subsequent intervention by the Bush White House (EPA interview 3/17/94; environmentalist interview 3/17/94).

A hastily arranged set of negotiations brought together key Bush advisors Boyden Gray and Michael Boskin (then counsel to the Quayle Competitiveness Council), Michael Elliot of EPA's Office of General Counsel, and environmentalists and state regulatory representatives. The eventual protocol "almost look[ed] like a stipulated set of ground rules for the Supreme Court" (EPA interview 3/17/94). It included provisions barring executive branch intervention and stakeholder lobbying (in forums other than the reg-neg), either during the reg-neg or after consensus was reached. Also stipulated were clauses obligating stakeholders to support any final consensus by agreeing not to litigate and by agreeing to unite in opposition to any defections. All provisions were to remain in force up to, and even after, issuance of the final regulation, as long as the final rules complied with the signed agreement (environmentalist interview 3/30/94; Wald 1991). With this additional piece of certainty, the reg-neg went forward. For environmentalists:

> this was an opportunity to pin down the [Bush] Administration. We spent a long time in the beginning of the reg-neg hammering out . . . the protocols. An essential protocol from the environmental standpoint is that if we

come to a negotiated agreement that the administration signed, then they are essentially honor-bound ... to propose that [agreement] as the rule. OMB doesn't get to change this after the negotiation. We saw this as a point of leverage in the reg-neg that we could not have done in a traditional notice-and-comment rulemaking (interview 3/17/94).

Within this context, participants were able to engage in the give and take of negotiation necessary to reach an agreement "in principle" with the occasional push or supporting effort by the entrepreneur.

THE COLLABORATIVE GAME IN ACTION

In June of 1991, three months after the EPA established the thirty-five-member Clean Fuels Advisory Committee (the official reg-neg roster), a weary director of EPA's Office of Mobile Services, Richard Wilson, spoke as if failure was imminent. Wilson expressed hope, nevertheless, that EPA could salvage something positive from the reg-neg by using the information developed thus far to "craft something down the middle so [the negotiating parties] can accept it and not have to litigate it." He estimated the probability at no more than 50–50 that an agreement, "at least in principle," would be reached (*Environment Reporter*, 6/14/91, 333; hereinafter cited as *ER*).

Pushed by approaching deadlines and Rosenberg's "dogged" pursuit of an agreement,[28] and knowing that the price of disagreement was the high-cost alternative of a standard rulemaking process, stakeholders reached a tentative agreement on the broad outlines of the program. Central to the agreement was a bargain struck between the oil and alternative fuel industries, on one side, and environmentalists and state regulators, on the other, over the means used to reach compliance. Environmentalists and regulators favored a gallon-by-gallon emissions standard which, in theory, would improve the enforceability of the program. In contrast, fuel producers wanted the flexibility to achieve compliance with the mandate through an "averaging-based" program which met reformulated standards by assessing a producer's aggregate gasoline contribution to a particular urban area. RFG producers could, in effect, end up violating pollution control standards in some portion of their total gasoline supply, but only if the violations were offset by supplying an equal or greater amount of RFG that was cleaner than the regulation required. In other words, as long as an RFG producer's overall supply of gasoline met stipulated pollution control standards *on average*, a producer was treated as being in compliance with reformulated gasoline standards. The averaging-based plan held potential merit not only for the oil industry's costs of compliance, but for the consuming public as well. Original EPA estimates of RFG compliance costs to consumers for the year 1995 were six cents per gallon, the equivalent of an annual program cost of $2.1 billion. Yet, according to Bill Rosenberg of EPA, a flexible "average-based" compliance program would reduce the costs of RFG to four cents per gallon (U.S. Congress. House. CAA Implementation Hearings, Part II 1991–1992, 16, 743).

Despite potential consumer savings, others at EPA and within the environmental community argued that averaging was not allowable in the CAAA. Several EPA officials also made it clear that they would not have proposed an averaging system for use with the RFG rule under a traditional notice-and-comment rulemaking process. Nor was there any doubt about the intent of environmental advocates and states to litigate the averaging provisions if adopted outside the reg-neg framework.[29] Yet, within the context of the reg-neg, the averaging issue became negotiable. From the perspective of environmentalists, several in EPA, and state regulators, the critical question was: What would industry trade in order to get the flexibility and cost savings likely to accompany an averaging scheme? Toward this end, these stakeholders used "averaging" in an attempt to extract concessions from industry in the areas of primary importance to them: emissions reductions and a higher degree of certainty with respect to regulatory enforcement.

Perhaps most remarkably, a reg-neg caucus of state regulators and environmental advocates were able to secure an agreement with industry that made more stringent the baseline from which emissions reductions would begin. Of pivotal importance to the reduction of VOCs was the need to contain fuel volatility, or the tendency of a fuel to evaporate; the greater the evaporation, the greater the release of VOC pollution. Reid vapor pressure (RVP) measures fuel evaporation on a pound-per-square-inch basis, and the CAAAs mandated that RVP standards be set as a baseline for emissions reductions.[30] The statute left ambiguous, however, just what that baseline was to be. Congress set "absolute" limits on the RVP standard in one section of the law, yet mandated a 15 percent reduction in the standards elsewhere. Industry contended that the "absolute" limits satisfied the 15 percent reduction requirement, since these "limits" constituted a substantial tightening of the RVP levels found in existing supplies of conventional gasoline. The caucus of environmentalists and state regulators, on the other hand, interpreted the law as requiring standards 15 percent *tougher* than the absolute limits. From their perspective, losing on this issue meant "an RFG program where we didn't get any benefits for the environment at least until the year 2000" (state regulator interview 3/21/94). For industry, losing entailed additional compliance costs of hundreds of millions of dollars (*ER*, 2/5/93). The coalition was able to persuade industry to opt for the more stringent standard as part of the overall exchange for greater operational flexibility (averaging) in implementing the rule.

A second trade-off focused directly on the use of averaging as a means to comply with emissions reductions. Again, the environmentalist–state regulator caucus negotiated agreements that increased from 15 to 16.5 percent the mandated reduction in volatile organic compounds (VOCs) and similar provisions for air toxics emissions standards. David Doniger of the Natural Resources Defense Council (NRDC) argued that because a gallon-by-gallon emissions standard forces industry to "shoot, to some degree, beyond the mark in order to have comfort that every gallon will meet [statutory] requirements," the nominal standard is actually more stringent than that specified by law. For example, in order to meet a mandated 15 percent reduction in VOCs, fuel refiners would not "shoot" for 15 percent, but would opt for an emissions reduction objective of 16 to 17 percent or more. With averaging, however, "there is a lessened need on the part of industry to shoot beyond the mark in order to maintain those margins [of safety]." In this respect, a switch to averaging, without a more stringent emissions reduction standard as compensation, was a "step backward" from the environmentalists' perspective since it was likely to result in fewer total emissions reductions (USEPA, NRDC, Doniger testimony, RFG Hearings 1991c, 34–36; EPA 1991b, 3).

Finally, environmental advocates and state regulators received increased certainty in the monitoring and enforcement systems of the program in return for their support of the averaging approach. The rationale was straightforward. Given that averaging offered additional opportunities for industry shirking, and given that prior "experience (at the state level) had shown that averaging programs were extremely difficult to enforce, . . . [regulators would only] agree to support an averaging program provided there [were] sufficient safeguards."[31] At issue were a number of technical matters involving the performance characteristics of gasoline as well as the operational dynamic, frequency, and permanency of the compliance monitoring system. Further, regulators wanted an "automatic ratchet" if compliance surveys revealed that performance averaging was not working as expected; the averaging program would either be "tightened" or, if violations persisted, withdrawn in favor of a gallon-by-gallon standard.

Not everyone was completely happy with the proposed agreement, however. Ethanol interests opposed the certification of RFG gasoline using a "simple" model or formula. Instead, they wanted a "complex" model that would "credit" ethanol-based RFG's reduction of air toxics and carbon monoxide (CO) pollution against its increased production of VOC and nitrogen oxide (NO_x) types of pollution. Other reg-neg participants refused to go along with the more complex model proposed by ethanol interests for several reasons. The general consensus was that there was not enough data available to define the complex model and still issue a timely rule. A full one-year delay was likely, introducing uncertainty into the start-up of the RFG program by its January 1995 mandate. Significantly, even the ethanol lobby's lead representative at the reg-neg, when questioned on this point, agreed that the simple model was the best available "model" of reformulated gasoline, given existing data.[32] Further, the information that was available showed that ethanol produced a net disadvantage to the environment, even with its significant carbon monoxide reductions factored into the model (Wald 1990). Finally, the ethanol lobby encountered staunch opposition from state and local regulators, who insisted that the RFG program strictly observe the NO_x and VOC provisions in the statute. Otherwise, states with urban smog problems would be forced to compensate for the concessions granted to ethanol producers by implementing other, more costly, pollution control measures (*ER*, 8/16/91; USEPA RFG Hearings, Majkut testimony 1991c, 17–18).

Nevertheless, most stakeholders felt they had much to gain from the tentative agreement. In case anyone needed a reminder of what "going down the alternative road" of traditional rulemaking and litigation entailed, David Doniger of NRDC promised litigation, the likely judicial slap at averaging, and a patchwork quilt of state-level fuel regulations to compensate for enforcement problems and to achieve emission targets: "Now this is the path, in my view, that would maximize industry's uncertainty, for a clear outcome to the judicial and state-level processes may take three years or longer. That prospect can be of little comfort to those facing a fixed deadline of January 1, 1995. This path would also maximize the rigidity of the rules industry would face, for there is no way performance averaging or the other flexibility features discussed above will survive outside of a [negotiated] agreement" (USEPA RFG Hearings 1991c, 20–28).

With great fanfare, the tentative agreement of July became the core of the "final agreement in principle" signed on August 16, 1991. At a press conference announcing the consensus, participants "applauded the negotiation process, the nearly litigation-proof agreement that resulted, and the production certainty in the makeup of vehicle fuels for the next decade" (*ER*, 8/23/91, 1141; *New York Times* 1991b). An informal commitment from Administrator Reilly granted ethanol interests an important concession in the area of NO_x emissions that assured the industry a larger market share.[33] Letters to the other stakeholders in the reg-neg indicating his decision completed the process, and it was enough to convince ethanol representatives to sign the agreement.[34] Nevertheless, despite Administrator Reilly's informal gesture and, importantly, a formal protocol governing after-the-fact pleadings, ethanol went straight to the White House and congress. The appeal challenged not only the viability of the agreement, but the legitimacy of reg-neg as a means to resolve disputes and arrive at workable rules.

STANDING FIRM FOR THE LONG TERM

Ethanol went to the top of the political hierarchy for assistance. Senate Minority Leader Bob Dole (R-KS), Senate Majority Leader George Mitchell (D-ME), Senator Tom Daschle (D-SD), and Clayton Yeutter, special counsel to President Bush, were enlisted to petition EPA for changes in the rule. Concerned that the informal nature of Administrator Reilly's letter would not guarantee sufficient market share, ethanol sought additional leeway in its ability to comply with a final rule. Ethanol fuels were going to have an extremely difficult time meeting the Reid vapor pressure (RVP) standards specified in the reg-neg agreement (on a pounds-per-square-inch basis). It was thus likely that they would be unable to access markets in certain regions of the country, particularly the Northeastern United States. What they sought was a one-pound waiver, so that if the RVP standard, for example, was eight pounds per square inch, ethanol fuels would be allowed a nine-pound-per-square-inch standard (*ER*, 3/27/92). The ethanol lobby maintained that the inclusion of the one-pound waiver elsewhere in the CAAA signaled general congressional intent to apply the waiver to the RFG program as well.[35]

Not surprisingly, the defection elicited a sharp response from other stakeholders, who united in defense of the reg-neg agreement (*ER*, 9/18/92; 4/16/93). State, local, and EPA regulatory officials reiterated their opposition to the waiver, arguing that it would only make urban smog problems worse in the nation's most polluted cities (*ER*, 4/7/92). Thomas Jorling, the New York State Commissioner of Environmental Conservation said, "There is a use for alcohol [e.g., ethanol] fuels, but I suspect they are limited to areas that don't have air pollution problems" (Wald 1992, D3). Other stakeholders were incredulous:

> [T]he ethanol industry can't meet the oxygen requirements [of the law] on a per-gallon basis because they splash-blend the ethanol. They can't do it with sufficient precision to meet the per-gallon requirements so they saw the averaging as a major advantage. ... But, if they want to play hardball, let's get into court and we'll throw the averaging out and we'll

throw the [presumed no net increase in] NO$_x$ out, and then they'll really be screwed. You won't see any ethanol in the RFG program if somebody wants to be really tough. That's what's so remarkable about them breaking with the reg-neg agreement. It's really remarkably greedy on their part. . . . They could end up much worse (environmentalist interview 3/17/94).

Fuel industry analysts weighed into the debate, characterizing as "highly exaggerated" ethanol interests' claims that the reg-neg-based RFG rule would "freeze" ethanol out of the alternative fuels market. As written, ethanol's market share was predicted to rise from 10 to 25 percent (*ER*, 4/7/92). A 1992 report issued by the Energy Information Administration found that not only was ethanol use up 35 percent from the previous year, it was up 1,000 percent from ten years earlier; the expectation was that under the existing rule ethanol use in 1995 would be double that for 1991 (*ER*, 9/18/92).

Key opposition to the defection came from the EPA itself and, in particular, Assistant Administrator Rosenberg. Calling the initial request "illegal," he refused to reissue the rule with the waiver. When President Bush chose to simply "wave a magic wand," as one EPA official stated, and grant the one-pound RVP waiver to ethanol, the EPA nevertheless continued to stand firm (Schneider 1992b). An EPA official made it clear that the battle over the RFG rule was not over:

We do have legally required formal process for changing a regulation. We will have to go through the whole process, including a public hearing. Who knows what issues will resurface when this rulemaking is reopened? . . . [A]ll bets are off that other parts of the reg-neg will remain. This could be a knock-down, drag-out fight. It will make for an interesting hearing. . . . They'd better put metal detectors at the door (*ER*, 10/16/92, 1596).

Eventual resolution of the ethanol request rested with the incoming Clinton Administration and the new EPA Administrator Carol Browner. After additional hearings and an extended period of public comment, the ethanol waiver was officially withdrawn in October 1993, and the RFG program was reported as a final rule *in keeping with the original reg-neg agreement* (*ER*, 10/15/93). At the same time, however, the EPA proposed a new Renewable Oxygenate Program (ROP) guaranteeing "that at least 30 percent of the gasoline sold in the . . . reformulated gasoline program . . . would have to be from renewable sources, which essentially means ethanol" (Noah 1993, A3; Schneider 1993a). While clean fuels competitors were furious, some observers argued that by offering the carrot of ROP to ethanol, EPA allowed the RFG rule to go forward, knowing that the ROP rule would be litigated and not likely survive judicial scrutiny.[36] Such a strategy, while clearly high-risk on the part of the EPA, nevertheless heightened its credibility as an organization genuinely interested in preserving the outcomes produced by collaborative processes, thereby enhancing its reputation for similar endeavors in the long term.

LESSONS LEARNED: THE AFTERMATH

Participants in national environmental politics have long recognized the costs associated with traditional notice-and-comment rulemaking, and the potential of collaborative games to minimize these costs and produce "win–win" benefits for all stakeholders. Yet with few exceptions, the playing of the collaborative game and the benefits of collaboration have remained theoretical conjecture. The substantial uncertainty accompanying collaboration succeeds in deterring participants from regularly engaging the collaborative format, especially in cases involving adversaries with a long history of bitterness between them.

What does it take to overcome the uncertainty that so predictably sabotages collaborative efforts? What is it that convinced the affected interests in the RFG case to play the collaborative game in the first place and, just as importantly, what sustained the collaborative process? The answer is that players must have a high level of confidence in the ability of the collaborative game to deliver anticipated benefits. The case of reformulated gasoline suggests the importance of pluralism by the rules. Assurance is provided not only through a preselection process (certain transaction-specific conditions had to be satisfied) and the inclusion of a representative universe of affected interests, but by a public sector entrepreneur respected by all participants, the credibility of the EPA in utilizing a reg-neg format in the past, and the use of formal binding rules to preempt appeals to political officials. These "rules" reduce uncertainty and convince affected interests to engage and to sustain the collaborative game.

The result, as most participants in the collaborative effort saw it, was a more efficient regulatory process and outcome. The final regulatory agreement provided greater cost effectiveness during implementation and was produced in a more timely manner with what seemed to be better information. To a large extent, in other words, stakeholders' original perceptions of collaborative games as a vehicle by which to reduce transaction costs[37] and achieve more of their organizational goals were realized.[38] Environmentalists and regulators felt they ended up with a rule that, when finally implemented, will be more stringent and easier to monitor and enforce. Thus, the rule delivered what they sought—a greater certainty of environmental results. EPA saved resources because industry pays the costs of administering the compliance survey/monitoring system. As well, the stringency of the final pollution control standards and the ease with which states could voluntarily opt in to the RFG program meant that individual states with severe urban smog problems would be less likely to promulgate their own *stricter* standards, and therefore less likely to incur the considerable political and administrative costs of making rules delivering little extra benefit to the environment.[39] The methanol and oil industries, though unable to reduce the uncertainty of delay, still were able to achieve considerable compliance cost savings with a more flexible, averaging-based compliance program. Industry was further able to win a guarantee of a month-by-month delay in compliance requirements commensurate with any delays in promulgation of the final rule.[40] Finally, the ownership by all but the ethanol interests translated into far less litigation—only a few cases have resulted over a few issues—"than would typically accompany a rule of this complexity."[41]

Certainly the dynamics of the regulatory process were different from a traditional notice-and-comment proceeding. Scientific information necessary for a good rule flowed more freely in the reg-neg format and created additional "filters" for data verification to the benefit of EPA. For example, an official from the Department of Energy (DOE) noted in an interview that the reg-neg format "was a vehicle by which the DOE could make sure that EPA was taking advantage of the expertise that was available at [DOE] national laboratories rather than taking it upon themselves to [develop the same data]" (3/23/94). In addition, according to this same official, DOE was able to contract with the National Petroleum Council to examine the RFG program and to develop the parameters (a model) for reformulated gasoline, the results of which were then shared with EPA. In conjunction with DOE, the automobile industry helped the EPA to assess the validity and selectiveness of the data offered by the oil and alternative fuels industries. Further, iterative opportunities to discuss and challenge the scientific information put forth by others during negotiating sessions forced stakeholders to defend their arguments and assumptions and helped to create the consensus needed to move forward in areas where substantial scientific uncertainty dominated the debate.

The reduction of information asymmetries also facilitated agreements on implementation and enforcement of the RFG regulation. On the one hand, the oil industry had the opportunity to demonstrate the importance of the relationship between compliance costs and an RFG program compatible with the existing national distribution system (industry interview 4/14/94). As an EPA official explained, "The information from reg-neg provided a reality check. We learned a lot about the distribution system of the oil industry, the pipeline systems, and vari-

ous aspects of how the industry actually works. . . . [That] knowledge
. . . helped ensure that the specific provisions of the rule were realistic
and implementable" (EPA interview 3/17/94). The final agreement
reflected industry concerns in this area by including the "least cost"
compliance option of fuel averaging.[42] Yet while industry was making
its argument for a workable rule, regulators and environmentalists
gained valuable information about how to develop a more enforceable
rule. Without the information on "how industry worked," it was im-
probable that the compliance monitoring system could have been designed with the rigor and detail found in the final rule, much less
accepted by industry without litigation.[43] Indeed, this open exchange
and face-to-face negotiation not only enhanced the ability to enforce
the rule, but created a sense of ownership among participants that
made less likely both litigation and noncompliance. So confident was
the industry in its ability to comply with the RFG program under the
more flexible program of averaging that they agreed to pay for the
compliance surveys.

The collaborative game also clearly facilitated bargaining and coalition building among participants to speed the process along. As industry struggled to solve the "averaging" puzzle, a member of the
states–environmentalist caucus determined that helping industry
would help their own cause as well. As described by one participant:

> I can remember [X] helping them in our own caucus. [This individual]
> was saying "How can we help industry on averaging? How can we put
> together a scheme on averaging that will be beneficial to them?" And I
> said, "Why do you want to help them? Why should we come up with the
> averaging solution? If they want flexibility, let them be smart enough to
> do it." The response was, "The sooner we help them to resolve this issue,
> the quicker we'll have an agreement, the quicker the rule will be out, and
> the quicker the environment will be cleaned up" (state regulator interview
> 3/21/94).

The willingness of traditional adversaries to cooperate in such a
manner also helped the EPA to educate stakeholders about the purposes and benefits of the RFG program. Participants came away with
an explicit understanding of what was required in terms of implementation and compliance. A large part of this stemmed from the new
lines of communication established among stakeholders during the
reg-neg and the extension of collaboration beyond the completion of
the official reg-neg. Thus, although the "final agreement in principle"
was just that—an eleven-page statement of principles to guide the
final rule instead of hundreds of pages of regulatory language—"there

developed a working relationship in which the spirit of the reg-neg carried beyond to the post-reg-neg stage as [EPA] developed . . . the actual language of the regulation."[44] In short, the reg-neg provided a venue where the rank ordering of "political" priorities could be clarified, the middle ground between contentious issues explored, and innovative compromises worked out and incorporated into the final regulatory program.

REPUTATION, CREDIBILITY, AND THE LIMITS OF COLLABORATIVE GAMES

Without entrepreneurial leadership, the EPA's credible commitment to the process, and a formal protocol, uncertainty among the stakeholders would have prevented the realization of these transaction cost reductions and the achievement of stakeholders' various objectives. It mattered that the key public sector entrepreneurs—Reilly and Rosenberg—evidenced support for the collaborative effort. Their high-level efforts to make the process work communicated important cues to stakeholders of the EPA's commitment to the collaborative effort as a legitimate form of rulemaking. The individual efforts of EPA's Rosenberg, in particular, held out to traditional combatants the likelihood that questions of cost and economic efficiency would receive a credible hearing alongside questions of rigorous pollution control. Indeed, his support for the averaging system as a consumer bonus of two cents per gallon was key to an agreement over averaging, more generally. His support added clout to the industry position and enhanced industry's interest in the compliance method; at the same time, with industry firmly behind averaging, the opportunity for the environmental advocate–state regulator caucus to extract more rigorous pollution emissions standards from industry, in exchange for going along with averaging, was enhanced. Likewise, Rosenberg's tireless efforts to break the deadlock over the RVP standard in June and July of 1991 were instrumental in forging the final agreement. It also mattered a great deal, particularly for the long-term credibility of the EPA as a facilitator of collaboration, that Rosenberg refused to change the rule for the benefit of ethanol interests following the intervention by the White House.

Rosenberg's efforts to protect the integrity of the negotiated agreement were key not only to his own credibility as a leader of reg-negs in the future, but also for ensuring the reputation of the EPA as an organization committed to collaborative efforts as a form of rulemaking. The successful communication of EPA's trustworthiness to other stakeholders was important as a means of bringing individuals to the table and ensuring that they come to the table again and again. By establishing the reg-neg as a legitimate form of decision making within the broader environmental policy-making arena, the EPA and its leaders were establishing or building upon a regulatory culture that would eventually define "how things are done" to stakeholders throughout the process.

Leadership and reputation together provided a framework within which stakeholders could trust each other. They facilitated collaboration within the hierarchy of the policy process by creating assurance that self-interested organizations would not act opportunistically to derail the reg-neg. Put another way, it brought the efforts of powerful, self-interested stakeholding organizations in line with the collective public policy goal of environmental protection. If stakeholders in the rulemaking process only required the clear perception of a more efficient means to develop the rule, the reg-neg would have proceeded without entrepreneurial leadership, without the backing of the EPA, and, importantly, without the effort to formally restrain appeals to higher political principals.[45] More significantly, the collaborative pattern emerging today would have begun to take hold many years ago; but it did not, and the RFG reg-neg would not have gone forward without these additional pieces of certainty for the participants.

Yet in the end, the RFG case also raises questions concerning the stability or durability of policy outcomes negotiated under the pluralism-by-the-rules scenario. The story demonstrates the fragility of the assurance afforded by entrepreneurial leadership, reputation, and even a formal binding agreement to preempt *ex post* intervention. The reg-neg protocol did not eliminate outside interference by hierarchically superior political principals as planned. Delays and uncertainty caused by the defection of ethanol producers naturally complicated the task of entrepreneurial leaders at the time and in the future, and raised questions about the ability of formal protocols to provide binding certainty within a game played by traditional, often bitter, adversaries. In the words of one industry stakeholder: "I told the administration point-blank that if you want to have additional [reg-negs] with this industry, honor the first one. . . . I won't say that we will not come to the table, but I will say that it will be much more difficult for us to reach meaningful compromise knowing that it's not a done deal" (industry interview 3/23/94).

Clearly, there is much about the American national political system that makes the collaborative approach to regulation an uncertain gamble. Elected officials can disrupt or facilitate a collaborative effort, responding in an ad hoc manner to important constituencies who trigger fire alarms. While preselection through transaction-specific conditions, entrepreneurial leaders, agency credibility, and formal binding rules can minimize some of these uncertainties, they cannot prevent them altogether.

Despite the difficulties caused by the ethanol lobby's defection, the degree of instability should be kept in perspective. The original reg-neg agreement is intact and the RFG program became fully operational as scheduled in January 1995.[46] Each development is a sign that pluralism by the rules holds potential for managing conflict in highly adversarial arenas and for improving the likelihood of enduring, stable regulatory outcomes, compared to no-holds-barred pluralistic alternatives. Moreover, as the costs imposed by conflict and hierarchy-based forms of regulation escalate, and given the continuing presence of the contextual changes that have made pluralism by the rules possible, pollution control stakeholders continue to encounter strong incentives to seek alternatives to no-holds-barred pluralism. Thus, although the task of piecing together the players, conditions, and leadership required to put collaborative games into play is no simple matter, the overarching incentive structure indicates that such rule-based arrangements might, in fact, become more common in the future. Finally, as the comments of the industry stakeholder offering advice to the Bush Administration indicate, traditional adversaries are developing a solid self-interest in collaborative processes that raises the stakes for politicians considering *ex post* intervention. Simply put, there is a high risk for the political principal who intervenes when collaboration produces a broad consensus among stakeholders.

CHAPTER NOTES

1. As quoted in Weisskopf (1989a, A18).

2. Despite population growth, the 210 tons of pollution dumped into the air in 1970 have been cut by a third. Emissions of lead have been reduced by 96 percent, large particulates by 62 percent, and carbon monoxide by 39 percent. Automobiles emit over 90 percent less carbon monoxide and hydrocarbons and 75 percent less NO_x than 1970 models (Weisskopf 1989a, A18).

3. Testimony of Donald Theiler, President of the State and Territorial Air Pollution Program Administrators (STAPPA), CAA Hearings, Part I (U.S. Congress. House. 1989, 346). As of 1988, fifty-six areas of the country were unable to attain the air quality standards for ground-level ozone (aka urban smog) mandated by the 1970 CAA, fifty-nine areas failed to meet carbon monoxide standards, and PM–10 standards were regularly exceeded in over 100 areas.

4. Testimony of Henry Waxman, chair of House Subcommittee on Health and Environment, CAAA Hearings, Part I (U.S. Congress. House. 1989, 1).

5. Ground-level ozone forms when emissions of volatile organic compounds (VOCs) and nitrogen oxides (NO_x) react in the presence of sunlight. It is estimated that mobile sources produce 50 percent of the nation's VOC emis-

sions and over 45 percent of the country's NO_x emissions (Walsh 1990, 217–18). In urban areas where smog is most problematic, they contribute even higher percentages of these two pollutants. For example, in the Northeastern states, motor vehicles emit 62 percent of the VOCs and 53 percent of the NO_x, while in Los Angeles mobile sources contribute 52 percent of VOCs and 76 percent of the NO_x (NESCAUM testimony, U.S. Congress. House. CAA Hearings, Part I, 335; California Air Resources Board 1990). The two main reasons behind the large volume of mobile source pollution are the large increase in vehicle-miles-traveled (VMT) and the emergence of "dirtier" gasoline in recent years.

    6. Oil companies increased the percentages of butane and toxic aromatic octane enhancers, while simultaneously allowing fuel volatility (or tendency to evaporate) to rise. See generally Waxman, Wetstone, and Barnett (1991, 1949–52, 1972–91). For the story of "dirty" gasoline, see Lyman (1990, C5) and Rothschild (1990, B3). For data on the increases in toxic compounds and volatility (the tendency to evaporate), see Rothschild (1990, B3); GAO (1987, 29–30); OTA (1989b, figure 3).

    7. Weisskopf (1989b, A8); Weisskopf (1990a); Waxman, Wetstone, and Barnett (1991, 1951–53). The USEPA (1990a) estimates that the minimum cost of securing additional reductions in VOC emissions from stationary sources is approximately $5,000 per ton (p. 5). Pollution control costs in the most polluted areas are much higher, however, and can range upwards of $25,000 per ton of pollution reduced (South Coast Air Quality Management District 1990, Sections 4–38 to 4–39). EPA estimated that mobile sources, on the other hand, can lower gasoline volatility and VOCs for as little as $140 per ton (USEPA 1990a, 24), as well as reap the benefit of reformulated gasoline for only "pennies per gallon" (USEPA 1990b). EPA's 1993 Regulatory Impact Analysis estimated that the majority of VOC reductions in the RFG program would be attained by the specified lower Reid vapor pressure for a cost of between $261 and $270 per ton, while the total cost per ton for reducing VOCs over Phase I and Phase II of the program was estimated at $3,075 per ton (GAO 1996, 21).

    8. President Bush's original June 1989 clean fuels proposal and both of the initial house and senate bills, H. R. 3030 and S. 1490, did not include a reformulated gasoline provision.

    9. Rep. Ralph Hall (D-Tex) and Rep. Jack Fields, Jr. (R-Tex).

    10. Weisskopf (1989c, A4); Kuntz and Hager (1990, 985). Rep. Henry Waxman (D-CA) disputed the emission-reduction numbers announced by Rep. Fields, arguing instead that the "true" emissions picture gave the "M–100" standard almost a three-to-one edge in the amount of pollution reduced, as opposed to the "M–85" standard (Hager 1989c, 2701). EPA, for its part, argued that "M–85 is a poor substitute for pure methanol, releasing 30 percent more of the ingredients in smog" (Weisskopf 1989c, A4). Waxman also noted the existence of data suggesting that the "M–85" standard "is no cleaner than conventional gasoline" (Hager 1989c, 2701).

    11. The VOC requirements apply during the summertime high-ozone season, while the air toxics requirement is a year-round requirement.

    12. Five "specified" fuel elements had to be included in the RFG model: the benzene content of the fuel cannot exceed 1 percent by volume, the aromatic hydrocarbon content cannot exceed 25 percent by volume, the fuel can contain

no lead, the fuel must contain detergents, and the oxygen content of the fuel must be at least 2 percent [Sec. 211(k)3(A)].

13. GAO (1990a, 4–5); *New York Times* (1991a; 1991c). The GAO report (1990a) listed oil industry estimates of $20 to $30 billion to reformulate all gasoline, while ARCO alone estimated its share of the conversion effort at $2 billion over a five-year period for all its gasoline (pp. 4–7).

14. *New York Times* (1990). "Cows, Bulls, and Clean Air [Mobil Oil op-ed advertisement], (December 13, A31).

15. U.S. Congress. House. CAAA Implementation Hearings (Part II) (1991–1992, 13).

16. In some instances, rules have been promulgated after nine years, and in others, such as the Clean Air Act of 1977 mobile on-board canister rule, rules have never been finalized. See Thomas (1987); McGarity (1992).

17. See Auto/Oil Air Quality Improvement Research Program (1993). *Phase I Final Report.* (May).

18. Rosenberg, CAA Oversight Hearings (U.S. Congress. House. 1991, 546); Thomas (1987).

19. See *Establishment of EPA's Regulatory Negotiation Project, Federal Register,* 48 (February 22, 1983, 7494), and Pritzker and Dalton (1990, 330–36). ACUS recommendation 82–4, 1 CFR §305.822–4 set forth criteria to guide agencies in determining whether reg-neg is appropriate for particular regulatory decisions, and suggested specific procedures for agencies applying the reg-neg approach. ACUS refined the recommendation in 1985 after studying agency experiences with reg-neg (see Recommendation 85–5, 1 CFR §305.85–5). The earliest congressional hearings concerning reg-neg occurred during 1980 (U.S. Congress. Senate. Regulatory Negotiation Hearings 1980). Following these hearings, proponents of reg-neg introduced the Regulatory Mediation Act of 1981, S. 1601, which sought to "establish an alternative rulemaking procedure which includes the establishment of regulatory negotiation committees."

20. A key concern of reg-neg proponents was that during congressional deliberations on the Negotiated Rulemaking Act of 1990, serious consideration was given to mandating the use of reg-negs for a broad array of rulemaking situations irrespective of any special, transaction-specific conditions. The fear was that such a broad and inappropriate application of reg-neg would not only diminish the likelihood of success, but inevitably lead to a backlash which might prohibit its use altogether (interview with environmentalist 3/30/94; EPA 3/17/94).

21. Kerwin and Furlong (1992, 113, 134) compared four EPA reg-negs to the most substantial 15 percent of all EPA rules adopted during fiscal years 1987–1990 and found that reg-negs, on average, took 778 days to complete, a time savings of eleven months (per rule) versus rules subjected to traditional rulemaking methods. Coglianese (1997), in the most in-depth study of reg-neg timeliness to date, finds that the fifteen EPA reg-negs are actually no more timely than traditional rulemaking methods.

22. Interviews with EPA #1 (3/17/94); EPA #2 (3/17/94); industry (4/14/94); industry (3/23/94). See also Fiorino and Kirtz (1985, 30); Harter (1982); Perritt (1986); Susskind and McMahon (1985); Waxman (1991).

23. Interviews with DOE (3/23/94); environmentalist (3/30/94); and industry (3/10/94; 4/14/94).

24. As the congressional battle over clean fuels made clear, fuel producers had much to gain from the "new" market in reformulated gasoline, especially ethanol and methanol producers. Even the oil industry, which faced additional compliance and retooling costs, could appreciate RFG as the least "bad" alternative when it came to defining clean fuels. Through utilization of their established distribution and marketing systems and the ability to pass through production costs to consumers (since it was a level playing field), the actual economic damage wrought by the introduction of RFG over the long term was expected to be minimal.

25. Schneider (1992a, B20); Shabecoff (1989, A14); Thomas (1987).

26. See Pritzker and Dalton (1990); USEPA (1987, 9–11); state regulator interview (3/21/94); environmentalist interview (3/30/94).

27. Costle (1993, 59); state regulator interview (3/21/94). In 1989, 2,200 rules were submitted to OMB for review from all government agencies. OMB found 1,638 rules (73.8 percent) consistent with its requirements and therefore ordered no changes. For EPA, however, only 97 of 201 rules (48.3 percent) were approved without change. See Executive Office of the President (1990, 636, 638). For a specific example, see Herz (1995). He tells the story of how the Bush White House, for reasons of politics, pulled out of a "roundtable" rulemaking process for the Title V "major source" permit program pursuant to the Clean Air Act Amendments of 1990.

28. Interviews (industry 9/20/94; EPA 3/17/94). "We in the oil industry were absolutely unwilling to give on the Southern state RVP issue in June [of 1991]. But Rosenberg was a guy you could trust. It was clear that he was sincerely concerned with getting a win–win deal for all parties. He drove the bargain forward through his sheer doggedness" (industry 9/20/94).

29. Interviews, environmentalist (3/17/94); EPA (3/17/94); state regulator (3/21/94). See also State and Territorial Air Pollution Program Administrators (STAPPA), Majkut testimony, USEPA RFG Hearings (1991c, 18); statement of Doniger, NRDC.

30. In general, higher RVP levels and warmer air temperatures create higher levels of VOC emissions.

31. STAPPA, Majkut testimony, USEPA RFG Hearings (1991c, 18–19).

32. USEPA RFG Hearings (1991c), Vaughn testimony, Renewable Fuels Association, p. 57. See also Majkut testimony, STAPPA; Wilson testimony/ EPA during same hearings.

33. Reilly issued a letter in which a 3.5 percent oxygenate level for ethanol-based RFG was "presumed" not to increase NO_x pollution except during the summer ozone season. The actual reg-neg agreement specified an oxygenate level of 2.1 percent for ethanol. The 2.1 percent standard is the level at which an ethanol-based oxygen content is generally considered safe for nitrogen oxide purposes. The presumption of no NO_x increase was limited to the first two years of the RFG program, or until further research demonstrated that ethanol-based oxygen contents greater than 2.1 percent would not increase NO_x pollution.

34. All stakeholders, including representatives of the ethanol industry, signed the final agreement in principle.

35. Wald (1992, D3). See also the analysis by EPA's Office of General Council (USEPA 1992, 8–10), for a specific rebuttal of the ethanol industry position.

36. Noah (1993); industry interview (4/14/94); environmentalist interview (3/17/94).

37. Environmentalists and consumer advocates do not necessarily perceive a reduction in their own, individual organizational costs, even when the comparison is a notice-and-comment rule that is then litigated (environmentalist interview 3/30/94; consumer advocate interview 3/25/94). Rather, they perceive that the "better" rules (more stringent regulations, faster implementation, and more rigorous monitoring processes) produced by reg-negs increase the certainty that more of their organizational goal—environmental protection—is delivered. The increased certainty of environmental results more than offsets the perceived increase in organizational costs.

38. Carnevale (1993), in an empirical study of the U. S. Postal Service, offers evidence for how consensus-based alternative dispute resolution (ADR) processes contribute to significant transaction cost savings.

39. Any such rules were likely to deliver "little benefit to the environment" because the gap between "stringent" federal and state requirements was going to be relatively small. State regulator interview (3/21/94).

40. See the "final agreement in principle," USEPA (1991b, 1). The month-by-month delay applied only to the "complex" model requirements of the RFG program scheduled to come into effect in 1997.

41. EPA interview (8/29/94). A total of five lawsuits were filed by American Petroleum Institute, Texaco, Fina Oil, Amerada Hess Corporation, and National Tank Truck Carriers, Inc. The first three petitions were consolidated into a single lawsuit. Coglianese (1996) disputes whether reg-negs actually reduce litigation. Focusing entirely on frequency with which EPA rules are litigated, he finds that four of twelve rules produced by reg-negs have been litigated—a rate of 33 percent that is within the range of litigation for EPA rules (from 19 percent to 44 percent) produced by the more traditional rulemaking process (see pp. 35–36). But, as the comment from the EPA official suggests, Coglianese's critique would be stronger if he investigated the *number* of lawsuits filed for each rule, rather than the frequency with which lawsuits are filed against individual rules. The perception that the RFG rule would have encountered additional litigation under a more traditional rulemaking appears to be the motivator in this case. As well, it can be argued that the key is still the perception by participants that litigation is imminent for the rule that is of particular concern to them at the moment, rather than some abstract average rate of litigation, and the perception that somehow reg-neg may be able to minimize, not necessarily eliminate, litigation for the rule they care most about.

42. Industry interview (3/23/94). Fuel refiners report initial RFG production costs range from three to ten cents per gallon. See Aeppel (1995).

43. Interviews with environmentalist (3/30/94); environmentalist (3/17/94); EPA (3/17/94). For example, the final agreement made provisions for a compliance survey program for the nine cities involving 120 unannounced surveys in the first year, eighty surveys in the second, sixty surveys in the third, and fifty in every year beyond (USEPA 1991b, 4). The number of required surveys is significantly larger than in a typical regulatory program (see GAO 1990b, 19).

44. EPA interview (3/17/94). Reg-neg participants were satisfied to outline the major points of their consensus agreement in the eleven-page document, then let EPA draft the rule using these guidelines and subject the proposed rule to public comment. The same format has been used in other reg-negs, including EPA's first one on Nonconformance Penalties (see Fiorino and Kirtz 1985, 35).

45. This, of course, is contrary to the expectations of much of the organizational economics literature, which is based on the premise that hierarchical organizations, like markets, move toward more efficient forms through competition. Hence, the role of organizational leaders is cast in minimalist terms (see, for example, Williamson and Ouchi 1981).

46. The U.S. Court of Appeals in Washington, D.C., blocked the Clinton Administration's Renewable Oxygenate Program (ROP) on April 28, 1995. The court said that the EPA lacked the statutory authority to create the ROP, a program designed to give the ethanol industry an automatic 30 percent share of the RFG market. See Noah and Kilman (1995).

6

Assuring Reductions in Acid Rain: The Case of Government-Imposed Markets

The acid rain program has succeeded in moving the idea of market-based regulation from theory to political reality and into the mainstream of political discussion as an alternate means to the end of environmental protection (Richard Ayres, Chair, National Clean Air Coalition, 1975–1990).

Acid rain became a national policy concern during the late 1970s. At that time scientists issued warnings about a possible link between long-range transport of sulfur dioxide (SO_2) and nitrogen oxide (NO_x) emissions and damage to aquatic as well as terrestrial ecosystems in West Germany, Northern Europe, Canada, and the eastern United States (NRC 1981). The concern was that SO_2 and NO_x, the primary precursors to acid rain, imposed an unprecedented and alarming acid burden on the forests, streams, and lakes in the affected areas. In the United States and Canada, the principal source of acid rain was believed to be the heavy concentration of industrial and utility plants in Midwestern states—hundreds of miles from the reported damage (Harrington 1989; NAPAP 1991; NRC 1986).

To environmentalists, the case of acid rain was clear-cut. Immediate action was required to stop the damage. To do otherwise would result in severe, perhaps irreversible, damage to fragile ecosystems. Equally clear-cut was the solution: a 50 percent reduction in SO_2 and NO_x emissions (10 million tons), using their preferred method of ensuring environmental quality—command and control. Many in the business community, on the other hand, were not convinced that there was an acid rain problem, that it required the drastic action implied by a 10-million-ton cut in emissions, or that the U.S. economy could afford the enormous cost of the cleanup (Clean Air Working Group 1987). In the case of congress, dozens of acid rain bills were introduced throughout the 1980s, all to no avail. The regional nature of acid rain, the high costs of controlling emissions using command and control,[1] scientific uncertainty,[2] and the unwillingness of the Reagan Administration to act made consensus building an extraordinarily difficult task. The issue of acid rain, "the single most complex and divisive issue in the congressional clean-air debate," joined a growing list of environmental issues in which congressional and regulatory gridlock was the rule (Bryner 1993; Hager 1989a, 2934; Kraft 1990).

Then on June 12, 1989, President Bush kept a promise made during the 1988 presidential election campaign. He proposed a new Clean Air Act whose centerpiece was an innovative market-based emissions-trading program designed to solve the acid rain problem. President Bush's program, designed in collaboration with national environmentalists, won accolades from all sides and quickly became the "engine" that moved the clean air debate forward.[3] By halving the emissions of sulfur dioxide and including rigorous compliance features, Bush was able to meet the demands of the national environmental community and key leaders in congress such as Senate Majority Leader George Mitchell (D-Maine) and Rep. Henry Waxman (D-Calif.), among others (interview with congressional staff, 3/18/94; Lawrence 1989, 2381). These stakeholders seized upon the acid rain provisions as the "good" part of the overall Clean Air Act proposal (Cohen 1992, 87, 178; Hager 1989b, 1464).

At the same time, the market-based trading scheme was attractive to industry and conservative members of congress because it adhered to the premise that "government intervention needed to be more decentralized, flexible, and efficient" and promised industry considerable compliance cost savings as opposed to command-and-control alternatives (Bryner 1993, 96). John Dingell (D-Mi), the chair of the House Energy and Commerce Committee through which clean air legislation must pass and a stalwart defender of industry prerogatives during the decade-long clean air deadlock, proclaimed the acid rain program an important breakthrough (Cohen 1992, 178).

The collaborative dynamic over "markets" was not limited to the lawmaking phase of the policy process. It extended into rulemaking and implementation as well. In fact, when all was said and done, acid rain was the only major title of the 1990 Act whose basic concepts emerged virtually unchanged and with near-unanimous support from the national environmental community, congress, the Environmental Protection Agency (EPA), the White House, and industry.[4]

What made this broad-based consensus on a market mechanism so remarkable was that for years many of these same stakeholders viewed incentives-based pollution control programs with disdain, if not outright hostility. Environmentalists viewed economists' claims regarding market-based pollution control mechanisms with extreme skepticism. From their perspective, market failure and the unwillingness of industry to clean up were the reasons an environmental crisis existed in the first place. Markets simply were not a legitimate way to fight pollution because they created licenses to pollute, created additional opportunities for shirking, and undermined the moral basis of society's fight against pollution (Heidenheimer et al. 1990; Kelman 1981). Further, proposals for fees or emissions trading generally fell on deaf ears in both congress and the Environmental Protection Agency. Senator William Proxmire offered an amendment to the Clean Water Act in 1971 allowing the use of discharge fees. It attracted no support (Eads and Fix 1984, 103). At EPA, support for markets was limited to the Office of Policy, Planning, and Evaluation (OPPE), especially the Regulatory Reform staff. More influential offices in the Office of Air and Radiation, such as the Office of Policy Analysis and Review (OPAR) and the Office of Air Quality Planning and Standards (OAQPS), fiercely opposed markets in most any form (Cook 1988; Levin 1982; Meidinger 1985). Even industry had long made clear their preference for regulatory relief and a rollback of environmental gains rather than the regulatory reform implied by markets (Eads and Fix 1984; Hays 1989). Others in industry were convinced that market mechanisms were not in their best interest. Instead, market mechanisms were only a more sophisticated way of extending the reach of government regulation that, in the end, would relegitimize pollution control as both environmentally effective and economically efficient (Meidinger 1985).

How do we explain the willingness of interests as diverse as the Natural Resources Defense Council, the National Clean Air Coalition, a sizable number of the utilities, key elites in EPA's air offices,[5] and Democrats in congress to support a method of pollution control explicitly recognizing both environment and economy? The short answer is that the specific shape of the acid rain market mechanism—a government-imposed market (GIM)—engendered support among traditional adversaries by promising transaction cost savings to each, thereby helping them to attain more of their organizational goals. Environmentalists and regulators perceived that they would obtain more environmental results sooner. For EPA regulators, the GIM was an opportunity to improve the agency's reputation as an advocate for the environment, while simultaneously incurring lower administrative costs. Industry expected lower compliance costs, greater autonomy, and ultimately enhanced responsiveness to changing markets and technological developments. Meanwhile, legislators and majority party leaders in congress anticipated an end to legislative gridlock, thus enabling them to deliver policies crucial to reelection efforts and to pass the party's policy agenda and to maintain the party's majority in congress.

Yet President Bush's ability to set the agenda with an acid rain program promising significant transaction cost savings solved only part of the policy-making puzzle. It was not by itself sufficient to induce the coalition of support needed to break the gridlock in congress. Although the benefits of supporting the GIM program were easily perceived by major stakeholders, the uncertainties of lawmaking in the postreform congress posed significant political risks to all concerned and complicated the management task facing the majority party leaders and committee-based legislators responsible for moving the proposal forward.

Under such conditions of uncertainty, legislators and stakeholders required assurance that the collaborative deal would hold together and that their stakes in the outcome would be honored. Otherwise, it was not clear why participants should abandon their traditional skepticism toward market-based regulatory mechanisms and accept the risks inherent in such support. Each group had an incentive to avoid the uncertainty of the collaborative effort and instead take their chances with either the high-cost alternative of command and control or, given the consistent inability of command-and-control acid rain proposals to pass congress, the very real possibility of no deal at all. Overcoming the collective action dilemma in congress necessitated an assurance mechanism based on a credible commitment to the collaborative game by legislative leaders, and an effort to restrain individual legislators and other political actors from intervening and manipulating agreements *ex post*.[6] Specifically, the effort was facilitated by a set of transaction-specific conditions, the entrepreneurial efforts of Senate Majority Leader George Mitchell and key (sub)committee chairs in the house, the use of unconventional lawmaking institutions,[7] and explicit legislative language designed to protect the agreement during congressional deliberation as well as afterward during bureaucratic rulemaking and implementation.

DEFINING GOVERNMENT-IMPOSED MARKETS

The goal of government-imposed markets is the same as that of command and control: to increase the certainty of environmental protection. But the method of achieving compliance is dramatically different. Government-imposed markets grant industry an extraordinary degree of autonomy. Government sets the broad parameters of the program and then "gets out of the way," leaving control over compliance strategies and choices of control technologies in the hands of industry. EPA "emphasis shift[s] from getting involved in the details of actual compliance decisions back to the basics. 'Are you in or out of compliance?' 'Are you emitting within your allowable levels or not?'" (interview with EPA 1/11/94).

The core of a government-imposed market is the emissions allowance trading system. In the case of acid rain, sulfur dioxide emissions are allocated among utilities according to the tons of sulfur dioxide emitted. Each ton of SO_2 is the equivalent of a single allowance. Daniel Dudek, a senior economist at the Environmental Defense Fund (EDF), likens the trading system to a checking account. Every polluter is given an initial deposit or allowance at the beginning of the year. At the end of the year, the emissions record is evaluated by EPA and actual emissions are compared against the number of allowances held by a polluting unit. In cases where a unit's emissions are less than the allowance deposited, an emissions credit is created. This credit can be transferred to another unit in the utility, sold to a different utility or interested party such as an environmental group, or "banked" for future use. If a utility's emissions exceed the total amount of allowances on deposit, then it has overdrawn its account and must make a new deposit to balance the account by purchasing surplus credits from other utilities (see Reynolds 1990, 40).

As part of the market-based component, permitting processes are streamlined and refocused on pollutants instead of industrial processes. Multiple checkpoints on the road to compliance are discarded in favor of a single checkpoint at the end of each compliance period. Industrial process modifications and product-design changes typically do not have to submit to new source review procedures; rather industry must only ensure that permissible aggregate levels of pollutants are maintained. Further, industrial facilities are relieved of the obligation to hold dozens and even hundreds of permits because government-imposed markets typically consolidate them into a single facility-wide permit.

The second element in a GIM is the idea of shared savings. Benefits of reduced compliance costs for industry must be shared with the environment. This can either be designed in from the start by imposing a higher level of emissions reduction as opposed to a command-and-control program, or made an integral part of every market transaction. In the latter case, every time industry overcontrols (i.e., reduces beyond what the law requires), they are granted emissions reduction credits at a level less than 100 percent. For example, buyers of credits may only receive 90 percent of the full value of the emissions credit. The remaining 10 percent is a benefit to the environment (see Kosobud, Testa, and Hanson 1993, *xi*).

Third, instead of being defined in terms of a technology standard (often expressed as an emissions rate or specified technology), GIM pollution goals are defined in terms of an emissions tonnage limitation—the idea of a closed system or an aggregate emissions cap.

The fourth element involves the assignment of property rights over the pollution being emitted. Establishing the emissions cap requires reliable emissions baseline data[8] or, at a minimum, agreement among stakeholders on the appropriate formulas to allocate pollution rights among the regulated community. However, since the focal point of control in a government-imposed market *is* government, property rights are contingent on government approval of allocation formula and are not granted in perpetuity to polluters.

Guaranteed enforceability is the final component of the government-imposed market framework. It consists of a rigorous monitoring program and automatic noncompliance penalties.

MINIMIZING RESISTANCE AND DELAY

The acid rain government-imposed market proposal promised to alter the incentive structure facing industry. Stakeholders perceived that the presence of production flexibility and freedom of choice in selecting compliance strategies would transform industry into a more constructive, cooperative force in the policy process. The change in attitudes was facilitated by the prospect of compliance cost savings, by providing a closer fit with the established psychology of business decision making, by turning environmental compliance into another factor of production, by making compliance obligations independent of the trading scheme, and through the presence of fewer rules.

Perhaps the most commonly cited reason for "why markets" concerned the cost savings associated with a system giving industry planners and compliance experts a large degree of freedom in their choice of compliance options.[9] Hahn and Hester (1987) estimated that EPA's limited experiences with emissions-trading programs saved more than $4 billion in control costs without adversely affecting the environment. The use of market incentives in a single program, EPA's lead phase-down for gasoline (1979–1988), saved an estimated $220 million as opposed to traditional command-and-control regulations "without compromising health benefits" (Whiteman 1992, 39). For acid rain, EPA calculated that emissions trading would lead to comparative compliance-cost savings of over $1 billion annually (USEPA 1990).

Savings were anticipated for a number of reasons. Instead of "one size fits all" regulations, the GIM allowed industry to custom-tailor strategies to individual firm and plant conditions. "[B]y giving firms with relatively low control costs an incentive to control above the level mandated by uniform regulation, while allowing firms with high costs to control less," the aggregate result was likely to be a "cost-effective reallocation of control burdens produc[ing] tens of billions of dollars of cost savings annually" (Stewart 1988, 159). Granting discretion to industry decision makers was also expected to increase the robustness of competition among the various alternatives (e.g., alternative fuels, a variety of scrubbers, emissions allowances, compliance packages that mix and match compliance technologies), thereby exerting downward pressure on the prices charged for *all* compliance options.

> The environmental compliance decision process was transformed from a one-time choice of hardware into a dynamic process where there were significant financial gains to be made from making right decisions, and significant financial penalties for making wrong decisions. Those seeking to provide compliance options, whether technological, fuel or financial, were quickly forced to reduce their claims to a very simple and understandable equation—what was the effective cost of each compliance option, calculated on a dollars per allowance basis? . . . The availability of options allows those who choose scrubbers to drive much better deals than if those same scrubbers were mandated by congress (Keenan testimony, U.S. Congress. Senate. Acid Rain Hearings 1993, 129–30).

Further, the proposed GIM relieved industry of its obligation to double-check with regulators at every step on the road to final compliance. Streamlined permitting systems and autonomy in determining the means of compliance led industry to anticipate transaction cost savings in the areas of required regulatory paperwork, fewer implementation delays since industry no longer had to bargain with regulators over acceptable control technologies, and an enhanced response capability to changing market conditions since compliance strategies did not have to be locked in at an early stage (interviews with industry 1/21/94; 2/22/94). Central to industry thinking was the perception that the relative lack of government involvement in compliance planning processes increased the probability that the rules of the regulatory game would stay intact long enough for investments in time, money, and expertise to bear fruit.

The psychology of government-imposed markets provided a closer fit with traditional modes of business decision making as well. There was widespread agreement in the case of acid rain that the "more rational and reasonable" market-based format made it easier for utility companies and the traditional supporters of business interests in congress to "swallow" the legislation (interviews with congressional staff, 1/7/94; 1/8/94; 3/18/94; environmentalist 1/13/94; industry 2/22/94; 3/21/94).

There's a whole psychology to this in terms of reactions you get from people. If we tell an industry that they must meet a 90 percent reduction, or they must put on this particular kind of technology, all of their energies and efforts are focused on telling us why that's the wrong requirement and why it shouldn't be as tight. If we tell them that we are setting up a market-based system [with] a lot of flexibility, well, initially all of their energy is spent trying to figure out how to set [up the program] in ways that they think can work. Then a lot of their energy goes into trying to figure out how to comply at least cost. . . . It changes the terms of discussion, and the negotiations we have with industry are much better and more constructive than the ones where we haven't given them any choices (interview with EPA 1/13/94).

Closely related to the business psychology–rationality relationship was the idea that market-based regulations transform environmental compliance into another factor of production much like raw materials, transportation, and labor costs (Stewart 1981). Emissions trading gives business the *opportunity* to marshal every facet of their expertise— environmental, safety, production, financial, and so on—toward solving compliance issues. By explicitly valuing pollution control outputs, emissions trading creates an *incentive* for firms to apply their expertise in the service of pollution control goals. Yet it is the competitive pressures of the marketplace that "*force* them to integrate pollution control into traditional corporate decision making."[10] Environmental compliance becomes another of the same genre of problems industry is used to dealing with: How do you, given these constraints, meet these goals at least cost and maximize profitability? As a result, compliance is no longer viewed with distaste by top corporate management because instead of being only a "fixed" cost, as with command and control, environmental compliance represents an opportunity to gain advantage over competitors (interviews with industry 1/21/94; 2/22/94; state regulator 1/12/94).

Government-imposed markets further facilitated the transformation of industry behavior by including compliance deadlines. By the program's start date in 1995, utilities had to demonstrate that their pollution emissions either matched or were less than their legal allotment of pollution allowances. The deadline was accompanied by automatic noncompliance penalties. The default provision created a litigation disincentive by changing industry's payoff from a strategy of resistance during rulemaking. With the acid rain program

[t]he utility industry has no reason to litigate. Why? We have [program] deadlines to meet. . . . From our standpoint, it pays to cut a deal. OK, so you can't get everything you wanted. In the past, if we didn't get everything we

wanted, we'd comment on the federal register rulemaking, then we'd litigate, then we'd appeal the litigation, then we'd appeal the appeal, we'd go on forever. In the meantime, . . . we wouldn't have to spend money on compliance. . . . [W]hen a scrubber costs a $100 million, . . . even in Washington, you can buy an awful lot of lawyer time. . . . You can go years before you have to pay for one scrubber. . . . That's not the case anymore. The law says "deadline." You don't meet it, you're in violation. I don't care what the reason is, you're in violation. So now it is in our interest to make sure the rules are out, to make sure they're as good as they can be and then live with them. . . . I know you wouldn't necessarily want to know the day on which you're going to die, but in my industry knowledge of specifics and knowing what you have to do is sometimes worth more than whatever it costs to get there.[11]

The new payoff was automatic noncompliance penalties that not only hurt financially—$2,000 for each allowance-ton of excess emissions (versus a market value of less than $200 per allowance-ton)— but also forced utilities to forfeit their property rights to an equivalent number of pollution allowances in the following year.[12] The second measure ultimately limited production capacity. From industry's perspective, choosing litigation was analogous to "shooting yourself in the foot" since it would not change the compliance obligation, but would remove the opportunity to comply using a least-cost trading scheme (interviews with EPA 1/12/94; 1/13/94). The acid rain program was therefore expected to have a measurable effect on the use of a conflict-oriented strategy by industry: a substantial reduction in the amount of litigation (interviews with EPA 1/11/94; industry 2/22/94).

A final factor anticipated to minimize private-sector resistance was the presence of fewer rules. GIMs minimize traditional points of conflict in the areas of permitting and applicable control technologies by making "[i]mplementation . . . [less] depend[ent] on substantive EPA rulemaking or EPA decisions on individual compliance approaches. . . . [Instead,] absolute responsibility for achieving the required sulfur dioxide reductions [rests] directly on each utility unit" (U.S. Congress. Senate. Senate Report Card 1993, 90). By transferring responsibilities, traditional industry complaints—over suboptimal control technologies, or the uncertainties of the permitting process that negatively affect a firm's long-term planning processes, or the fact that rules may be targeting the least polluting part of the plant or the part of the manufacturing process where reducing emissions is most costly—lose merit because if mistakes are made, industry has only itself to blame. Much like the laws of physics, where the presence of friction creates additional energy demands, giving industry fewer decision points to react against offers fewer opportunities for friction to develop (see Mashaw and Harfst 1990, 228).

Regulators and environmentalists perceived that transforming business into a more constructive player during rulemaking and implementation would redound to their benefit as well. First, the timeliness of rule implementation was likely to improve, given less "friction" and less litigation (U.S. Congress. Senate. Senate Report Card 1993, 90).

Second, public sector enforcement costs were expected to decline, given less litigation and because the combination of results-oriented public control and immediate, significant financial penalties for noncompliance redefined the concept of compliance. Instead of a resource-intensive, multiple-checkpoint game, compliance under GIMs "revolved completely around whether or not on the expected date of the requirement [for emissions reductions] . . . you were reducing your emissions or not. If you were, you were in. If you weren't, you were going to be subject to really draconian sanctions" (interviews with environmentalist 1/7/94; EPA 1/11/94). The measure of compliance— whether polluters had enough allowances in their checkbooks to cover their emissions—was such a specific, unambiguous requirement that "[r]egulatory intervention . . . can be targeted surgically on noncompliers; the vast majority of sources, those that comply, are not burdened with costly regulatory transactions, nor are precious regulatory resources diverted by the need to impose redundant reviews of each complying source's compliance strategy" (Goffman 1993b, 2).

Third, introducing compliance cost savings into the regulatory equation created opportunities for shared savings, providing additional environmental benefits. National environmental advocates consider the shared-savings concept critical to the expanded use of market-based regulatory mechanisms. "[I]f industry and government are willing to include shared savings as a basic design principle, they'll see more environmentalists hopping aboard the markets bandwagon" (interview with environmentalist 2/11/94; 1/13/94). An EPA official involved in the acid rain program and the certification of the Southern California RECLAIM program noted that in both cases environmental groups told industry point-blank, "If we're going to allow you this additional flexibility to save money and take some risks as to whether this program will work, then we want part of the savings to go toward the environment" (interview 1/13/94). The acid rain program's "shared" savings with the environment equaled three million tons of *additional* pollution reduction (approximate) (interviews with environmentalist 1/7/94; EPA 1/13/94).

Fourth, regulators perceived that the acid rain program decreased the ability of all parties to blame the bureaucracy for program failure.[13]

The acid rain program "took the uncertainty off the government and put it on industry. . . . [In the past,] if things were delayed [or] . . . if we didn't get environmental protection, it was the government's fault. What we wanted to do when we wrote this law was turn that equation around. The government didn't create the pollution; the government shouldn't be at fault if it is not cleaned up. The industry created it; the industry should clean it up" (interview with EPA 1/11/94).

Finally, major stakeholders expected to see broader and continuous technology innovation for environmental purposes, thus expanding the range of policy options and increasing the probability of environmental program success over the long term.[14] In the words of a leading EPA official: "It is important to meet environmental goals as efficiently as possible, but that's the easy part and everybody's aware of that. . . . [But] forget why industry is interested in markets and forget economic efficiency. There are more subtle reasons why, from a regulator's perspective, there are advantages to using these market-based approaches. . . . [One] reason is that it is one of the best ways to get technology innovation" (interview 1/13/94).

Market-based mechanisms induce technological innovation by providing both the latitude and incentives for industry to apply its entrepreneurial energies in search of more efficient and more effective environmental technologies.[15] Instead of being constrained by "politicized bureaucratic rulemaking," the enhanced flexibility afforded by markets "helps sources harness the complex, widely dispersed and ever-changing information needed to select optimal [control] strategies, [and] . . . permits sources to respond immediately and directly in applying new ideas and approaches" (Goffman 1993b, 2–3). Likewise, the opportunity to sell the emissions credits gained from increased technology efficiency (i.e., overcontrol) rewards firms for successful innovations. Thus, instead of a regulatory game where "industry hides what they can do because if the regulators find out they'll make me do it, the incentives are flipped over completely, and suddenly it becomes useful to be able to do it" (interview with environmentalist 1/13/94). Further, the incentive to innovate is not confined to the regulated community, given that "the whole market is open to whoever can develop a better mousetrap. . . . Instead of just having a few folks at EPA trying to find a solution, . . . millions of people who have the lure of potential profit [will be] engaged in finding solutions to environmental problems."[16]

Policy options multiply because compliance planners have the freedom to choose from a virtually unlimited array of technologies and approaches (interview with EPA 1/11/94). In the acid rain program, industry can choose from a broad assortment of single technologies, or they can opt for various packages of technologies such as high-sulfur coal and emissions allowances; or lower efficiency scrubbers, allowances, and low-sulfur coal; or fuel mixing, where natural gas and coal are cofired. This opens up a new market for middling technologies able to reduce emissions by 25 percent, or 50 percent, or 70 percent "because in a market-based system like this they're useful, and they're not useful in the command-and-control system which says, 'Either you're uncovered, in which case you can belch away, or you're covered, in which case you have to meet 95 percent'" (interviews with environmentalist 1/13/94; EPA 1/13/94). Markets also allow compliance planners to fine-tune the timing of their control-technology investment decisions. Instead of being locked in to a bureaucratically imposed deadline for a technology application, industry can choose short-term emissions-trading and banking strategies until more efficient or less costly capital-intensive control technologies become available (interview with EPA 1/11/94). As well, industry may find it more cost effective to reduce emissions by tinkering with *existing* control technologies or making changes in technologies not traditionally associated with the business of pollution control, such as equipment valves, pipe connections, and so on (interviews with industry 4/14/94; 2/22/94; EPA 12/10/93).

All of these factors affect the investment climate for environmental technologies in a positive manner. Investment uncertainty diminishes because government regulators no longer "make the market" through their control over best available control technology (BACT) certification. Investment bankers are thus able to avoid the "what is BACT today may not be BACT tomorrow" syndrome—a key reason for lagging rates of investment in environmental technologies over the past decade.[17] Hence, market risk is more understandable to investors, given that the success of a particular technology is tied more directly to technical efficiency and cost-effectiveness factors than to seemingly arbitrary decisions of regulators. Moreover, although the demand for innovation is still partly dependent on the passage of new laws, the continuous innovation dynamic (especially the "time-shifting" feature) is likely to smooth the severe market volatility associated with command-and-control arrangements. Instead of punctuated equilibriums (narrow windows of opportunities targeted on mandated deadlines and precipitous falloff in demand once deadlines are passed), market demand for control technologies is likely to be spread more evenly over time. Investor risk is lessened since they have longer time frames in which to recapture investment returns on specialized plant and machinery equipment, human resource training, and so on. Environmental technology innovation should accelerate in both cases, since relative decreases in financial risk should push lending rates down and contribute to lower cost compliance technologies.

In each of these cases, the market-based flexibility central to a government-imposed market was instrumental in transforming industry into a more compliant, willing participant in the regulatory process. Resistance and delay on the part of the regulated community and their allies were expected to be minimized by the prospect of lower compliance costs, relative freedom from government direction once the game started (vis-à-vis command and control), a more rational regulatory framework, the possibility that environmental compliance activities might be a new way to establish competitive advantage, and avoidance of draconian noncompliance penalties. Meanwhile, anticipated ancillary benefits flowing from the new incentive structure gave environmental advocates and regulators reasons of their own to support the acid rain GIM: the promise of quicker environmental results, shared savings with the environment, a higher likelihood of broader and accelerated development of environmental technologies, a lower incidence of blame affixed by industry and their allies in congress, and reduced enforcement-based transaction costs.

Of more interest to regulators and environmentalists, however, was the inclusion of components designed to decrease the uncertainty surrounding the capture of the environmental gains (results) implied by the acid rain emissions-trading program.

> The acid rain program was a bargain that environmentalists were willing to take a risk on. We wanted a program with big environmental reductions, and this market-based program promised it. But our support was conditional. If we couldn't get the parts of the program that guaranteed environmental results, like the cap on emissions, more stringency in the monitoring system, and so on, the deal was off (interview with environmentalist 2/11/94).

INCREASING THE CERTAINTY OF ENVIRONMENTAL RESULTS

Government-imposed markets include an emissions "cap." Emissions caps set an aggregate limit on the pollutant being regulated. Defining program goals in such a way provides a clear advantage to those stakeholders most concerned with environmental protection: since "you know how many tons are going to be emitted into the air, . . . there is a lot more certainty that program goals will be reached."[18] Within the context of acid rain legislation, it is doubtful that a bill without an emissions cap on sulfur dioxide emissions would have succeeded. National environmentalists consider this a fundamental precondition to their support of market-based programs (interviews with environmentalists 1/8/94; 1/13/94; 2/11/94).

Regulators anticipated additional transaction cost savings in the areas of information search, program specification, and program negotiation when the regulatory game focuses on environmental results. In particular, regulators expected to avoid the continual writing and negotiation mode associated with command and control (see Chapter 3). An example using the 1990 Clean Air Act Amendments is illustrative. Title I specified tougher standards for "new" stationary sources and "lower[ed] the definition of what constitutes a major source [which] results in much broader coverage of the New Source Review program."[19] Under a command-and-control scenario, increasing the stringency of emissions-reduction goals makes the regulatory task more difficult, since regulators generally lack basic information regarding control technologies able to meet the new Clean Air Act mandates. Therefore, regulators have to collect pertinent information. Yet the information search process entails a transaction-cost-intensive industry-by-industry game of technology specification and bargaining, the effect of which is only magnified by forcing regulators to include more sources within the definition of major sources. A market-based program, on the other hand, does not require regulators to gather detailed information on control technologies. Instead, regulators can specify a schedule of gradual reductions and then "get out of the way," thus minimizing the need for resource-intensive negotiations with industry.[20]

Some regulators also believed that shifting the basic focus of regulatory activity from source-specific to aggregate levels of pollution could help to minimize the high "sunk costs" in personnel (industry-dedicated pollution control specialists) and organizational structure (a rigid, multiunit structure) associated with command-and-control arrangements (see Chapter 2) (interviews with state regulator 3/1/94; EPA 1/11/94). While the types of expertise remained the same—engineers, instrumentation specialists, chemists, field inspectors, and so on—their expertise would be applied in a more generalist fashion *across* industries. At the same time, the GIM arrangement offered regulators an opportunity to collapse agency structure from multiple organizational units, each with a narrow industry-specific mission, into a more streamlined organization.

From the regulators' perspective, these changes were significant. Generalists and a streamlined organization offered the potential for enhanced agency responsiveness to external variations in demand for regulatory services. As demand varied, expert resources could be "flexed" (transferred) from one area to another more readily and at lower organizational cost than with a comparable command-and-control-based arrangement. In addition, regulators anticipated lower administrative costs. Given that human resources could be utilized across a broader array of tasks, fewer people would be needed to accomplish the overall regulatory mission. Finally, overhead operating expenses could be reduced by eliminating the duplication of tasks, personnel, and physical infrastructure (i.e., copiers, office space, etc.) found under the command-and-control multiunit, industry-by-industry organizational structure.

However, even given these expected benefits, there was still the matter of ensuring accountability. Major players in national pollution control politics, other than a few neoclassically trained economists and some Republican party ideologues, did not believe that market-based mechanisms were self-enforcing. Most believed that devolving authority for compliance decisions to private-sector agents reinforces the information asymmetry favoring industry, thus giving industry additional opportunity to misrepresent private information (i.e., shirk) (Kettl 1993; Miller 1992, 213–14). Therefore, regulators, environmentalists, and powerful players in congress, many of whom have staked their reputations on being in the vanguard of the command-and-control movement, were unwilling to let markets go forward without quid pro quos in the area of clearly specified property rights and rigorous monitoring systems. Otherwise, the environmental results implied by the emissions cap were virtually meaningless, since regulators would have no way of measuring and enforcing the GIM program.[21]

Solving the problem of measurement and enforceability, however, entails development of an emissions inventory, an airshed budget, and an emissions and allowance tracking system. An emissions inventory provides information on the mix of industry contributing to the pollution problem and the levels of pollution contributed by individual industrial facilities. An airshed budget (nationally, regionally, facility-wide) sets the emissions "cap"—the upper bounds of the emissions inventory—and allocates the regulatory burden[22] among polluters.

The emissions and allowance-tracking system is a way to keep everything straight. It provides a way to monitor allowance trading and pollution emissions—the two chief prerequisites of a legally enforceable system of pollution-based property rights. In both the RECLAIM and acid rain market-based programs, industry reports emissions-allowance trades to centralized data banks and must install continuous emissions monitors (CEMs) to physically track emissions. Acid rain program rules require emission data points every fifteen minutes and the electronic transmission of this data to EPA. The tracking system, thus defined, serves four main purposes. It monitors the aggregate level of emissions, allowing regulators to assess whether the emissions budget is balanced. The tracking system also provides a way for regulators to assess whether enforcement action is needed, since the database tracks allowances held by individual polluters and actual levels of pollution being emitted. In this way, regulators know which polluters are in compliance and which are not. Moreover, regulators can use this data to monitor the distribution of pollution. An important concern here is whether "hot spots"—high density concentrations of pollution sources posing high human health risks —exist. Finally, rigorous emissions monitoring creates a database protecting the buyers of emissions credits. Claims of pollution reductions made by sellers can be verified against the database, thus providing more certainty in the allowance-trading marketplace (i.e., prevents counterfeiting).

The preferred type of "rigorous" monitoring system requires the installation of CEMs on individual sources and automatic electronic reporting of emissions data to the regulatory agency in charge of the program.[23] More generally, however, an acceptable monitoring system means an emissions-monitoring technology that is replicable within a reasonable margin of statistical error (EPA, Mayer, Great Lakes RETC 1994), or a program where the incidence of physical inspections and data-reporting requirements are markedly higher than in a comparable command-and-control program.[24] Achieving this degree of accuracy often means that market-based monitoring programs closely resemble a command-and-control approach. In the case of the acid rain program, "this is the area where there is the highest degree of specificity" (interview with EPA 1/11/94).

Making the trade-off of flexibility for a more intensive monitoring regime says nothing about the transaction costs encountered by regulators in making such a system credible. Conventional wisdom has always suggested that market-based approaches increase public sector monitoring costs. In fact, with the acid rain program, most stakeholders perceived this to be the case, given the resource-intensive nature of the tasks required to make the monitoring system credible—setting up the allowance-trading tracking system, increasing the frequency of reporting and site inspection requirements, and analyzing the massive amounts of data produced by the system. Yet several players in the acid rain drama suggested that monitoring costs do not always increase or, at a minimum, that there is much less of a relative increase in transaction costs in contrast to command and control than conventional wisdom admits. Regulators involved with the Southern California RECLAIM program and with acid rain, where CEMs and electronic data reporting are mandated, perceive that their program monitoring costs are lower than those in a command-and-control-based approach (interviews with state regulator 3/1/94; EPA 1/11/94).[25] There is also anecdotal evidence of industry's willingness to pay monitoring costs that traditionally have been borne by the public sector in exchange for a more flexible, market-based, or averaging-based program.[26] Further, even when stakeholders perceive that GIMs increase government's monitoring costs, they are quick to point out the various side benefits accompanying the creation of emissions inventories and more rigorous monitoring systems. Benefits include higher quality databases that create a basis for better rules in the long run,[27] a wider application of CEMs that help regulators establish a higher threshold of credibility and accountability,[28] and, in theory, the potential for windfall environmental benefits.[29]

THE SPECIAL CASE OF CONGRESS AS STAKEHOLDER

The consensus over the acid rain GIM program ultimately provided a vehicle by which individual members and majority party leaders in congress could achieve more of their bottom lines as well. Government-imposed markets are uniquely suited to serve a broad variety of electoral connection needs for individual legislators, both inside and outside of the majority party in congress. In a congress whose everyday dynamic is increasingly shaped by the reality of deficit politics (Kettl 1993) and concerns over international economic competitiveness, regulatory programs that solve policy problems using least-cost methods of compliance while limiting the role of government are attractive to fiscal and regulatory reform-oriented conservatives who typically have little interest in supporting environmental protection. At the same time, the Bush Administration's acid rain proposal provided a window of opportunity for legislators concerned with the environment to move forward on an issue that had become "the" crucible of environmental progress during the 1980s. Finally, market-based environmental policy can protect the electoral connection of other legislators by minimizing their risk exposure to heterogeneous district constituencies. Especially in cases where there is an approximate balance among competing interests, hence a high degree of uncertainty as to which policy vote holds the greatest electoral payoff, political value accrues to pragmatic policy solutions able to satisfy preferences across diverse constituencies. Government-imposed markets thus provide some politicians with a way to hedge their bets by promising environmental quality while at the same time displaying sensitivity to the cost concerns of the business community (interview with congressional staff, 1/18/94).

Moreover, by successfully bridging the gaps among competing sets of interests, the acid rain GIM helped facilitate the two main goals of Democratic (majority) party leaders in congress: "to help formulate and pass the party's policy agenda and to maintain the party's majority in Congress" (Canon 1992, 9). Achieving these goals requires successful coalition building in support of party goals (where "success" includes final passage of said law) and sensitivity to the policy needs of individual legislators (Jones 1981; Sinclair 1983). As just discussed, government-imposed markets meet the test of sensitivity quite well. Further, by attracting such widespread support, markets eased the leadership's coalition-building task. Not having to devote as many coalition-building resources in support of acid rain meant they were able to target scarce resources toward some of the more problematic titles (e.g., mobile sources and air toxics), thus helping to ensure passage of the act.

In terms of majority party goals, delivering new clean air legislation and a legislative solution to acid rain, in particular, had long been a priority item on the Democratic party policy agenda.[30] A new Clean Air Act provided an opportunity to advertise this fact, as well as the long history of party support for pollution control more generally. Even if President Bush walked away with much of the credit, it still served an overarching institutional need directly connected to the majority party goal of maintaining control of congress. Passing acid rain legislation helped to satisfy the public clamor to get something done.[31] Democratic party leaders were thus able to show that congress was responsive to the general public. Given the Democrats' long, virtually unbroken tenure as the majority party in both chambers of congress and their inevitable identification with legislative success or failure, the success of clean air legislation was likely to help them maintain their majority in congress.

TAKING RISKS WITH PLURALISM BY THE RULES

The general problem of policy innovation for stakeholders was that the rancorous history of environmental politics and traditional actor preferences for specific types of regulatory arrangements other than government-imposed markets introduced considerable uncertainty into the long-range policy picture. Participants to the deal simply had no way of knowing whether the "other" side was sincere in their willingness to forgo past preferred positions, or whether they were only waiting until later in the policy process to reconstruct the deal more to their liking. Thus, while there was clear agreement that the GIM bridged the gaps among interests in this case, there was also a high degree of uncertainty that naturally accompanies such an innovative accord throughout the policy process. In addition, as described in Chapter 2, lawmaking in congress is a riskier, more uncertain proposition today than in years past. Successfully pushing the arrangement through the legislative gauntlet and beyond required the presence of certain conditions aiding the manageability and legitimacy of the game, committed political leadership in both houses of congress, the use of unconventional lawmaking methods, and explicit legislative language which locked in key parameters of the market-oriented program.

MANAGEABILITY AND LEGITIMACY

The deliberations surrounding acid rain fit the "rule" concerning transaction-specific conditions. A decade of deadlock created an opening for an innovative solution to the problem of acid rain. The lack of progress using traditional command-and-control proposals motivated key members of the environmental lobby to develop a new, more politically palatable market-based program. The incorporation of markets without the sacrifice of environmental gains earned the explicit sponsorship of the Bush Administration as well as the blessing of key congressional leaders from Senate Majority Leader George Mitchell to Rep. Henry Waxman and John Dingell in the house. As well, by clearly defining the major parameters of the regulatory program, the final legislation ensured that the primary concern of the rulemaking process would be with how the program would be implemented, rather than what the program goals and standards should be.

Policy implications were, for the most part, limited programmatically to the EPA Air Office, specifically to the utility industry, and geographically to the Midwest and Eastern United States, the areas of the country suffering from the highest concentrations of acid rain production and impact.

There were no hard and fast deadlines driving the legislative stage of acid rain deliberation, but there were clear, consistent signals from political and interest-group leaders on all sides of the debate that this was a "must do" agenda item. During rulemaking the process was facilitated by deadlines similar to those found in the reformulated gasoline program: a congressional deadline for a final rule and a statutory deadline specifying the program's start date. Of most importance, particularly for industry, was how the design of the acid rain program—the linkage among the market, compliance deadline, and penalty components—created incentives to accelerate rather than stymie the rulemaking process.

Interests were readily identifiable, with major interest groupings centered in the environmental community, the coal industry, the utility industry, and EPA and state regulators. The environmental lobby, despite initial reservations by some members of the National Clean Air Coalition, gave strong support to the original Bush–EDF proposal and to subsequent negotiating decisions taken by representatives from EDF and NRDC during the legislative and rulemaking phases of the policy process. EPA leadership from Administrator Reilly, Assistant Administrator Rosenberg, and Eileen Brenneman, the Air Office manager in charge of the acid rain rulemaking, were sufficient not only to overcome initial Air Office objections to the Bush–EDF proposal, but to sustain agency cohesiveness such that by the end of the rulemaking key career officials formerly opposed to the program evinced strong support for the plan. Cohesiveness for the utility industry was more problematic. Power producers split into two broad categories: those in opposition (known as the "dirties") and those more willing to support the market-based package as a reasonable, cost-efficient alternative (the "progressives").

A factual database was available to frame policy discussions and resolve most major issues. Evidence from earlier market-based pollution control programs supported cost-savings claims, while the political embrace of markets by environmentalists signaled a willingness to accept such claims as fact. Utilities were clearly a primary source of the pollutants responsible for acid rain. Significant improvements in continuous emissions-monitoring technologies, supported by extensive testing data, facilitated the resolution of pollution measurement and program assessment issues.[32]

Fundamental values did not appear to be at stake in this case either. The Bush–EDF proposal codified the level of environmental protection that the national environmental lobby was supporting. This victory was backed by a second layer of statutory protection: individual utilities could not purchase additional emissions allowances if regulators determined that such a purchase violated ambient air quality standards designed to protect human health. Utility industry stakeholders, long accustomed to the protection from competition afforded by government control over pricing and market share, were hard put to argue against additional government intervention on philosophical grounds. At the same time, industry opposition to the acid rain program stemmed more from the belief that acid rain was a nonproblem with respect to the environment than from opposition to the market-based plan per se. Industry officials consistently lauded the market-based program's sensitivity to their concerns over efficiency and autonomy. Moreover, despite the added compliance costs imposed by acid rain regulations, utilities faced no imminent danger of going out of business, given their protected status within the state-level system of public utility commissions.

MANAGING UNCERTAINTY THROUGH UNCONVENTIONAL LAWMAKING

Both houses of congress used unconventional lawmaking to move acid rain and the Clean Air Act amendments through the legislative process. Inside the U. S. House of Representatives, John Dingell, chair of the Energy and Commerce Committee, was unable to craft a Clean Air Act consistent with his proindustry preferences. From the beginning Dingell was forced to engage in lengthy backroom negotiations with the two principal subcommittee chairs—Henry Waxman (Health and Environment) and Philip Sharp (Energy and Power). These private negotiating sessions "produced most of the substantive work on the [clean air] bill, . . . [including] surprise, broad-ranging agreements on the four major titles of the bill: urban smog, motor vehicles, acid rain, and air toxics" (Hager 1990b, 1551).

Of even more interest was the way they chose to enforce their bargains. Each legislator was generally confident of having the votes to prevail on the floor of the house, but none was willing to risk the possibility of damaging amendments at the floor stage. The fear of uncertainty prompted them to bind their compromise agreements all the way through conference with the senate (Hager 1990a, 1062; 1990c, 1643–45). Yet Dingell, Waxman, and Sharp knew that binding committee agreements on a bill of such major importance were probably not enough to ensure safe passage through the uncertain waters of congressional decision making. There were early indications that the bill might run into trouble on the floor and later in conference because the house had not invited the White House to sit in on their backroom negotiations as the senate had done. Concern was that the White House might use that as an excuse to "play a wild-card role" on any compromises with which they disagreed (Hager 1990a, 1058). The key players in the house therefore enlisted the support of the leadership via the Rules Committee. Specifically, the Rules Committee was asked to grant a restrictive rule to help keep their bargains intact. The Rules Committee did just that when they issued House Resolution 399 on May 23, 1990. H. R. 399 protected the committee agreements by preventing amendments to the four major bargains in the areas of urban smog, automobile tailpipe standards and inspection and maintenance programs for motor vehicles, air toxics, and acid rain.[33]

Unconventional lawmaking was evident in other areas as well, particularly activist majority party leadership. House Speaker Thomas Foley is credited with forging a key compromise on the floor of the house between Dingell and Waxman on the matter of a "production mandate" for clean cars (Hager 1990c, 1645). Further, the leadership structured the timing of bill referrals to Ways and Means and the Public Works committees in such a way that made it difficult for them to thoroughly assess the massive 1,000-plus-page bill and committee report, much less devise effective responses to encroachments on their respective jurisdictions.[34] Finally, many house members feared that Dingell "still harbor[ed] a desire to stall or even kill the [clean air] bill" and that he was only waiting until the conference proceedings "to force weakening changes in the legislation" (Hager 1990d, 2291). In hopes of forestalling such an outcome, the house leadership took action that gave it the leverage it would need to "roll over Dingell" if he tried to circumvent their wishes to see the bill produced in a timely fashion. The leadership sent Dingell a clear message of their intent to protect the deal by creating an inordinately large, diverse conference delegation consisting of more than 130 members from eight different committees, some of whom were Dingell's "bitter philosophical enemies" (p. 2292). Dingell, in fact, delayed the conference with the senate by more than a month in an attempt to exclude house members hostile to his own viewpoint. In the end, however, Speaker Foley intervened on behalf of the house rank-and-file members and allowed them to participate in conference proceedings.[35]

The net result of all this unconventional lawmaking was an "easy" house vote for "a sweeping rewrite of the nation's clean air laws. . . . The long-awaited floor showdown that some lobbyists had promoted as the environmental vote of the decade evolved at times into a bipartisan love-in, with members clamoring to take credit for a series of compromise amendments that passed largely on overwhelming votes."[36]

Meanwhile, over in the senate, Majority Leader George Mitchell stripped the Environment and Public Works Committee of jurisdiction and entered into backroom negotiations with the minority party leadership, key Environmental and Public Works Committee leaders and members, and the White House (Cohen 1992; Bryner 1993). The compromise was introduced as the Mitchell–Dole substitute in the form of an amendment to replace the original committee bill on clean air. This negotiated version eventually passed the senate on April 7, 1990, by an 89–11 margin.[37] Like Rep. Dingell, Majority Leader Mitchell tried to reduce the uncertainty of lawmaking by binding the participants in the backroom bargaining process to support the deal through the floor stage. Another part of the Mitchell–Dole–White House strategy for protecting their clean air deal centered on a signaling game that provided clear decision cues for other legislators. Any amendments threatening major changes were identified as "dealbusters" capable of killing clean air legislation and therefore to be voted down. The "dealbuster" strategy succeeded in all cases but one.[38]

In short, senate behavior was as unconventional as house lawmaking activities in the case of acid rain and clean air. Both examples provide additional corroboration for the general thesis proposed by others—the committee system as traditionally conceived is increasingly unable to manage lawmaking in a postreform congress whose most common element is high transaction costs. Therefore, majority party leaders and (sub)committee chairs with jurisdictional authority over a particular bill are taking advantage of the power void, choosing unconventional institutions to minimize uncertainty and help ensure successful passage of major legislation.

FINALIZING THE DEAL WITH EXPLICIT LEGISLATIVE LANGUAGE

Paradoxically, at the same time unconventional lawmaking reduces the uncertainty of congressional decision making, its ad hoc nature increases uncertainty by introducing broad variation into the timing and procedural rules of the legislative game. One way to minimize these uncertainties is "to craft legislation in explicit terms. Bargains or winning positions can be set in concise terms so each member involved in the negotiations has some certainty about the ultimate legislative product" (Khademian 1993, 12). The operating principle becomes "trust, but verify" that legislation is structured so as to guarantee results throughout the policy process (interview with congressional staff, 1/18/94).

Again, the acid rain bargain is a case in point. As already described, there was a broad consensus among key legislators that a market approach to acid rain was desirable so long as they could somehow guarantee the results implied by the GIM. Therefore, legislators went to great lengths to protect the integrity of critical program elements with explicit legislative language (interviews with congressional staff, 1/7/94; 1/18/94; state regulator 1/12/94). In the words of a senior EPA official: "This program was worked out in great detail during the debate in congress. ... [A] lot of the issues ... are specified in the legislation" (interview 1/13/94).

Two of the more important issues settled in congress along these lines concern the allocation of emissions allowances, or pollution property rights, and the rules for trading allowances. Title IV includes not only specific "baseline" formulas that allocate emissions among utilities, but also a list of all Phase I utilities along with their allowance entitlements. There is an explicit rejection of any permanent transfer of pollution property rights to the private sector. The issue of how new power plants and clean states will access the allowance market in future years is clearly specified as well. Further, the statute provides a reserve pool of allowances designed to add liquidity to the allowance market. The intent is to help "jump-start the market," thus accelerating the use of trading and increasing the probability of lower compliance costs in the early years of the program. As part of this, congress mandated that EPA hold auctions on a yearly basis.

Another example of statutory specificity centers on congressional concern for the credibility of the market-based system. "[Congress] had a lot of questions about how do you certify the trades? What are the possibilities of cheating? What will the document look like? When I get an allowance, will I be able to counterfeit it? We had detailed discussions about these issues because we were worried that if the system could be skirted [i.e., "gamed"], then we had nothing. The deal was only as good as the paper it was written on" (interview with congressional staff 3/18/94). In the end, congress reduced the uncertainty surrounding these questions by explicitly mandating the most rigorous monitoring technology available (continuous emissions monitors), increasing the frequency of reporting emissions data, requiring instantaneous electronic reporting directly to the EPA, and requiring a central EPA-based allowance-tracking system.

IMPLEMENTING THE ACID RAIN PROGRAM: PRELIMINARY EVIDENCE OF REDUCED TRANSACTION COSTS

Few pollution control programs have had greater expectations of results, both environmental and economic, than the acid rain program of the 1990 Clean Air Act. Although it is still too early to pass definitive judgment on the program's performance, preliminary results are in keeping with stakeholder expectations of transaction cost savings.

Emissions reductions are occurring earlier and are greater than expected, as many utilities have chosen to overcontrol their emissions during Phase I (years 1995–2000) (U.S. Congress. Senate. Senate Report Card 1993, 73). After receiving utility permit applications and reviewing Phase I compliance plans, EPA estimates that a total of 11–13 million tons of allowances will be banked during Phase I (EPA 1994, 17).

Compliance cost savings are greater than expected and almost "an order of magnitude lower" than pre-1990 scrubber-based compliance costs.[39] Initial "prerule" EPA analyses predicted that emissions trading would reduce annualized compliance costs by approximately 20 percent, or $1 billion, versus a traditional command-and-control approach once the program was fully operational (U.S. Congress. Senate. Senate Report No. 228 1989, 303). The estimated yearly cost of the emissions trading program—$4 billion—was based on expected allowance values in the range of $500 to $700 per allowance (Fulton 1992). Yet emissions allowances traded in the range of $150 to $450 per allowance at the first EPA-sponsored Chicago Board of Trade auction in March 1993, was even lower during the March 1994 auction (U.S. Congress. Senate. Senate Report Card 1993, 73), while the (weighted) average successful bid during the March 1997 auction was $110.36. In February 1994, EPA revised their compliance cost estimates. They now project annualized utility compliance costs in the range of $2.2 billion, more than 50 percent less than command and control (USEPA 1994, 18).[40] Some individual utilities are actually experiencing "negative compliance costs. . . . The total costs of generating electricity while reducing SO_2 emissions [are] less than they had been to emit SO_2 at significantly higher levels" (Keenan testimony, U.S. Congress. Senate. Acid Rain Hearings 1993, 130). Senator Joseph Leiberman (D-Conn), in his opening statement to the acid rain implementation hearings, notes the significance of these developments: "This . . . may be the first time in the history of the [Senate Environment and Public Works] Committee that industry witnesses will actually discuss how a new congressional mandate is decreasing the cost of pollution control" (p. 2).

Stakeholders have also observed a distinct change in the attitudes of industry during implementation. Rather than adopting their typical obstructionist pose, the utility industry has been forthcoming with information, willing to help pay for a more rapid installation of EPA's allowance-tracking system, and has been the moderating force in settlement negotiations (interviews with environmentalist 1/7/94; EPA 1/11/94). Likewise, industry has rechanneled its expertise into making the market work; "Rather than seeing themselves as victims of legislative environmental excess, [utility managers] have worked quickly to understand and exploit the leverage which the market provided them" (Keenan testimony, U.S. Congress. Senate. Acid Rain Hearings 1993, 133). Further, litigation on program rules has been minimal and has covered relatively minor issues in all but a few instances.[41] These developments suggest that the market dynamic as well as the independence of the compliance obligation from the trading program are having their expected effect. In other words, they minimize resistance and delay by diverting industry energies into constructive activities precisely because the payoffs for a resistance-based strategy are not what they used to be.

Expectations in the area of accelerated technological innovation are also being met. New control technologies, improved efficiencies and modifications of existing technologies, innovative own–build–operate scrubber management arrangements, and "the sudden emergence of middling technologies . . . that take 40 percent out, or 50 percent, or 60 percent of the emissions out" are ascribed to the use of markets in the acid rain program (interviews with environmentalist 1/13/94; EPA 1/11/94). For example, "[m]ost of the scrubbers being built in Phase I at existing plants have sulfur-removal efficiencies greater than the 90 percent reduction required at new plants by the New Source Performance Standards. In fact, the vendor at one plant is guaranteeing 98 percent sulfur removal. Additionally, at other [older] facilities, where it was previously not thought possible, utilities are finding ways to burn the very-low-sulfur Powder River Basin coal or to burn mixtures of coal and natural gas" (EPA, Shapiro testimony, U.S. Congress. Senate. Acid Rain hearings 1993, 45–46).[42]

Finally, regulators are convinced that EPA resource needs are less than what they would have been under a comparable command-and-control arrangement. Although there are almost 2,000 people in the EPA Air Office (headquarters and regions) and an estimated 20,000 government regulators nationwide charged with specifying, monitoring, and enforcing air pollution regulations, there are less than 100 people total involved in acid rain program implementation (including state-level personnel). Yet the acid rain program

> will get over 40 percent of the emission reductions under the Clean Air Act. . . . That's because [it is cutting] 10 million tons of SO_2 and 2 million tons of NO_x. . . . Granted, air toxics are worse [from a health-based perspective], and you can't always compare pollutants on a pound-for-pound basis. But still, that's a huge segment of the reduction that's going to be done by only a few percent of the people. The ability to get that kind of leverage in emissions reduction is just phenomenal. . . . That's a tremendous government benefit for resources applied (interview with EPA 1/11/94).

In sum, there is not only widespread consensus among major stakeholders that government-imposed markets minimize transaction costs; preliminary evidence indicates that these lower costs translate into stakeholders meeting more of their own organizational goals. Environmentalists get more of the public good of environmental quality. Industry experiences lower pollution control compliance costs, thus making for a healthier bottom line. EPA is viewed as a more effective advocate for environmental protection while expending fewer resources, while politicians seeking reelection can claim credit for a successful government program.

Therefore, it is not surprising that stakeholders across the board view the acid rain program as a successful enterprise (interview with utility industry official 1/21/94). One stakeholder describes EPA Air Office attitudes in terms of "loving the acid rain program. . . . The Office of Policy, Analysis, and Review in the Air Office views it as a huge success story. In their minds it is a classic example of trading working" (interview with EPA 1/10/94). Deputy Assistant Administrator Michael Shapiro reports that EPA is "happy with the market program" because it contains all the "prerequisites" for a successful regulatory program: "accountability, enforceability, and meaningful penalties" (U.S. Congress. Senate. Acid Rain Hearings 1993, 48). Congress awarded acid rain program implementation an "A" in November 1993 at the same time that it graded EPA's overall Clean Air Act implementation effort as a "B–" (U.S. Congress. Senate. Senate Report Card 1993).[43] An EPA official working closely with the implementation of the program says point-blank: "The acid rain program is working. . . . I do not get people calling me up and screaming at me about acid rain. In many ways, it is such a success, it is not even on our radar screens. We spend our time on problems, and the problems tend to be in these other areas where we are still doing it the old-fashioned command-and-control way" (interview 12/10/93).

The acid rain program is by no means a perfect program. It is described by some stakeholding elites as "struggling," "suffering growing pains," and "unclear whether the trading system will ever get off the ground." There are lawsuits on such arcane yet important issues as substitution, reduced utilization, and the level of accuracy required for the continuous emissions monitors. Likewise, it is still unclear in most states whether state public utility commissions, whose policy decisions are critical to the long-term success of the acid rain emissions allowance-trading program, will embrace trading or hamstring it (U.S. Congress. Senate. Acid Rain Hearings 1993; Bohi and Burtraw 1991; GAO 1994b). Others express concerns over whether EPA has adequate expertise in the monitoring, accounting, and data evaluation areas so critical to program success (interview with environmentalist 2/11/94). President Clinton's assistant administrator for the Air Office, Mary Nichols, listed the general lack of EPA expertise in "auditing and accounting . . . the requirements of financial systems" as a key reason why the allowance-tracking system has taken so long to develop (Nichols, letter to Sen. Leiberman 1994). Further, the fact that EPA felt compelled to change one of the core rules in 1993 had a chilling effect on market activity and made clear how quickly uncertainty can be reintroduced into the regulatory picture. Although the chilling effect on the allowance-trading market was short-lived and the substantive importance of the rule "disappears" at year 2000 (once Phase II starts), stakeholders are concerned that EPA's willingness to "change the rules in the middle of the program" will negatively affect industry's willingness to support government-imposed markets in the future (U.S. Congress. Senate. Senate Report Card 1993, 86–87).

Nonetheless, these concerns are set against the background of the larger message sent by stakeholders familiar with the program: acid rain implementation is relatively troublefree, especially when compared to traditional command-and-control-based pollution control programs. In fact, it is working well enough that a broad cross section of stakeholders think congress should give serious consideration to more government-imposed markets in the future.[44] From its initial conception in the Bush White House, through lawmaking, rulemaking, and implementation, the experience of the acid rain GIM challenges important preconceptions of environmental politics. It demonstrates that environment and economy are not necessarily irreconcilable objectives and that erstwhile adversaries can collaborate (and are collaborating) in pursuit of regulatory arrangements offering both more of their own group objectives and the national policy objective of cleaner air. Senator Max Baucus, former chair of the Senate Environment and Public Works Committee, sums it up as follows:

> In the big picture, I view Title IV of the Clean Air Act Amendments as an historic accomplishment in environmental law. As policy, it is an innovative approach to a complicated environmental and economic problem, and it also shows that all who are concerned with the environment can work together (U.S. Congress. Senate. Acid Rain Hearings 1993, 4).

By no means can the collaboration surrounding acid rain be construed as a pure form of collaboration absolutely devoid of conflict. However, when compared against the norm in American pollution control politics—bitter, protracted disputes among interests, between political parties and political institutions—the case of acid rain is striking. It is best characterized as collaborative policy making due to strong bipartisan cooperation in both the House and the Senate, interinstitutional cooperation between the Senate and the White House, early efforts involving the national environmental community and the White House, strong support of the acid rain provisions by environmentalists once it reached congress, the cooperative attitudes of EPA officials during lawmaking, strong support from fiscal conservatives and regulatory reform conservatives, and the tacit support of "progressive" utilities.

Significantly, the design of the government-imposed market was all of a piece with the collaborative behavior of the stakeholders. Market flexibility, streamlined permitting, the emissions cap, rigorous monitoring, automatic penalties, shared savings, and compliance obligations independent of the trading scheme aligned incentives and gave participants tangible stakes in the policy outcome, whether in terms of economic efficiency or environmental results. However, and perhaps more importantly, because the acid rain GIM aligned incentives among organizational players interested in fundamentally different bottom-line goals, the incentive of transaction cost savings was not enough to overcome the collective action dilemma facing decision makers in the postreform congress. In a policy game where bitter adversarialism reigns supreme and opportunities for *ex post* opportunism abound, trust was in short supply. Therefore, assurance mechanisms designed to protect each participants' stake in the outcome were needed to surmount the legislative gauntlet and to minimize the possibility of a reconstructed program later in the policy process. Without such assurances, the probability lessens that even collaborative GIMs will survive the policy process. Hence the glowing, albeit preliminary, reviews of program performance would not be possible, and without proven performance, especially in the area of environmental results, the political future of market-based pollution control mechanisms is questionable (interviews with state regulator 1/12/94; 3/1/94; EPA 1/11/94; 1/13/94; environmentalist 1/13/94; 2/11/94).

CHAPTER NOTES

1. For example, EPA, the Office of Technology Assessment, and industry estimate the costs of acid rain control bills introduced in the 99th Congress to be anywhere from $3 to 9 billion annually for one major bill and as high as $17 billion annually for another. Projected emission reductions from electric utilities corresponding to these cost impacts, made by EPA and the Office of Technology Assessment (OTA), range between 7 and 9 million tons per year for SO_2 and between 2 and 4 million tons per year for NO_x (taken from Clean Air Working Group 1987, 22–23).

2. In 1989, Resources for the Future reported that "a firm scientific consensus on acid rain has not emerged. It seems fairly clear that the acidity in rainfall and in deposited particles is much higher than it used to be, and that the main source of the acid compounds is coal combustion. But the extent and severity of ecosystem damage resulting from acidity are uncertain, especially in terrestrial ecosystems. Also uncertain is the extent to which emissions reductions will help [solve the problems posed by acid deposition]" (Harrington 1989, 11).

3. Cohen (1992, 91); Senator Leiberman, U.S. Congress. Senate. *Report Card on the 1990 Clean Air Act Amendments*, hereinafter cited as U.S. Congress. Senate. Senate Report Card (1993, 1).

4. U.S. Congress. Senate. Acid Rain Hearings (1993); Cohen (1992); Gutfeld (1992); interviews with congressional staff (1/5/94); industry (1/21/94); environmentalist (1/13/94).

5. By most counts, EPA Air Offices have changed dramatically in the past few years and are now much more likely to be advocates of market-based approaches like the one used with acid rain (interviews with EPA 1/7/94; 1/13/94). One stakeholder who has been watching air pollution control politics since the early 1980s characterizes the transformation as follows: "The final administration formulation of the acid rain program was far broader than anything the EPA Air Offices would have ever dreamed of, far broader than anything they were comfortable with, and filled with provisions they would have died on their swords over if it would have done any good. But that was the administration's proposal that was going to congress. We had been waiting ten years for an acid rain bill. It did have a ten-million-ton reduction. This was the big moment and [the Air Office] got behind it, not just with their rhetoric, but in the end with their bodies, hearts, and souls. In the end they found religion. It took me a long time to decide for myself whether they were saying it as faithful civil servants because that was their job, whether they were saying that because they knew where their bread was buttered and that's what their assistant administrator [William Rosenberg] and administrator [William Reilly] wanted, or whether they had really internalized it and believed it. And it wasn't really until Rosenberg was gone and they were still pretty much acting and talking the way they had been, you know, pretty much open and supportive of the acid rain program and other things, that I concluded that they really were sincere. They really had found religion" (interview 1/10/94). See the internal USEPA *Memorandum on Summary and Recommendations Resulting from the Analysis of EDF's Acid Rain Proposal* (June 2, 1989) for a good example of how EPA originally preferred a much more restricted version of the acid rain emissions-trading program.

6. Kreps (1992); Miller (1992); Weingast and Marshall (1988).

7. "Institution" is used in much the same way as regulatory or legislative "contract" and is the same as David Canon's (1992) extension of McCubbins and Sullivan's (1987) work. Institutions are defined as "the rules of the game that constrain individual choices and provide incentives for individual action, with the clarification that this definition encompasses the activities of the leadership" when applied to congress (p. 2).

8. Emissions baseline is defined as the "ambient pollutant concentration level that exists in the baseline area at the time of the applicable baseline date. As only those emissions reductions not currently required by law are creditable, regulatory agencies [or elected officials, as in the case of acid rain] establish an emissions baseline against which surplus reductions can be calculated" (Dudek and Palmisano 1988, 231, footnote 22).

9. Portney (1990, 70–75); Stavins et al. (1991); see Tietenberg (1985) for a survey of studies estimating cost savings of emissions-trading arrangements compared to a command-and-control benchmark.

10. Local regulator, Inman, Great Lakes RETC (1994), emphasis added; interviews with EPA (1/8/94; 1/13/94).

11. Interview with industry (1/21/94).

12. The deterrence penalties within the acid rain program are considered the toughest ever applied to an air pollution control program (Reynolds 1990).

13. According to a veteran EPA decision maker, a chronic problem with command and control is that "nobody ever hears much about the low-cost compliance examples, but you're always going to hear a lot about the high-cost examples. It's a tremendous advantage [for regulators] to be able to say, 'You did not have to pay those high costs. You had a lot of other options. [EPA] gave you the latitude to find another way to do it, so don't say we locked you into doing something which was stupid; we didn't.' That's another reason why EPA has an incentive to pursue market-based programs" (interview 1/13/94).

14. Breyer (1982); Dudek and Palmisano (1988, 216); GAO interview (2/25/94); Kneese and Schultze (1976); NACEPT (1991); Porter (1993); state regulator interview (3/1/94); Shapiro testimony, U.S. Congress. Senate. Acid Rain Hearings (1993). Most stakeholders interviewed for this project cite the enhanced technology-innovation effects of markets as an important reason for why markets are emerging as a viable alternative to command and control, and why they support government-imposed markets. Not surprisingly, however, several environmental advocates and some regulators either find little merit in the market-based innovation argument or are satisfied with the rate of innovation derived from the performance-standards approach (interviews with EPA 2/16/94; state regulator 1/10/94).

15. According to Richard Abdoo, Chairman of the Wisconsin Electric Power Company, when "we have some degree of certainty that we know what we're dealing with. . . . we collectively unleash the ingenuity, the creativity, and the challenge among the engineers, and the scientists, and the business community to work to accomplish the objective in the most efficient manner" (U.S. Congress. Senate. Acid Rain Hearings 1993, 14).

16. Daniel Dudek, senior economist, Environmental Defense Fund, as quoted in Reynolds (1990, 40). In the same article, Dudek also predicts that "[a]s we look to the future this kind of technological innovation is critical if we are going to continue the pace of environmental progress" (p. 40).

17. NACEPT (1991); Nikkila, SCAQMD, in USEPA (1993b, 162).

18. Interviews with environmentalists (1/13/94; 2/11/94); EPA (1/10/94; 1/11/94; quote, 1/13/94); state regulators (1/12/94; 3/1/94). "The emissions limitations [for SO_2] must be met . . . whether or not the trading system functions as expected. Inefficient trading may fail to achieve some of the cost savings that were expected, but it will not fail to achieve the nationwide reductions in pollution mandated by the statute. Compliance is an obligation independent from the trading scheme" (U.S. Congress. Senate. Senate Report Card 1993, 72).

19. "Although data on the extensiveness of the impact is limited, existing EPA source data suggests that going from 100 tons per year to 50 tons per year doubles the sources covered and going to 25 tons per year doubles it again" (Calcagni 1993, 191). In "extreme" ozone nonattainment areas like Los Angeles, the 1990 CAAA defines a major source as any source emitting 10 tons of pollution per year. See Levin and Elman (1990) for a discussion of why market-based mechanisms are particularly well-suited to pollution control problems covering large numbers of sources.

20. Interviews with EPA (12/10/93; 1/13/94); state regulator (3/1/94). For example, in the Southern California "RECLAIM program, there's a system in place . . . where industry has to make emissions reductions on the order of 8 percent every year. . . . Absent the RECLAIM program, you would have had to go out industry-by-industry and say, OK, we want you to achieve by x year an 80 or 90 percent reduction [i.e., this is what it will take for the Los Angeles area to meet the urban smog attainment goals of the 1990 CAAA]. . . . We could not have done that because we couldn't have pointed to [control] technologies that they could use. . . . We simply did not have enough information. . . . We achieved more reductions as a result of RECLAIM than we would have simply by slogging through and going after [the problems] industry-by-industry" (interview with EPA 1/13/94).

21. Interviews with environmentalists (1/11/94; 1/13/94; 2/11/94; 3/30/94); EPA (1/8/94); congressional staff (3/18/94).

22. Allocation of the regulatory burden entails the determination of emissions "baselines," the first step toward establishing property rights. See footnote 8 for a definition of baseline.

23. A growing number of state and federal regulators, environmentalists, and members of congress are satisfied that CEM technology for certain pollutants, especially sulfur dioxide (SO_2) and nitrogen oxide (NO_x), is now more than adequate to meet their requirements for a rigorous monitoring system (interviews with state regulator 1/12/94; state regulator 3/1/94; environmentalist 2/11/94; EPA 1/11/94; congressional staff 3/18/94). Many stakeholders, however, are skeptical that CEMs are advanced enough for anything more than a few air pollutants.

24. Interview with environmentalist (3/30/94); Mahoney (1992). The Massachusetts IMPACT emissions-trading program for volatile organic compounds (VOCs), NO_x, and carbon monoxide (CO) is an innovative example that accepts a number of different kinds of monitoring systems or technologies. Program design encourages CEM technology, but does not require it, by applying a multiplier effect to emissions credits earned by polluters according to the type of monitoring system employed. Polluters who install CEMs qualify for a higher multiplier than other types of compliance assessment testing methods, hence keep more of every credit earned (Massachusetts Department of Environmental Protection, Air Pollution Control Regulations, Chapter 310 CMR, Appendix B, p. 152.5).

A key reason why environmentalists and regulators insist on high levels of accuracy here concerns the problem of third-party enforcement. Trading pollution commodities differs from a typical market where buyers and sellers can both measure the commodity being exchanged. In a pollution control commodity market only the seller knows the "true" size of the emission credit. And buyers of credits have little interest in the accuracy of seller's measurements since all the buyer needs is a valid certificate stating they have purchased the right to x number of allowances. Therefore, environmentalists and regulators insist on third-party enforcement because buyers and sellers of pollution rights are not exchanging anything tangible; they are only exchanging "paper." It's "a commodity program with no ability to see or verify the commodity. [Buyers] are being delivered boxes but are not allowed to open the boxes" (interview with environmentalist 2/11/94).

25. Of course, since these technological advances are not exclusive to

market-based arrangements, any form of regulatory contract using them as part of the monitoring package will experience lower transaction costs vis-à-vis the past. However, the acid rain program experience suggests that markets are likely to see a broader application of CEMs as opposed to traditional command-and-control programs.

26. EPA (1994); interviews with EPA (1/11/94); environmentalist (3/30/94); industry (12/1/94); e.g., the reformulated gasoline rule and the coke ovens emissions rule pursuant to the 1990 CAAA.

27. Interviews with EPA (1/13/94); state regulator (3/1/94); comments of Roger Kanerva, environmental policy advisor to the Illinois EPA, and Daniel Dudek, senior economist for EDF (Great Lakes RETC 1994). The higher quality of data is the direct result of increased frequency of reporting, hence improved statistical reliability, and the production of a "real live" emissions-inventory database. The point is critical precisely because under command and control "we never really knew what emissions were going to be. . . . [That's why] a key benefit of markets is the new emissions-inventory database . . . [It] offers the potential of getting away from such 'blind' policy making" (Kanerva, Great Lakes RETC 1994). With both the RECLAIM and acid rain market-based programs "[t]here's much more monitoring and compliance tracking . . . than in command-and-control types of pollution control programs because the regulators and the environmental groups want assurance that these emissions reductions are really taking place" (interview with EPA 1/13/94).

28. Interviews with EPA (12/10/93; 1/11/94); environmentalists (1/10/94; 1/13/94). Michael Shapiro, EPA deputy assistant administrator, testified that the acid rain program offers "unprecedented accountability" (U.S. Congress. Senate. Acid Rain Hearings 1993, 8). With respect to the point on wider application: "For a long while people wanted to have continuous emissions monitors put on power plants under the command-and-control system. They should be there. But it never happened. It happened on new [power plants] but it didn't happen on the older ones until the acid rain emissions-trading program came along, and as part of that package the government said you're going to have to do this" (interview with environmentalist, 1/13/94). As of 1988, CEMs were installed at only 1,065 facilities, or about 11 percent of the 10,000 major sources where EPA estimates that CEMs are feasible. As a result, EPA and the states continue to rely primarily on on-site inspections to detect violations. Yet on-site inspections suffer from significant credibility and accountability problems because "in many situations the inspector, using his training and experience, judges a facility's compliance status without empirical evidence of the quantity, rate, or concentration of pollutants emitted. Inspectors often assess facility compliance by visually observing emissions and by reviewing operating equipment, records, and pollution control equipment. Because of the uncertainties involved in making these judgments, inspectors are often unable to determine whether sources are in compliance" (GAO 1990b, 17, 19). By contrast, senior EPA compliance officials report that CEMs are ten times more likely to detect violations than on-site inspections, while some state officials—most notably regulators in Pennsylvania, a state which has made substantial use of monitors since 1984—estimate that CEMs may be up to fifty times more effective than on-site inspections (GAO 1990b, 18). Although precise comparisons of the effectiveness of these different detection methods are difficult to make, both state and federal regulators agree that the detection potential of CEMs is much greater than that of inspections because monitors measure and record emissions directly and accurately; provide near-continuous coverage of facility emissions through 24-hour-per-day operation and measurement of more than 90 percent of a facility's annual emissions; and detect violations at night, during adverse weather, and of invisible gaseous emissions that periodic inspection cannot catch (GAO 1990b, 18–19).

29. Results come from both the new acid rain program requirement for CEMs on utilities' bypass stacks and the changeover to the allowance-based emissions-trading system (interview with EPA 1/11/94). In the latter example, the acid rain program starts from a zero-emission level and gives out allowances according to baseline formulas based on historic levels of utility emissions. Command-and-control programs, on the other hand, start at the top; they always take credit for emissions reductions. Given that industry wants to be in compliance, the incentive in command and control is to underreport emissions. "EPA got a lot of sheepish calls from [the utility industry] saying, 'Um, well, that's what we reported but during that time period we were having trouble with our scrubbers and our emissions rates were really higher and therefore, we ought to use a higher rate to calculate our allowances.' You wouldn't believe. We had hundreds of calls from people who wanted adjustments upward in their allowable emissions, [people who were saying] that they hadn't accurately reported their emission rates in the past because the 'game' before was to underreport. For the acid rain program the 'game' is to overreport and so I don't know what the truth is, whether they really were higher or they really were lower" (interview with EPA 1/11/94).

30. In 1981, Senate Majority Leader Mitchell was the first in a long succession of Democrats to propose an acid rain control bill. The fight to reauthorize the CAA began in 1980, yet was stymied throughout the 1980s for a number of reasons, not least of which was the fierce opposition of the Reagan Administration and Rep. John Dingell (D-MI), chair of the House Energy and Commerce Committee.

31. "Democrats in particular wanted a big environmental victory to take home" (Pytte 1990b, 3587).

32. Since the late 1970s, a wealth of information has been collected concerning the science of acid rain. This data, however, played a limited role in the final agreement, since industry and environmentalists remained at odds over the severity and urgency of the environmental problems attributed to acid rain, as well as the certainty of the linkage between midwestern power plants and ecological damage in the northeastern United States. Significantly, the National Acid Precipitation Assessment Program study, commissioned during the early 1980s for the specific purpose of answering such questions, was not concluded until after the acid rain program became law.

33. The rule protected the committee agreements in several other ways as well. No other amendments to the bill could be offered "except the amendments printed in the supplemental report of the Committee on Rules accompanying this resolution or as specified [within H. R. 399]" (p. 2667). "Said amendments shall not be subject to amendment" (p. 2667), and floor debate was compressed to eight hours for the entire bill (U. S. Congress, Senate 1993, A Legislative History of the Clean Air Act Amendments of 1990, Volume II, pp. 2667–89).

34. For example, Title I included "conformity" provisions that allow highway projects in ozone nonattainment areas to be reviewed by the EPA for "conformity" with the CAA. Projects that do not meet "conformity" standards, *as determined by the EPA,* can have their funding cut off (interview with EPA, 12/10/94). The Public Works Committee argued unsuccessfully that proper jurisdiction over the issue belonged to the Department of Transportation and therefore Public Works should have ample opportunity to influence this particular part of the law (Hager 1990b, 1551–52).

35. CQ Weekly Report (6/30/90, 2044). Obviously, the unconventional lawmaking examples cited here actually helped Energy and Commerce push their bill through the house. Yet in each case it is the transaction costs of lawmaking in the postreform congress that create an additional degree of dependency of committees and committee chairs on party leadership, thereby "provid[ing] the leadership with more leverage over the legislative process" (Canon 1992, 3). This is a distinctive change from textbook congress days when committee autonomy was such that committees and committee chairs rarely needed leadership assistance to work their will on the entire chamber.

36. Acid rain provisions were reported out of the House Energy and Commerce Committee on a 42–1 vote, while the final house vote on the entire 1990 CAAA package passed on May 23, 1990, by a 401–21 margin. See Hager (1990c, 1643).

37. It is not clear what part the acid rain title played in Mitchell's decision to strip the bill from committee and conduct backroom negotiations with the White House, minority party leaders, and select members of the Senate Environment and Public Works Committee. Mitchell's fear was that the whole of the clean air bill leaned too heavily toward the environmental side of things and as a result would not pass the senate (Bryner 1993; Cohen 1992). This is the reason why environmentalists complained vociferously about how the backroom negotiations would only weaken the bill (see Hager 1990f) and why they "stormed the floor" with "dealbuster" amendments trying to restore at least some of the bill's provisions to their former stringency (Hager 1990g, 738). A close review of the evolution of the acid rain title through its various incarnations—the original Bush proposal, the Senate Environment and Public Works Committee version, the Mitchell–Dole compromise version, and the final senate version—shows that the proposal changed little from start to finish in the senate. In addition, the acid rain title was the subject of limited amending activity on the floor of the senate. The vast majority of what floor activity there was consisted of senators seeking extra allowances for their home state utilities. In other words, legislators had discovered a new way to deliver political pork, in this case the cash value of emissions allowances. Significantly, only two of these amendments passed before Sen. Pete Domenici (R-NM) convinced the leadership to go back behind "closed doors" and hammer out one final deal among the various allowance seekers (interview with congressional staff 3/30/94; Kuntz 1990, 1060). Finally, acid rain was the target of only a single "dealbuster" amendment—the Byrd amendment that sought to compensate

high-sulfur coal miners for expected job losses—that was eventually defeated (Kuntz and Hager 1990).

38. See Hager and Kuntz (1990, 900–06); Hager (1990g, 738–40). The lone successful "dealbuster" was Senator Tom Daschle's (D-SD) amendment on reformulated gasoline (Kuntz and Hager 1990, 986).

39. Bartels testimony, U.S. Congress. Senate. Acid Rain Hearings (1993), 116; Electric Power Research Institute (EPRI) (1993); EPA (1994).

40. EPRI estimates projected savings for electric utilities and their customers to range from $1.7 to $2.3 billion annually (U.S. Congress. Senate. Acid Rain Hearings 1993, 67).

41. See Bartels testimony, U.S. Congress. Senate. Acid Rain Hearings (1993, 117). This was also a more general theme throughout my interview data (EPA 3/25/94; 1/11/94; 1/7/94; environmentalist 1/13/94; environmentalist 1/7/94; industry 1/21/94).

42. Regulators familiar with the market-based RECLAIM program in Southern California observe the same dynamic and attribute the advances in environmental control technologies to the use of a market-based approach (interview with state regulator 3/1/94).

43. The Senate Committee on Environment and Public Works awarded this grade of "A" ("excellent") to only one other major program—Title VI, the Stratospheric Ozone Protection Program. Significantly, this is the other major title in the 1990 CAA premised on market-based principles.

44. U.S. Congress. Senate. Acid Rain Hearings (1993). See testimony of Richard Abdoo, chairman and CEO, Wisconsin Electric Power, 14; Patrick Arbor, Chairman, Chicago Board of Trade, 24–25; Senator Max Baucus, 4; Joseph Goffman, Environmental Defense Fund, 21–22; Gerald Keenan, senior vice president, Palmer Bellevue Corporation (financial services industry), 127; Senator Joseph Leiberman, 2; Michael Shapiro, acting assistant administrator for EPA's OAR, 46. See also GAO (1994b). This assessment dominates my interview data as well.

7

Preventing Pollution through the Collaborative Search for Better Information

The Administrator of the EPA must follow rules of nine major statutes, none of which were designed to work with one another. There is no integrating principle built into all this statutory armor. Each is written to stand alone, as if the world were made entirely of air or water or some other target of concern. No word in all this law directs EPA to simply find the combination of policies across all programs that will garner the maximum benefit to the environment for every dollar of cost expended (William Ruckelshaus, former EPA administrator, U.S. Congress. Senate. Taking Stock Hearings 1993, 207).

In July 1989, a chance meeting of old acquaintances planted the seeds of the first joint exploratory venture between federal regulators and industry in American pollution control politics. During an airplane ride from Chicago to Washington, the acquaintances—James Lounsbury from EPA and Deborah Sparks from Amoco Oil—exchanged notes regarding a regulatory system that is costly for both regulators and the regulated, yet where much pollution is uncontrolled. The existing system is notorious for problems such as the use of activity-based measures as proxies for environmental results,[1] overlapping and contradictory regulatory mandates, and the assignment of regulatory priorities according to public perceptions of human health and environmental risks, which often has the perverse effect of directing scarce agency and industry resources toward cleanup issues with the lowest risks. Further, each side encounters double jeopardy with cross-media pollution transfers. After cleaning up in one media, pollution is often encountered again in another media, along with the added costs of rulemaking, compliance, and enforcement activities. Beyond this, it is widely agreed that the "cheap, easy pounds" of pollution associated with large, stationary industrial sites have been cleaned up and that future environmental progress will require, among other things, greater regulatory intrusiveness into upstream industrial processes, as opposed to traditional end-of-pipe controls (USEPA 1990e).

Frustrated with the uncertainty of environmental results and the high transaction costs surrounding conventional methods of pollution control, Lounsbury and Sparks engaged in a brainstorming exercise where the guiding premise was: "If we could be king and queen for a day, wouldn't it be nice if we could restructure the world of environmental analysis?"[2] By the time they arrived in Washington, they had settled on a joint government-industry exploration of an entire industrial facility emphasizing pollution prevention, particularly waste minimization. The proposal encountered initial resistance from both organizations. Amoco officials feared that giving regulators relatively unrestricted access to one of their oil refineries was a "stupid" strategic move sure to increase their regulatory burden. EPA officials were concerned that collaboration might elicit charges it was "sleeping with the enemy." But in both cases—in Amoco's case within days—authorization was granted to proceed with the joint project.

From such inauspicious beginnings was launched the two-and-a-half-year Yorktown Pollution Prevention Project (YPPP), focusing on Amoco's Yorktown, Virginia, oil refinery. The YPPP sought relief from the high costs of a command-and-control system of regulation through the production of better information. The first step involved establishing an *actual* emissions profile, or emissions inventory, of refinery pollution according to chemical type, quantity, source, and medium of release. The emissions-inventory information would then be used to develop pollution reduction options, to evaluate and prioritize the options, and to identify and evaluate barriers and incentives[3] to implementing the various alternatives (Amoco/USEPA Yorktown Pollution Prevention Project, Executive Summary 1992, *ii–iii*; hereinafter cited as Yorktown ES 1992).

Government and industry stakeholders expected that a rigorous review of the emissions data and their relationship to existing regulatory requirements would allow them to test the hypothesis that a collaborative, whole-facility approach to pollution control, while requiring a high-cost information search phase, was ultimately a more cost-effective and environmentally effective approach.[4] Just as in the cases of acid rain and reformulated gasoline, the promise of transaction cost savings was instrumental in bringing participants to the negotiating table.

But the Yorktown story is about more than transaction cost savings. Federal regulators and corporate America had little reason to trust each other's motivations. They had no way of knowing whether the other's interest in the win–win outcome implied by the collaborative endeavor was genuine or served merely as a vehicle to advance some hidden agenda. The uncertainties prompted stakeholders to seek assurance that their interests and investments would be safeguarded. Otherwise, each had an incentive to avoid the collaborative game and instead choose the known costs of the regulatory status quo. Participants needed a mechanism by which they could build the trust necessary to initiate and sustain the collaborative game.

Unlike the other cases, however, participants stopped short of insisting on the full pluralism-by-the-rules framework. Formal binding rules were absent from the proceedings, while Amoco Oil refused to grant environmental advocates full participant status in the venture. Creating the trust necessary to solve the initial collective action problem and propel the collaborative game forward depended instead on an assurance mechanism based largely on bureaucratic leadership, transaction-specific conditions, and, to a more limited extent than the other cases, organizational reputation. Significantly, however, the absence of key pieces of the pluralism-by-the-rules framework, together with the premature departure of the senior EPA official in charge of the project, conspired to transform the final story of Yorktown from one of success to failure. For in the end, without all the pieces in place, uncertainty overwhelmed the proceedings and the collaborative effort succeeded only in discovering rather than delivering a variety of transaction costs savings.

LOWER COSTS THROUGH PREVENTION AND INTEGRATION

The proactive, integrated approach to pollution control envisioned for the Yorktown Pollution Prevention Project deviated from the existing superstructure of regulatory control. The pollution prevention aspect of the project aimed to reduce or eliminate pollution at its source without creating new risks of concern. Chief components included waste minimization (source reduction), materials and process substitution, and recycling.[5] By contrast, traditional approaches achieve pollution reduction goals through the management, containment, and treatment of waste (emissions) *after* it has been generated, typically by requiring end-of-pipe controls.[6] The second major goal focused on integrated or multimedia pollution control, as opposed to the single-media fragmented approach promoted by virtually every major federal environmental statute. A multimedia approach looks comprehensively at an industrial facility's pollution releases, at the relationship among various pollutants in order to calibrate values for interpollutant trading, and at whether regulatory solutions actually solve a particular pollution problem or merely shift its harmful effects into another media.

Operationalizing a combined pollution prevention–integrated approach requires an intensive information search process. At Yorktown, not only did state and federal regulators have to overcome the information *asymmetry* favoring industry in the area of industrial processes, but all stakeholders faced a large information *deficit* regarding facility-wide pollution emissions and health risks. Participants accepted these costs as necessary because they anticipated that the new information would create a basis for more "intelligent and efficient" decisions leading to significant transaction cost benefits.[7] Put differently, stakeholders perceived that the collaborative game could produce a new set of regulatory rules which would apply compliance resources to the areas delivering "the biggest bang for the buck," thereby reducing the most and worst pollution at the least cost (see also the Management Institute for the Environment and Business 1993, 3; hereinafter cited as MIEB 1993).[8]

REDUCING POLLUTION-BASED INFORMATION DEFICITS

Reaping transaction cost benefits required, first and foremost, erasure of the information deficit (a measurement problem) regarding the relationship of industrial processes and various emissions to the actual facility emissions profile.[9] "Existing estimates of environmental releases were not adequate for making a . . . multimedia, facility-wide assessment," in part because when "good" data existed, as in the case of water and solid-waste pollution, "[it] did not include adequate chemical-specific characterization of . . . discharge[s]."[10] Moreover, these estimates covered only 11 percent of the facility's total pollution (Yorktown ES 1992, 3–5, Figure 2.5). Given monitoring difficulties and the fact that some sources were not regulated, data were unavailable for fugitive emissions; pollution from uncontrolled sources such as valves, flanges, and pump seals;[11] and other significant pollution sources within the refinery.[12] As well, the Toxic Release Inventory (TRI)—the de facto national inventory for air toxics releases—did not adequately identify air emissions, given estimating inaccuracies and the limited focus on specific chemicals (See Figure 7.1). For instance, although TRI targets more than 300 chemicals, at the Yorktown site it covered only 9.2 percent of the total air toxics (hydrocarbons) released and 4.7 percent of the total releases to all media.[13]

The other part of the information-deficit problem stems from the lack of coordination among environmental statutes. Technically, this is not an information deficit, since emissions data are reported regularly

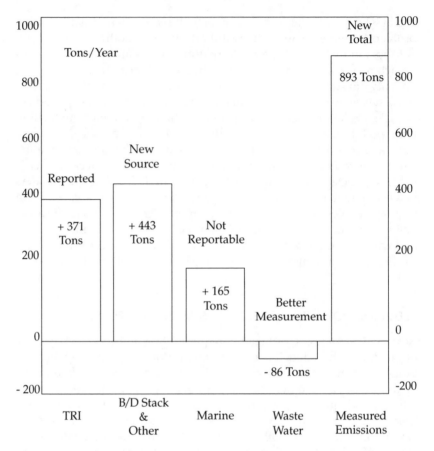

Source: Amoco/USEPA Yorktown Pollution Prevention Project, Executive Summary (1992), Figure 2.7.

Figure 7.1   1989 TRI Inventory Compared to Measured Air Toxics Emissions

by industry. Yet the final effect is the same: regulators and industry each have an incomplete understanding of the cumulative effect of refinery emissions on the environment (and public health) and the net impact of regulatory rules on facility emissions. This is because the information that does get reported, "is reported in different units, under discrete [single-media] programs for air, water, and waste. There is no coherent attempt to look at all the emissions data and say 'what's going on here?'"[14]

The participants in the [Yorktown] project naively took an engineering view of the world and said, 'If we had good data, we would make better decisions.' . . . We said 'Let's get a coherent set of data about a site, measured in the same units, at one point in time, on all the different media.' Then we'll put that out on the public table and anybody who wants to can look at different alternatives, at policy choices, and so on. We'll at least have a set of data for testing hypotheses. . . . [We expected that] good data and good science would triumph (interview with industry 12/1/94b).

Developing a comprehensive emissions inventory was valuable to government regulators and to Amoco because it offered an opportunity to rationalize the regulatory rules and compliance decision-making activities affecting the refinery complex. Transaction cost benefits were expected in three principal areas: the creation of a better match of regulatory rules to pollution problems, the avoidance of double jeopardy through pollution prevention, and the improvement of Amoco's cost structure related to environmental compliance activities.[15]

Stakeholders expected that a comprehensive database would provide a basis for smarter rules which would improve the match of regulations with pollution problems. Put differently, better information reduced the probability that regulatory solutions were either over- or underdesigned.[16] Smarter rules, in turn, would shift participants' focus toward actual environmental performance and away from regulatory rules as proxies for environmental results (see Chapter 3). The avoidance (or minimization) of token compliance means that organizational resources devoted to environmental regulations would be more efficiently targeted in service of environmental policy goals. Instead of an enforcement system predicated on the question, "Have you complied with the rules as written?" regulator concern is directed at a more fundamental inquiry, "Have you cleaned up?" Focusing enforcement resources in such a way increases the certainty that when a violation or case of noncompliance is found, the net result of a successful enforcement action will be an improvement in environmental conditions, rather than simply compliance with rules disconnected from environmental results. Industry, on the other hand, experiences greater certainty that the money spent complying with regulatory mandates actually produces its intended result—environmental protection.

Better information was also expected to help with the design of pollution prevention measures. Regulators liked the pollution prevention aspect because, by definition, there are substantial environmental benefits. There is either less pollution, the same level of pollution (risk) for less cost, or in cases of outright elimination, a permanent solution to pollution problems. Pollution prevention also produces transaction cost benefits because it obviates or diminishes the need for resources devoted to the second-order problem of double jeopardy (Rabe 1986). As noted previously, double jeopardy occurs when single-media regulations transfer pollution across media—from air to land, or water to air, and so on. For example, "wastewater treatment plants built to satisfy federal water quality requirements are now among the biggest sources of toxic air emissions at industrial facilities and in some urban areas" (Browner 1993, 7). As a result, stakeholders must contend with the costs of writing, implementing, enforcing, and complying with regulations twice instead of once.[17]

Amoco perceived that the new information would lead to greater cost effectiveness in their environmental permitting activities.[18] The detailed, prescriptive, single-media focus of command-and-control-based permits often mandate overlapping and contradictory actions on the part of the regulated community. Not only are such outcomes inefficient in terms of paperwork and personnel requirements,[19] but in emergency situations they are of little practical use.[20] Amoco believed the new information would produce substantial cost savings through the creation of a consolidated, streamlined system of permits encompassing all media. EPA regulators and environmentalists agreed that integrating regulatory requirements "saves industry time and trouble by giving them one set of signals from government" (interview with EPA 11/2/94; 11/3/94; 11/9/94; environmentalist 11/11/94a). Further, Amoco perceived that treating pollution releases within an integrated framework would spur innovative technical solutions that, while in certain cases would increase pollution for one media, would result in an overall improvement of environmental quality.[21]

Amoco officials further anticipated that reducing the information deficit would enhance corporate management's ability to control the environmental compliance part of their business (interviews with industry 11/8/94a; 11/8/94b). Committing substantial organizational resources to the collaborative effort and the creation of a "real live" emissions profile would signal managers to be more vigilant toward the relationship between environmental compliance activities and the production process, while simultaneously giving managers the information or tools needed to be more vigilant. The expected payoffs from improved management technologies were several. They included improvements in process innovation, production efficiencies, materials substitution, and ultimately bottom-line operating costs at the Yorktown refinery. As well, there was the chance to develop health and environmental risk assessments of various pollutants that might then lead to a greater appreciation of how an alternative and more flexible compliance pathway could provide results equal to or better than the traditional system of regulation, yet at significantly lower cost.[22] Finally, managers could develop a better idea of what each dollar of compliance activity was buying in the way of pollution reduction, thus increasing the certainty associated with pollution control expenditures.

OVERCOMING INFORMATION ASYMMETRIES

Most federal environmental statutes accept that how businesses manage upstream industrial processes—those processes or decisions prior to end-of-the-pipe pollution—is the private sector's domain. But what comes out of the pipe is EPA's business. EPA, in other words, regulates discharges, yet does not necessarily get to tell industry how to operate the facilities (interviews with EPA 11/1/94b; 11/1/94a). Yet significant numbers of environmentalists and regulators believe that sustained environmental progress requires permanent changes in the culture and decision-making practices of industry, whether in terms of product formulations, overall management technologies, upstream production processes, or other traditional ways of doing business.[23] Much like the aim of a government-imposed market, the objective here is to transform environmental compliance activities into another factor of production.

The problem is that getting industry to divulge information on upstream production processes is costly. Regulators encounter high information-search and program-specification costs not only because industry controls pertinent information, but also because industry resists regulations which intrude on their decision-making autonomy.[24] Nor is it clear that command and control is a feasible option, given the complexity of many industrial processes. Regulators must choose from hundreds and even thousands of possible solutions, yet with limited expertise to guide their decisions (compared to industry).

Regulators involved in the Yorktown project expressed appreciation for how collaborative games can alleviate problems of asymmetric information concerning upstream production processes (interviews with EPA 11/1/94a; 11/1/94b). This is largely because collaboration makes it more likely that industry will voluntarily share information and, more generally, play a helping, constructive role during rulemaking and implementation. By enlisting industry's expertise in the service of environmental policy goals, regulators saw collaboration as a way to leverage scarce public sector resources and to effect the permanent changes in industry's culture and decision-making procedures necessary for sustained environmental progress.[25]

REDUCING THE UNCERTAINTY OF COLLABORATION

The expectation of transaction cost savings was not enough, however, to drive affected interests toward a joint exploratory venture. The collaborative undertaking was risky. Rival stakeholders with conflicting interests were likely to act opportunistically. Such a possibility made uncertain the achievement of promised benefits. The uncertainty was compounded by the history of bitter environmental policy wars. In the case of the Yorktown Pollution Prevention Project, building the trust necessary for resolving the collective action dilemma required a supportive framework capable of offering stakeholders assurance that their stakes in the joint exploratory venture would be honored. It required the presence of certain transaction-specific conditions, reputation on the part of public entrepreneurs, and the growing credibility of the EPA as a supporter of collaborative efforts. Within this context, participants were able to mount a good-faith effort in both their search for information and the give and take of negotiation necessary to reach a consensus agreement. As with the cases of regulatory negotiation and government-imposed markets, moving the joint venture forward relied on the occasional push or supporting effort by the entrepreneur.

MANAGEABILITY AND OPPORTUNITY

The Yorktown project was an attractive candidate for the collaborative format because it either met or, as a basic premise, accepted a series of conditions lowering the difficulties (uncertainty) likely to be encountered during negotiations.

First, fundamental values were not at stake. The project's starting point was the existing regulatory framework and primary emphasis was on improving the ability of that framework to achieve both environmental results and cost effectiveness. Cost effectiveness was not to be valued ahead of environmental protection or human health concerns unless *consensus* existed that a stringent (safe) level of protection was in force and added increments of risk reduction beyond that level were of marginal value.

Second, the driving force behind the Yorktown effort was the creation of a well-developed factual database to frame the discussion and resolution of pertinent issues. Participants collected massive amounts of data on the refinery's pollution patterns, their relationship to various industrial processes and practices, as well as to existing regulatory rules. Thus, participants were in a better position to assess cause and effect between industrial processes and levels of pollution. They were also better equipped to make decisions in the areas of solution feasibility and cost effectiveness, among others.

Third, the scope of the project was limited, hence the number of interdependent or related issues was limited, too. The project involved only a single industrial facility of medium size and examined only pollution control and cost-related issues. Actions taken during negotiations reinforced the project's adherence to this transaction-specific condition, particularly when all participants, including the executive peer review council, agreed to downsize the possible solution set from fifty to a more manageable set of twelve alternatives.

Fourth, the site-specific, voluntary nature of the venture, the goal of integrated pollution control, and the location of the oil refinery in a Clean Air Act attainment area made it unlikely that Yorktown would have immediate, direct, or broader ramifications for agency-wide policy.[26]

Fifth, affected interests were identifiable, few, and cohesive; or in EPA's case, they appeared to be cohesive to other participants. As will be described in detail, EPA's management team created the perception of cohesiveness at the beginning and was, in fact, able to maintain cohesiveness until late in the project when the top-level EPA leader with ultimate responsibility for the project left the agency. On Amoco's side, once senior management overcame some initial reservations and decided to pursue the project, their manager, Howard Klee, was entrusted with broad authority to make decisions on the company's behalf. Rounding out the slate of participants were state regulators from Virginia's Department of Environmental Quality.[27]

Beyond issues of manageability, opportunity also existed to craft the creative compromises critical to collaborative games. From the initial conception of the Yorktown joint venture, innovation and creativity were basic ground rules; to the extent feasible, the project intended to examine all possible solutions and combinations of solutions. Further, not only did the project have the blessing of executive branch officials, the central questions of concern to participants focused more on how best to achieve environmental goals, rather than the substance of the goals themselves.[28]

ENTREPRENEURS AND REPUTATION

In a multimedia project such as the YPPP, entrepreneurial public sector leaders and managers must be able to "sell" the benefits of working together to the individual stakeholders, both those inside the public agency and those private-sector and state-level actors outside the organization. They must inspire participants to transcend the sort of self-interested behavior that can result in shirking (see Miller 1992). The skill and reputation of entrepreneurial public sector managers created assurance and facilitated the YPPP in three main ways: by convincing outsiders (Amoco) to participate, by inducing *ex ante* cooperation inside the EPA hierarchy, and by sustaining collaboration over time.

Senior management at EPA, in particular Assistant Administrator for the Office of Policy, Planning and Evaluation (OPPE) J. Clarence Davies and EPA Administrator William Reilly, were professional environmentalists with a track record of commitment to innovative ideas and collaborative methods. Thirteen years of leadership at the Conservation Foundation[29] firmly established their reputations as stakeholders skilled at finding common ground among industry, government, and environmentalists.[30] For his efforts, Reilly was known as "the great includer" (Weisskopf 1988). In his confirmation hearings before the senate, Reilly reiterated the call for more collaboration and suggested that future progress in the battle against environmental degradation depended on it (Shabecoff 1989). He also made it clear early in his tenure at EPA that he planned to promote greater use of pollution prevention approaches. Toward this end, the EPA christened the Office of Pollution Prevention in January 1989.[31] Further, Reilly carried through on his promise to infuse the EPA with a greater appreciation for risk assessment as a method of redirecting agency priorities (see USEPA 1990e; *Economist*, 3/30/91).

For his part, Davies "was a very strong supporter of the Yorktown project."[32] He "ha[d] spent basically his entire professional career trying to promote an integrated, organic statute that looked at the whole pollution picture as opposed to a fragmented single-media approach."[33] While at EPA, he sought ways to focus the agency's resources where they would get the biggest payoff, concentrating especially on the risk reduction (health and environmental), feasibility, and cost components of various pollution control options (interview with EPA 11/3/94a).

It was clear that Davies and Reilly were committed to innovation and collaboration. In fact, the perception that the Yorktown project "had enough senior management support at EPA" helped to convince Amoco's leadership that the project had both merit and a relatively good chance for success. The commitment of senior agency leaders was envisioned as more than enough to keep the project moving forward if "rough water" (internal agency resistance) was encountered.[34]

Nevertheless, there was still the matter of inducing meaningful participation inside the EPA hierarchy. Given the multimedia focus of the project in an agency devoted to predominantly single-media issues and the lack of a specific congressional mandate (e.g., deadline),[35] affected stakeholders in the program offices needed assurance that their stakes were credible. For example, at the time of the project's inception, resources of the Office of Solid Waste and Emergency Response (OSWER) were heavily focused on meeting congressional rulemaking deadlines, while the Air Office was engaged in 1989 and 1990 Clean Air Act reauthorization battles (interview with EPA 11/1/94a). Within this context, the Yorktown Project was but one of approximately 5,000 proposals occupying space on the EPA's master workplan.

Creating the organizational energy needed to pull the proposal from the workplan required the blessing of senior management and the reputation of the manager in charge of day-to-day project supervision. The latter case of entrepreneurship involved a midlevel OPPE manager, Mahesh Podar.

> Mahesh had a strong interest in [Yorktown] and he had the kind of stature in the organization to push this project and keep people interested. . . . [Over the years,] he had established good relations with the program offices necessary to make the YPPP effort go. People knew him as a guy you could trust. . . . He also . . . was successful in convincing others to kick in money. This helped the OPPE to leverage their own scarce resources (interview with EPA 11/1/94b).

More importantly, the reputation of organizational principals—Reilly and Davies—signaled to agents within EPA that the project enjoyed conceptual support at the highest levels. The YPPP also provided Davies a chance to put his voluminous philosophical musings on the subject of multimedia pollution control into action. As EPA's assistant administrator for OPPE, he therefore had both an administrative and a personal stake in seeing the program succeed. Further, Davies' close association with Reilly at the Conservation Foundation created the perception that he was vested with real organizational power. Such a notion ran contrary to conventional conceptions of the OPPE assistant administrator position because the OPPE had long been the "weak sister" in the EPA organizational structure.[36]

Finally, sustaining the project over time required entrepreneurs who could facilitate collaboration on a day-to-day basis and a champion among EPA's senior managers. Participants in the joint venture generally credit the comanagement team of Mahesh Podar (EPA) and Howard Klee (Amoco) with providing the "entrepreneurial dynamic . . . that drove the project forward, that kept it moving. They were very committed to it."[37] Moreover, while Podar's trustworthy reputation within EPA was integral to keeping the project afloat, his task was complicated by the fact that "it went against the general grain of the agency in terms of organization, in terms of general attitudes toward polluters, and so on" (interview with EPA 11/3/94a). At the same time, the active support of a senior level "champion" or "godfather"— Assistant Administrator Davies—inside EPA was critical, if for no other reason than that he "kept it alive and defended it against potential threats from other EPA offices" (interviews with EPA 11/3/94; 9/27/94; 11/1/94a; industry 12/1/94b).

EPA CREDIBILITY

Davies' and Podar's efforts to overcome the collective action dilemma and sustain the collaborative effort were inevitably enhanced by the stewardship of EPA administrators Ruckelshaus, Thomas, and Reilly during the 1980s. Each EPA leader fostered the development of EPA's reputation as an agency credibly committed to greater collaboration among stakeholders. The reputation stemmed not only from their exhortation and symbolic support for collaborative efforts, but from the successful use of both public–private partnerships involving locally based stakeholders and negotiated rulemaking as a legitimate replacement for notice-and-comment rulemaking.[38] In short, EPA's recent history helped to reduce uncertainty for the prospective participants in the Yorktown Pollution Prevention Project.

In terms of specific agency commitment to a Yorktown-like project, however, organizational reputation played a more limited role for several reasons. Although the agency was in the process of strengthening its commitment to pollution prevention, as evidenced by a new office for pollution prevention established only months prior to the inauguration of the project, the Yorktown collaboration was a "groundbreaking, first-of-its-kind" arrangement (interviews with EPA 11/3/94a; GAO, 11/9/94; industry 12/1/94b). It was unique because not only was it the first time Amoco and EPA had worked so closely together, but it was the first collaborative project to undertake a comprehensive whole-facility, multimedia study of pollution based on a factual (rather than estimated) emissions profile of an industrial facility. The innovative design of YPPP meant stakeholders had no past experiences by which to gauge the depth of EPA's specific commitment.[39]

THE *LACK* OF FORMAL BINDING RULES

Stakeholders never made any specific commitments to implementation during the Yorktown joint venture.[40] Yet the open-ended nature of the project left this an open question along with other options. The possibility existed that if all went well, project participants would choose to extend the venture into the implementation stage in order to capture the gains from collaboration. Influencing this calculation was the expectation by key participants that despite organizational differences in perspective, the joint development and subsequent sharing of a "better" database would lead stakeholders toward "reasonable, rational" conclusions and ultimately to the selection and implementation of pollution prevention options providing clear benefits for all.[41] Contrary to the expectations of the assurance mechanism argument, none of the parties asked for special guarantees constraining *ex post* appeals to political principals or protecting against *ex post* manipulation of consensus agreements.[42] More specifically, Amoco agreed that EPA actions would not be restricted regarding use of the information derived from the project, either during or after the project, and that Amoco would receive no special treatment with respect to pending or potential future enforcement actions. Likewise, Amoco agreed to forgo any guarantees regarding their ability to supplant existing regulatory requirements with more cost-effective alternative paths to compliance that might develop as a result of the project.[43]

WORKING TOGETHER TO DISCOVER WIN–WIN SOLUTIONS

In late October 1989, EPA, Amoco, and the Virginia Department of Environmental Quality agreed to move ahead with the Yorktown joint venture. Project principals set up an independent peer review committee to ensure quality control and the credibility of project conclusions. Resources for the Future, a Washington, D.C., think tank, was hired to manage the committee's work. Included on the committee were academics and scientists, as well as environmental advocates from the Conservation Foundation and the Chesapeake Bay Foundation (a local Virginia group).

Participants then defined the objectives and scope of the project. Stakeholders faced considerable uncertainty, given the initial commitment to working together "with only a vague sense of knowing what it was we were going to do," and not knowing whether others would bargain in good faith and share the information required to make the project successful (interview with industry 12/1/94a). As a result, the first five months were spent getting acquainted and overcoming the awkwardness of a collaborative effort involving traditional adversaries. It was a trust-building exercise. The inaugural hurdle for the project comanagers from EPA and Amoco was establishing enough trust among workgroup members that the parameters of the study could be established. Amoco's senior leadership was particularly uncomfortable with the idea of collaborating with government regulators. Sharing information with their traditional adversary might only add to their regulatory burden. Or, in light of EPA's scarce resources, EPA might well be unable to follow through on their commitment, in which case Amoco's investment in time and money would produce nothing of value (interviews with environmentalist 11/11/94a; industry 12/1/94a; 12/1/94b). On this latter count, the entrepreneurial skill of the EPA comanager, Mahesh Podar, in cobbling together the agency resources needed to make the project viable, was instrumental in allaying Amoco's initial concerns (MIEB 1993, 5; interview with EPA 11/1/94a).

Virginia regulators faced a steady barrage of in-house commentary questioning the value of the joint venture. Many of their colleagues could not conceive of Amoco in anything other than duplicitous terms. State regulators involved in the project had their own concerns regarding Amoco's intentions. Not having experienced sustained contact with industry before, they were not sure whether the traditional stereotypes of industry were valid or not and were not sure what to expect (interviews with state regulators 11/7/94a; 11/7/94b).

EPA participants, for their part, were generally skeptical of Amoco's underlying motives. Much like state-level critics of the project, the workgroup's federal regulators were veterans of environmental policy wars. Although frustrated with the inefficiencies and "the transaction costs from constantly fighting and litigating,"[44] industry was still the stereotypical enemy committed to fighting or avoiding regulation and only able to conceive of pollution in self-interested terms. EPA thus saw Amoco as credibly committed to the collaborative effort as a way to reduce the regulatory burden on the refinery. But they had difficulty believing that Amoco's end goal of improving both cost effectiveness *and* environmental protection was genuine (interviews with EPA 11/2/94; 11/3/94b). Howard Klee, Amoco's co-manager on the project, had to repeatedly assure EPA of Amoco's interest in both the economic and environmental aspects of the venture. Convincing EPA participants that Amoco was committed to environmental protection took five months (interview with industry 11/8/94b; 12/1/94a).

MOVING TOWARD A CONSENSUS AGREEMENT

The early brainstorming, negotiation, and trust-building sessions produced an agreement in March 1990 that the Yorktown Project was worth doing. Participants announced an initial set of goals:

- inventory refinery pollution releases to define their chemical type, quantity, source, and medium of release,

- develop options to reduce releases,
- evaluate, rank, and prioritize the options for reducing or preventing pollution, and
- identify and evaluate barriers and incentives to implementing the various alternatives.

The next several months were spent getting stakeholders, including each of the respective EPA program offices (e.g., Office of Solid Waste; Office of Air and Radiation), to approve the goals as well as Amoco's proposed methodologies for monitoring, sampling, and evaluating the data from the refinery. While most EPA staff were supportive of the project and the workplan, there was concern over the monitoring methodologies for measuring air emissions flows and ultimately for attributing pollution to various sources within the refinery complex.[45] The testing methods, though jointly determined by Amoco and regulators, "were quite different" from the methods traditionally used by EPA's technical office—the Office of Air Quality Planning and Standards (OAQPS)—in North Carolina (interview with EPA 11/3/94b). As one way to ameliorate these concerns, Amoco tried to convince EPA to conduct "parallel monitoring and sampling (i.e., parallel to the efforts of Amoco personnel), but EPA claimed not to have the budget to [accomplish the task]."[46] Still needing official approval from the OAQPS staff, the monitoring protocols were given to OAQPS for further review. Despite persistent efforts by the Yorktown comanagers to obtain the official sign-off in the spring of 1990 (including several trips to North Carolina), no "definitive response" was forthcoming. After interpreting the lack of OAQPS response as neutrality and a tacit acceptance of the appropriateness of the proposed testing methods, the project continued.[47]

A formal workplan was then released in September 1990, detailing how the collaborative venture would proceed. The first phase entailed the collection of emissions data. A sampling and monitoring program consisting of almost 1,000 samples was taken during the Fall of 1990 over a two-week period when the refinery was at peak capacity.[48] The monitoring "snapshot"[49] was followed by a seven-month period in which independent laboratories tested each air, water, groundwater, solid waste, and soils sample for the presence of fifteen to twenty chemicals. By this point, and in a pattern that would continue for the remainder of the project, regular attendance and active involvement was limited to a core group of participants from Amoco, Virginia, and EPA's OPPE, OSWER, and Pollution Prevention offices. EPA's Air Office "only sporadically attended [monthly workgroup meetings] and never sent any of their technical people" (interviews with EPA

11/1/94b; 11/1/94a; 11/2/94; industry 11/8/94b; 12/1/94b; state regulators 11/7/94a; 11/7/94b).

In March 1991, almost a year and a half into the project, stakeholders convened a three-day brainstorming and review session in Williamsburg, Virginia. The review group included more than 120 people, including additional staff from Virginia's Department of Environmental Quality, EPA, and Amoco, as well as the executive peer review group. The workshop focused its efforts in three main areas: (1) a review of the refinery's pollution release information and detailed air and groundwater dispersion modeling studies, (2) an examination and selection of alternative environmental technologies to manage the refinery's multimedia pollution problems, and (3) development of screening criteria to help prioritize selected pollution prevention options.[50] In determining alternative pollution reduction options, participants focused broadly on the entire pollution prevention hierarchy—source reduction, recycling, treatment, and safe disposal—rather than limit possible choices of "how" to manage pollution only to source reduction.[51] Workshop participants were convinced that the collaborative format provided quicker coverage of pollution reduction options and the consideration of broader issues such as the consequences of managing crossmedia pollution transfer problems and future liability impacts in a "more comprehensive [fashion] than either government or industry alone would normally do" (p. 8). Working together, participants identified fifty potential release reduction options.[52]

During the Spring and Summer of 1991, project members pared the original fifty-item list to twelve pollution management options.[53] The workgroup used a multidimensional decision tree known as the Analytical Hierarchy Process to develop a more careful quantitative analysis of the final options.[54] Criteria used in the ranking process included human health risk, environmental impact, cost, timeliness, risk reduction potential,[55] benzene exposure reduction potential, status in the pollution prevention hierarchy, transferability to other industrial facilities, the effect of a particular pollution reduction option on other media, impact on liability, safety, and whether options were technically feasible now[56] or offered potentially large pollution reductions.

> [E]ach of these factors was assigned a numerical score or weight . . . [within the] decision tree hierarchy. That was probably the most agonizing part of the entire project. . . . [Yet] it was important because it served to focus people on the real issues. It started out with everybody figuring, "Well, we're never going to agree on what's the best thing to do." For one thing, the private sector takes a different view on the importance of cost versus what the agency has to consider. We tried to quantify that. Indeed [regula-

tors and industry] assigned different weights to the dollars versus the environmental impacts, the matter of "is this technically feasible or not," and so on for the various different criteria. As the owner and operator of the refinery, we care about technical feasibility a whole lot. That wasn't of as much concern to EPA (interview with industry 12/1/94b).

After each of the stakeholding organizations analyzed the final twelve options, using their individually assigned weights for the various criteria, each rank-ordered the options. Much to everyone's surprise, EPA, Amoco, and state regulators agreed on "which options were the most effective and which were least, regardless of their ranking criteria or institutional viewpoints."[57] The consensus top priority was a set of four pollution management options targeting marine barge-loading losses, the installation of secondary seals on gasoline storage tanks to capture fugitive vapor losses, improvements in leak detection and repair programs, and upgrades for what are called "blowdown" stacks (which was one part of a larger program designed to control benzene emissions from refinery wastewater sources). These four steps would prevent or capture almost 6,900 tons of emissions annually at a cost of $510 per ton, while simultaneously reducing the exposure to benzene by 87 percent (see Table 7.1).[58]

Stakeholders also discovered a number of instances in which regulations were poorly matched to the emissions profile of the facility. For example, in the particular case of benzene, a carcinogenic by-product of oil refining and Yorktown's main pollution problem, EPA rules issued in 1990 required Amoco to build a $31 million water-treatment system to capture benzene vapors emanating from wastewater.[59] But data gathered by the joint exploratory venture showed "that EPA's basic assumptions in requiring such a system—assumptions based largely on a 1959 study of benzene emissions from pools of dirty water . . .—were wrong for this refinery. Fumes and evaporation of benzene from the plant's dirty water was, in fact, twenty times less than the 1959 study predicted" (Solomon 1993, A6). At the same time, the project's monitoring efforts uncovered a far more serious, and unregulated, benzene problem at the refinery's loading docks (marine barge-loading area).[60] Given the estimated $6 million capital construction cost of controlling barge-loading emissions, the refinery could have saved $25 million while concurrently cleaning up five times more pollution (Solomon 1993).

Using these revelations, participants turned their attention to the existing regulatory reality governing pollution control at the refinery. They found that existing and anticipated regulations mandated actions ranked as least preferred by each participant. Compliance with these

TABLE 7.1 Comparison of Different Environmental Management Options

Selection Criteria for Release Reduction Projects	Number of Projects	Material Released[a]	Total Release Reduction (Tons/Yr)	Capital Cost $MM	Annual Cost $MM	Benzene Exposure Reduction %	Average Cost $/Ton
1. Existing and Expected Regulatory Requirements[b]	8	VOC/HC	7,300	53.6	17.5	99	2,400
2. Cost-effective Release Reduction	6	VOC/HC Listed HW	7,500	10.7	3.8	87	510
3. Cost-effective Benzene Exposure Reduction	6	VOC	7,100	13.2	4.2	90	590
4. Multiple Criteria[c]							
4a. Work Group (Top 4)	4	VOC	Four options were consistently selected as most effective in different ranking exercises.				
4b. Amoco (Top 4)	4	VOC					
4c. EPA/Virginia (Top 4)	4	VOC					
5. Most favored—All Rankings, All Evaluators	4	VOC	6,900	10.2	3.5	87	510

[a]VOC = Volatile Organic Compounds; HC = Liquid Hydrocarbons; Listed HW = Solid, Hazardous Waste

[b]Regulatory and statutory programs considered include benzene NESHAP, ozone nonattainment, likely Clean Air Act requirements under MACT (maximum available control technology), and HON (hazardous organic NESHAP) rules.

[c]Multiple criteria included release-reduction potential, benzene exposure-reduction potential, cost, impact on liability, transferability to other facilities, status in pollution prevention hierarchy, etc.

Source: Amoco/USEPA Yorktown Pollution Prevention Project, Executive Summary (1992), Table 1.3, p. 25.

laws produced environmental protection on the order of 7,300 tons per year and cut exposure to benzene by 99 percent. Achieving these reductions entailed an average cost to the private sector of $2,400 per ton, or $17.5 million annually. Yet participants agreed that the last increment of pollution reduction—400 pounds—provided such marginal environmental and human health benefits that "going the final mile" was unnecessary. Put differently, stakeholders agreed that if they could redesign and rationalize the regulatory system, they would reduce 94.5 percent of the refinery's pollution output and 87 percent of the risk of exposure to benzene instead of 99 percent. Moreover, the costs of cleaning up at these levels equaled 20 percent of existing annual compliance costs and 19 percent of existing capital expenditures. Over a five-year period, choosing the consensus alternative for a single refinery would save Amoco $70.5 million per year on compliance-related activities and an additional $43.4 million in capital costs, for a total of $113.9 million.

In the middle of the deliberations over how to apply the data, however, and as part of a nationwide campaign to enforce lead pollution laws, EPA fined Amoco $5.5 million for violating lead standards at the Yorktown refinery. The enforcement action "shattered . . . the carefully nurtured trust," "shook Amoco's faith" in EPA as a trustworthy partner, and "came awfully close to derailing [the project]," as much because of the way in which the action was announced as because of the problematic nature of the charges (Solomon 1993; interviews with state regulators 11/7/94a; 11/7/94b; industry 11/8/94b).

> [Amoco was] not steamed up because there was an enforcement action brought, or that it was directed at Yorktown. . . . [T]hat was one of the risks going into [the project]. But we were really steamed up about the way it was handled. EPA published a press release on a Friday afternoon and the first we heard about it was when the guys at the refinery got a call from a local reporter saying, "What's all this about a big lead problem at the Yorktown facility?" By then it was 5 PM Washington time and everyone had gone home for the day. If you're trying to do business with somebody and you get that kind of treatment, it gives you serious reservations. "Is this somebody that I really want to do business with?" . . . [Another problem] related to the alleged lead contamination. We had collected, many, many samples, all analyzed by that point, and EPA had that data. The data showed there was no lead contamination problem. So there may be reasons for having the enforcement action, but it sure wasn't because there were big lead problems at the Yorktown refinery.[61]

The enforcement flap elicited an unprecedented intervention by EPA Administrator Reilly; he called Amoco's chairman, H. Laurance

Fuller, to apologize for not giving Amoco prior warning of the enforcement action and to ask that Amoco not quit the Yorktown Project.[62] The interest of EPA's top official alleviated the concerns of senior managers at Amoco's Chicago headquarters over the depth of EPA's commitment to Yorktown.[63] Yet, just as important to getting the collaborative effort back on track and moving forward, say stakeholders, was the entrepreneurial tenacity and clear commitment displayed by the two project comanagers at the next meeting. According to one workgroup member, the EPA comanager, Mahesh Podar, unequivocally stated, "We're just going to go forward and not let this derail what we were going to do" (interviews with EPA 11/2/94; industry 11/8/ 94b; state regulators 11/7/94a; 11/7/94b).

Having salvaged the joint venture for the moment, the comanagers gathered the Yorktown workgroup in Annapolis to assess the policy implications of the study. A draft version of the project's executive summary was circulated among the stakeholders as well as the peer review committee during the Fall of 1991, when another, far more serious, technical objection emerged.

WAITING UNTIL THE LAST MINUTE

The EPA Air Office's technical staff from OAQPS—the office which had seemingly given the Yorktown Project their tacit blessing fully eighteen months before—decided at the last moment to question the appropriateness of the monitoring methodologies used during the project. To a senior EPA official, the actions were inexcusable: "'They tried to submarine the whole thing. It was ludicrous that a minute before midnight they complained about technical problems they could have addressed' more than a year before when the two comanagers had pressed them to approve the testing procedures" (as quoted in Solomon 1993). Yet the Air Office staff was largely a nonparticipant in the Yorktown effort. Intervention occurred only after OAQPS realized the report's damaging effects on its reputation (interviews with EPA 11/2/ 94; MIEB 1993, 10). "[W]hen the final [draft] report was scheduled to come out [the Air Office] realized that their rules were going to look really stupid. They were inefficient in terms of dollars per pound of pollution reduced."[64]

By insisting that the report not be published without significant changes and qualifications, the Air Office jeopardized the possibility not only that any final report would be issued, but also that implementation would occur. The increased likelihood of failure, and therefore no opportunity to capture the transaction cost savings implied by the project's conclusions, spurred the involvement of senior EPA management once again. Given the departure of the Yorktown Project's main EPA champion, Assistant Administrator Davies, only months before, Deputy Administrator Hank Habicht assumed the primary leadership role for the agency during a series of meetings involving original workgroup participants and recalcitrant OAQPS officials.

> [W]e were ready to release the final report and you basically had one program office saying over our dead body—a clear case of loggerheads. Mahesh [Podar] had reviewed it with his management at OPPE. They were ready to release it. Amoco had reviewed it. We were done. . . . Hank Habicht served as a mediator and really a catalyst to get this damned thing resolved. . . . [He mediated] six months' worth of incredibly detailed wordsmithing and rewriting of the final report (interview with industry 12/1/94b).

In the end, Michael Shapiro, the acting assistant administrator for the Air Office, also intervened and told OAQPS officials, "Look, you can't stop the project. Not following through will make EPA look bad and will be a waste of our invested resources" (EPA 11/3/94b; industry 12/1/94b; 11/8/94b; MIEB 1993).

Ultimately, the entrepreneurial efforts produced results. In May 1992 a final revised report outlining the earlier consensus agreement on pollution reduction options was released for public consumption. The fundamental issues underlying the EPA–Amoco disagreement over monitoring methodologies remained unresolved. Instead, each side simply logged their positions into the final report. As one participant observed, it was a good example of how pollution control "engineers can make lawyers look like very reasonable people. . . . The [OAQPS technical staff] thought the Amoco protocol for measuring emissions wasn't adequate. The Amoco people thought the OAQPS people were all wet" (interview with EPA 11/2/94). Nor were the conclusions criticizing the inefficiencies of air pollution regulations removed from the final report; rather, the wordsmithing exercise deleted references to specific program elements (Solomon 1993).

Nevertheless, the success of the salvage operation was limited because publication of the final report became the end point of the collaborative game; the information and policy suggestions produced by the joint exploratory venture were never transformed into the on-the-ground transaction cost savings implied by the report's conclusions. The failure to go to implementation was a testament to the price exacted by OAQPS for letting the final report go forward. "[OAQPS] basically said, 'We'll accept making it a public document, but let's leave it as a report because we are not willing to act on the recommendations right now' " (interview with EPA 11/2/94).

Lessons Learned: Theoretical and Practical

As in the other cases, Yorktown Project participants were motivated by the prospect of transaction cost savings and the achievement of more of their organizational bottom line, whether environmental protection or gains in economic efficiencies. Significantly, however, the case departs from expectations in that resolving the collective action dilemma required only the leadership, transaction-specific conditions, and organizational reputation components of the pluralism by the rules. Taken together, the three-part assurance mechanism was enough to engender the perception that participants were credibly committed to talking—to bargaining in good faith, sharing information, and creating a facility-wide emissions inventory against which to test hypotheses predicting both better cost and environmental effectiveness. In addition, sustaining the collaborative game necessitated persistent trust-building efforts by the two entrepreneurial comanagers,[65] the presence of a senior EPA "champion" able to defend and promote the project inside the EPA hierarchy, and a leader's (Reilly) willingness to reiterate commitment and restore trust at critical moments. The incomplete version of pluralism by the rules was enough to carry the project to a preliminary consensus agreement regarding the rationalization of the refinery's regulations. The stage was also set for a final report identifying areas where all parties could save on transaction costs. To this extent, participants' initial reason for coming together, the perception that collaboration could lead to transaction cost savings, was validated. Yet the Yorktown collaboration failed in that the recommendations were never implemented, hence transaction cost savings were left on the table.

The failure of the Yorktown case study clarifies the importance of the missing elements of the pluralism-by-the-rules framework: formal binding rules and inclusion. In both the acid rain and reformulated gasoline case studies, there was little doubt that the collaborative ventures, once started, would be implemented. The prospect of implementation carried with it the uncertainty arising from *ex post* enforceability problems and thus created a clear imperative to use formal binding rules to protect stakes. Without such formal agreements delimiting participants' ability to defect or to manipulate arrangements *ex post*, stakeholders faced high uncertainty as to what the outcomes would be, especially whether or how their organizational investments would produce the transaction cost returns of most importance to them. The uncertainty stood as a disincentive to collaborative ventures between traditional adversaries.

Nevertheless, in the Yorktown venture, Amoco purposely refused to ask for a formal set of binding rules because they believed that the credible commitment of senior EPA leaders was enough to guarantee broader organizational commitment to the bargaining *and* implementation phases of the project. It was not until roughly six months into the project that they began to realize how fragmented EPA truly was, how poorly developed the lines of communications among the various pieces of the organization were, and how tough it was going to be for top-level leadership to deliver on their commitment to an integrated pollution control project, even on such a small, site-specific scale. Despite the obstacles posed by EPA's organizational fragmentation, the trust engendered during the project by entrepreneurial leadership successfully held the deal together. On this count it is significant that the ultimatum issued by the Air Office, and their subsequent attempt to rewrite the conclusions to better reflect their programmatic preferences, did not occur until *after* Yorktown's senior-level EPA "godfather," Assistant Administrator Davies, had left EPA.

> The [Air Office] blow-up would not have happened if Terry [Davies] had been there. . . . [His departure] took away a senior-level, day-to-day kind of visible support that would have resolved some of these things. . . . Without having an assistant administrator in place, at a level equal to the leader of the Air Office, there wasn't any way to get those offices to come in and face the issues.[66]

Further, notwithstanding attempts to mount a final salvage operation by several EPA leaders cognizant of the need to protect EPA's reputation (with respect to future collaboration), the damage had been done. The wordsmithing changes in the report directly affected Amoco's stake by restricting the kinds and amounts of transaction cost savings they could gain via implementation. Amoco thus faced a situation in which it had less incentive to move forward into implementation and increased uncertainty as to the trustworthiness of a key bargaining partner.

The other case studies demonstrate that stakeholders could have avoided or at least minimized the uncertainty caused by the loss of leadership by using formal binding rules to protect against opportunistic behavior.[67] In subsequent collaborative arrangements modeled after Yorktown's core concepts (site-specific, integrated pollution prevention), there is evidence that when implementation is assumed from the outset stakeholders insist on formal binding rules. The private sector, in particular, wants formal *ex ante* guarantees allowing them to reap the benefits of their collaborative efforts.[68] Otherwise, it makes little sense for them to participate. There is simply too much uncertainty that, after all is said and done, one of two things will happen: regulators will use the information to increase the regulatory burden, or there will be no change in the regulatory status quo (interviews with state regulators 11/7/94a; 11/7/94b). In the latter case, industry and government will have spent millions of dollars (Amoco spent $1.7 M on the Yorktown study; EPA spent approximately $600,000), yet face the very real possibility that they cannot apply the knowledge gained to capture transaction cost savings. Specifically, industry seeks a guarantee that once consensus agreements on alternative compliance pathways for industrial facilities are reached, such as at the Yorktown refinery, they can choose the alternate compliance path in lieu of the existing regulatory structure if they, not government regulators, deem it worth their time and effort.[69] As well, they seek to "lock in" the credibility of their regulatory counterparts.

> [Within the Common Sense Initiative], we've presented a set of principles ... aimed at ... practical issues that say, "Hey EPA, if we are going to get involved with this collaborative process and dedicate the kind of effort needed to make it work, we want some assurances up front that this process is sincere and that it will be successful. For instance, we don't want to spend a year or two developing all these great guidelines and ideas directly with environmentalists and states and EPA, and then at the eleventh hour find out that [EPA's] Office of General Counsel won't buy into it and cans the whole process. ... We don't want to have in the eleventh hour, after everyone has operated in good faith, EPA backing down in the face of threatened lawsuits from whatever group or organization decides to challenge the agreement. ... We want EPA's assurance that they will demonstrate a sense of fairness as well as some backbone in these decisions once they are made (interview with industry 12/1/94a).

Environmentalists participating in the Common Sense Initiative (CSI) express similar concerns. They worry that the end point of collaborative games will ultimately allow industry to achieve their goals of cost effectiveness and rationalization of the regulatory framework, while ignoring environmental protection.[70] "[I]t's clear that environmentalists are concerned about guaranteeing that their efforts in CSI and other collaborative efforts won't go to waste. If they put all this energy into this they want to see it bear fruit; they want to be assured that something will come of it. ... Otherwise, they won't bother" (interview with environmentalist 11/11/94a).

Another piece of uncertainty is also important in explaining the lack of implementation at Yorktown: the failure to develop credible commitment on the part of certain stakeholders inside the bureaucratic hierarchy and the exclusion of powerful environmental interests. Both violate the principle of inclusion so important to the dynamic of collaborative games.

First, the Yorktown collaboration illustrates how difficult it is to overcome the organizational fragmentation of EPA and engender credible commitment on the part of various program offices, especially when the task concerns integrated pollution control. In an agency dominated by the well-established, discrete jurisdictional prerogatives of program offices (e.g., air, water, solid waste), and where the specific statutory goals mandated by congress overwhelm everything else, the prevention-oriented, multimedia focus of YPPP offered EPA program officials few institutional rewards for participation. As a direct consequence of congressional mandates, some program offices lacked the time and resources to pursue such an innovative collaborative venture. For example, OSWER's assistant administrator liked the Yorktown Project and wanted to support it, yet had little opportunity to do so.

> [B]y comparison [to Davies], it sounds like the assistant administrator for OSWER . . . didn't want to see Yorktown succeed. But it wasn't anything like that. It was just who had more opportunity at the time, and Terry Davies did. OSWER's assistant administrator had Superfund reauthorization breathing down his neck, and RCRA requirements [to push out the door]. . . . He was hounded on a daily basis: "Where's the damn rule? Where's the damn deadline? Where's the hearing today?" . . . People were staying up all night to just meet the basic deadlines (interview with EPA 11/1/94a).

Thus, even when members of EPA wanted to give the project sufficient time and attention to make it succeed, they were prevented from doing so by a prioritization process defined largely by outside political principals.

The Air Office's technical staff in North Carolina—OAQPS—presented a different problem. From their vantage point, the Yorktown Project did not appear to be in their best interest. The collaborative effort stretched the limits of their "core" knowledge regarding air monitoring and sampling protocols. Essentially, the Air Office was being asked to abandon traditional methods of measuring and assessing air pollution issues.

> There were [established] standards of proof and information-collection protocols associated with media-specific and source-category-specific regulation. . . . Then you look at the bigger picture, the world of pollution prevention and integrated pollution control, and the problem becomes "how do you validate the information?". . . [In the] media-specific world, [for example,] EPA has people that have been working in the oil refining industry for years. They've got a method in their mind. It might not be the right method, but they've got a method. . . . [I]t's hard for those people

to see the bigger picture. . . . That's what was playing out in the Amoco project toward the end (interview with EPA 11/3/94b).

In other words, this was a fundamental challenge to OAQPS's role as the agency expert in setting air pollution control standards. Relying on different monitoring and sampling methodologies not only threatened their preconceived worldview regarding how pollution control standards should be set, it raised the possibility that OAQPS had been doing it wrong all along. Moreover, there were no definitive signals from their own assistant administrator in the Air Office, Bill Rosenberg, that the Yorktown venture was a high-priority matter.[71] They thus had difficulty seeing how such a project might redound to their benefit and were left unconvinced that they had a credible stake in the outcome. In the end, these concerns were borne out; the use of different methods led to results questioning the efficacy of existing Air Office rules.

Second, Amoco's discomfort in collaborating with adversaries led them to prevent national and local environmentalists from playing a coequal role in the project. Amoco believed environmental advocates were too much of a "wild card" to credibly commit to such a project, irrespective of EPA leadership's will and skill. They pursued this strategy despite advice to the contrary from fellow industry elites, some of whom had more experience in dealing with environmental groups in partnership efforts. Instead, "[two] token environmentalists . . . from nonthreatening groups" were relegated to a peripheral role as advisors on the peer review committee (interviews with environmentalist 11/11/94; state regulator 11/7/94b). In the end, however, this strategic miscalculation caught up with Amoco. The failure to include environmentalists—a critical and powerful player in the regulatory drama— in the core negotiations cast a pall of illegitimacy over the project's conclusions and compounded the difficulties experienced by EPA in moving the project forward to implementation. For while adding environmentalists to the collaborative mix complicates negotiations and makes consensus building tougher, it ultimately protects government regulators from charges of collusion and capture and decreases the uncertainty associated with implementation once consensus is reached.

Subsequent actions taken by Amoco indicate they seem to have learned this lesson. A long-time observer of national environmental politics "considers this one of the major successes of the Amoco [Yorktown] Project: [Amoco] seem[s] to be willing to work with environmental groups now."[72] EPA has likewise taken steps to strengthen the commitment of the organization and leadership to Yorktown-like collaborative arrangements through the highly visible leadership of Administrator Carol Browner on the Common Sense Initiative (USEPA 1994a). "CSI . . . is her initiative, it is her legacy to the agency. It is something that is brought up at nearly every senior staff meeting. . . . Browner has made it clear that this is not just a fun intellectual exercise; if we find things that all parties agree are important things to do and that require some sort of policy change or procedural change of regulations, then we will take a very hard look at that" (interview with EPA 11/9/94). Others report that Browner is using the Common Sense Initiative "to create a serious management structure for supporting collaborative multimedia approaches so that you don't get all the way to the end of a two-year project and have offices inside EPA say, Gee, we can't live with this. We can't make this work."[73] Finally, recent overtures by congress show nascent acceptance of key principles found in the Yorktown joint venture that will aid agency leaders' attempts to reprioritize resources toward areas where they will have the greatest impact.[74]

In the final analysis, however, the failure of the Yorktown Pollution Prevention Project to go to implementation may prove less important than its overall impact as a model for defining and discovering new, lower (transaction) cost ways of doing business in the environmental policy arena.[75] The value of Yorktown for EPA's comanager on the project, Mahesh Podar, is that "[it] shows that EPA and industry can work together . . . [to] find more effective ways to meet environmental objectives" (Solomon 1993, A6). To others, the three-way consensus on the most effective options confirmed the more general and, according to some, naive premise that "given the same data [government and the private sector] were both likely to come to the same conclusions. . . . The top management of Amoco still talks quite a bit about this particular experience" (interviews with industry 11/8/94a; GAO, 11/9/94). From the perspective of environmental advocates, "the lesson out of the Amoco project" and other collaborative efforts is straightforward: "We've gained a much better understanding of industry and can understand where the environmental opportunities are and what some of the problems are. The problem with the more traditional regulatory process is that . . . we've had a very hit-or-miss approach to environmental regulations, and the result is that we're missing a huge amount of pollution" (interview with environmentalist 11/11/94b). For others, Yorktown signals an appreciation of how bureaucratic "red tape," in the shape of an intensive information search process, can provide positive instead of negative policy results by ultimately yielding a more rational, efficient system of regulation focused primarily on environmental results rather than regulatory rules (interviews with EPA 11/1/94b; GAO, 11/9/94; Hahn 1995).

CHAPTER NOTES

1. Examples include the numbers of regulations and permits issued, inspections conducted, or enforcement actions taken. The General Accounting Office (GAO) documented "the insufficiency of activity-based measures alone" in their 1988 general management review of EPA. They gave the example of Puget Sound, which "was a program success story according to activity-based indicators: All water pollution discharge permits had been issued, all applicable waivers of program requirements were being processed, and so on. However, once EPA shifted its attention to environmental accomplishments, it found that shellfish beds were being closed at an increasing rate, contaminated sediment was being found almost wherever researchers looked, and fish tumors and other signs of poor biological health abounded" (from GAO 1991, 25–26).

2. Lounsbury, as quoted in Solomon (1993, 1).

3. For example, technical, legislative, regulatory, institutional, and economic factors (Yorktown ES 1992, *iii*).

4. The YPPP sought both to prevent the release of pollution and to develop a "whole facility" integrated approach, as contrasted to a "one pipe at a time" approach to environmental regulation (interviews with industry 12/1/94a; EPA 11/1/94a).

5. GAO (1991). EPA's Scientific Advisory Board defines pollution prevention as "changes in raw materials, products or technologies of production which reduce the use of hazardous materials, energy, water, or other resources and/or the creation of pollutants or destructive results, without creating new risks of concern" (USEPA 1990).

6. Dr. Thomas Hauser (1993), executive director of the American Institute of Pollution Prevention, notes that since its inception in 1970 over 90 percent of EPA resources targeted command-and-control-based end-of-pipe solutions (p. 19).

7. See testimony of Thomas Jorling, Commissioner of the New York Department of Environmental Conservation, U.S. Congress. Senate. Taking Stock hearings (1993, 158–59). His testimony draws on a joint exploratory venture in New York involving a Kodak facility (in Rochester, New York). The goal: an integrated whole-facility pollution management/prevention program.

8. With respect to the value of targeting regulatory resources on the "worst" pollution and most-cost-effective solutions, Thomas Jorling notes: "The fact is, none of us, neither the EPA nor the states, have the ability to satisfy all of those textbook [statutory] workloads that are out there. We all make judgments about what's at the bottom end of that system and apply our resources to the top end" (testimony, U.S. Congress. Senate. Taking Stock hearings 1993, 158–59, 162).

9. The Yorktown oil refinery was in an attainment area for air pollution. Several participants suggested that refineries or large industrial facilities located in nonattainment areas would have smaller information deficits than found at Yorktown.

10. Yorktown ES (1992, 3–4). Interviews with industry (12/1/94b, 11/8/94b); EPA (11/1/94a; 11/1/94b; 11/2/94).

11. Industrial facilities such as refineries may have as many as 10,000 fugitive emissions sources. There is general agreement that "[d]irect measurement of each of these sources is not practical" (Yorktown ES 1992, 4).

12. The most prominent example of an unregulated area at the Yorktown refinery involved the barge-loading dock area (virtually all product is shipped over water using marine barges), which accounted for approximately 20 percent of total benzene emissions (Yorktown ES 1992, 7). These particular emissions would have been covered if the refinery had been located in a nonattainment area.

13. Yorktown ES (1992, 6–7). TRI reporting is based on *estimates*, not actual measurements. Criteria pollutants such as carbon monoxide, nitrogen oxide, sulfur dioxide, and particulate matter (PM–10) are not reportable in the TRI. TRI reports covered 728 tons (the sum total of "reported," "new source," and "better measurement" columns in Figure 7.1) out of a total 7,905 tons of air toxics released to the environment, or 9.2 percent. Total pollution releases entering the environment from the Yorktown refinery equaled 15,380 tons per year. Therefore the 728 tons of air toxics covered by TRI represent 4.7 percent of the total releases to all media. Calculations based on Figure 2.5 and Figure 2.7 of the Yorktown ES (1992).

14. Interviews with industry (12/1/94a); environmentalist (11/11/94a). See also Davies (1990); Irwin (1990).

15. See testimony before the U.S. Congress. Senate. Petroleum Refinery Hearings (1992) by Amoco's Richard E. Evans, Vice President, Refining and Engineering (pp. 76–79) and J. C. Klasing, General Manager, Environmental Affairs and Safety (pp. 160–64).

16. The problem of incomplete regulatory contracts does not disappear; rather, there is relative improvement. In particular, EPA saw the Yorktown project as an opportunity for learning how to write "smarter" permits that encouraged people to prevent pollution (interviews with EPA 11/1/94; GAO 11/9/94). This is also one of the primary rationales behind EPA's push to develop the Common Sense Initiative under Administrator Browner.

17. "Pollution prevention can also play an important role in allowing the federal government to avoid future environmental liabilities. Years of neglect and inappropriate disposal practices have resulted in costly environmental liabilities, particularly at Department of Energy and Department of Defense facilities. The Congressional Budget Office estimates that the costs of hazardous waste cleanup and regulatory compliance activities at these and other federal facilities could exceed $150 billion over the next three decades" (GAO 1991, 34).

18. Interviews with industry (11/8/94a; 11/8/94a; 11/10/ 94; 12/1/94b).

19. Interviews with GAO (11/9/94); industry (11/8/94); state regulator (11/7/94). See also the proposed Beyond Compliance Emissions Reduction Act of 1994. The core of this industry initiative focuses on reducing the "transactional and time costs associated with existing environmental regulations, . . . [such as] reduced paperwork and other administrative burdens," in exchange for "provid[ing] the benefits of significant pollution prevention" (p. 1).

20. For example, "[u]nder the Oil Pollution Act of 1990, [oil companies] are required to have a spill response plan. However, the legislation jointly delegates implementation authority to the EPA and the Coast Guard, therefore we are required to have two plans, one for [each]. There is almost 100 percent overlap in these documents because the way the regulations are written they are extremely prescriptive about not only what has to be in the plan, but where it has to be. And to make matters worse, the states have another requirement. So we now have three oil pollution plans in very big volumes sitting at the refinery. These are supposed to be available for employees so that if there's a spill someone will know what to do, . . . the fact is now that there is so much paper these are not useful. They're counterproductive because the things are so thick, self-prescriptive, and complicated that somebody with good intentions wanting to find out something would have a heck of a hard time doing it in a timely way. . . . [And as a result,] they would not be used in an emergency" (interview with industry 12/1/94b).

   21. Howard Klee, Jr. (1993), the director of regulatory affairs for Amoco, reported that "[f]rustration with our inabilit[y] to implement innovative solutions to environmental problems within the regulatory framework led Amoco to initiate the joint pollution prevention initiative in Yorktown" (p. 25). He gave two examples to illustrate the point, one of which concerned "Amoco's production of terephthalic acid, which is used to make polyester. One of the outputs is a wastewater stream that is very difficult to treat. Over the years, Amoco . . . developed a wastewater treatment technology that consumes less energy, generates natural gas, produces less solid waste, and takes up less land. Although the multimedia benefits of this process reportedly (**see endnote) far outweigh the EPA-approved process, it does not quite meet the existing water-quality standards, and [therefore] cannot be constructed in this country" (p. 25). Endnote: The quote is from a transcription of Klee's comments. The word "reportedly" is used to indicate that Klee's claims are based on Amoco data. It is not clear that EPA regulators would interpret the Amoco data in the same manner.

   22. Interviews with industry (11/10/94; 12/1/94a; 12/1/94b). "It is widely acknowledged among environmental experts in industry, in academia, and in government that pollution prevention has the potential to yield effective environmental protection at a fraction of the cost of conventional end-of-pipe controls. Moreover, pollution prevention often produces significant ancillary benefits for a company by initiating and sustaining vigilance over the production process. Increases in production efficiency, improvements in yield, and overall cost reductions have been achieved by companies of all sizes in numerous industries" (MIEB 1993, 3). Part of the potential for cost savings derives from the substitution of materials or new industrial processes for existing practices (GAO 1991, 34). For example, Chevron's Save Money and Reduce Toxics (SMART) program saved the company $3.8 million during its first year (1987). A key part of the savings stemmed from the substitution of nonhazardous for hazardous compounds of drilling mud. (Chevron disposed of 44 percent less hazardous waste during 1987 as opposed to the previous year.) Similarly, Dupont used a pollution prevention survey at one of its major facilities to identify and implement changes in their industrial processes that led to both emissions reductions and $15 million in annual cost savings. The survey was part of an enforcement settlement with EPA (interview with EPA, 11/2/94). For other examples, see Dorfman, Muir, and Miller (1992), Hirschhorn and Oldenburg (1991), Smart (ed.) (1992), and the journal *Pollution Prevention Review*.

23. Interviews with EPA (11/9/94); environmentalist (11/11/94b); Levin and Elman (1990, 9); Mazmanian and Press (1994).

24. Strock, Helliker, and Chan (1991, 323–24). Regulators also generally lack the statutory authority to reach upstream.

25. Jorling testimony, U.S. Congress. Senate. Taking Stock hearings (1993, 158–59); interviews with EPA (11/1/94a; 11/1/94b; 11/3/94a; 11/9/94); environmentalist (11/11/94b). EPA has also started to use enforcement actions to force companies into conducting whole-facility audits and installing pollution prevention programs (see Kling and Schaeffer 1993).

26. Virginia's Department of Environmental Quality viewed the Yorktown effort as more of an "agenda setting" exercise. The outcome might eventually affect the way the state regulated and permitted large industrial sites, but the immediate effects would be limited to the Yorktown site itself (interviews with state regulators 11/7/94a; 11/7/94b).

27. "Initially Virginia was not invited to participate. We had to fight for and make a place for ourselves at the table" (interview with state regulator 11/7/94a). However, "[o]nce Virginia joined, it was fine; the others welcomed us" (interview with state regulator 11/7/94b).

28. Less clear in this case was the willingness of congressional members with vested interests in the regulatory status quo to give the Yorktown Pollution Prevention Project their approval. None of the Yorktown participants interviewed for this case study noted any interference, unexpected or otherwise, from political officials in congress in response to the following question: "During the Yorktown Project were there any unexpected surprises, difficulties, or resistance from the interested parties, including elected officials?" The actions of Senator Max Baucus (D-MT), chair of the Senate Environment Committee, after the conclusion of the project suggest that he probably would have supported a bill to implement the final conclusions if consensus had been reached (e.g., U.S. Congress. Senate. Taking Stock Hearings 1993; his support for site-specific "pilot projects" based on the Yorktown experience in the proposed rewrite of the Clean Water Act during the 103rd Congress; also interview with GAO 11/9/94). Over in the U.S. House of Representatives, however, it is not clear if Rep. Henry Waxman (D-CA), the chair of the Subcommittee on Health and the Environment, would have supported such a dramatic departure from the status quo. In fact, it is plausible that the exclusion of environmentalists, the constituent group of most importance to Rep. Waxman, would ultimately have led him to oppose implementation.

29. Reilly was president from 1975 to 1989. Davies was the executive vice president from 1976 to 1989.

30. In the mid-1970s, the Conservation Foundation initiated a series of dialogue groups among traditional adversaries on specific public topics. The issue receiving the most emphasis was integrated pollution control under the Toxic Substances Control Act (TSCA). The "residual" product of these collaborative efforts was *Business and the Environment: Toward Common Ground*,

edited by Leonard, Davies, and Binder, and published in 1977. A second edition of the book (same title), edited by Kent Gilbreath, followed in 1984. Reilly also led the national consensus-building effort on wetlands, begun in July 1987 (Weisskopf 1988). Three good examples of significant research sponsored by the Conservation Foundation, focusing on collaboration and innovation in environmental policy, are Gail Bingham (1986) *Resolving Environmental Disputes: A Decade of Experience*; Barry G. Rabe (1986) *Fragmentation and Integration in State Environmental Management*; and Nigel Haigh and Frances Irwin (eds.) (1990) *Integrated Pollution Control in Europe and North America*. The Conservation Foundation also was the driving force behind the collaborative "no-net-loss" wetlands effort during the 1980s. Finally, the Conservation Foundation operates RESOLVE, an organization designed to facilitate collaboration among traditional adversaries by using alternative dispute resolution techniques and negotiated rulemaking (reg-neg).

31. "By establishing an office of pollution prevention, EPA Administrator William K. Reilly has made it an agency priority, second only to the enforcement of environmental laws. . . . 'What we are trying to do is articulate pollution prevention across the board,' said Hank Schilling, assistant administrator of the Office of Pollution Prevention." As part of this broader agency-wide effort, EPA's Office of Research and Development released to Congress a Pollution Prevention Research Plan in March 1990 that, unlike past pollution prevention approaches, focused on a multimedia problem set. See *Environment Reporter* (5/4/90, pp. 130–31).

32. Interviews with EPA (11/3/94a; 11/1/94b; 11/2/94; 11/3/94b); environmentalist (11/11/94).

33. Interview with industry (12/1/94b). See for example, Davies and Davies (1975); Leonard, Davies, and Binder (1977); Davies (1983); Davies (1985); Davies (1990).

34. Interviews with EPA (9/27/94; 11/1/94a; 11/1/94b); industry (12/1/94a); MIEB (1993, 5).

35. Guruswamy (1989, 463, 487–89); see also *Inside EPA* (1989) for a recounting of jurisdictional clashes encountered in the case of EPA efforts to implement pollution prevention programs.

36. Interviews with EPA (1/10/94; 1/13/94; 11/3/94a). See also Cook (1988); Davies (1990); Marcus (1980).

37. Interviews with EPA (11/2/94;11/3/94a; 11/3/94b); state regulators (11/7/94a; 11/7/94b); industry (11/8/94b).

38. USEPA (1990d); Ruckelshaus (1985); Schneider (1992a, B20); Shabecoff (1989, A14); Thomas (1987). The trend continues today with the stewardship of Carol Browner. According to EPA Deputy Administrator Hank Habicht, a key part of this has to do with instilling a "new" culture within EPA that does away with the "us versus them" attitude of old, encourages innovation and creativity, and focuses more on strategic planning and pollution prevention. The last point on pollution prevention is especially important, says Habicht, given the "crucial" connection between pollution prevention and the international competitiveness of American industry (see *Environment Reporter* 11/22/91, 1794).

39. Some might argue that the agency's past record of failure in sustaining integrated (multimedia) pollution control initiatives indicates a negative reputation and a general lack of organizational commitment to this particular aspect of the Yorktown Project. But Amoco officials made it clear that they saw little connection between the agency's past integrated pollution control failures and the proposed Yorktown Project. To them, it was like comparing apples to oranges. The earlier EPA efforts were internally focused, not directed at a specific industrial site like a refinery complex, not developed with the active involvement of industry, nor based on an actual emissions inventory (interviews with industry 11/8/94a; 11/8/94b; 12/1/94b). For a brief review of EPA efforts in the area of integrated pollution control, see Davies (1990).

40. Interviews with EPA (11/2/94; 11/3/94a); state regulator (11/7/94a); industry (11/10/94; 12/1/94a; 12/1/94b); MIEB (1993, 9, 12).

41. Interviews with EPA (11/1/94a; 11/3/94a; 11/9/94); industry (11/8/94a; 11/10/94; 12/1/94b).

42. "There were no signed contracts and no agreement on 'Well, gee, if you do this we'll do that, or if you don't do this we won't do that, none of that kind of stuff.' About the only thing we did do was get together and shake hands and said, 'OK, we'll try to work together and see what we can come up with,' recognizing that at any time anybody could say, 'This is not working, I quit'" (interview with industry 12/1/94a).

43. Of course, Amoco could use the information derived during the course of the venture to improve the effectiveness of its environmental compliance activities and management technologies, as long as they stayed within the bounds of the existing regulatory structure.

44. Interviews with EPA (11/1/94a; 11/3/94a; 9/27/94).

45. MIEB (1993, 7). The protocols for monitoring said how often they sampled, when they sampled, which direction the wind was blowing, and so on. Data derived from historical reporting on the refinery's pollution levels were also used.

46. MIEB (1993, 7); interview with EPA (11/1/94b). The Yorktown emissions sampling and monitoring program cost "about $1 million" of the $2.3 million total project cost (Amoco/USEPA Pollution Prevention Project 1992, 4).

47. Solomon (1993); interviews with EPA (11/1/94b; 11/2/94); state regulators (11/7/94a; 11/7/94b); industry (11/8/94b; 12/1/94b).

48. Water and groundwater sampling took longer. "The final release inventory was assembled by using a combination of sampling, measurements, dispersion modeling, and estimates based on emission factors" (Amoco/USEPA Pollution Prevention Project 1992, 4–5). The total number of samples was 959, with 630 air samples, 143 for groundwater, 110 for surface water, 39 for soils, and 37 in the area of solid waste (Amoco/USEPA Pollution Prevention Project 1992, Figure 2.2).

49. As opposed to measured annual values.

50. "Breakout" brainstorming sessions were held on such various topics as (a) process changes to reduce emissions, (b) groundwater protection, (c) criteria for ranking alternatives, (d) permitting issues, (e) general obstacles and incentives, and (f) maintenance and operating practices (see Amoco/USEPA 1991, "Pollution Prevention Workshop," #PB92228543).

51. Source reduction is what the Pollution Prevention Act of 1990 "emphasi[zes] . . . as the primary, if not the exclusive, means to accomplish pollution prevention" (Amoco/USEPA Pollution Prevention Project 1992, 1, 9)

52. The options ranged from producing a single type of gasoline to technical options for particular equipment or processes such as the installation of seals on storage tanks, the reconfiguration of the benzene emissions-control system, the reduction of barge-loading emissions, and the creation of more rigorous leak detection and repair programs for process equipment (e.g., valves, flanges, pump seals) (Amoco/USEPA Pollution Prevention Project 1992, 8). The "project focused on pollution and potential risks posed by normal operation of the refinery and chronic exposure to its releases into the environment. . . . [The study of] emergency and upset events [and their possible] catastrophic consequences," was not included for a variety of reasons (see Amoco/USEPA Pollution Prevention Project 1992, 2). Most solutions focused on air emissions because almost 90 percent of refinery emissions were released into the air.

53. See Table 3.2 on pp. 26–28 of Amoco/USEPA Pollution Prevention Project (1992).

54. Although "[p]rojects designed to comply with several current or anticipated regulations were also included" (Amoco/USEPA Pollution Prevention Project 1992, 8) and "[a]ll options were considered legally acceptable, [the ranking exercise was stripped of regulatory reality in that] no specific regulatory requirements were imposed on the decision-making process" (p. 11).

55. "Due to the inherent uncertainties in risk assessments, the Project focused on *relative* changes in risk compared to existing levels, rather than establishing absolute risk levels" (Amoco/USEPA Pollution Prevention Project 1992, 1–2). For an introduction to risk assessment, risk management, and comparative risk analysis, see Stephen Breyer (1993), Adam Finkel and Dominic Golding (eds.) (1994) and the entire volume of the *EPA Journal* 19 No. 1 (January–March 1993), especially Sheila Jasanoff, "Relating Risk Assessment and Risk Management" (pp. 35–37), and Wendy Cleland-Hamnett, "The Role of Comparative Risk Analysis" (pp. 18–23).

56. "Time and budget constraints limited technology choices to conventional, proven solutions rather than exploring innovative alternatives" (Amoco/USEPA Pollution Prevention Project 1992, 9).

57. Amoco/USEPA Pollution Prevention Project (1992, 11); MIEB (1993, 10). Interviews with EPA (9/27/94); industry (12/1/94b); state regulators (11/7/94a; 11/7/94b).

58. According to project participants, "the driving forces in this prioritization were cost and relative risk reduction, as measured by benzene exposure" (Amoco/USEPA Pollution Prevention Project 1992, 11). As part of this, the workgroup discovered that some pollution prevention measures actually pay for themselves by capturing a product (such as hydrocarbons) valued at more than the cost of compliance. Further, source-reduction options "were more cost effective than most treatment and disposal alternatives. Nevertheless, source reduction alone was not adequate to achieve all the desired or legally required release reductions" (p. 9).

59. Interview with industry (12/1/94b). Solomon (1993, A6), lists a $41 million *estimated* cost. There was a thirteen-year lag between the time the rules covering the capture of benzene vapors from the wastewater source were originally mandated by the 1977 Clean Air Act Amendments and their final promulgation in 1990.

60. The Yorktown refinery is located in an attainment area for air pollution and, as a result, does not have to comply with the more rigorous set of regulations (i.e., pollution control standards) imposed on nonattainment areas like Los Angeles, California. The point is significant because refinery barge-loading dock areas located in nonattainment areas *are* regulated.

61. Interview with industry (12/1/94b). The issues actually listed in the official enforcement action focus primarily on a disputed interpretation of Resource Conservation and Recovery Act rules involving the state of Virginia and Amoco. The two parties had been discussing the issue, but not making much progress, for two years prior to the July 1991 EPA action. Further, Amoco "hadn't been making leaded gasoline in years. The lead contamination was from an old land application, . . . a remediation effort. Everybody knew it was there; Amoco wasn't trying to hide anything. It was a debate over what to do to get rid of the old lead problem" (interviews with state regulators 11/1/94a; 11/1/94b).

62. Reilly also "[r]ecus[ed] himself from any further dealings on the lead fine" (Solomon 1993, A6).

63. Solomon (1993); interview with industry (12/1/94b). Others involved in the Yorktown project argue that although "Amoco was very upset, the chances were still better than 50–50 the project would have gone on anyway" even had Reilly not intervened (interview with EPA 11/3/94a).

64. Interview with EPA (11/1/94b). The report also "said that some air programs . . . were not effective because they put so many constraints on the regulated community that innovation was stifled and compliance was much more expensive than it needed to be" (interview with industry 12/1/94b).

65. Without first establishing trust within the confines of this effort, information-sharing efforts would have suffered, but they didn't.

66. Interview with industry (12/1/94b). An EPA official agreed, "It all fell apart after [Davies] left" (interview 9/27/94). Another EPA participant, while in essential agreement that "his leaving set the project back," was less certain that Davies' leadership would have been able to override the Air Office defection (interview 11/2/94).

67. Depending on the nature of the binding rules used, they might require the consent of congress or, at a minimum, a ruling from EPA's Office of General Counsel (OGC) waiving the application of existing environmental laws and regulations. During Yorktown, there was no procedure to do this "even if [the existing laws] were contradicted by an EPA-sanctioned study" (Solomon 1993, A6).

68. Interviews with EPA (11/2/94); industry (11/8/94a; 11/10/94; 12/1/94a; 12/1/94b). For example, the "4-P" collaborative effort involving Amoco, Dow Chemical, Natural Resources Defense Council, and EPA; EPA's Common Sense Initiative focusing on six industrial sectors; industry testimony during research on applications of the Yorktown study to other pollution control

issues, as conducted by the Senate Environment and Public Works Committee and the General Accounting Office in 1993 (interview with GAO 11/9/94).

69. Interviews with industry (11/9/94; 12/1/94a); EPA (11/9/94); environmentalist (11/11/94b). See also the proposed Beyond Compliance Emissions Reduction Act of 1994.

70. Letter from more than a dozen environmentalists and environmental justice groups to EPA Administrator Carol Browner (10/28/94).

71. The Air Office suffered from some of the same constraints as OSWER. Their resources were overwhelmed by the legislative passage and the implementation of the massive 1990 Clean Air Act Amendments.

72. Interview with environmentalist (11/11/94). In late 1994, Amoco joined with the Natural Resources Defense Council (NRDC), EPA, Dow Chemical, and state regulators from New Jersey to establish the "4-P" joint exploratory venture (Project Summary 1994). They are likewise playing a leading role in the Common Sense Initiative launched by EPA, industry, environmentalists, environmental justice groups, and state regulators in July 1994.

73. Interview with EPA (11/2/94). See also Browner (1993). "Pollution Prevention Takes Center Stage," *EPA Journal* 19 No. 3 (July–September), pp. 6–8. The INFORM (1992) report *Environmental Dividends: Cutting More Chemical Wastes* (by Dorfman, Muir, and Miller) notes that in 1982 pollution prevention "was merely an idea optimistically whispered about. . . . Today, 10 years later, it stands front and center stage—a clear call to an environmentally sound future" (p. *xi*). See Kling and Schaeffer (1993) for a brief discussion of the depth and breadth of EPA's "Flagship" pollution prevention programs.

74. For example, passage of the 1990 Pollution Prevention Act; Taking Stock hearings (U.S. Congress. Senate 1993) focused on the high costs and general ineffectiveness of many federal pollution control statutes as well as policy innovations promising to provide better environmental results for less cost, including market-based incentives, risk assessment, pollution prevention, integrated pollution control, and collaboration among the major stakeholders; Senator Max Baucus (D-MT) and Senator John Chafee (R-CT) sponsorship of the Clean Water Act "safe havens" concept modeled after the Yorktown Project; intensive study by Senate Environment and Public Works Committee of the policy implications of the Yorktown case study in 1993; Senator Patrick Moynihan's (D-NY) endorsement of risk assessment (see Moynihan 1993); the attempts of the 104th Congress to pass risk-assessment legislation for environmental regulation.

75. See comments of Randall Browning (Amoco) in Mintz (1994); interviews with EPA (11/3/94b); industry (11/10/94).

8

Reinventing the Regulatory Game

Increasingly, politicians, policy analysts, environmentalists, the regulated community, and regulators are deciding that standard ways of conducting business in the environmental arena are simply not good enough. New methods of ensuring environmental progress are needed.[1] The question of which regulatory methods best meet this need is open to debate.[2] It is very much reminiscent of the period when contemporary environmentalism first came to the fore. At that time, many agreed that the old pollution control strategy of relying on the states for policy performance was flawed, and that the federal government needed more power if environmental protection was to have meaning. But forging solutions was another matter, and it remained an open, contested question for years. In the cases studied here, the high costs and ineffectiveness of hierarchy and its concomitant dynamic of no-holds-barred pluralism are open to question and in need of solutions.

Because the collaborative game appears to offer significant relief, participants in pollution control politics are cautiously testing its potential. To stakeholders, the transaction cost benefits associated with collaboration are readily apparent. Collaborative games are a way to reinvent government, to move beyond the conflict game where all sides have spent a lot of time and a lot of resources blocking opponents' initiatives and canceling each other out. Participants in pollution control politics "fe[el] that if we [can] take just a fraction of the resources we're using to disagree and focus that energy on finding common ground, we [can] all create a better future for the environment and economy."[3]

The three cases illustrate the dimensions of the new collaborative game. Collaborative games share power and information among public and private sector stakeholders; emphasize flexible compliance arrangements in exchange for greater rigor in monitoring systems; rely on consultation, consensus, and a concerted search for better information; and seek out creative compromises providing win–win solutions. In short, collaborative games make explicit the connection between politics and administration and seek to channel the political dynamic accompanying regulatory decision making into arrangements delivering more bang for the regulatory buck. The cases lend support to

Bardach and Kagan's (1982), Ayres and Braithwaite's (1992), and Scholz's (1991) contention that if the institutional design is right, principals and agents in political and administrative games will support effective administrative games.[4]

Just as important, however, is the need to understand why collaboration is not being used on a larger scale. While collaboration yields important benefits in the form of transaction cost savings, playing the game poses added uncertainties for participants that are difficult to surmount. As attractive as the prospective savings are, uncertainty concerning the outcome of the collaborative game is more powerful, and the set of conditions required to overcome that uncertainty are hard to come by. This is pluralism by the rules. Collaboration is not necessarily evidence that the pluralists got it wrong; its limited use is evidence of how correct they were in seeing the limits of the American political system. But the fact that collaboration is occurring, and that it is occurring in the most conflictual regulatory arena in American government, even if on a limited scale, points out how conventional wisdom often ignores developments having significant ramifications for how American society solves public policy problems. More importantly, the contextual changes that have made pluralism by the rules possible—by heightening participants' perceptions of the damaging relationship between high transaction costs and their own organizational goals—are still present, giving pollution control stakeholders continuing incentives to engage the collaborative format.

Employing pluralism by the rules to reach public policy goals teaches a number of basic lessons and raises several questions important to the study of public policy and public administration. The lessons include the real potential for success and the difficulty of reinventing government in the collaborative mold. Questions arise in the areas of bureaucratic leadership, democratic accountability, representativeness, and the overall viability of collaborative games.

THE PROMISE OF COLLABORATIVE GAMES

The first lesson centers on the promise of collaborative games; there is real potential for improving the efficiency of government. Such a conclusion directly challenges Moe's (1989) thesis that when powerful, competing interests collide, ineffective bureaucracy necessarily results. Just as importantly, levels of success are measured not by theoretical conjecture, but in most cases by empirically verifiable transaction cost savings. Results are evident in a number of areas.

Process costs   Stakeholders generally agreed that information search and program specification costs were roughly comparable to or lower than alternatives, while the intensity of program negotiations using the collaborative format raised negotiation costs, particularly for smaller groups. According to participants, however, the key was the amount of value received for the costs incurred. The relative willingness to share information and the ability to discuss and confront others' positions and data meant that EPA and state regulators not only had access to (controlled) more information, but also were in a better position to assess its quality. The Yorktown Project's generation of massive amounts of new data overcame scientific information deficits. It also created a basis for the discovery of common ground in the area of risk assessment. The opportunity to directly shape the details of regulatory outcomes let state regulators and industry explain and incorporate their expertise on implementation matters and, in some cases, transformed skeptical participants into staunch supporters of outcomes (interview with industry 1/21/94). In each case, participants perceived that the development of additional information and credible stakes translated into better specified, more workable regulatory programs able to improve cost effectiveness, shift the focus of the implementation game from regulatory rules to environmental results, and reduce the uncertainty associated with environmental results.

Implementation Costs Legislation and regulations communicate to stakeholders how implementation is to be achieved, the level and distribution of compliance costs, the basis upon which compliance is determined, and ultimately whether an organization's interests are reflected in the final agreement. These legal parameters directly affect transaction costs experienced during implementation. Regulators like the added rigor of monitoring arrangements produced by the reformulated gasoline (RFG) and acid rain collaborations because it increases the certainty of (non)compliance patterns, making it harder for polluters to shirk successfully and making the achievement of program goals more likely. Put differently, regulators see the added rigor as a valuable additional tool in the fight against pollution—it helps them locate, classify, and efficiently target enforcement resources on those polluters who consistently and even egregiously violate program standards, and it helps them do it in quicker fashion. Compliance costs paid by the regulated community are also lower vis-à-vis alternatives with the RFG reg-neg and acid rain government-imposed market, while the Yorktown joint exploratory venture projected compliance savings in the tens of millions over the first few years of implementation. Likewise, EPA officials in charge of the acid rain program make the case that program administration costs devoted to implementation are less under the market-based arrangement than for a comparable command-and-control arrangement (see Chapter 6). Further, the early evidence suggests that the flexibility afforded to industry with government-imposed markets is positively affecting program adaptability, both in terms of accelerated rates of technological and managerial innovation and the ability of industry to shift gears in tandem with changing information and markets. Finally, collaborative games are encountering lower levels of resistance, limited litigation, and attitudinal changes in which the regulated community channels energy into making programs work instead of fighting their existence. Similarly, the willingness of reformulated gasoline stakeholders, many of whom are traditional adversaries, to unite in opposition to the defection of the ethanol lobby illustrates the remarkable potential of collaborative games for transforming participant behavior into a powerful supporting mechanism for regulatory decisions.

Timeliness   Timeliness is important for environmentalists and regulators charged with protecting the environment, for state regulators needing to comply with federal mandates, and for industry planning activities, especially when regulations create new markets or when the default mechanism imposes severe, automatic penalties for noncompliance. Of particular importance to enhanced timeliness are the behavioral transformations effected through stakeholders' "ownership" of outcomes and, at least with acid rain, the separation of compliance obligations from the emissions-trading program. Instead of obfuscation, litigation, and delay, the dynamic is one where participants willingly channel their energies into making programs work. The positive effect of collaborative games on timeliness is evident in several areas. Not only did the market-based acid rain program break a decade-long congressional deadlock on acid rain pollution, the explicit legislative language protecting participants' stakes helped the acid rain program successfully meet the congressionally imposed rulemaking deadline. The potential of reg-neg to meet initial stakeholder expectations of improved rulemaking timeliness is clear as well. Prior to the ethanol defection, the RFG rule was well on its way to the final stages of the rulemaking process within nine months after the 1990 Clean Air Act Amendments passed. Congressionally scheduled program start dates have also been met for the acid rain and reformulated gasoline programs. These "successes" are in keeping with the conventional wisdom that collaboration reduces delay compared to traditional methods of decision making (see Kerwin and Furlong 1992). Yet a recent in-depth examination of fifteen EPA reg-negs by Coglianese (1997) disputes conventional wisdom regarding timeliness. He finds that reg-negs, on average, take as long as traditional rulemakings. To the extent that this revelation affects participants' expectations regarding the overall mix of benefits accruing from collaborative games, such games will be harder to initiate.

Environmental Results   Environmental progress and environmental performance can be difficult to measure. Environmental advocates, their legislative allies, and regulators often measure success in this area by the number of legislative breakthroughs where environmental goals are codified into law, the stringency of pollution control standards, and the number of enforcement actions. However, as amply demonstrated in prior chapters, there is significant uncertainty here—laws may not be implemented for a variety of reasons, standards may be consistently and widely violated, and the number of EPA enforcement actions may tell us more about political control of the bureaucracy than the effects of pollution control programs on environmental quality.

Players in national pollution control politics have gravitated toward collaborative games in part because collaboration promises to reduce the degree of uncertainty associated with promised environmental results by speeding up rulemaking and implementation processes; improving the rigor of monitoring programs, including emission caps within environmental programs; transforming industry resistance into active facilitation of program goals; defining compliance in terms of environmental results rather than regulatory rules; or expanding environmental protection through shared savings with the environment.

Ascertaining environmental progress and performance by using such criteria, however, suffers some of the same problems as the more traditional criteria already noted. Objectively, it is hard to know whether a particular program design is better or worse than another possibility. For example, will a more rigorous monitoring program actually lead to better environmental results? Will an emissions cap ultimately limit the production of targeted pollutants as intended? Will a focus on environmental results rather than regulatory rules produce better environmental quality? Objective answers to such questions may not be forthcoming until years later, if at all.

But for the purpose of understanding politics, the important thing is that the players involved in collaborative games perceive that the environment will be better off with collaborative processes and programs designed via collaboration, whether compared to the historical norm of command-and-control programs or in relation to traditional notice-and-comment rulemaking processes. In each of the three cases studied here, participants expected progress toward a cleaner environment because they perceived that collaborative games increased the level of certainty surrounding promised environmental results. Greater frequency of pollution data transmission using continuous emissions monitoring for sulfur dioxide pollution (acid rain) and sixty to eighty compliance surveys per year in the RFG program (as opposed to the norm of one or two) produce higher quality databases upon which to judge program effectiveness. In addition, the acid rain program's aggregate emissions cap for sulfur dioxide pollutants firmly connects program rules to environmental results. Further, "smarter" regulations developed for acid rain and the Yorktown Project defined compliance success in terms of actual environmental results, rather than rule-based proxies disconnected from results. As part of this, the Yorktown effort discovered a series of unregulated, yet significant, pollution problems that, when added to the regulatory mix by using an integrated pollution prevention approach, could be resolved without increasing the regulatory burden on Amoco Oil. As well, incentives provided by the acid rain government-imposed market framework are inducing utilities to reduce pollution much faster than originally anticipated.

Finally, there are shared savings. The expected cost effectiveness of the government-imposed market for acid rain created bargaining latitude for environmentalists. They were able to ask for, and receive, greater pollution reductions than the utility industry had previously been willing to support under a comparable command-and-control arrangement. Moreover, although the Yorktown Project never made it to implementation, the significant size of the savings—$113 million in five years—gave room for maneuvering in the same fashion; the potential was there. Participants could have agreed *ex ante* to devote 10 to 15 percent of any compliance cost savings to defraying the costs of program negotiations and the extensive monitoring effort, and to paying for additional, locally based, environmental protection programs.

THE DIFFICULTY OF REINVENTING THE REGULATORY GAME

Reinventing government regulation in order to produce such transaction cost savings is not easy, especially when the new game departs so dramatically from the norm of no-holds-barred pluralism (see DiIulio, Garvey, and Kettl 1993). Collaborative games are not spontaneously generated and maintained by virtue of incentive alignments, or "getting the incentives right." Although it is true that potential transaction cost savings are a powerful motivator and are critical to understanding the overall game dynamic, putting the game into play requires a set of rules—pluralism by the rules. The "rules" foster the credible commitment needed to move the collaborative game forward. They reduce the uncertainty and risks associated with the collaborative game by selectively promoting collaboration and by structuring participant behavior to minimize the likelihood of *ex post* opportunism. They also spread power among the major stakeholders of the policy network by recognizing the implicit property rights (power) that information asymmetries and complex interdependence confer on each, creating credible stakes in decision-making processes and regulatory outcomes for all. Through the reduction of uncertainty and the creation of credible stakes for all, the "rules" carve the political space within which the creative compromises leading to transaction cost savings and win–win outcomes can be crafted. In this way, pluralism by the rules expands the policy space within which partisan mutual adjustments are possible beyond the original, limited set of possibilities found with traditional pluralism.

But catalyzing the game—surmounting the initial collective action problem—is not an easy task. A series of objective conditions must be met. The regulatory program must comply with several transaction-specific conditions. There needs to be an agency with an established reputation of support for the collaborative format and for fair dealing when unexpected contingencies arise. All the major players must want to play, and they must all agree to a set of binding rules structuring opportunities and constraints during the bargaining and specification stages of the game, as well as after the signing of any consensus agreement. Discovering a regulatory program that satisfies one or perhaps even two parts of the institutional framework is challenge enough, let alone a program that complies with every institutional component.

What is equally clear is that stable, enduring outcomes are difficult to achieve, even with pluralism by the rules guiding stakeholder behavior and protecting their stakes. Two of the three case studies show the difficulty of effecting credible commitment from the many interests engaged in the game, much less maintaining that commitment over time. The story of reformulated gasoline demonstrates the fragility of the assurance afforded by the reputation and skills of an entrepreneurial leader and even of a formal binding agreement to preempt *ex post* intervention. Delays and uncertainty caused by the defection of ethanol producers naturally complicated the task of transaction leaders and raised questions about the ability of formal protocols to provide binding certainty within a network composed of traditional, often bitter, adversaries. The Yorktown Project, on the other hand, suffered a series of challenges necessitating continual trust-building by the project's two entrepreneurial comanagers and senior EPA leaders. In the end, the EPA's Air Office scuttled the deal, demonstrating that enduring collaboration on *integrated* pollution control is likely to require one of two things: a prior congressional blessing along the lines of an alternative compliance pathway or, as has been suggested for years, an internal reorganization of EPA that shifts authority away from the single-media program offices.[5]

Nevertheless, in the RFG case the degree of instability should be kept in perspective. Despite the difficulties caused by the ethanol lobby's defection, the original reg-neg agreement is intact and the RFG program became fully operational as scheduled in January 1995.[6] Each development is a sign that collaborative networks hold potential for managing conflict in highly adversarial arenas and improving the likelihood of enduring, stable regulatory outcomes compared to no-holds-barred pluralistic alternatives. Moreover, as the acid rain and reformulated gasoline outcomes make clear, traditional adversaries are developing a solid self-interest in collaborative processes which necessarily raises the stakes for politicians considering *ex post* intervention. Simply put, there is a high risk for the political principal who intervenes when collaboration produces a broad consensus among stakeholders.

RECONCEIVING THE ROLE OF BUREAUCRATIC LEADERS

Transforming the potential of collaborative games into improved policy performance hinges on how well the public sector leverages its resources by tapping into the expertise and information of others. Under such an arrangement, the interlinkages among organizations become more important, as does the role of the political and administrative leaders responsible for connecting organizations and shepherding regulatory transactions through the legislative or administrative thickets.[7] Just as incentives alone are not enough to catalyze and sustain collaborative games, the institutional components of the pluralism-by-the-rules framework only take us so far; something more is needed. Success in catalyzing, sustaining, and implementing collaborative games requires a new conception of the role of public sector leaders and managers in the policy process: the idea of active, entrepreneurial leadership.

Traditional conceptions of leadership, dating back to the Progressive era and drawing primarily from orthodox public administration theory, conceive of public leaders as guardians of the public interest, with the public interest necessarily defined by elected officials (Goodnow 1900; W. Wilson, 1887). Because politics is treated as separate from, and superior to, administrative decision making, administrative leaders are essentially mechanistic "tools" who, by virtue of limited discretion, are consigned to the faithful implementation of their superiors' commands. In this view, bureaucratic leadership is an oxymoron, connoting nothing of the active exercise of power and strategic discretion normally accorded the term "leadership."[8]

Pluralism by the rules, on the other hand, accepts that the politics/ administration dichotomy is false. Bureaucratic decision making is unavoidably political in nature.[9] The chief task for the leader is to mobilize, coordinate, and sustain the political interaction among affected interests and to, in effect, share authority in the selection and design of the means to policy ends. Leaders must learn to match regulatory transactions with the conditions under which pluralism by the rules is possible and cajole participants into joining. They hold primary responsibility for maintaining the collaborative effort when the unexpected occurs or when questions arise regarding a particular player's commitment to the game. Ultimately, they must possess the skill and prescience to forge the creative compromises that keep *public* goals intact, while simultaneously allowing players to reap their individual transaction cost benefits.[10]

Success necessitates dynamic, entrepreneurial leadership cognizant of the constraints placed on the exercise of power by the consensual nature of the authority relationship in regulatory politics. Leaders must thus be able to persuade as much as or more than command.[11] Leaders must convince potential game participants that collaboration is possible, that their stakes in the outcomes will be respected and protected, and that at every step of the process, if they cooperate in good faith, others will do likewise. In short, entrepreneurial leaders must be able to "sell" the benefits of participating in collaborative games to the individual stakeholders and thereby inspire transaction participants to transcend the sort of self-interested behavior that can result in shirking. Otherwise, the potential gains from trade, in this case more of both collective public policy goals and individual organizational goals, will go unrealized.

At the heart of this conception of leadership is the ability to convey trust, to convey credible commitment to both the process of collaboration and the goals of the process, before, during, and after collaborative games. Credible commitment is necessary because leaders are asking participants to accept the additional risks and uncertainties accompanying collaboration. Participants need to know that public agencies are in the game for the long run, and leadership, along with a general agency reputation of support for collaborative games and fair dealing, is the primary instrument for signaling such long-term commitment.

Leaders demonstrate credible commitment through reputation, rhetoric, and authoritative action. Reputation derives from an established record of (1) trustworthiness when dealing with others; (2) support for collaborative methods; (3) acceptance of agency goals, in this case environmental protection; and (4) sensitivity to, and acceptance of, the organizational goals of primary importance to all game participants. A trustworthy leader, for example, is likely to possess a track record of resolving issues in a fair manner rather than taking advantage of circumstances to advance self-interests at the expense of others. Sensitivity to others' goals refers to a leader's willingness to recognize the legitimacy of all participants' goals, even those organizations whose principal focus is economic growth and the pursuit of profit, goals which have little direct relation to pollution abatement. The reputation might come, at least in part, from past professional experiences, such as Bill Rosenberg's employment in the private sector, or William Reilly and Terry Davies' time with the Conservation Foundation. Or it might stem from long service within a public agency or in congress, such as the cases of EPA's Mahesh Podar[12] and Senator George Mitchell, respectively.

Leadership rhetoric and exhortation provide overt signals in support of collaborative game processes and goals. As Philip Selznick (1957) says, leaders must infuse organizations with value and convince potential participants that collaborative games are an important agency priority, enough so that the chance is relatively small that an effort will be abandoned in midstream.

Leaders also need to display a willingness to use the authority of their position to promote, protect, and enforce collaborative deals. In general terms, this means establishing and supporting agency programs and decision-making processes that match their rhetoric. EPA Administrator Reilly's (Bush Administration) creation of a Pollution Prevention Office is a good example, as is Carol Browner's (Clinton Administration) efforts to integrate collaborative decision making more fully into EPA's management structure. More specifically, as was seen in the Yorktown Project, active promotion of a collaborative effort prior to its formal engagement can be crucial in getting collaborative games off the ground, particularly when trust among participants is low or when the specific style of collaborative game is new and hence entails additional uncertainty. Promotion requires leaders to communicate with potential game participants and cajole them into joining collaborative efforts. Leadership action may also be required to hold deals together whenever "rough water" is encountered, whether during the bargaining phase or afterward during implementation of consensus agreements. "Rough water" is when the decisions of participants, or events external to the collaborative game, threaten to either derail the process by destroying the trust within collaborative games or significantly alter the consensus agreement after the fact. Strong links between a leader's ability to calm rough water and the maintenance and successful conclusion of collaborative games are found in all three case studies: in the actions of EPA leaders throughout the Yorktown Project, the intervention of Reilly just prior to the signing of the reformulated gasoline reg-neg agreement, Rosenberg's diplomacy to salvage the RFG rulemaking from deadlock, the refusal of Rosenberg and Reilly to capitulate to presidential pressure after the ethanol lobby defected from the RFG agreement, and the willingness of majority party leaders in both the house and senate to use unconventional lawmaking methods to promote and protect the acid rain emissions trading program.

The entrepreneurial leader is much more than a "simple" broker— a passive, neutral "referee" who enforces procedural rules to ensure a level playing field and mediates outcomes reflecting the balance of interests of nongovernmental parties.[13] Instead, entrepreneurial leaders occupy the role of a "complex" broker; they hold a dual responsibility— to broker a workable compromise, yet without forgoing a fundamental obligation to inject government's perception of the public interest into the proceedings. The parameters assigned by elected officials are still the chief constraint upon bureaucratic leaders' discretion. From this perspective, bureaucratic leadership is about discovering, catalyzing, and implementing effective means to externally defined ends, not whether the overarching policy goal of environmental protection is appropriate or not. If collaborative game participants are inclined to ignore the policy goals set by congress, bureaucratic leaders can use their veto power over the proceedings to pressure participants into rethinking their positions or, if need be, to stop the game altogether (therefore switching it back to the notice-and-comment format).[14]

In cases where congressional intent is less than clear or is in conflict with executive branch preferences, public sector leaders need to have a clear sense of agency goals—what the public interest is—and they need to articulate those goals prior to engaging the collaborative format. Doing otherwise increases the chance that leaders will default into the "simple" broker role, which increases their exposure to manipulation by private interests, thereby diminishing their ability to protect some notion of a broader public interest.[15] Industry, environmentalists, and EPA officials count this as one of their major concerns (or complaints) about the collaborative games conducted by EPA. In too many instances EPA is marching into collaborative games without stopping to consider its goals or interests, independent of other participants.

Thus far, the conception of entrepreneurial leaders assumes a naive trust that leaders will do everything in their power to protect the public interest as defined by their political superiors—even after prolonged, intimate contact with their private-sector counterparts. Yet James Madison's warning that people are both ambitious and lacking in angelic qualities is equally applicable here (*Federalist #51*). Legitimating collaborative games and the exercise of entrepreneurial leadership by unelected bureaucratic leaders requires some sort of mechanism by which they can be held accountable.

HOLDING REINVENTED GOVERNMENT ACCOUNTABLE

Finding better ways to hold government agencies accountable for their decisions is central to the effort of reinventing government. Outcomes that make it difficult for elected officials to intervene, when combined with shared power and the need for bureaucratic discretion implied by creative dealmaking, have important implications for democratic accountability. Do collaborative games, by emphasizing efficiency and effectiveness, compromise our ability to hold public sector decision makers accountable? To the extent that this question is answered in the affirmative, the more difficult it will be to reinvent government in the collaborative mold, since the added uncertainty is likely to deter legislators from sponsoring or endorsing collaborative games.

Traditional conceptions of accountability place the power to decide and shape policy firmly in the hands of elected officials. Bureaucracies are constitutionally charged with the faithful execution of laws and are legally empowered to act only to the extent permitted by presidential and congressional delegations of authority. Accountability is achieved to the extent that bureaucracies and their decisions are responsive to elected officials. Administrative law doctrines and the Administrative Procedure Act of 1946 guide agency decisions and provide a measure of accountability by, for example, "prohibiting government officials from delegating their policymaking authority to persons or institutions that are not politically accountable" (Perritt 1986, 486), limiting *ex parte* contact, and forcing the agency to provide a factual record and rationale in support of final rules. Judicial review is then available for those administrative decisions which either belie legislative intent or violate these legal procedural requirements. The role of government agencies in the administrative process is that of an authoritative, third-party decision maker; affected interests are given the opportunity to plead their case before the bureaucracy, but in the end must abide by agency conclusions (Fiorino 1988; Perritt 1986).

By contrast, collaborative games define accountability more broadly. The traditional model of top-down accountability is melded with a controlled degree of bottom-up accountability to the stakeholders in a particular transaction. Control over the process of deciding the shape of regulatory programs is shared with interested, nongovernment parties. The presumption is one of equality among the players sitting at the negotiation table. Theoretically, "controlled" accountability means that bureaucratic responsiveness to bottom-up demands are constrained by the specific grant of statutory authority from democratically elected politicians, the same procedural constraints just described, and the courts as a venue of last resort. As well, the presence of countervailing interests, in this case environmentalists and industry, keep the negotiations honest, since deviations from congressional intent will likely cause the aggrieved party to litigate, trigger a fire alarm, or otherwise act in a manner designed to protect its interests.

The danger is that granting entrepreneurial bureaucratic leaders too much discretion under such conditions may make a mockery of accountability. There are three chief areas of concern. First, the additional information, or expertise, developed through collaborative games and shared among participants may not flow upward to members of congress and the president. Second, the close contact afforded by collaborative games creates additional opportunities for agency leaders to cultivate clienteles. In the worst-case scenario, stakeholders will take advantage of the information asymmetry and added opportunities for discussion to conceive of win–win deals having little or nothing to do with the broader policy goals laid down by elected officials. The problematic outcomes will not trigger any alarms and congress will not be alerted that anything is wrong, however, since the major players with the interest and resources to monitor and report on such things are beneficiaries and will necessarily refrain from such actions.[16]

Moreover, police patrol oversight is unlikely to uncover the problem either. The more formal police patrol oversight is costly and congressional resources are finite. In addition, "happy" collaborative games which produce satisfied stakeholders give legislators no opportunity to satisfy constituent groups, while oversight in a conflict-laden area gives legislators ample opportunity to solve problems, satisfy unhappy constituent groups, and ultimately strengthen their electoral connection. As a result, congressional oversight will tend to gravitate toward those environmental and regulatory issues loaded with conflict.

The third potential problem with respect to accountability involves the blurring of the line of authority from members of congress to EPA administrators. Technically, the authority relationship remains intact. The actions of bureaucratic officials are constrained by substantive grants of authority and the Administrative Procedure Act. Nor is the "delegation doctrine" of administrative law violated.[17] Operationally, however, the authority relationship is more tenuous. By agreeing *ex ante* to be bound by any conclusions grounded in consensus, agencies necessarily give up their traditional role of authoritative, third-party decision maker with complete control over regulatory program design. Within the collaborative format,

> [t]he administrative agency agrees to act as the theoretical equal of the other parties by sitting at the table to negotiate and resolve issues. A decision is not made until the affected interests . . . consent to it. The

agency is not delegating decision authority to affected interests but is participating as one of them, with the same authority to block or promote consensus as any other party. What distinguishes the agency is that it is the only party with the authority to withdraw ... and propose a rule as its own [using the more conventional, adversarial, formal process of notice-and-comment rulemaking]. The equality of the parties ... is in this sense a fiction, but it can be sustained if the agency and the other parties accept it (Fiorino 1988, 769).

The pitfall is that once the collaborative game is in full swing, and considerable agency resources and reputation are invested, there is the possibility that a "consensus-minus-one" could develop in which the agency is the lone dissenter because it views the solution as suboptimal or even illegal. Under such circumstances, how likely is it that bureaucratic officials will act responsibly by exercising their right to withdraw and use their legal authority to issue a different rule? Endowed with limited resources, facing the additional costs of a notice-and-comment rulemaking, and knowing that withdrawal assures litigation and damages their reputation of commitment to collaborative games, such decision makers face powerful incentives to acquiesce to the near consensus, even if it means a suboptimal, perhaps illegal outcome narrowly responsive to established clientele groups.

Given these potential problems, some method of keeping tabs on outcomes is needed. What might effective accountability look like with a collaborative mode? How do we know it when we see it? The first and best method of assessing accountability is to focus on the measurable transaction cost results and compare them to statutory goals (and, in a case like the Yorktown Project, assess outcomes against existing statutes). Were rulemaking deadlines met? Is the program being implemented on schedule? Does the rule maintain congressionally specified environmental standards or, as in the case of the RFG rule, are they more rigorous? Is the outcome meeting pollution-reduction goals in a timely fashion, or are polluters reducing pollution slower or faster than originally planned? Are there any shared savings with the environment which stretch the benefits of the original program into other areas of environmental protection? What are the rates of innovation for control technologies? Is industry reaping significant compliance cost savings as expected? What are the administrative costs of operating the program? What about the rates of compliance versus noncompliance by the regulated community? All of these are appropriate measures of program performance that can be used to assess the accountability of collaborative games.[18]

In cases like the acid rain emissions-trading program, a good measure of accountability is built into the regulatory game through explicit legislative language. Outcome assessments are possible. But such laws are difficult to produce and may be the exception rather than the rule (Katzmann 1990). As well, in the other collaborative games examined here, the measurable results like increased monitoring rigor or improved efficiency of pollution reductions are produced *after* legislative action. Given the uncertainty surrounding the final form of such accountability measures and the differing incentive structures facing democratic principals and bureaucratic agents, the accountability problem—the problem of controlling bureaucratic preferences—never completely disappears. But ensuring accountability is an issue in any arrangement where power is delegated, and as Lowi (1993) admits, "delegation of power is an inevitable and necessary practice in any government"(p. 149; Schoenbrod 1993).

Nevertheless, the uncertainty surrounding accountability may be mitigated to the extent that senior management and entrepreneurial transaction leaders at EPA evoke a professional ethos and reputation guided by an environmental ethic which seeks to balance environmental and economic concerns. In practice, the "new" breed of environmental professional would display an overarching concern for efficiency and program results, whether in terms of industry's compliance costs or agency objectives, but with the bottom line defined as equivalent or better environmental results than are required by the statute in question. The presence of such professionals would affix greater certainty to the kinds of decisions made by the bureaucracy. When added to the other guarantor of accountability—the active participation of constituency groups important to a legislator's electoral and/or policy interests—the new professionals might well solve enough of the accountability problem that members of congress will endorse or allow a greater number of administratively based collaborative games to go forward.

ACCESSING REINVENTED GOVERNMENT

Another difficulty in reinventing the regulatory game involves the question of access. The reinventing government movement preaches customer service. But just how much input should the customer have?[19] Too much means the process is likely to bog down, buried in a morass of detailed, customized demands for responsiveness. Too little may produce decisiveness, but create the impression of an elite-driven, non-democratic process. Collaboration presents a picture of decision making where participation is limited to a select, elite few. Those with the power to block or impede policy outcomes are invited to sit at the negotiating table. Everyone else is relegated to the role of bystander, unable to access, much less influence, deliberations concerning the details of the regulatory game. The question becomes: Does everyone who needs to be at the bargaining table have a chance to participate or, at a minimum, have the opportunity to influence collaborative outcomes? Or are collaborative games simply a replay of the "heavenly chorus" pluralist dynamic described by E. E. Schattschneider (1960), except that major national environmental groups are now part of the elite circle of interests invited to play?

Keeping in mind the transaction-specific conditions under which collaborative endeavors are most likely to surmount the collective action dilemma, initial access may or may not be a problem. Much depends on whether stakeholders are free to select the "interest" grouping they wish to be affiliated with, or must accept classification according to some predetermined formula or government criteria. A recent example involving EPA—the Common Sense Initiative—suggests that EPA, by acceding to the demands of environmental justice groups to be treated as an interest separate from national environmentalists, is willing to entertain flexibility in this area and accept a reasonable degree of self-definition. Likewise, the level of satisfaction with the lead representative of your interest grouping may affect the perceived degree of fair representation extant for any one game. Further, to the extent that uncertainty affects the identification process, poor evaluation of the primary stakeholder base may result and increase the likelihood that the inclusivity rule will be violated. As the Yorktown study demonstrated, inclusivity is the key to implementing the recommendations flowing from a collaborative effort.

Douglas Amy (1987) and others, however, warn that an overarching focus on initial access, and its corollary concern of inclusivity within a collaborative framework, misses the point. Amy critiques the use of collaboration, which includes environmental mediation and dispute-resolution techniques, by cautioning that it can be a subtle but powerful form of political control by established economic interests which co-opts public interest "voices" in the name of consensus outcomes. Because of these pitfalls, Amy suggests that collaborative efforts should play no more than a minor role in the development of regulation relative to the traditional means of legislation, standard notice-and-comment rulemaking, and, if necessary, litigation. However, the question of inclusion within the collaborative format, and the accompanying danger of co-optation, needs to be framed against the actual context of public interests' access to, participation in, and influence over outcomes within traditional lawmaking and regulatory proceedings.

The collaborative games at issue here met the same test of democratic representation imposed by a republican form of government as any other piece of legislation. The broad outlines of the regulatory programs were not determined by a select group of interests during implementation; rather they were the product of congressional deliberation. In the RFG case it was congress, not EPA, that determined who would bear the costs of air pollution cleanup by creating the program and setting specific pollution reduction goals. Consumers of gasoline in the nine "dirty" cities were going to bear the cost of cleanup regardless of the rulemaking process selected. Add to this the fact that the reg-neg produced a program saving consumers considerable amounts of money at the pump, and it becomes clearer that angry consumers did not have a case against collaboration and its outcome as much as they did against the congress which created the program in the first place.[20] Even the Yorktown Project, a bureaucratic-level initiative proposing changes in how the goals set by congress were achieved, proposed to do nothing more than substitute an integrated regulatory program designed to achieve the same or better environmental results than required by existing statutes.

Nor is it clear that the general public, consumers, or other public interest "voices" representing various facets of the American citizenry are better represented in regulatory efforts adhering to traditional notice-and-comment rulemaking processes, or that the potential for powerful political players to dominate such processes is any less. In practice, notice-and-comment rulemaking is also elitist, perhaps even more than a reg-neg. The power to "flesh out the bare-bones laws" produced by congress rests in the hands of an unelected bureaucracy (Reich 1990), and that power has been enhanced by a trio of administrative law cases—*Vermont Yankee, Chevron v. NRDC,* and *Heckler v. Chaney*—over the past two decades.[21] Further, although public comments are open to all citizens, rules are not equally responsive to every facet of the affected political spectrum. Instead, like reg-negs, and to the extent possible, rules are shaped to avoid judicial review and to placate powerful groups (interviews with EPA 1/7/94; 3/17/94). In addition, most major rules end up in the hands of the judges, who, as Shep Melnick (1983) and Judge David Bazelon of the D. C. Circuit Court, among others, point out, are ill-equipped to deal with the technical issues underpinning much environmental litigation. Moreover, the lack of broad public access to negotiated rulemakings should not be overstated. Basic procedural protections under the Administrative Procedure Act, such as public notices in the federal register, public comment periods, public hearings, and the opportunity for judicial review are integral parts of any reg-neg (Perritt 1986, 485–86).

Finally, Justice Antonin Scalia's majority opinion in *Lujan v. Defenders of Wildlife* (1992) not only makes it much more difficult for regulatory beneficiaries such as environmental and consumer interests to gain standing to sue in response to administrative actions, but fundamentally challenges the constitutionality of congressionally mandated citizen suit provisions—a key vehicle for advancing the power and interests of public interest advocates within the regulatory arena during the 1970s and 1980s.

Taken together, these developments place significant authority for regulatory outcomes in the hands of unelected bureaucratic officials, who may or may not be responsive to the policy preferences of public interest advocates. The fact that public interest advocates have formal access to a traditional notice-and-comment rulemaking is mitigated by the substantial uncertainty over whether their voice will actually be heard *during* the proceedings. The problem is compounded by the severely diminished opportunities for access and influence afforded public interest advocates *after* agency decisions have been finalized. This is the "context" that needs to be compared against the collaborative reg-neg mechanism—an alternative institutional arrangement which secures public interest advocates an official seat at the bargaining table and affords them considerable, multiple opportunities to shape regulatory outcomes. As Amy (1987) suggests, it may not be much of a guarantee if co-optation occurs, but compared to the constraints on access and influence imposed by contemporary administrative law, collaboration may be one of the better games in town for representing a broad variety of interests.

An equally important question revolves around the matter of sustained access.[22] Can environmental and consumer advocates continue active involvement in collaborative efforts over the long term? Stakeholders involved in the RFG reg-neg and the Yorktown Pollution Prevention Project were virtually unanimous in their concern over the resource intensity of the negotiation phase of the decision-making process. Senior officials from the stakeholding organizations typically have responsibility over a wide number of pollution control regulatory matters. But the collaborative game forced them to focus on a very small part of their larger decision-making universe for the better part of several months. Unsurprisingly, staffing problems were more acute for environmental and consumer interest groups, who typically must rely on a small handful of expert staff, as opposed to the battery of personnel employed by industry and government. Participants from consumer and environmental advocacy organizations also complained of the financial burden, with some suggesting that even successful regulatory negotiations are more costly for them than the litigation which typically accompanies notice-and-comment rulemaking.[23]

Moreover, environmentalists and consumer advocates encounter a further potential disadvantage related to the quality of the expertise brought to bear. Given the overt reliance of collaborative endeavors on better technical information, a reasonable standard for meaningful (full) participation requires participants fluent in the arcane language of economic and scientific analysis.[24] Although national environmental groups have made great strides in this regard over the past decade, it is generally recognized that scientific analysis is not one of their strengths. For example, fundamental to the Yorktown effort was a comparative risk assessment/analysis used to sort through the health risks posed by different pollutants and different areas of the facility. Yet risk analysis, even though it is fast becoming central to national regulatory debates, is precisely one of the areas where the environmental community's "level of sophistication is relatively low, and to the extent that it becomes central to negotiations they are going to be outgunned by industry. . . . [From this perspective, collaborative games] not only rely on a tool [i.e., analysis] that handicaps environmentalists, they also downgrade the tools at which they're best, mobilizing their memberships, lobbying on the Hill, litigation, and so on . . . There is a real conflict there."[25]

Compounding the problem of a disparity in expert resources, at least in cases relying on risk analysis/assessment, is the high degree of uncertainty and the normative implications accompanying the decision-making process. "[T]he ranking process is inherently subjective and value-laden, requiring individuals or the team as a whole to compare problems along many dimensions at once. . . . Technical analysis can provide some of the raw material for making these judgments but ultimately the decisions are of the type that some would call policy decisions;" they are political in nature.[26] The subjectiveness of such a decision-making process reinforces the need for inclusivity in collaborative games, since environmental groups, community-level environmental justice groups, and consumer interests will want to inject their own insights colored by their own values and biases.

REINVENTED GOVERNMENT AND PUBLIC BACKLASH

Also requiring attention is whether the public perceives it has ample opportunity to access and influence collaborative games. The issue is important because it affects the public's willingness to accept the outcomes produced by collaborative games. In the particular case of reformulated gasoline, collaboration might have facilitated the efficient development of the regulation, but was efficiency gained at the expense of representativeness for gasoline consumers, a fair distribution of the cleanup burden, and "good" public policy? The motoring public in Milwaukee and points across the country seemed to think so. Shortly after sales of reformulated gasoline began in Milwaukee, newspaper headlines reported that state and federal officials were being inundated with thousands of consumer complaints regarding the effects of RFG. Reformulated gasoline was perceived to be the culprit in everything from nausea, headaches, and respiratory problems to lower gas mileage to the destruction of small two-cycle engines in snowmobiles, snowblowers, and chain saws. Rather than purchase the reformulated gasoline in the Milwaukee area, consumers were driving outside of the metropolitan area to find conventional gasoline. The unexpected behavior translated into more pollution as people traveled greater distances to buy fuel.

An EPA hearing into the matter resulted in the expression of tremendous anger by the consuming public against the regulation imposed by the national government. The public evinced clear concern that the collaborative effort responsible for the regulation was a rigged inside game played by national policy elites. Although consumer interests were officially represented by Edwin Rothschild of Citizen Action during the actual rulemaking effort, the general impression in the audience was that a lone representative was incapable of adequately representing the millions in the motoring public affected by the rule. As a result, the American motoring public was being forced to foot the bill for cleaning up urban smog, an "outrage" for some who failed to "see why the small guy should pay the price." At the same time, people were suspicious that a game which places environmentalists in agreement with the oil and auto industries and with state and federal regulators represents an "unholy alliance" of interests more likely to produce policy outcomes contrary to the public interest. Lost in the uproar was the fact that, when compared with alternative methods for reducing similar amounts of targeted pollutants, RFG was "the low-hanging fruit"—a policy mechanism able to reduce pollution for low cost (per each unit of pollution reduced). Yet consumers who had to pay the price seemed not to care. It certainly was not efficient from their perspective; rather, it had a direct, highly visible, and negative effect on their pocketbook. There were also questionable, perhaps serious, health consequences for Milwaukee residents.[27]

Again, however, we should not overstate the relationship between the public backlash against the reformulated gasoline program and the collaborative game per se.[28] Citizen dissatisfaction applies equally well to other cases of pollution control regulation directly affecting the motoring public, either behaviorally or through their pocketbooks. Prominent recent examples include the growing revolt against the 1990 Clean Air Act Amendments' centralized inspection and maintenance program for automobiles and the employee commute option program, which tries to encourage (critics would say coerce) motoring publics living in suburban areas to restrict vehicle miles traveled. As Joseph

Minott, the executive director of the Clean Air Council in Philadelphia, laments, motorists "are like hyperactive children. They just keep shouting 'No, no, no!' no matter what's suggested." Others suggest that laws which prevent people from driving their cars as they see fit are "meant to be broken."[29] In short, what may look, smell, sound, and feel like good public policy to policy experts and organized interests in Washington, D. C., may be viewed as intrusive, unfair, and dangerous by the American public and thus may encounter staunch resistance, regardless of whether it is the product of a collaborative game or the more traditional no-holds-barred pluralism.

The uncertainty of the public's behavior at the end of collaborative games is only exacerbated by the more formalized patterns of backlash found in the steady fragmentation of grassroots "voices" concerned with environmental policy. From the left side of the political spectrum, the concentrated power of the green lobby is facing serious challenges from both disaffected environmental activists and the environmental justice movement. The former criticize national environmental groups for being too willing to compromise on core beliefs and seek politically feasible, inevitably marginal policy gains, instead of attacking the root causes of environmental degradation—the advanced industrial economy and its fundamental allegiance to economic growth (Brower 1995; Foreman 1987; Kassiola 1990; Sale 1986). The disaffection is spurring the growth of splinter groups and factions such as Ecotage, a radical offshoot from Earth First, a group many consider to be a relatively radical group to begin with.[30] The growth of these groups and the debate within the larger environmental community over the propriety of collaborating with erstwhile adversaries is certainly not new.[31] What is new "is that some of those grassroots groups who traditionally wanted the role of being outsiders . . . to provide the 'left' end point and so make it safe for the others to come in toward the middle, now want to serve both roles. They both want to be that 'left' end point and participate in national-level bargaining games" (interview 3/23/94).

The latter aspect of the environmentalist grassroots explosion—the environmental justice movement—seeks to focus greater attention on social equity concerns. It is driven by the perception that the pollution burden falls disproportionately on poor, minority populations, especially in urban areas and heavily polluted industrial corridors like Louisiana's cancer alley. Aggrieved advocates argue that existing laws have done little to alleviate the inequities. Advocated remedies include elevation of the EPA to cabinet-level status, mandatory use of environmental justice as a policy-making value, greater local control over policy and policy implementation, and official representation as a separate entity within the collaborative game framework (Bosso 1994; Bullard 1993; LaDuke 1993; Moore and Head 1993).

Pressure for change and devolution in environmental policy making is also coming from the other side of the political spectrum. In recent years, hundreds of property-rights groups have organized in response to environmental laws in which government officials "have asserted a prerogative to make decisions for individuals, . . . prohibiting tens of thousands of citizens . . . from making their own best bargains" regarding the purchase and disposal of private property, thus encroaching on the most basic of liberties (Bovard 1994, as quoted in Bethell 1994, A10). Particularly outrageous to property rights advocates is the perceived unwillingness of the federal government to act in good faith where citizens have suffered from regulatory "takings"—the devaluation of property as a direct result of government action without compensation—related to wetlands and endangered species regulations.[32] The push for regulatory rollback and reform has been aided by a spate of recent books and reports detailing how environmental policies are often based on "junk" science and the exaggerated claims of environmental advocates (Wildavsky 1994; Ray 1990), the tendency to expend the vast majority of resources in preventing exposure to relatively low-level health risks (USEPA 1987b 1990e), the prevalence of regulatory horror stories (Phillips 1994), the relatively small contributions of man-made pollution vis-à-vis "natural" pollution,[33] and the adaptive, resilient qualities of nature (Easterbrook 1995).[34]

The challenge from below has serious implications for the viability of collaborative games at the national level. Extending participation to environmental justice representatives and others adds costs and makes negotiation more difficult, not only because new voices have been added to the mix, but because ideology, communication, iteration, and cohesiveness issues are likely to hamper the good-faith negotiation and creative deal making required to make the collaborative game successful.

In the first instance, grassroots groups have a propensity to display steadfast allegiance to ideology at the expense of pragmatism. As a result, there is a higher threshold of what is negotiable and what is not. Placing a premium on "keeping the true faith" makes it that much less likely such groups will conform to the informal rules and decorum governing the collaborative negotiation process. For example,

> We had one meeting where the grassroots organization came in and said, "We need a, b, c, and d," and they presented (a) and explained it, and industry said "That's pretty reasonable, we can do that." They then presented (b) and received the same positive response, and on down the line. The grassroots organization got their entire agenda accepted by the larger

group of stakeholders during the morning session, and then they gave a speech at noon calling everybody "Fat pigs, lazy dogs, corrupt, biased, bigoted, you know, a whole string of names." The group walked away with zero. Nothing! Nothing! (interview 3/23/94).

Ideological myopia may also translate into geographical myopia more readily than for groups with national constituencies. When the primary concern is local or regional (e.g., a single watershed or industrial complex) and the goal is customized, parochial solutions, there are fewer incentives to treat the problem as but one part of a much larger national pollution problem.

Coupled with the ideology factor are additional communication difficulties. The reliance of collaborative games on the language of technical expertise means that grassroots groups are likely to encounter many of the same "expertise" deficits already plaguing national environmentalists.

Moreover, grassroots groups tend to suffer from the "here today, gone tomorrow" syndrome, especially when compared to the relatively small coterie of established national groups that have dominated environmental politics over the past two decades (Browne 1988; Weber 1993). Until the high degree of flux in the composition of the grassroots universe shows signs of consolidation, it will be hard both to identify which groups need to be included and to know whether the included groups are iterative players capable of, much less interested in, taking a longer-term view of policy issues. The lack of consolidation also makes it harder to assure that the designated representative for an "interest" category is vested with authority sufficient to deliver the support of all groups within its representative category. As such, it challenges the transaction-specific condition of hierarchical representation, or cohesiveness, crucial to the playing of the collaborative game.

Clearly, the rise to prominence of grassroots groups on both sides of the political spectrum places policy makers squarely in the horns of a dilemma. Adhering to the inclusiveness principle may introduce enough uncertainty into the collaborative effort that expected transaction cost savings are placed in jeopardy. At the same time, excluding these players from the game risks additional uncertainty and derailleure after the fact, given the nascent power of grassroots organizations to influence outcomes. In both cases, incentives to play the collaborative game at the federal level may be seriously diminished.[35]

CONTINUING PRESSURE TO PLAY COLLABORATIVE GAMES

Recognizing the difficulties of reinventing government by using a collaborative format says nothing about the pressure to play collaborative games. Chapter 2 discusses how changes in the larger institutional context pressure pollution control stakeholders to seek alternatives to the dominant conflict game. The context helps participants to recognize the critical link between the high transaction costs imposed by no-holds-barred pluralism and their inability to maximize their own organizational goals. Significantly, the contextual changes that have made pluralism by the rules possible are still present. Participants therefore still have strong incentives to continue experimenting with and improving upon collaborative regulatory arrangements.

First, the high costs and uncertainties imposed by an open administrative decision process and judicial activism persist. Second, more of American industry is encountering the pressures of the international marketplace. In 1970, at the beginning of the contemporary environmental era, international transactions (exports plus imports) equaled 12.7 percent of the U.S. gross national product. By 1985 the figure almost doubled to 21.3 percent, while by the mid-1990s, over 25 percent of the American economy involved international transactions.[36] In addition, the pace of economic and technological change has quickened, and along with it the need for innovation and the capacity for rapid adjustment of products and services to emerging market niches (Hurst 1995; Porter 1993).

Third, the approximate balance of power among the environmental lobby and their industry counterparts has been sustained over time. While many national environmental advocacy groups suffered sizable membership and revenue losses during the early 1990s, their power was sufficient to ensure gridlock and prevent erosion of past statutory gains. Moreover, threats to environmental progress posed by the Republican capture of congress in 1994 have been instrumental in reversing membership and revenue trends, and preserving environmentalists' substantial political clout at both ends of Pennsylvania Avenue.

Fourth, the hostility the 104th Congress expresses toward EPA's mission of environmental protection should be kept in perspective. The emergence of David McIntosh (R-Ind.), the former chief of staff for the Quayle Competitiveness Council, as the chair of the National Economic Growth, Natural Resources, and Regulatory Affairs Subcommittee is a good example. In his aggressive attempts to oversee and hamper EPA decision making, Rep. McIntosh exudes an intensity of purpose and moral fervor perhaps unmatched in EPA's history. But his actions are an extension of, rather than a departure from, the larger historical pattern. The political–bureaucratic nexus as it affects EPA has always been fraught with difficulty and high costs for EPA as competing officials in congress and the presidency try to influence agency decisions. The battle for control intensified during the late 1970s, throughout the 1980s, and into the 1990s. As a result, EPA officials are accustomed to constant, often hostile, scrutiny by elected officials; the institutional memory is that of an agency under siege. Seen in this light, the behavior of Republican politicians is much less a change than a continuation of a game in which elected politicians seek to impose their will on bureaucratic agents.

Fifth, majority party lawmakers in the 104th Congress still face the same electoral and institutional imperatives as before. In order to maintain their party majority in congress, Republicans need to produce legislative results for which they can claim credit.[37] In their quest for legislative results, congressional Republicans have responded to the uncertainty of legislative decision making by employing unconventional lawmaking methods—just like their Democratic Party counterparts before them. Bills regularly reached the house floor protected by closed and otherwise restricted rules limiting or foreclosing debate and amendments.[38] Committees produced bills constructed through backroom negotiations, often with substantial assistance and policy guidance from the house leadership. Program funds were appropriated without authorizing legislation (Evans and Oleszek 1995, 8–9). President Clinton and key members of congress used a leadership summit to resolve differences on budgeting priorities. Major policy issues were shepherded through the house under the watchful eye of an aggressive, hands-on "supercommittee . . . made up of the cadre of leaders closest to the speaker."[39]

Under the direction of House Speaker Newt Gingrich, Republicans reorganized the U.S. House of Representatives in order to give party leaders greater control over the unwieldy decision-making process and thus facilitate passage of their agenda. Republicans reduced the number of subcommittees and staff, violated the norm of seniority in several key committee chair assignments, outlawed proxy voting in committee, and, compared to past congresses, granted greater power to both committee chairs[40] and the house leadership, particularly the speaker.[41]

Changes in congressional structure and the use of unconventional lawmaking methods helped the GOP leadership in the U.S. House of Representatives enforce party unity and pass most items on the Contract With America by sweeping vote margins.[42] The Republican freshman class in the house was a major contributor to the strong party cohesion. It "display[ed] such unswerving loyalty to [Speaker] Gingrich that Democrats habitually refer[red] to the newcomers as 'Newtoids'" (Doherty 1995, 915).

But the moves to centralize power in the house were not always successful, nor did they prevent individual members from pursuing constituency interests when they conflicted with majority party priorities. "Attempts to comprehensively realign committee jurisdictions to reflect Republican policy interests . . . mostly failed, primarily because of opposition from constituency interests and the personal power agendas of individual members" (Evans and Oleszek 1995, 3). By the Summer and Fall of 1995, barely six months after regaining control of the U.S. House of Representatives, Republicans started experiencing greater difficulty procedurally shepherding issues through the house. Working without a script, and in sharp contrast to the disciplined march through the Contract With America, the behavior of GOP leaders and the rank-and-file membership fell into the more familiar historical pattern of "intraparty warfare." Driven by the inherent tension between governing and representation, member responsiveness to the more parochial concerns of their individual home districts began interfering with majority party priorities, especially when it came time to translate proposed budget cuts into fiscal reality (Doherty 1995; 1996; Katz 1996; Rubin 1995). Appropriations bills "became bogged down with pet policy riders, generating several internecine fights and making the majority unable to govern" (Kozszuk 1996, 7). Southern Republicans defected on farm legislation reducing aid to cotton growers in the region (Rogers 1995a). GOP leaders further acquiesced to a threat by Rep. Gerald Solomon (R-NY), chair of the House Rules Committee, "that the Republican delegation from New York would . . . vote against the entire budget" if provisions reducing federal dairy subsidies to New York farmers were not removed from the larger budget bill (Rosenbaum 1995, A1). In late November 1995, the Republican leadership was "dealt a surprise blow" when the defection of twenty-five rank-and-file Republicans succeeded in derailing an $80.6 billion spending bill because it did not spend enough money on veterans' programs (Rogers and Georges 1995).

Moreover, the freshman class is turning out to be "more diverse than its stereotype suggests. Interviews with many find them more willing to accept compromises, even on such party priorities as the Republicans' seven-year, $245 billion package of tax cuts. . . . Having cast politically tough votes for a balanced budget, many of the Republicans do not want to campaign [in 1996] with nothing to show for it. Says first-term GOP Representative Charles Bass of New Hampshire: 'The freshman class has a stake in this being a productive Congress'" (Calmes 1995, A22; Georges 1996).

Further, for the vast majority of environmental protection policies, legislative stalemate and, once President Clinton is factored in, overall gridlock are the rule once again. The GOP's environmental agenda in congress threatens to undermine the existing regulatory superstructure by excluding environmentalists from policy-making arrangements and rolling back regulations in a number of areas.[43] Early evidence suggests, however, that the attempted revolution in the environmental arena is going to mimic the early Reagan years, in which Republican attempts to reverse the course of environmental regulation were largely rebuffed, the environmental movement was reinvented, and the high costs of conflict were painfully evident to all.

The philosophical differences between the moderate and conservative wings of the Republican Party and the accompanying inability of the party leadership to enforce party discipline to the point where their agenda could move forward "became particularly apparent in disputes over how much to loosen environmental regulations" (Katz 1996, 8). In July 1995, proposals for comprehensive regulatory reform stalled and died in the senate as much due to the opposition of moderate Republicans like Senator John Chafee (R-RI), chair of the Environment and Public Works Committee, as to anything else.[44] Prospects for passage of other legislation designed to roll back environmental regulations banning the production of chlorofluorocarbons (CFCs), the chemical many scientists consider the major destroyer of the earth's ozone layer, were "problematic at best" (Stevens 1995, A13). Further, a sizable bloc of GOP moderates (sixty-three members) broke ranks with the house leadership to help stop initiatives designed to defund EPA enforcement activities (Rogers 1995b). Likewise, what some describe as a "dramatic overhaul" of the Endangered Species Act faced such formidable opposition from "GOP environmentalists . . . [that] Speaker Gingrich decided against bringing the bill to the floor" (*Congressional Quarterly Weekly Report* 1996, 36). The standstill was so complete that by January 1996, a full year after taking power, virtually all major environmental initiatives remained stalled *in congress*, including measures to revise the federal hazardous waste cleanup program (Superfund), the Clean Water Act, the Endangered Species Act, federal grazing policy, and the Safe Drinking Water Act (Katz 1996).

The defeats and growing dissension among Republican legislators led some members of the Republican Party hierarchy like House Budget Committee Chairman John Kasich (R-Ohio) to argue that Republicans needed "to rethink [their] environmental policy" and instead to design and pass legislation closer to the center of the political spectrum (Rogers 1995b, A16; Cushman 1995, 1996; Freedman 1996a; Noah 1995c). Congressional Republicans experienced a modicum of success while using a more centrist approach during the second session of the 104th Congress. In October 1996, a broad package of legislation on parks and public lands was signed into law. In the area of pesticide legislation, congress and the president agreed to significantly loosen regulatory restrictions concerning carcinogens in processed foods by scuttling the Delaney Clause.[45] Agreement was also reached on a revised version of the Safe Drinking Water Act, which eased regulatory requirements for small-town drinking water systems while simultaneously increasing water authorities' public disclosure requirements concerning water-borne chemicals (Noah 1996).

Moreover, there is little philosophical difference between the Republican chair of the Senate Environment Committee, John Chafee (RI), and Senator Max Baucus (MT), the Democratic party's committee chair in the 103rd Congress. Both are staunch, generally pragmatic defenders of environmental prerogatives who like policies favoring the environment and the economy, not one at the expense of the other (U.S. Congress. Senate. Taking Stock hearings 1993; Baucus 1993). As the Environment Committee chair during the early 1980s, Chafee aggressively investigated decisions taken by the EPA. In fact, environmentalists consider him a more committed, "bolder" advocate for the environment than Baucus. The League of Conservation Voters, the watchdog group that monitors congressional voting records on environmental issues, rates Chafee higher than Baucus, with a 90 percent favorable voting record as opposed to Baucus's 79 percent rating (Noah 1994). Chafee has effectively used his position in the senate to slow and block the progress of the GOP environmental agenda (Benenson 1995c; Kozszuk 1996). Moreover, if GOP reform initiatives do happen to pass congress, President Clinton has made it clear that he will not hesitate to use the presidential veto power. In the Fall 1995 budget battles, the massive Republican budget cuts for EPA were targeted as one of three issues guaranteed to trigger a veto.[46] Nor is Clinton likely to sign the new Republican version of the Clean Water Act, a piece of legislation he has contemptuously labeled the "Dirty" Water Act.

With gridlock as the rule on virtually all pollution control issues,[47] the existing command-and-control superstructure stays intact, hence existing laws are not rationalized and industry keeps on paying high compliance costs. Yet with international competitiveness concerns continuing unabated, cost and adaptability imperatives do not diminish; rather, they are heightened. Environmentalists and regulators see little further progress in the battle against pollution. Oversight of EPA continues to intensify as legislators hostile to EPA's basic mission seek to influence agency decisions. Given the prominence of federal deficit politics and the willingness of both Republicans and the Clinton Administration to pursue a balanced budget, EPA can expect its budget to be cut even further during the latter half of the 1990s. Thus EPA decision makers face added incentives to seek more cost-effective ways of meeting agency objectives. In addition, states remain stuck between a rock and a hard place. They continue to face hostility from industry in their attempts to implement high-cost, federally mandated environmental priorities and mandates, but with ever fewer dollars.

In short, the high-transaction-cost context within which pollution control decision making occurs continues to provide participants with substantial incentives to devise alternative regulatory arrangements promising each a greater share of their primary organizational goals. In fact, the *failure* of two major efforts at regulatory relief little more than a decade apart is likely to convince more industry officials to accept the staying power of the environmental lobby and environmental values within the American electorate. When considered together with the persistence of contextual incentives, it is plausible to expect that the rate at which players seek out and engage the collaborative dynamic will increase during the latter half of the 1990s and on into the next century.

CHAPTER NOTES

1. Benenson (1995a); Easterbrook (1995); Freedman (1995); John (1994); NAPA (1995); Rabe (1994).

2. Breyer (1993); Bryner (1995); Mazmanian and Morell (1992). More generally, see Kettl (1993); Goodsell (1985); Gormley (1991); Osborne and Gaebler (1993); Salamon (ed.) (1989).

3. Michael Catania, executive director of the New Jersey Nature Conservancy, as quoted in *Environment Reporter* (5/13/94, pp. 67–68). Catania's statement is in reference to the Stockton Alliance, a consortium of business, environmental, and consumer groups in New Jersey seeking better ways to resolve environmental problems. Members of the effort include the New Jersey–American Water Company, Mannington Mills, Mobil Oil, the Sierra Club, the New Jersey Conservation Foundation, Citizens United, New Jersey Audubon, Rutgers University Environmental Law Clinic, First Fidelity Bank, the Pinelands Preservation Alliance, and DuPont.

4. See Scholz (1991, 132). This is not Scholz's central concern. Rather, his central question is: If cooperative regulatory enforcement produces better policy effectiveness, why do the beneficiaries and other policy supporters not favor the most effective means of administrating their policies (p. 116)? He ultimately concludes that optimal institutional choices at the administrative level generate so much uncertainty in the broader political game that political actors prefer deterrence and policy *ineffectiveness* to cooperation and policy *effectiveness*.

5. See NAPA (1988; 1995). The Yorktown case study is an example of how congress controls EPA's organizational commitments and how difficult it is to devote agency resources to the goal of integrated pollution control. The lack of communication and coordination between program offices—a big complaint of state-level regulators and industry at Yorktown—occurs because

functional fragmentation fits well with the congressional committee structure. Agency decision makers care about fulfilling the needs and wishes of their primary clientele, congressional committees, because they provide agency funds and personnel, and committees are likely to be pushing compliance with the requirements and deadlines of specific single-media-based legislation of most import to them.

6. The U. S. Court of Appeals in Washington, D.C., blocked the Clinton Administration's Renewable Oxygenate Program on April 28, 1995. The court said that the EPA lacked the statutory authority to create the program, which was designed to give the ethanol industry an automatic 30 percent share of the RFG market. See Noah and Kilman (1995, B8).

7. The case studies illuminate the key role of leadership, particularly bureaucratic leadership, in explaining regulatory outcomes. While some work on regulation has given attention to the role of leaders, particularly the treatment of economic deregulation by Derthick and Quirk (1985) and Don Kettl's (1983) work on the Federal Reserve, the role of bureaucratic leadership is often neglected in institutional studies within political science.

8. "In the formal analyses of public policies and public policy making, public executives are, for the most part, analytic phantoms without personal goals, specific motivations, or a *raison d'etre*" (Lynn 1987, 4).

9. Appleby (1949); Waldo (1948). Leaders "participate actively in both formulating and implementing public policy" (Terry 1995, 12).

10. Barnard (1936). Burns (1978, 19–20), defines leadership in similar fashion. Leaders induce "followers [or subordinates] to act for certain goals that represent the values and the motivations—the wants and needs, the aspirations and expectations—of both leaders and [subordinates]" (p. 19). From this perspective, leadership is an aspect of power, but unlike naked power-wielding, it is inseparable from the subordinate's needs and goals.

11. Neustadt (1960) and Huitt (1961, 337) offer similar conclusions in the differing contexts of the presidency and the role of senate majority leader, respectively. The lack of formal power and the corresponding power resources of others force leaders to rely on their powers of persuasion in order to achieve political goals.

12. In cases of specific games, day-to-day agency management of the game itself is often critical and, therefore, to the extent that midlevel agency managers/leaders in charge of collaborative games possess a reputation of commitment and trustworthiness, the reputation component is strengthened.

13. Latham (1952); Truman (1951). Within the pluralist perspective, the administrator "is not an active responsible agent making a positive contribution to policy formulation and implementation; rather, he is a blank slate upon which are written the demands of external groups and interests" (Burke 1986, 19).

14. In this sense, ultimate accountability for regulatory outcomes is no different than under traditional conceptions of public bureaucracy's role in the policy process; accountability rests squarely with the government agency in charge of the transaction.

15. It also increases the uncertainty associated with the collaborative game

for participants outside the agency, since they do not have a clear conception of what the agency's bottom line is.

16. A plausible case can be made that the stakes, and the possible benefits, for disadvantaged and unorganized constituents are too small to expect their participation in a "fire-alarm" system, particularly when the primary discourse involves the arcane language of environmental science and pollution control. Nor does it make sense for self-interested maximizing politicians to factor these constituents' demands into their reelection calculus. Their influence on the electoral outcome is too small to be considered.

17. Nongovernment negotiators "play only an advisory role to the agency; the agency retains the final decision-making authority" (Perritt 1986, 486; Harter 1982, 109).

18. It should be recognized, however, that since these are fundamentally environmental policies, questions concerning the costs borne by industry or assessments bearing on program adaptability should not be analyzed separately from those aspects having direct bearing on the realization of environmental results. An example of a problematic outcome is where industry experiences compliance cost savings at the same time that environmental results are negligible or far less than legislation promises. Or industry is granted significant flexibility in order to maintain their responsiveness to changing market conditions, but without due compensation for the environmental side of the equation (e.g., more rigorous monitoring or data-reporting arrangements).

19. I agree with Michael Barzelay, who argues that it is inappropriate to characterize the regulated community as customers in the traditional sense, given that use of the term implies deference on the part of regulators to the demands of the regulated and thus misconstrues the nature of their relationship to each other. Regulations are designed to achieve public interest as defined by elected officials. The demands of the regulated and the idea of quasivoluntary compliance (coproduction of regulatory outcomes) should be considered only insofar that they do not damage the integrity of the regulatory relationship itself (remarks made at the National Public Management Research Conference, University of Wisconsin–Madison, September 30–October 2, 1993). For a brief overview of problems and issues related to customer-oriented government, see DiIulio, Kettl, and Garvey (1993, 48–54).

20. In light of these realities, it is interesting to note that the motoring public had *avoided* pollution control programs imposing such direct, visible costs in earlier versions of the Clean Air Act. Congress chose instead to focus on measures having a direct impact on "big" business, primarily major stationary sources and the elimination of tailpipe emissions in new motor vehicles. Gasoline and, by extension, the motoring public were targeted only after it was realized that twenty years of such cleanup efforts had failed to reduce urban smog to acceptable levels in many U. S. cities.

21. *Vermont Yankee Nuclear Power Corp. v. Natural Resources Defense Council* (435 U.S. 519, 1978) enhances administrative discretion by preventing lower courts from imposing additional procedural requirements on regulatory decision processes to ensure unbiased findings of fact. As long as agencies adhere to the procedural requirements imposed by the Administrative Procedure Act

or the statute in question, the courts have no authority to intervene on procedural grounds. *Chevron v. Natural Resources Defense Council* (467 U.S. 837, 1984)
involves the scope of judicial review related to agency interpretation of laws.
The Chevron Doctrine says that when congressional intent is either muddled
or ambiguous, or there are several competing intents within the statutory
language *and* legislative history, courts must defer to agency expertise as long
as regulators have adopted a permissible construction of the statute (Schwartz
1994, 213–15). Given the tendency for congress to delegate authority to agencies
using broad, ambiguous language (Katzmann, 1990), the power of unelected
bureaucratic officials to implement their preferred interpretation of legislative
intent is greatly enhanced, not least because the Chevron Doctrine severely
diminishes the possibility of judicial review as a final check on their policy-
making authority. *Heckler v. Chaney* (470 U.S. 821, 1985) provides regulators
with greater discretion in the area of nonenforcement or bureaucratic inaction.
The upshot is that if an agency's "nonaction" in a particular case is challenged
in court, the courts are less likely to review the case, thus leaving the original
agency decision intact.

   22. See Amy (1987), USEPA (1987a); Kerwin (1994); Stewart (1981, 1347–
50).

   23. USEPA (1987, 10–11). Interviews with consumer advocate (3/25/94);
environmentalist (3/30/94). See also Polkinghorn (1995) and Kerwin and Langbein (1995, 36).

   24. Or, at a minimum, ready access to experts one can trust. This is not
a new problem by any means. Marc Eisner (1993) points out that the role
assigned to scientific experts by the social and environmental regulatory revolution of the 1960s and 1970s is "unprecedented." A particular administrative
format can give groups access to policy making and rulemaking but can "not
give the interested parties the expertise necessary to make significant
contributions . . ." (p. 130).

   25. Interview with EPA (11/3/94). See also Baumgartner and Jones (1993).
Policy venues—"the institutional locations where authoritative decisions are
made concerning a given issue"—can be critical for determining final outcomes
(p. 32). Particular venues "confer general advantage on business or specific
groups" (p. 35).

   26. The National Academy of Public Administration (1995, 142). Recent
congressional debate over risk-based decision making in environmental policy
"has been based on the assumption that environmental policy could or should
be essentially science-driven. That assumption is flawed in two respects; first,
scientific tools available today are not precise enough to yield crisp answers
about risk; and second, subjective, value-laden decisions influence every step
of the process. Neither risk assessment nor environmental policy can be made
objective. . . . [but] they can be improved (NAPA 1995, 35).

   27. The Wisconsin Department of Natural Resources conducted extensive
air-sampling tests (130 total) in response to the concerns over possible added
health risks associated with RFG. They found that the levels of chemicals
detected in the air were all below federal health standards (Eggleston 1995).

   28. As evidence of how reg-negs are unable to prevent conflict after rulemaking, Coglianese (1997) cites the negative reaction of Milwaukee residents

to the final RFG rule and the adversarial response of internationally based stakeholders in Venezuela and Brazil. However, as discussed in the main text, the Milwaukee reaction, or "conflict," likely has less to do with collaboration and its effect on the final rule than it does with the original policy endorsed by congress. Similarly, it is not clear that any rulemaking method, collaborative or otherwise, could ever be inclusive enough to stop conflict that has its roots in international, as opposed to domestic, affairs.

29. The intensity of the backlash in areas of the country such as California, Pennsylvania, Maryland, Maine, New York, and New Jersey as well as major metropolitan areas like Chicago and Milwaukee has led regulators, elected officials, and environmentalists alike to fear that these minirebellions may become "tripwires" leading to congressional revision and emasculation of the entire Clean Air Act. In order to keep the political damage to a minimum, EPA is attempting to avoid confrontation and is working closely with the states to grant them greater flexibility in meeting the mandates. Aeppel and Solomon (1994, B1); Aeppel (1995, A1). Interview with EPA (12/10/93).

30. Ecotage believes that "[w]e must make this an insecure and uninhabitable place for capitalists and their projects. This is the best contribution we can make towards protecting the earth and struggling for a liberating society" (Foreman 1987, as quoted in Ray 1990, 166).

31. See McCloskey (1990). Dryzek and Lester (1989) categorized environmental groups and approaches to the environmental problematique.

32. Bovard (1994); McCoy (1995a; 1995b); Western (1995); Yandle (1995). See Florence Williams (1993) and David Helvarg (1994) for an opposing view.

33. Pollution emitted by volcanoes, naturally occurring chemical compounds, and fissures in geological structures are examples of "natural" pollution (see generally Easterbrook 1995).

34. All of this dovetails with what might be termed the resurgence of the de Tocquevillian ethic of civic responsibility. In policy areas across the board (e.g., education, crime, welfare, and public housing), publics are mobilizing against the perceived results of government regulation, general intervention, and the imposition of values contrary to their own. They are seeking to reclaim the right to control, or at least profoundly affect, the substance and execution of policy. General examples of the phenomena include the populist fervor supporting the presidential bids of both Pat Robertson and Jesse Jackson in 1988, the ascendancy of the Religious Right into a position of considerable influence within the Republican Party, the "takeover" of the 1994 Virginia Republican Party convention by the home schooling movement, and Ross Perot's independent candidacy in 1992 (see Hertzke 1993). A specific illustrative example occurred in the New York City school system a few years ago, where the introduction of the "Children of the Rainbow" curriculum provoked a citizens' revolt. Parents vehemently objected to condom instruction for fourth-graders and the aggressive effort to mainstream "alternative lifestyles." The uproar led to the resignation of the school system's chancellor and the abandonment of the offensive curriculum. Similar grassroots, community-based environmental management efforts are springing up throughout the Western United States (Jones 1996). For the theme of civic rejuvenation and innovation, more generally, see Broder (1994), and Sirianni and Friedland (1995).

35. The inclusion of environmental justice interests in EPA's ongoing Common Sense Initiative, which targets several industrial sectors, provides a number of important case studies where the added dynamic of the grassroots element can be assessed in greater detail.

36. United States Bureau of the Census (1982–83a; 1982–83b; 1995a; 1995b).

37. Key members of the Republican leadership, including Senate Majority Leader Bob Dole and House Speaker Newt Gingrich, evince clear recognition of the need to pass the Republican agenda in the runup to the Fall 1996 elections. Also evident is a growing frustration in both the majority party leadership and members of the rank-and-file, including some freshmen Republicans, at their inability to fulfill their agenda. For extensive discussion of these points, see the *Washington Post* series on the December 1995 budget negotiations and eventual deadlock which shut much of the government down for the second time in less than two months (Maraniss and Weisskopf 1996, January 18–20). See also Calmes (1995); Doherty (1996); Freedman (1996a); Kozszuk (1996); Rogers (1995a).

38. The actual number of restricted rules is in dispute and depends upon whether one accepts the Republican or Democratic Party definition of a restrictive rule. Republicans claim that 72 percent of all Contract With America measures were reported with open rules, while Democrats claim the number is actually 26 percent. This compares to 23.5 percent open rules in the 1981–1982 session of congress and 13.6 percent during the 1985–1986 session. For an extensive discussion of differences in definition and restricted rules during the 104th Congress, see Evans and Oleszek (1995, 18–22).

39. Rogers (1995a, A14). See also Cloud (1995); Kozszuk (1996); Maraniss and Weisskopf (1996).

40. The Subcommittee Bill of Rights, the cornerstone of the 1970s committee reforms, has essentially been repealed. Instead of encouraging strong subcommittee chairs, the GOP system encourages strong committee chairs. Standing committee chairs now have the power to (1) choose their subcommittee chairs, (2) assign members to subcommittees, (3) hire all majority party staff, and (4) control the committee's budget (Cloud 1995; Evans and Oleszek 1995, 13).

41. The speaker assumed the authority to name and remove (at least implicitly) all standing committee chairs. The speaker was given additional control over the majority party's committee on committees (the Steering Committee) through new appointment powers. He essentially controlled one-fourth of the votes in the Steering Committee. The speaker's appointment powers were further enhanced when he was given the right to select the chair as well as all members of the Rules Committee. Committee chairs were also subjected to six-year term limits. "Rotating the chairs was intended to diminish the potency of seniority in committee leadership selection, increase the number of lawmakers who gain insight and expertise from serving as committee leaders, and reduce the informational and other advantages that can accrue to long-serving committee chairs" (Evans and Oleszek 1995, 7). See Evans and Oleszek (1995) for an exhaustive review of committee system and house rule changes in the 104th Congress.

42. On the thirty-three roll call votes involving the Contract With America, fewer than five Republicans, on average, broke with the party position (Evans and Oleszek 1995, 6). For example, "[t]he [House] leadership lost only five of its members on the welfare vote, eight on revamping the federal regulatory process, and ten on the deficit-reducing budget reconciliation bill" (Doherty 1996, 119). See also *Congressional Quarterly Weekly Report* (1995), "Passage of Contract Bills," Vol. 53 (April 8), p. 1006; Salant (1995).

43. Benenson (1995b); Bryner (1995); Hosansky (1995). A few examples illustrate the point. "Congress has forbidden the EPA to finalize its improved radon standard [affecting drinking water] through spending restrictions in the EPA appropriations bill" (Natural Resources Defense Council 1995, 2). Senate Bill 1316 delays a new arsenic rule until 2001 and, according to the Natural Resources Defense Council, weakens environmental protection by "mak[ing] the proposed rule 10 times less protective than that proposed by the Bush administration" (p. 2).

44. Hebert (1995); Katz (1996). Senator Chafee expressed "serious reservations" about the bill before the senate, regarding it as a "prescription for litigation and bureaucratic gridlock" (Benenson 1995c, 1836).

45. The Delaney Clause, in effect since 1958, promotes a zero-tolerance standard for potentially carcinogenic substances that scientists have long believed out of date (Noah 1996).

46. Compared to the previous year, budget proposals that have passed the house in 1995 cut EPA's budget by roughly one-third for the next fiscal year, while the main senate budget bill cuts EPA's budget by approximately 20 percent (Rogers 1995b).

47. Gridlock, of course, might be overcome if the overarching political context changes to the point at which the balance of power shifts and overwhelms the ability of the national environmental lobby to block and impede Republican initiatives during the lawmaking process. One way this might occur is if the Republicans can capture the presidency, while also adding significant numbers of antiregulatory, antienvironmental legislators to their totals in congress. Yet even under such a worst-case scenario, overwhelming the environmental lobby is highly unlikely, at least in the near term. Recent gains in membership rolls and group revenues suggest environmentalists will easily retain their capacity to slow and stop what they see as antienvironmental proposals during the latter stages of the policy process.

9

Coping with the Brave New World of Policy Administration

Collaboration is occurring in American politics despite the significant obstacles posed by an adversarial political culture, a fragmented interest group system, and an open political system. Moreover, collaboration is appearing where we would least expect it—in the most combative of all regulatory arenas—pollution control politics. The reality of collaboration, along with continuing efforts across the United States to reinvent government by using administrative arrangements emphasizing many of the same elements found in collaborative games, challenges theory. It suggests that greater scholarly efforts should be devoted to discovering the conditions under which such alternative institutional arrangements can help to resolve complex regulatory dilemmas.

CHOOSING COLLABORATION INSTEAD OF CONFLICT

The cases examined here are not isolated phenomena. EPA has used the reg-neg format almost twenty times to date with a great deal of success in reducing rulemaking delays, effecting tougher rules, monitoring programs, and the like. Other federal agencies, including the Federal Aviation Administration, the Department of Transportation, and the Nuclear Regulatory Commission, among others, have been using reg-neg, too.[1] Congress gave its official blessing to reg-neg with passage of the Negotiated Rulemaking Act of 1990 (Public Law 101–648). In the Fall of 1993, President Clinton endorsed the concept by issuing an executive order directing all government agencies to start using regulatory negotiation more often.[2] Amoco Oil has moved on from the Yorktown Project to forge a new collaborative partnership which includes Dow Chemical and EPA, and most importantly the Natural Resources Defense Council. EPA has developed the Common Sense Initiative (CSI) in league with corporate America, state regulators, national environmentalists, and locally based environmental justice groups. Their goal: to encourage innovation by providing flexibility and to rationalize existing regulatory rules for each industrial sector through the use of a place-by-place approach to achieving pollution control standards (USEPA 1994a). EPA's Project XL (Excellence and Leadership), announced in 1996, is a series of pilot projects that follows the lead of CSI and is modeled on the Yorktown Pollution Prevention Project that was the subject of Chapter 7. Project XL authorizes site-based stakeholder collaboratives "to allow industrial facilities to replace the current regulatory system with alternative strategies if the result achieve[s] greater environmental benefits" (EPA Reinvention Assessment, U.S. Congress. House. 1996, 10). Similarly, environmentalists, regulators, industry, and politicians banded together in the Great Printers Project to create "smarter, faster and cheaper" ways of combating pollution in the Great Lakes region (Council of Great Lakes Governors 1994).

In the Western United States, more than 70 coalitions of environmentalists, ranchers, county commissioners, federal and state government officials, loggers, skiers, and off-road-vehicle enthusiasts are cooperating in an attempt to improve ecosystem and public, as well as private, lands management arrangements (Johnson 1993; Jones 1996; McClellan 1996). The collaborative arrangements work within the larger framework of national laws, not in lieu of them, to prevent degradation; to provide long-term, holistic solutions to complex local problems; and to enhance the degree of local oversight and implementation expertise. Collaboration is viewed as a way to customize one-size-fits-all national laws to the particular conditions of individual ecosystems and communities (Applegate Partnership 1996). Dan Daggett, a member of the Toiyabe Wetlands and Watersheds Management Team in Nevada, not only finds hope in alternative consensus-based mechanisms, seeing them as harbingers of progress in the battle against environmental degradation; he decries the futility of conventional politics, lawsuits, and, by implication, traditional administrative arrangements used to manage the environment. Explains Daggett,

> [t]hat's why ... when it's time for the biennial bloodletting we call elections, I won't be leafleting neighborhoods, calling voters or putting up signs. I'll be out in the world of trees and grass and bugs and streams. Sleeves rolled up, I'll be with one of a number of groups of ranchers, vegetarians, wise-users, and Earth First!ers I've been working with for a couple of years now. Together, we'll be celebrating small successes that can be measured in green meadows, healing riparian areas and increased biodiversity. ... I had been a soldier in the environmental wars for so long—22 years—I had forgotten how uplifting it is to be part of a group of people who don't paint the world in shades of guilt and look for someone to blame. ... And we get better results than the politicians do when they try to solve our problems for us (Daggett 1995, 1–2).

Others like Daniel Kemmis, the mayor of Missoula, Montana, endorse the burgeoning use of collaborative efforts by pointing to the limited capacity of centralized, federal management, and the futility of the conflict-based, "us versus them" approaches adopted by ideologues on both sides of environmental issues.

> I do not believe . . . that any solution coming from one end of the political spectrum or the other is going to have the capacity to do what this landscape requires. The danger is that one ideology or another will win a temporary victory because we did not work hard enough to find common ground (as quoted in Jones 1996, 2).

The use of collaborative methods is growing at other levels of government as well. Chapter 1 notes examples of collaboration in Texas, Massachusetts, Colorado, and Wisconsin. Barry Rabe's (1994) book, *Beyond NIMBY*, examines the phenomena in the United States and Canada within the context of local hazardous waste siting decisions.[3] DeWitt John (1994), in *Civic Environmentalism*, explores state-level collaborative games designed to resolve environmental issues associated with wetlands in the Florida Everglades, pesticides in Iowa, and energy conservation in Colorado.[4] Carmen Sirianni and Lewis Friedland (forthcoming) document the growth of collaborative methods in natural resources decision making as part of a larger project focused on the emergence of a more participatory, inclusive, and deliberative form of democracy. In the Ricelands Habitat Venture involving Ducks Unlimited, the National Audubon Society, the California Commissioner of Reclamation, and the California Rice Industry Association, among others, rice farmers agreed to alter traditional practices so that their fields can be turned into wetlands during the winter months, thereby providing critical wintering habitat for migrating waterfowl along the Pacific Flyway (Reinhold 1992). In New York, the Department of Environmental Conservation is conducting joint exploratory ventures creating integrated pollution management and prevention programs.[5]

Nor is the propensity to adopt alternative institutional arrangements like collaborative games limited to the world of environmental policy. The growing use across the United States of community policing methods which rely heavily on citizen input, innovative school choice and charter school initiatives which devolve authority to parents and teachers,[6] and more generally, various models of "reinvented" government suggest that whether we like it or not, policy makers and administrators *are not* waiting on scholars to decide whether such arrangements are appropriate or not. They are choosing alternative institutional arrangements that defy the traditional Weberian/Progressives approach to bureaucracy, whether it is in terms of including more bottom-up citizen input, sharing power with private-sector groups; adopting holistic, integrated approaches to pollution control; or practicing catalytic government that ultimately blurs the line between private and public spheres of action. In short, because practice *is* running ahead of theory, the challenge to theory is real, not imagined, and we need to figure out what it means. To the extent that traditional scholarship ignores such developments, political science is hampered in its ability as a discipline to explain and assess, much less understand, significant, interesting political–institutional phenomena such as collaborative decision-making arrangements.

EXPLOITING THE NATURAL LIMITS OF COLLABORATIVE GAMES

Despite the willingness of policy makers and administrators to continue selecting collaboration in lieu of the dominant game of no-holds-barred conflict, and despite the propitious conditions in the broader institutional context, there are natural limits to how often the collaborative game format can be employed—and employed successfully. The transaction-specific conditions outlined in Chapter 4—interest cohesiveness, scope of the rule, opportunity to play, ideological restrictions, and so on—reduce uncertainty and improve the chances for sustained, successful collaboration. Yet they also ensure selectiveness. Out of the possible universe of regulatory transactions, only a few will meet enough of the criteria to make good candidates for the collaborative game.

Moreover, even after these special conditions have been met, stakeholders still face overwhelming uncertainty. The uncertainty is likely to be enough to convince many potential participants to discount their projected savings to the point where engaging the collaborative game does not make sense. The previous discussion on instability, accountability, and access demonstrates some of the reasons why players in pollution control politics might be unwilling to take the risks associated with collaboration. The instability found in the reformulated gasoline and Yorktown Project examples show how participants can disrupt and stop collaborative games when they are unable to perceive themselves as having an adequate stake in outcomes. Questions concerning accountability illustrate the unavoidability of uncertainty whenever democratic principals delegate authority to unelected subordinates. With respect to access for smaller groups, especially public interest groups, playing the collaborative game entails proportionately more resources than their industry or government counterparts. As such, the uncertainty related to prospective benefits looms larger in their decision calculus because they have so much more at stake. Nor do potential players know whether others will bargain in good faith, share useful information, or respect the integrity of jointly negotiated agreements once they are signed.

Solving the collective-action dilemma and sustaining collaboration in a high-transaction-cost world requires the presence of the full pluralism-by-the-rules framework—transaction-specific conditions, entrepreneurial leaders, agency credibility, formal binding rules, and adherence to the inclusiveness doctrine. The "rules" reduce the overwhelming uncertainty and risks facing potential participants of collaborative games. At the same time, the rules further narrow the reach of collaborative games by forcing participants to align transaction-specific conditions with the rest of the "rules," thus increasing the difficulty of getting it right.

Yet while the "rules" can minimize uncertainty, they cannot prevent it altogether. As noted in Chapter 8, the growth of groups and the fragmentation of voices introduces greater objective difficulties into the collaborative game framework; thus, satisfying the transaction-specific conditions will be harder. In addition, the potentially hostile behavior of the general public and grassroots elements during implementation adds ever more uncertainty. If carefully negotiated win–win deals can be undone by negative public reactions and determined outside parties, regardless of whether the facts and evidence support the collaborative outcome, incentives to choose collaboration necessarily diminish. The continued existence of uncertainty in such an open and hostile policy-making environment places natural limits on the frequency with which pollution control stakeholders will engage collaborative games.

Exploiting the full potential of collaborative games in American pollution control politics—making sure that the natural limits are actually reached—is likely to require several things. There needs to be a track record of success, a compilation of game results clearly demonstrating the link between pluralism by the rules and transaction cost reductions. The more convinced potential participants are that such a framework can produce tangible, verifiable results, the less risk they will assign to the collaborative format and the less inclined they will be to opt for the high-cost status quo of no-holds-barred pluralism.

More activist, entrepreneurial leaders need to be appointed to administrative posts, while scholars need to devote greater intellectual energies to defining and understanding the entrepreneurial administrative leader concept so that public administration graduate schools can better prepare future managers and leaders for the realities of an increasingly nonhierarchical, interdependent world. On the latter count, a reexamination of the political leadership literature might be a prudent place to start. How can more broadly accepted principles of leadership be grafted onto the administrative leader's role in the policy process without violating the fundamentally subservient role of the bureaucracy to congress and the White House?

Another way to ensure that the full potential of collaborative games is exploited involves the creative sharing and disbursement of the financial and environmental gains derived from collaborative games, or what economists call side payments. As we saw in the case of acid rain, shared savings with the environment are critical for convincing environmentalists to abandon conflict in favor of collaboration during the legislative stage. Yet in games played in the administrative sphere and, as already outlined, the intensive, short-term demand for group resources implied by the collaborative format poses a funding problem for public interest groups. The expected benefits—shared savings with the environment—are nonfungible. Environmental gains do not compensate for the economic costs of playing the game.[7] Hence, initiating administratively based collaborative games when conditions are appropriate will be enhanced to the extent that public interest groups have at least a portion of their participation costs offset through either government funds or a formula which shares expected compliance cost savings between industry and such groups.[8] Likewise, the willingness of regulators to play collaborative games might be facilitated through a promise to fund additional pollution monitoring costs out of industry's compliance cost savings.

An example illustrates how this might work. Environmental justice groups in America's heavily polluted industrial corridors and urban areas want laws more responsive to local conditions. A collaborative forum could be convened which would include environmental justice advocates, regulators, local government officials and environmentalists, major polluters in the geographical area of concern, and perhaps consumer advocates and Chamber of Commerce representatives. They could use existing statutes as a baseline against which success would be measured, set shared savings with the environment as a basic ground rule, and distribute economic proceeds to offset the participation costs of environmental justice representatives and the added monitoring costs incurred by regulators. Compliance cost savings could also pay for pollution prevention and control technologies for unregulated small businesses in the immediate area whenever such a choice promised greater efficiency. Or perhaps small businesses (small pollution sources) could tap the expertise of environmental professionals to help them with their compliance paperwork and planning. In any case, the aggregate savings should be capped at a reasonable level, perhaps in the neighborhood of 10 to 30 percent,[9] in order to ensure that industry (out of whose pocket the money comes) still has a significant incentive to play. Further, both financial and environmental savings must target local areas suffering from high exposure to pollution and its accompanying health risks.[10]

Finally, the problem of democratic accountability must be resolved. Affected interests, but especially politicians and the general public, must be convinced that pluralism by the rules is not simply a newer, more sophisticated way to promote special-interest government by the few. Failure here will make it harder for congress to delegate authority to public bureaucracies and harder for the general public to accept pluralism by the rules as a legitimate form of government decision-making. In the world of contemporary politics, convincing the general public is critical. Better informed, "hyperactive" publics, the surge in grassroots involvement, and the push for smaller government behind the GOP successes in 1994 national and state elections suggest that politics as usual is producing unsatisfactory outcomes. As a result, the citizens who must live with the day-to-day consequences of public policy are now demanding decision-making arrangements giving them more creative control over policy, especially how that policy will be achieved. Accommodating such demands is likely to require greater use of institutional arrangements which empower citizens and stakeholders at the state and local levels of government. The inclusive, participative emphasis of pluralism by the rules provides a forum that moves in this direction—but it will not move very far unless concerns over accountability are properly addressed.[11]

The challenge for theory, therefore, is to accept the reality that alternative institutional arrangements that defy the traditional Weberian/Progressives approach to bureaucracy are here to stay for the foreseeable future. Rather than simply refute the reinventing government phenomena by defending the orthodoxy (see Ron Moe 1994), a more prudent course of action is to dig into the empirical specifics of the phenomena in question (J. Q. Wilson, 1989, *xii*, 12) and see if a new, coherent set of principles can be devised for organizing and controlling bureaucracy in the brave (and perhaps chaotic) new world of 21st century policy administration. In terms of the accountability equation, the challenge is to see if theory can be constructed which reconciles the three main threads of accountability: (1) responsiveness to top-down, elected officials, (2) performance (efficiency), and (3) responsiveness to bottom-up demands by those citizen–stakeholders affected by a particular policy or program. Current approaches emphasize parts of the accountability equation, but not the equation in its entirety.

Traditional public administration theory emphasizes top-down responsiveness to elected officials, assumes efficiency (performance) as a product of proper bureaucratic design, and, by definition, ignores the possibilities for enhanced democratic accountability flowing from alternative bureaucratic designs incorporating varying degrees of bottom-up responsiveness. Yet a growing body of research challenges all three positions. Light (1995) finds that the application of orthodox principles of administration, particularly hierarchy and span of control, "thickens" government, thereby increasing the distance between hierarchical authority and bureaucratic action. The added "distance" makes government less accountable by lessening the ability of democratically elected officials to control the bureaucracy. Others note how specific principles lead to various bureaucratic dysfunctions that necessarily interfere with accountability (see Knott and Miller 1987). The transaction cost element of the pluralism-by-the-rules framework challenges the second claim that efficiency necessarily derives, or follows, from the use of hierarchical regulatory arrangements. Michael Barzelay (1992), with the help of Babak Armajani, finds that government bureaucracies which integrate bottom-up demands from customers into administrative arrangements can be accountable and effective. Insights such as these are not news to public sector practitioners; they know from first-hand experience that orthodox public administration principles do not always bring about accountability, in terms of either responsiveness or efficiency.

At the same time, however, research into the alternative institutional arrangements comprising the reinventing government movement tends to place primary emphasis on performance (efficiency) and responsiveness to bottom-up demands of citizens and stakeholders. Less attention is generally paid by proponents of reinvented government to the correspondence between the preferences of elected officials as expressed in legislation or executive policy decrees, and the final policy results produced by reinvented government, or for the potential of such arrangements to succumb over time to agency capture or corruption.

Fleshing out the meaning of democratic accountability in the brave new world of policy administration can go a long way toward resolving what Don Kettl (1992) identified as "public administration's greatest dilemma—how to elicit effective performance and political accountability in the public sector" (p. 3). What does effective accountability look like in a world of shared power, results-oriented management, flattened hierarchies, and catalytic government? What does it mean to compromise accountability? Can institutional arrangements be designed which meet all three criteria? Put differently, is it possible for administrative arrangements to be responsive to both top-down and bottom-up political demands, while also delivering efficient performance? If there are trade-offs among the three, can thresholds be defined which maintain some optimal balance among the criteria and beyond which positive gains for one criterion are likely to be offset by diminishment of one, or both, of the other two elements of the accountability equation?

This research also suggests that scholars, policy makers, and practitioners need a better understanding of the conditions under which various regulatory arrangements work best. Collaborative games are only one of many different keys to improving regulatory effectiveness and ensuring environmental progress in the future—at the federal level or otherwise. Given the restrictions imposed by pluralism by the rules and uncertainty more generally, under other conditions different arrangements are needed. Much like other policy arenas in the 1990s,[12] the diversity of policy problems encountered in the environmental arena precludes the universal application of a *single* "set of prescriptions concerning the best way to regulate."[13] Instead, the key is to find the right policy for the job. Discovering which policies are right for the job requires that greater intellectual effort be devoted to exploring the empirical conditions under which each form of organizational arrangement is best utilized and why. The overarching goal of such a research agenda should be to produce information and models capable of helping national, state, and local governments to assess and prescribe regulatory arrangements that can help them achieve greater efficiency and effectiveness in environmental protection programs, yet without compromising environmental quality or democratic accountability.

CHAPTER NOTES

1. Other agencies using reg-neg include the Occupational Safety and Health Administration, the Federal Trade Commission, and the departments of Interior, Agriculture, and Education. See Pritzker and Dalton (1990, 8–9).

2. "[T]he overall proportion of agency regulations adopted using negotiated rulemaking remains . . . small—less than one-tenth of a percent" (Coglianese 1996, 20).

3. In a study of government efforts to site hazardous waste facilities, Rabe (1994) demonstrates the effectiveness of locally based collaborative efforts. Decision-making arrangements involving industry, government, and the affected communities have produced positive results in siting such waste in the United States and Canada. The key is that these collaborative efforts are constructed at the local level, rather than imposed by a central government whose experts identify the "best" location for the waste site. Direct participation of the general public in the process has been essential to the success.

4. John (1994) argues that the real innovation and progress in environmental protection—a "new paradigm" of environmental policy making called civic environmentalism—is centered at the state level of governance. Civic environmentalism relies on the collaborative dynamic and, much like the collaborative games described herein, emphasizes bottom-up participation and assistance in policy design, information sharing, iterative negotiations, and a willingness to choose from a broad variety of nonregulatory and noncoercive policy approaches. Cases of policy making that involve examining pesticides in Iowa, energy conservation in Colorado, and wetlands in Florida are used to make the point that significant future progress in the battle against environmental degradation may well require broader application of the new collaborative paradigm. See also Mazmanian and Morell (1994).

5. Testimony of Thomas Jorling, Commissioner of the New York Department of Environmental Conservation, U.S. Congress. Senate. Taking Stock Hearings (1993, 158–59).

6. President Clinton's budget proposal to the 105th Congress in January 1997 proposed an additional 3,000 charter schools by the year 2000.

7. However, a plausible argument can be made that tangible successes in cleaning up the environment might offset the costs of participation by attracting additional dues-paying members to the group.

8. The General Services Administration Advisory Committee Rule, finalized in 1987, removes prior restrictions on the compensation of committee members for decision-making efforts like negotiated rulemakings. The rule *allows*, but does not *require*, compensation in the way of daily wages and reimbursement for travel expenses, including per diem, whenever committee work takes the individual away from home. Substantive legislation can, of course, still mandate such compensation during rulemaking procedures if it will enable that party to better express its needs and positions (General Services Administration, 1987).

9. Each transaction's particular constellation of interests would have to come to agreement on just what constituted a "reasonable" level of shared savings during the initial phase of the game. The definition of "reasonable," for example, might vary, depending on the expected magnitude. As the aggregate size of industry's expected compliance cost benefits grow, they might be more willing to devote additional funds to the shared savings category.

10. The collaborative games format in this case also helps to alleviate the problems associated with funding public sector innovations in a time of general fiscal scarcity. Given the local character of the game, the list of transaction-specific conditions governing the pluralism-by-the-rules framework should be enlarged to include consideration of possible transboundary pollution effects.

11. The potential of collaborative games at state and local levels of government is supported by other research as well. See footnote 5.

12. Education policy is a prime example. Virtually everyone agrees that the primary and secondary public school system is not meeting key educational objectives, whether in terms of basic educational skills or the skills needed for economic and social success in the 21st century. But until relatively recently, the possibilities for meaningful reform were narrowly restricted to such options as additional money for teachers, supplies, and infrastructure; standardized testing; and restructured curriculums. The basic organizational form—neighborhood schools controlled by a centralized bureaucracy (except where busing was deemed necessary for racial equity purposes)—was left unquestioned.

Debate during the 1990s, however, ranges the spectrum from private school choice (vouchers) (e.g., Milwaukee and Cleveland) to charter schools in over a dozen states (e.g., Michigan and Colorado), magnet schools in Kansas City, public schools managed by private companies, and greater local control by principals and parents (e.g., Chicago and recent initiatives in Los Angeles).

13. Ayres and Braithwaite (1992, 5). See also Kettl (1993). Kettl examined the wide embrace given to privatization and competition prescriptions in recent years. He concluded that "the cases in this book . . . teach an important lesson: the competition prescription is scarcely a cure-all for government's problems of size and efficiency" (pp. 199–200).

Bibliography

Aberbach, Joel 1990. *Keeping a watchful eye: The politics of congressional oversight.* Washington, D.C.: The Brookings Institution.

Abramson, Rudy 1989. Administration reviving plan to require clean alternative auto fuels, Reilly says. *Los Angeles Times.* (October 18), A9.

Ackerman, Bruce A., and Richard B. Stewart 1985. Reforming environmental law. *Stanford Law Review.* 37, 1333–65.

Ackerman, Bruce A., and William T. Hassler 1981. *Clean coal/Dirty air.* New Haven, Conn.: Yale University Press.

Adler, Jonathan H. 1992. Clean fuels, dirty air: How a (bad) bill became law. *The Public Interest*, 108 (Summer), 116–31.

Adler, Robert 1994. The clean water act: Has it worked? *EPA Journal.* 19 (Summer), 10–14.

Aeppel, Timothy 1995. Not in my garage: Clean air act triggers backlash as its focus shifts to driving habits. *Wall Street Journal.* (January 25), A1.

Aeppel, Timothy, and Caleb Solomon 1994. Clean air fuel ignites revolt among drivers. *Wall Street Journal.* (December 13), B1

Alchian, Armen A., and Harold Demsetz 1972. Production, information costs, and economic organization. *American Economic Review.* 62: 777–95.

Allardice, David R. 1993. Preface. eds. David R. Allardice, Richard F. Kosobud, William A. Testa, and Donald A. Hanson. *Cost effective control of urban smog.* Chicago, Illinois: Federal Reserve Bank of Chicago, i–ii.

Allardice, David R., Richard F. Kosobud, William A. Testa, and Donald A. Hanson. eds. 1993. *Cost effective control of urban smog.* Chicago, Illinois: Federal Reserve Bank of Chicago.

Allardice, David R., Richard H. Mattoon, and William A. Testa 1993. Industry approaches to environmental policy in the Great Lakes region. A Federal Reserve Bank of Chicago working paper (WP-1993-8) (July), 26.

Allison, Graham T. 1969. *Essence of decision: Explaining the Cuban missile crisis.* Boston, MA: Little, Brown and Company.

Amoco/USEPA Pollution Prevention Project 1991. Pollution prevention workshop. Yorktown, Virginia (#PB92228543).

Amoco/USEPA Pollution Prevention Project 1992. Executive summary. Yorktown, Virginia (#PB92228519).

Amy, Douglas J. 1987. *The politics of environmental mediation.* New York: Columbia University Press.

Amy, Douglas J. 1990. Environmental dispute resolution: The promise and the pitfalls. eds. N. J. Vig and M. E. Kraft. *Environmental Policy in the 1990s.* Washington, D.C.: Congressional Quarterly Press, 211–234.

Appleby, Paul 1949. *Policy and administration.* Tuscaloosa, AL: University of Alabama Press.

Applegate Partnership 1996. An open letter to the environmental community [letter to the editor]. *High Country News.* 2 (http://www.hcn.org/home_page/dir/email_letters.html).

Arrandale, Tom 1992. Junk science and environmental regulation. *Governing.* (June), 82.

Arrow, Kenneth 1969. The organization of economic activity: Issues pertinent to the choice of market versus nonmarket allocation. In *The analysis and evaluation of public expenditure: The PPB system.* (Vol. 1) U.S. Joint Economic Committee, 91st Congress, 1st Session. Washington, D.C.: U.S. Government Printing Office, 59–73.

Auto/Oil Air Quality Improvement Research Program 1993. *Phase I, Final Report* (May).

Axelrod, Robert 1984. *The evolution of cooperation.* New York: Basic Books.

Ayres, Ian, and John Braithwaite 1992. *Responsive regulation: Transcending the deregulation debate.* New York: Oxford University Press.

Bacow, Lawrence S., and Michael Wheeler 1984. *Environmental dispute resolution.* New York: Plenum Press.

Badaracco, Joseph L., Jr. 1985. *Loading the dice: A five-country study of vinyl chloride regulation.* Cambridge: Harvard Business School Press.

Banks, Jeffrey S., and Barry R. Weingast 1992. The political control of bureaucracies under asymmetric information. *American Journal of Political Science.* 26 (May), 509–24.

Bardach, Eugene, and Robert A. Kagan. eds. 1982. *Social regulation: Strategies for reform.* San Francisco, CA: Institute for Contemporary Studies.

Bardach, Eugene, and Robert A. Kagan 1982. *Going by the book: The problem of regulatory unreasonableness.* Philadelphia: Temple University Press.

Barnard, Chester 1938. *The functions of the executive.* Cambridge, MA: Harvard University Press.

Barrett, Paul M. 1992. Environmental lawsuits face tough standard. *Wall Street Journal.* (June 15), A3.

Barzelay, Michael, with Babak J. Armanjani 1992. *Breaking through bureaucracy: A new vision for managing government.* Berkeley, CA: University of California Press.

Baucus, Max 1993. An environmental renaissance. In *The clean air marketplace 1993: Conference proceedings.* Washington, D.C.: U.S. Environmental Protection Agency (September 8–9), 139–145.

Baumgartner, Frank R., and Bryan D. Jones. 1993. Agendas and instability in American politics. Chicago, IL: The University of Chicago Press.

Becker, Gary 1983. A theory of competition among pressure groups for political influence. *Quarterly Journal of Economics,* 47, 371–400.

Benenson, Bob 1995a. House easily passes bills to limit regulations. *Congressional Quarterly Weekly Report.* 53 (March 4), 682.

Benenson, Bob 1995b. GOP sets the 104th Congress on new regulatory course. *Congressional Quarterly Weekly Report*. 53 (June 17), 1693–1701.

Benenson, Bob 1995c. Bill to scale back process gets bipartisan nod. *Congressional Quarterly Weekly Report*. 53 (June 24), 1836.

Berke, Richard L. 1990. House panel reaches accord on cleaner gasoline. *New York Times*. (May 21), B11.

Bernstein, Marver H. 1955. *Regulating business by independent commission*. Princeton, NJ: Princeton University Press.

Berry, Jeffrey M. 1989. Subgovernments, issue networks, and political conflict. In eds. Richard A. Harris and Sidney M. Milkis. *Remaking American Politics*. Boulder, CO: Westview Press, 239–260.

Berry, Michael A. 1984. A method for examining policy implementation: A study of decisionmaking for national ambient air quality standards, 1964–1984, (unpublished dissertation at the University of North Carolina).

Bethell, Tom 1994. Fix Washington before it enslaves us all. *Wall Street Journal*. (December 2), A10.

Beyond Compliance Emissions Reduction Act of 1994 [proposed] 1994. Executive summary.

Bingham, Gail 1986. *Resolving environmental disputes: A decade of experience*. Washington, D.C.: The Conservation Foundation.

Bohi, Douglas R., and Dallas Burtraw 1991. Avoiding regulatory gridlock in the acid rain program. *Journal of Policy Analysis and Management*. 10: 676–84.

Bosso, Christopher J. 1987. *Pesticides and politics*. Pittsburgh, PA: University of Pittsburgh Press.

Bosso, Christopher J. 1994. After the movement: Environmental activism in the 1990s. In eds. N. J. Vig and M. E. Kraft. *Environmental Policy in the 1990s*. 2nd ed. Washington, D.C.: CQ Press, 31–50.

Bovard, James 1994. *Lost rights: The destruction of American liberty*. New York: St. Martin's Press.

Braithwaite, John 1985. *To punish or persuade: Enforcement of coal mine safety*. Albany, NY: SUNY Press.

Breyer, Stephen 1982. *Regulation and its reform*. Cambridge, Mass.: Harvard University Press.

Breyer, Stephen 1993. *Breaking the vicious circle: Toward effective risk regulation*. Cambridge, Mass.: Harvard University Press.

Broder, David 1994. The citizens' movement. *Washington Post*. (November 15).

Brower, David 1995. *Let the mountains speak, let the rivers run*. Washington, D.C.: Island Press.

Browne, William 1986. Instability and change in an issue subsystem. eds. Allan Cigler and Burdett Loomis. *Interest Group Politics*. 2d. ed., Washington, D.C.: Congressional Quarterly Press, 183–201.

Browne, William 1988. *Private interests, public policy, and American agriculture*. Lawrence, Kansas: University Press of Kansas.

Browner, Carol 1993. Pollution prevention takes center stage. *EPA Journal*. 19 (July–September), 6–8.

Brownstein, Ronald 1980. Resource conservation and recovery act: Four years old and still not off the ground. *Amicus Journal*. 1 (Spring), 13–15.

Bryner, Gary C. 1987. *Bureaucratic discretion: Law and policy in federal regulatory agencies.* New York: Pergamon Press.

Bryner, Gary C. 1993. *Blue skies, green politics: The clean air act of 1990.* Washington, D.C.: Congressional Quarterly Press.

Bryner, Gary C. 1995. Rethinking environmental regulation: Assessing critiques of environmental regulation. Presented at the Annual Meeting of the Midwest Political Science Association. Chicago, Illinois (April 6–8).

Buchanan, James, and Gordon Tullock 1976. Polluters' profits and political response: Direct controls versus taxes. *American Economic Review.* 65, 139–47.

Bulkeley, William M. 1994. Pushing the pace: The latest thing at many companies is speed, speed, speed. *Wall Street Journal.* (December 23), 1.

Bullard, Robert D. 1993. Anatomy of environmental racism. In ed. Richard Hofrichter. *Toxic Struggles: The Theory and Practice of Environmental Justice.* Philadelphia, PA: New Society Publishers, 25–35.

Burke, J. 1986. *Bureaucratic responsibility.* Baltimore, MD: Johns Hopkins University Press.

Burns, James MacGregor 1978. *Leadership.* New York: Harper and Row.

Burton, Lloyd 1988. Negotiating the cleanup of toxic groundwater contamination: Strategy and legitimacy. *Natural Resources Journal.* 28 (Winter), 105–143.

Business Week. 1983. Environmentalists more of a political force. (January 24), 85–6.

Calcagni, John 1993. Title I of the Clean Air Act Amendments of 1990 and implications for market-based strategies. In eds. David R. Allardice, Richard F. Kosobud, William A. Testa, and Donald A. Hanson. *Cost Effective Control of Urban Smog.* Chicago, Illinois: Federal Reserve Bank of Chicago.

Calmes, Jackie 1995. Fight over balanced budget could prove to be defining moment for Gingrich and his agenda. *Wall Street Journal.* (December 6), A22.

Calvert, Randall, Matthew D. McCubbins, and Barry R. Weingast 1989. A theory of political control and agency discretion. *American Journal of Political Science.* 33, 588–611.

Canon, David T. 1992. Unconventional lawmaking in the United States Congress. Presented at the Annual Meeting of the American Political Science Association, Chicago, Illinois (September 3–6).

Carnevale, David G. 1993. Root dynamics of alternative dispute resolution: An illustrative case in the U.S. Postal Service. *Public Administration Review.* 53 (September–October), 455–61.

Carroll, Vincent 1995. Junk science fuels tailpipe policy. *Wall Street Journal.* (March 23), A14.

Carson, Rachel 1962. *Silent Spring.* Greenwich, Conn.: Fawcett Crest Books.

Chappie, Damon M., et al. 1990. Pollution control 20 years after earth day: A retrospective on federal environmental programs. *Environment Reporter,* 21 (May 4), 123–28.

Chubb, John E., and Paul E. Peterson 1989. American political institutions and the problem of governance. In eds. J. E. Chubb and E. Peterson. *Can the Government Govern?* Washington, D.C.: The Brookings Institution, 1–43.

Clean Air Working Group 1987. *Acid rain: The rush to judgment: A perspective for the 100th Congress.* Washington, D.C., 24.

Cleland-Hamnett, Wendy 1993. The role of comparative risk analysis. *EPA Journal.* 19 (January–March), 18–23.

Cloud, David S. 1995. GOP, to its own great delight, enacts House rule changes. *Congressional Quarterly Weekly Report.* 53 (January 7), 13–15.

Coase, Ronald H. 1937. The nature of the firm. *Economica*, 4 (November), 386–405.

Coase, Ronald H. 1952. The nature of the firm. *Economica*, 4 (November, 1937), 386–405. Reprinted in eds. G. J. Stigler and K. E. Boulding. *Readings in price theory.* Homewood, Ill.: Richard D. Irwin.

Coase, Ronald H. 1972. Industrial organization: A proposal for research. In ed. V. R. Fuchs. *Policy issues and research opportunities in industrial organization.* New York: National Bureau of Economic Research, 59–73.

Coglianese, Cary. 1997. Assessing consensus: The promise and performance of negotiated rulemaking. Duke University Law Journal.

Cohen, Richard E. 1992. *Washington at work: Back rooms and clean air.* New York: Macmillan.

Cohen, Steven A. 1986. EPA: A qualified success. In eds. Sheldon Kamieniecki, Robert O'Brien, and Michael Clarke *Controversies in Environmental Policy.* Albany, N.Y.: SUNY Press, 174–195.

Collie, Melissa, and Joseph Cooper 1989. Multiple referral and the 'new' committee system in the House of Representatives. In eds. Lawrence C. Dodd and Bruce I. Oppenheimer. *Congress reconsidered.* 4th ed., Washington, D.C.: CQ Press, 245–72.

Commons, John R. 1934. *Institutional economics.* Madison, Wisconsin: University of Wisconsin Press.

Congressional Quarterly Weekly Report 1990. Environment: Clean air conferees finally named. 48 (June 30), 2044.

Congressional Quarterly Weekly Report 1995. Passage of contract bills. 53 (April 8), 1006.

Congressional Quarterly Weekly Report 1996. Issue: Endangered Species Act. 54 (January 6), 36.

Cook, Brian J. 1988. *Bureaucratic politics and regulatory reform: The EPA and emissions trading.* Westport, Conn.: Greenwood Press.

Cook, Mary Etta, and Roger H. Davidson 1985. Deferral politics: Congressional decision making on environmental issues in the 1980s. In eds. Helen M. Ingram and R. Kenneth Godwin. *Public policy and the natural environment.* Greenwich, Conn.: JAI Press.

Costle, Douglas M. 1993. Regulation: Improving regulatory decision making. In *Science, Technology, and Government for a Changing World.* The Concluding Report of the Carnegie Commission. (April), 57–9.

Council of Great Lakes Governors 1994. *The great printers project: Recommendations to make pollution prevention a standard practice in the printing industry.*

Council on Environmental Quality 1982. *Environmental quality: Thirteenth annual report.* Washington, D.C.: U.S. Government Printing Office.

Council on Environmental Quality 1985. *Environmental quality: Sixteenth annual report.* Washington, D.C.: U.S. Government Printing Office.

Council on Environmental Quality 1989. *Environmental quality: Twentieth annual report*. Washington, D.C.: U.S. Government Printing Office.

Crandall, Robert 1983. *Controlling industrial pollution*. Washington, D.C.: The Brookings Institution.

Culhane, Paul J. 1981. *Public lands politics: Interest group influence on the Forest Service and the Bureau of Land Management*. Baltimore, MD: Johns Hopkins University Press.

Cushman, John H., Jr. 1995. Moderates soften GOP agenda on environment. *New York Times*. (October 23), A1+.

Cushman, John H., Jr. 1996. GOP backing off from tough stand over environment. *New York Times*. (January 26), A1+.

Cyert, Richard M., and James G. March 1963. *A behavioral theory of the firm*. Englewood Cliffs, N.J.: Prentice-Hall.

Daggett, Dan 1995. It's un-american, or at best unwestern, but cooperation works. *High Country News*, 27 (October 16), 1–3 (http://www.hcn.org/pseudo/1995/oct16/dir/Opinion__It's__unAme.html)

Dahl, Robert 1961. *Who governs?* New Haven: Yale University Press.

Davies, J. Clarence 1983. The effects of federal regulation on chemical-industry innovation. *Law and Contemporary Problems*. 46: 41–58.

Davies, J. Clarence 1985. Coping with toxic substances. *Issues in Science and Technology*. 1: 71–9.

Davies, J. Clarence 1990. The United States: Experiment and fragmentation. In eds. Nigel Haigh and Frances Irwin. *Integrated Pollution Control in Europe and North America*. Washington, D.C.: The Conservation Foundation, 51–66.

Davies, J. Clarence, and Barbara S. Davies 1975. *The politics of pollution*. 2d ed., Indianapolis, IN: Pegasus.

Derthick, Martha, and Paul J. Quirk 1985. *The politics of deregulation*. Washington, D.C.: The Brookings Institution.

DiIulio, John J., Jr., Gerald Garvey, and Donald F. Kettl 1993. *Improving government performance: An owner's manual*. Washington, D.C.: The Brookings Institution.

Doherty, Carroll J. 1995. Time and tax cuts will test GOP freshman solidarity. *Congressional Quarterly Weekly Report*. 53 (April 1), 915–16.

Doherty, Carroll J. 1996. GOP's first half is marked mostly by sound and fury. *Congressional Quarterly Weekly Report*. 54 (January 20), 119–38.

Dorfman, Mark H., Warren R. Muir, and Catherine G. Miller 1992. *Environmental dividends: Cutting more chemical wastes*. New York: INFORM, Inc.

Douglas, Mary, and Aaron Wildavsky 1983. *Risk and culture: An essay on the selection of technical and environmental dangers*. Berkeley, CA: University of California Press.

Downs, Anthony 1967. *Inside Bureaucracy*. Washington, D.C.: The Brookings Institution.

Downs, Anthony 1972. Up and Down with Ecology: The Issue-Attention Cycle, *The Public Interest*, 28: 38–50.

Dryzek, John S., and James Lester 1989. Alternative Views of the Environmental Problematic. In ed. James Lester. *Environmental Politics and Policy: Theories and Evidence*. Durham and London: Duke University Press, 314–30.

Dudek, Daniel J., and John Palmisano 1988. Emissions Trading: Why Is this Thoroughbred Hobbled? *Columbia Journal of Environmental Law*, 13: 217–56.

Dunlap, Riley E. 1990. Trends in Public Opinion Toward Environmental Issues, 1965–1990, ms, 38

Dunne, Nancy 1992. Complacency Breeds Contempt. *The London Financial Times*, (June 17), 12.

Eads, George C., and Michael Fix 1984. *Relief or Reform: Reagan's Regulatory Dilemma*. Washington, D.C.: The Urban Institute Press.

Easterbrook, Gregg 1995. *A Moment on the Earth: The Coming Age of Environmental Optimism*. New York: Viking Press.

Economist 1990. Business and the Environment: Seeing the Green Light, (October 20), 88–93.

Economist 1991. Lexington: William Reilly's Green Precision Weapons, (March 30), 28.

Edelman, Murray 1964. *The symbolic uses of politics*. Urbana, IL: University of Illinois Press.

Eggertsson, Thrainn 1990. *Economic Behavior and Institutions*. Cambridge: Cambridge University Press.

Eggleston, Richard 1995. DNR Reports Similar Air Qualities for Conventional, Reformulated Gas, *Wisconsin State Journal*. (April 1), D3.

Eisner, Marc A. 1993. *Regulatory Politics in Transition*. Baltimore and London: The Johns Hopkins University Press.

Eisner, Marc A., and Kenneth J. Meier 1990. Presidential Control versus Bureaucratic Power: Explaining the Reagan Revolution in Antitrust. *American Journal of Political Science*. 34: 269–87.

Elman, Barry S., Tom Tyler, and Michael Doonan 1992. Economic Incentives Under the New Clean Air Act, ms, 21.

Environment Reporter 1988. Thomas Tells of Frustration with OMB, Predicts More Rules But Urges Prevention, 19 (December 9), 1617.

———. 1990. After Twenty Years of Pollution Control, EPA Gears Up for Switch to Pollution Prevention, 21 (May 4), 130–31.

———. 1990. EPA Issues Rule Aimed at Cutting Urban Smog, 21 (June 8), 311.

———. 1991. Reformulated Fuel Negotiations Begin; Committee Raises Enforcement, Credits Issue, 21 (March 22), 2090–91.

———. 1991. Reformulated Gasoline, 22 (May 17), 126–7.

———. 1991. Consensus Still Not Reached on Proposal for Reformulated Gas, Oxygenated Fuels, 22 (June 14), 333–34.

———. 1991. Air Act's Oxygenate Limits for Gasoline Could Be Hard to Meet, Industry Report Says, 22 (July 5), 557.

———. 1991. Weaker EPA Proposal on Fuels Could Lead to State Regulation, Environmentalist Says, 22 (July 19), 645–6.

———. 1991. Reformulated Fuels Negotiation Near End, But Agreement on Proposal Not Yet Assured, 22 (August 16), 1051–52.

———. 1991. Traditional Antagonists Agree on Makeup of Cleaner, Reformulated Fuel, 22 (August 23), 1141–42.

———. 1991. Environmentalists Turn to Alternate Solutions as Federal Policies Fail, Sierra Club Chief Says, 22 (October 25), 1615–1616.

———. 1991. Disclosure, Pollution Prevention Crucial to U.S. Business Competition, EPA Official Says, 22 (November 22), 1794.

Environment Reporter 1992. Senator, Ethanol Producers Delay Gas Rule; States, Environmentalists Charge 'Bad Faith,' 22 (March 27), 2635.

———. 1992. Critics of Ethanol Make Their Case, 22 (April 7), 2730–31.

———. 1992. Environmentalist, Oil Industry, Others Team Up to Fight Break for Ethanol Makers, 23 (September 18), 1429–30.

———. 1992. Top Air Official at EPA Said to Consider Vapor Pressure Waiver for Ethanol Illegal, 23 (September 25), 1470–71.

———. 1992. [President] Bush Grants Evaporative Limit Waiver for Ethanol, 23 (October 9), 1544–45.

———. 1992. Supplemental Rule-Making on Ethanol Not Likely to be Easy, EPA Staffer Says, 23 (October 16), 1596–97.

———. 1992. Browner Urges Consensus on Rules, Permits, 23 (December 25), 2099.

Environment Reporter 1993. EPA Releases Reformulated Gasoline Rule for Publication, 23 (February 5), 2632–33.

———. 1993. Reformulated Fuel Proposal, Cleared by OMB with Ethanol Provisions Intact, 23 (February 19), 2711.

———. 1993. Groups Voice Complaints, Fear of Increased VOC Emissions, 23 (April 16), 3162.

———. 1993. Browner Says Cooperation with Industry Enhances Environmental Policy Development, 24 (June 18), 322.

———. 1993. Ethanol Waiver Proposed by EPA Under Bush Withdrawn, 24 (October 15), 1138–39.

———. 1994. Business, Environmental Group Coalition Suggests Ways to Improve Regulatory Climate, 24 (May 13), 67–8.

Erskine, Hazel 1969. The Polls: Pollution and Its Costs, *Public Opinion Quarterly*, 36, 121–23.

Esposito, John C. et al. 1970. *Vanishing Air*. New York: Grossman Publishers.

Evans, C. Lawrence, and Walter J. Oleszek 1995. Congressional Tsunami? Institutional Change in the 104th Congress, presented at the Annual Meeting of the American Political Science Association, Chicago, Illinois (August 31–September 3).

Evans, Peter B., Dietrich Rueschmeyer, and Theda Skocpol. eds. 1985. *Bringing the State Back In*. New York: Cambridge University Press.

Executive Office of the President 1990. *Regulatory Program of the United States Government: April 1, 1990–March 31, 1991*.

Faber, Daniel, and James O'Connor 1989. The Struggle for Nature: Environmental Crises and the Crisis of Environmentalism in the United States, *Capitalism, Nature, Socialism*, 2 (Summer), 12–39.

Federal Register 1983. *Establishment of EPA's Regulatory Negotiation Project*, 48 (February 22), 7494.

Federalist 51 1961. *The Federalist Papers: Alexander Hamilton, James Madison, John Jay*. New York: Times Mirror, 320–25.

Fenno, Richard F., Jr. 1973. *Congressmen in committees*. Boston: Little, Brown and Company.

Finkel, Adam M., and Dominic Golding 1994. *Worst Things First? The Debate over Risk-Based National Environmental Priorities.* Washington, D.C.: Resources for the Future.

Fiorina, Morris 1981. Congressional Control of the Bureaucracy: A Mismatch of Incentives and Capability. In eds. Lawrence C. Dodd and Bruce I. Oppenheimer *Congress Reconsidered.* Washington, D.C.: CQ Press.

Fiorino, Daniel J. 1988. Regulatory Negotiation as a Policy Process. *Public Administration Review.* (July/August), 764–72.

Fiorino, Daniel J., and Chris Kirtz 1985. Breaking Down Walls: Negotiated Rulemaking at EPA. *Temple Environmental Law and Technology Journal.* 4: 29–40.

Fisher, Roger, and William Ury 1981. *Getting to Yes.* Boston, MA: Houghton Mifflin.

Foreman, Dave 1987. *Ecodefense: A Field Guide to Monkeywrenching.* 2d ed., Tuscon, AZ: Ned Ludd Books.

Freedman, Allan 1995. DeLay Aims at Regulations. *Congressional Quarterly Weekly Report.* 53 (February 11), 451.

Freedman, Allan 1996a. GOP Trying to Find Balance After Early Stumbles. *Congressional Quarterly Weekly Report.* Vol. 54 (January 20), 151–153.

Freedman, Allan 1996b. On the Second Session Agenda. *Congressional Quarterly Weekly Report.* Vol. 54 (January 20), 152.

Freudenburg, William R., and Robert Gramling 1994. Bureaucratic Slippage and Failures of Agency Vigilance: The Case of the Environmental Studies Program, *Social Problems,* 41 (May), 214–39.

Friedland, Lewis A. 1996. Electronic Democracy and the New Citizenship, *Media, Culture, and Society,* 18, 185–212.

Fulton, William 1992. The Air Pollution Trading Game. *Governing.* 5 (March), 40–45.

Gais, Thomas L., and Jack L. Walker, Jr. 1991. Pathways to Influence in American Politics: Factors Affecting the Choice of Tactics by Interest Groups, Presented at the Annual Meeting of the Midwest Political Science Association, Chicago.

Gais, Thomas L., Mark A. Peterson, and Jack L. Walker, Jr. 1984. Interest Groups, Iron Triangles and Representative Institutions in American National Government. *British Journal of Political Science.* 14, 161–85.

General Accounting Office 1979. *Improvements Needed in Controlling Major Air Pollution Sources.* Report to the Subcommittee on Environmental Pollution, Committee on Environment and Public Works, U.S. Senate (January 2) (CED–78–165).

General Accounting Office 1987. *EPA's Efforts to Control Vehicle Refueling and Evaporative Emissions.* Report to the Chairman, Subcommittee on Health and the Environment, Committee on Energy and Commerce, U.S. House of Representatives (RCED–87–155).

General Accounting Office 1988. *Environmental Protection Agency: Protecting Human Health and the Environment Through Improved Management.* Report to the Congress (August 16) (RCED–88–101).

General Accounting Office 1990a. *Gasoline Marketing: Uncertainties Surround*

Reformulated Gasoline as a Motor Fuel. Report to the Chairman, Subcommittee on Energy and Power, Committee on Energy and Commerce, U.S. House of Representatives (June) (RCED–90–153).

General Accounting Office 1990b. *Air Pollution: Improvements Needed in Detecting and Preventing Violations.* Report to the Chairman, Subcommittee on Oversight and Investigations, Committee on Energy and Commerce, U.S. House of Representatives (September) (RCED–90–155).

General Accounting Office 1991. *Environmental Protection: Meeting Public Expectations with Limited Resources.* Report to the Congress (June) (RCED–91–97).

General Accounting Office 1994a. *Toxic Substances Control Act: EPA's Limited Progress in Regulating Toxic Chemicals.* Testimony before the Subcommittee on Toxic Substances, Research and Development, Committee on Environment and Public Works, U.S. Senate (May) (RCED–94–212).

General Accounting Office 1994b. *Air Pollution: Allowance Trading Offers an Opportunity to Reduce Emissions at Less Cost.* Report to the Chairman, Environment, Energy, and Natural Resources Subcommittee, Committee on Government Operations, U.S. House of Representatives (December) (RCED–95–30).

General Accounting Office 1994c. *Superfund: Status, Cost, and Timeliness of Hazardous Waste Site Cleanups.* Report to the Chairman, Committee on Energy and Commerce, U.S. House of Representatives (September) (RCED–94–256.

General Accounting Office 1995. *EPA and the States: Environmental Challenges Require a Better Working Relationship.* Report to the Ranking Minority Member, Committee on Governmental Affairs, U.S. Senate (April) (RCED–95–64).

General Accounting Office 1996. *Motor Fuels: Issues Related to Reformulated Gasoline, Oxygenated Fuels, and Biofuels.* Report to the Honorable Tom Daschle, Minority Leader, U.S. Senate (June) (RCED–96–121).

General Services Administration 1987. Advisory committee rule. *Federal Register.* 45:926–34.

Georges, Christopher 1996. Discord Over Tax Cuts is Beginning to Blemish GOP Freshmen's Perfect Picture of Budget Unity. *Wall Street Journal* (January 4), A12.

Gilbreath, Kent. ed. 1984. *Business and the Environment: Toward Common Ground.* 2d. ed., Washington, D.C.: The Conservation Foundation.

Glicksman, Robert, and Christopher H. Schroeder 1991. EPA and the Courts: Twenty Years of Law and Politics. *Law and Contemporary Problems.* 54 (Autumn), 249–310.

Goffman, Joseph 1993a. Senior Attorney for the Environmental Defense Fund. *Personal correspondence.*

Goffman, Joseph 1993b. The Performance Challenge: Markets Mechanisms for Both Efficiency and Equity, remarks at the AWMA-EPA Conference on New Partnerships: Economic Incentives for Environmental Management; Rochester, New York (November 3), 1–3.

Goodnow, Frank J. 1900. *Politics and Administration.* New York: Macmillan.

Goodsell, Charles T. 1985. *The Case for Bureaucracy: A Public Administration Polemic.* Chatham, N. J.: Chatham House Publishers.

Gormley, William T. 1989. *Taming the Bureaucracy: Muscles, Prayers, and Others Strategies.* Princeton, N. J.: Princeton University Press.

Gormley, William T., Jr. 1991. Two Cheers for Privatization. In ed. W. T. Gormley, Jr. *Privatization and Its Alternatives.* Madison, WI: University of Wisconsin Press, 307–318.

Gottlieb, Robert, and Margaret FitzSimmons 1991. *Thirst for Growth: Water Agencies as Hidden Government in California.* Tucson, AZ: University of Arizona Press.

Gottlieb, Robert, and Helen Ingram 1988. The New Environmentalists, *The Progressive,* 52 (August), 14–15.

Granovetter, Mark 1985. Economic Action and Social Structure: The Problem of Embeddedness. *American Journal of Sociology,* 91 (November), 481–510.

Great Lakes Regional Emissions Trading Conference 1994. Chicago, Illinois: Federal Reserve Bank of Chicago (January 27–28).

Greve, Michael S. 1992. Introduction: Environmental Politics Without Romance. In eds. Michael S. Greve and Fred L. Smith. *Environmental Politics: Public Costs, Private Rewards.* New York: Praeger Publishing, 1–18.

Greve, Michael S., and Fred L. Smith eds. 1992. *Environmental Politics: Public Costs, Private Rewards.* New York: Praeger Publishing.

Guruswamy, Lakshman 1989. Integrating Thoughtways: Reopening of the Environmental Mind? *Wisconsin Law Review.:* 47, No. 3, 463–537.

Gutfeld, Rose 1992. Environmental Group Doesn't Always Lick 'Em; It Can Join 'Em and Succeed. *Wall Street Journal.* (August 20), B1+.

Hager, George 1989a. Bush's Tough Acid Rain Bill Puts Midwest on the Spot. *Congressional Quarterly Weekly Report.* 47 (November 4), 2934.

Hager, George 1989b. Bush Sets Clean Air Debate in Motion with New Plan. *Congressional Quarterly Weekly Report.* 47 (June 17), 1464.

Hager, George 1989c. Bush's Plan for Cleaner Fuels Scaled Back by House Panel. *Congressional Quarterly Weekly Report.* 47 (October 14), 2700–01.

Hager, George 1990a. Clean Air: War About Over in Both the House and the Senate. *Congressional Quarterly Weekly Report.* 48 (April 7), 1057–59, 1062–63.

Hager, George 1990b. House Plans to Act Quickly on Clean Air Amendments. *Congressional Quarterly Weekly Report.* 48 (May 19), 1551–52.

Hager, George 1990c. Easy House Vote on Clean Air Bodes Well for Bill's Future. *Congressional Quarterly Weekly Report.* 48 (May 26), 1643–45.

Hager, George 1990d. Cannons of the Conference Room Draw Clean Air Battle Lines. *Congressional Quarterly Weekly Report.* 48 (July 21), 2291–93.

Hager, George 1990e. Conferees in Holding Pattern Over Clean Air Proposals. *Congressional Quarterly Weekly Report.* 48 (July 28), 2399–2400.

Hager, George 1990f. Senate-White House Deal Breaks Clean-Air Logjam. *Congressional Quarterly Weekly Report.* 48 (March 3), 652–54.

Hager, George 1990g. Clean-Air Deal Survives First Senate Assault. *Congressional Quarterly Weekly Report.* 48 (March 10), 738–40.

Hager, George, and Phil Kuntz 1990. Senate-White House Deal Survives Another Test. *Congressional Quarterly Weekly Report.* 48 (March 24), 900–06.

Hahn, Robert W. 1995. Regulatory Reform—The Whole Story. *Wall Street Journal.* (February 27), p A14.

Hahn, Robert W., and G. L. Hester 1987. The Market for Bads: EPA's Experience with Emissions Trading. *Regulation* (Nos. 3/4). 48–53.

Hahn, Robert W., and Robert N. Stavins, 1991. Incentives-Based Environmental Regulation: A New Era from an Old Idea? *Ecology Law Quarterly,* 1–42.

Haigh, Nigel, and Frances Irwin. eds. 1990. *Integrated Pollution Control in Europe and North America.* Washington, D.C.: The Conservation Foundation.

Hamilton, Martha 1992. Making a Product's Cost Reflect Pollution's Costs. *Washington Post.* (Nov. 29), H1+.

Hammond, Thomas H. 1984. Organizational Structure and Bureaucratic Politics, ms, 45.

Hammond, Thomas H., and Jack H. Knott 1993. Who Controls the Bureaucracy? Presidential Power, Congressional Dominance, and Bureaucratic Autonomy in a Model of Multi-Institutional Policymaking, paper presented at the Annual Meeting of the American Political Science Association, Washington, D.C. (September 1–4).

Hammond, Thomas, and Gary Miller 1985. A Social Choice Perspective on Expertise and Authority in Bureaucracy. *American Journal of Political Science.* 29: 1–28.

Harrington, Winston 1989. Acid Rain: Science and Policy, working paper published by Resources for the Future, Washington, D.C.

Harris, Richard A. 1989. Politicized Management: The Changing Face of Business in American Politics. In eds. Richard A. Harris and Sidney M. Milkis. *Remaking American Politics.* Boulder, CO: Westview Press, 261–286.

Harter, Philip J. 1982. Negotiating Regulations: A Cure for Malaise. *Georgetown Law Journal.* 71: 1–113.

Hauser, Thomas 1993. Session 2: Pollution Prevention and the Clean Air Act [comments], in *The Clean Air Marketplace 1993: Conference Proceedings.* Washington, D.C.: U.S. Environmental Protection Agency (September 8–9), 19–20.

Hawkins, Keith, and John M. Thomas 1984. The Enforcement Process in Regulatory Bureaucracies. In eds. K. Hawkins and J. M. Thomas. *Enforcing Regulation.* Boston: Kluwer Nijhoff Publishing, 3–22.

Hayes, Michael T. 1992. *Incrementalism and Public Policy.* New York: Longman.

Hays, Samuel 1989. *Beauty, Health, and Permanence: Environmental Politics in the United States, 1955–1985.* Cambridge and New York: Cambridge University Press.

Healey, Jon 1993. From Conflict to Coexistence: New Politics of Environment. *Congressional Quarterly Weekly Report.* (Feb. 13), 309–13.

Hebert, H. Josef 1995. Democrats Have Blocked Regulatory Reform Bill, GOP Concedes, *Wisconsin State Journal.* (July 22), 4A.

Heclo, Hugh 1978. Issue Networks and the Executive Establishment. In ed. Anthony King. *The New American Political System.* Washington, D.C.: The American Enterprise Institute, 88–120.

Heidenheimer, Arnold J., Hugh Heclo, and Carolyn T. Adams 1990. Environmental Policy, in A. J. Heidenheimer, H. Heclo, and C. T. Adams *Comparative Public Policy: The Politics of Social Choice in Europe and America*. 3rd ed. New York: St. Martin's Press, 308–344.

Helvarg, David 1994. *The War Against the Greens: The Wise-Use Movement, the New Right, and Anti-Environmental Violence*. San Francisco, CA: Sierra Club Books.

Hertzke, Allen D. 1993. *Echoes of Discontent: Jesse Jackson, Pat Robertson, and the Resurgence of Populism*. Washington, D.C.: Congressional Quarterly Press.

Herz, Michael 1995. The Attorney Particular: Governmental Role of the Agency Counsel General. In ed. Cornell Clayton. *Government Lawyers*. Lawrence, KS: University of Kansas Press, 143–179.

Hird, John A. 1994. *Superfund: The Political Economy of Environmental Risk*. Baltimore, MD: Johns Hopkins University Press.

Hirschhorn, Joel S., and Kirsten U. Oldenburg 1991. *Prosperity Without Pollution: The Prevention Strategy for Industry and Consumers*. New York: Van Nostrand Reinhold.

Hoberg, George 1992. *Pluralism By Design: Environmental Policy and the American Regulatory State*. New York: Praeger Publishers.

Horn, Murray J. 1995. *The Political Economy of Public Administration*. Cambridge: Cambridge University Press.

Horowitz, Donald L. 1977. *The Courts and Social Policy*. Washington, D.C.: The Brookings Institution.

Hosansky, David 1995. Bliley Likely to Steer Panel Away from Activist Past. *Congressional Quarterly Weekly Report*. 53 (January 7), 36–8.

Huitt, Ralph K. 1961. Democratic Party Leadership in the Senate. *American Political Science Review*. (June), 333–344.

Hurst, David K. 1995. *Crisis and Renewal: Meeting the Challenge of Organizational Change*. Boston, MA: Harvard Business School Press.

Ingram, Helen M., and Dean E. Mann 1989. Interest Groups and Environmental Policy. In ed. James Lester. *Environmental Politics and Policy: Theories and Evidence*. Durham and London: Duke University Press, 135–57.

Ingram, Helen, and Steven Rathgeb Smith. eds. 1993. *Public Policy for Democracy*. Washington, D.C.: The Brookings Institution.

Inside EPA 1984. OMB Concerned with Costs, Delays EPA Action on Benzene Toxic Air Rules, (April 20), 4.

Inside EPA 1985. OMB Has Been Sitting On EPA's Superfund Feasibility Study Guidance, (March 22), 12.

Inside EPA 1989. Congressmen to Push Mandatory High-Level EPA Pollution Prevention Office, (November 3).

Inside OMB 1982. OMB, After 7-Month *Review*. Again Stalls Plans to Okay Radwaste Guidelines, (July 16), 8.

Irwin, Frances 1990. Introduction to Integrated Pollution Control. In eds. Nigel Haigh and Frances Irwin. 1990. *Integrated Pollution Control in Europe and North America*. Washington, D.C.: The Conservation Foundation, and Bonn: Institute for European Environmental Policy, 3–30.

Jasanoff, Sheila 1990. *The Fifth Branch: Science Advisors as Policymakers*. Cambridge, Mass.: Harvard University Press.

Jasanoff, Sheila 1993. Relating Risk Assessment and Risk Management. *EPA Journal*. 19 (January–March), 35–37.

Jensen, Michael C. 1983. Organization Theory and Methodology, *The Accounting Review*. 8, 319–37.

Jensen, Michael C., and William Meckling 1976. Theory of the Firm: Managerial Behavior, Agency Costs, and Ownership Structure. *Journal of Financial Economics*, 3 (October), 305–60.

John, DeWitt 1994. *Civic Environmentalism: Alternatives to Regulation in States and Communities*. Washington, D.C.: Congressional Quarterly Press.

Johnson, Kirk. 1993. *Beyond polarization: Emerging strategies for reconciling community and environment*. Seattle, WA: The Northwest Policy Center at the University of Washington.

Jones, Charles O. 1975. *Clean Air: The Policies and Politics of Pollution Control*. Pittsburgh, PA: Pittsburgh University Press.

Jones, Charles O. 1979. American Politics and the Organization of Energy Decision Making, *The Annual Review of Energy*, 4, 99–121.

Jones, Charles O. 1981. House Leadership in an Age of Reform. In ed. F. H. Mackaman. *Understanding Congressional Leadership*. Washington, D.C.: Congressional Quarterly Press, 117–134.

Jones, Lisa 1996. Howdy, Neighbor!: As a Last Resort, Westerners Start Talking to Each Other. *High Country News*. 28 (May 13), 1–5 (http://www.hcn.org/1996/may13/dir/Feature_Howdy,_nei.html).

Jorgensen, Dale W., and Peter J. Wilcoxen 1990. Environmental Regulation and U.S. Economic Growth. *Rand Journal of Economics*, 21 (Summer), 314–40.

Joskow, Paul L. 1991. The Role of Transaction Cost Economics in Antitrust and Public Utility Regulatory Policies. *The Journal of Law, Economics, and Organization*, 7 (Special Issue), 53–83.

Kagan, Robert A. and John T. Scholz 1984. The 'Criminology of the Corporation' and Regulatory Enforcement Strategies. In eds. K. Hawkins and J. M. Thomas. *Enforcing Regulation*. Boston: Kluwer Nijhoff Publishing, 67–96.

Kassiola, Joel J. 1990. *The Death of Industrial Civilization*. Albany, NY: SUNY Press.

Katz, Jeffrey 1996. With Few Initiatives Completed, Jury on 104th Still Out. *Congressional Quarterly Weekly Report*. 54 (January 6), 8–9.

Katzmann, Robert A. 1990. The American Legislative Process as a Signal. *Journal of Public Policy*, 9, 287–305.

Keane, J. 1991. *The Media and Democracy*. Oxford and Cambridge, MA: Polity/Basil Blackwell.

Kelman, Steven 1981. *What Price Incentives? Economists and the Environment*. Boston, Mass.: Auburn House.

Kenski, Henry C., and Helen M. Ingram 1986. The Reagan Administration and Environmental Regulation: The Constraint of the Political Market. In eds. Sheldon Kamieniecki, Robert O'Brien, and Michael Clarke. *Controversies in Environmental Policy*. Albany, N.Y.: SUNY Press, 275–298.

Kerwin, Cornelius M. 1994. *Rulemaking: How Government Agencies Write Law and Make Policy*. Washington, D.C.: Congressional Quarterly Press.

Kerwin, Cornelius, and Scott R. Furlong. 1992. Time and rulemaking: An empirical test of theory. *Journal of Public Administration Research and Theory.* 2: 113–136.

Kerwin, Cornelius M., and Laura Langbein. 1995. An evaluation of negotiated rulemaking at the Environmental Protection Agency: Phase I. Prepared for the Administrative Conference of the United States (September).

Kettl, Donald F. 1983. *The Regulation of American Federalism.* Baltimore and London: Johns Hopkins University Press.

Kettl, Donald F. 1992. *Deficit Politics: Public Budgeting in Its Institutional and Historical Context.* New York: Macmillan Publishing.

Kettl, Donald F. 1993. *Sharing Power: Public Governance and Private Markets.* Washington, D.C.: The Brookings Institution.

Khademian, Anne M. 1992. *The SEC and Capital Market Regulation: The Politics of Expertise.* Pittsburgh: University of Pittsburgh Press.

Khademian, Anne M. 1993. The New Dynamics of Legislating and the Implications for Delegating: What's to be Expected on the Receiving End? paper presented at the National Public Management Research Conference, University of Wisconsin-Madison (September 30–October 2).

Klee, Howard, Jr. 1993. Session 2: Pollution Prevention and the Clean Air Act [comments], in *The Clean Air Marketplace 1993: Conference Proceedings.* Washington, D.C.: U.S. Environmental Protection Agency (September 8–9), 25–7.

Kling, David J., and Eric Schaeffer 1993. EPA's Flagship [Pollution Prevention] Programs. *EPA Journal.* 19 (July–September), 26–30.

Kneese, Allan V., and George Schultze 1976. *Pollution, Prices, and Public Policy.* Washington, D.C.: The Brookings Institution.

Knott, Jack H., and Gary J. Miller 1987. *Reforming Bureaucracy.* Englewood Cliffs, N. J.: Prentice-Hall.

Kosobud, Richard F., William A. Testa, and Donald A. Hanson 1993. Introduction, in D. Allardice et al. *Cost Effective Control of Urban Smog.* Chicago, Illinois: Federal Reserve Bank of Chicago.

Kozszuk, Jackie 1996. Republicans' Hopes for 1996 Lie in Unfinished Business. *Congressional Quarterly Weekly Report.* 54 (January 6), 6–52.

Kraft, Michael E. 1990. Environmental Gridlock: Searching for Consensus in Congress. eds. Norman J. Vig and Michael E. Kraft. *Environmental Policy in the 1990s.* Washington, D.C.: Congressional Quarterly Press, 103–124.

Kraft, Michael E. 1994. Environmental Gridlock: Searching for Consensus in Congress. eds. Norman J. Vig and Michael E. Kraft. *Environmental Policy in the 1990s.* Washington, D.C.: CQ Press, 97–120.

Kreps, David M. 1992. Corporate Culture and Economic Theory. eds. J. A. Alt and K. A. Shepsle. *Perspectives on Positive Political Economy.* Cambridge: Cambridge University Press, 90- 143.

Krupp, Frederic D. 1986. New Environmentalism Factors in Economic Needs. *Wall Street Journal.* (November 20).

Kuntz, Phil 1990. Clean Air Bill: Dozens of Small Favors That Came Wrapped in a Big Package. *Congressional Quarterly Weekly Report.* 48 (April 7), 1060–61.

Kuntz, Phil, and George Hager 1990. Showdown on Clean-Air Bill: Senate Says 'No' to Byrd. *Congressional Quarterly Weekly Report.* 48 (March 31), 983–87.

LaDuke, Winona 1993. A Society Based on Conquest Cannot Be Sustained: Native Peoples and the Environmental Crisis. ed. R. Hofrichter. *Toxic Struggles*. 98–106.

Latham, Earl 1952. *The group basis of politics*. Ithaca, NY: Cornell University Press.

Lave, Carter B., and Gilbert S. Omenn 1981. *Clearing the Air: Reforming the Clean Air Act*. Washington, D.C.: The Brookings Institution.

Lawrence, Christine C. 1989. Lines Drawn in Opening Round Over Cleaning Nation's Air. *Congressional Quarterly Weekly Report*. (September 16), 2381.

Lazarus, Richard J. 1991a. The Neglected Question of Congressional Oversight of EPA: *Quis Custodiet Ipsos Custodes* (Who Shall Watch the Watchers Themselves). *Law and Contemporary Problems*. 54 (Autumn), 205–39.

Lazarus, Richard J. 1991b. The Tragedy of Distrust in the Implementation of Federal Environmental Law. *Law and Contemporary Problems*. 54 (Autumn), 311–74.

Leonard, H. Jeffrey, J. Clarence Davies, III, and Gordon Binder. eds. 1977. *Business and the Environment: Toward Common Ground*. Washington, D.C.: The Conservation Foundation.

Levin, Michael H. 1982. Getting There: Implementing the 'Bubble' Policy. In eds. E. Bardach and R. A. Kagan. *Social Regulation: Strategies for Reform*. London: Transaction Books, 59–92.

Levin, Michael H., and Barry S. Elman 1990. The Case for Environmental Incentives. *The Environmental Forum*. (January/ February), 7–11.

Levy, Richard E., and Robert L. Glicksman 1989. Judicial Activism and Restraint in the Supreme Court's Environmental Law Decisions, *Vanderbilt Law Review*. 42, 343–422.

Light, Paul 1995. *Thickening Government: Federal Hierarchy and the Diffusion of Accountability*. Washington, D.C.: The Brookings Institution.

Lindblom, Charles E. 1959. The Science of Muddling Through. *Public Administration Review*. 19 (Spring), 79–88.

Lindblom, Charles E. 1977. *Politics and markets*. New York: Basic Books.

Lindblom, Charles E. 1979. Still Muddling, Not Yet Through. *Public Administration Review*. 39 (November/December), 517–526.

Litan, Robert E., and William D. Nordhaus 1983. *Reforming Federal Regulation*. New Haven and London: Yale University Press.

Loeb, Alan 1993. Remarks to AWMA-EPA Conference on New Partnerships: Economic Incentives for Environmental Management, 1993 Air and Waste Management Association-U.S. EPA Conference, Rochester, New York (November 3).

Long, Norton E. 1947. Power and Administration. Reprinted in ed. F. E. Rourke (1986). *Bureaucratic Power in National Policy Making*. 4th ed., Boston: Little, Brown and Company, 7–16.

Lord, William B. 1979. Conflict in Federal Water Resource Planning, *Water Resources Bulletin*, 15 (October), 1226–1235.

Lowi, Theodore M., Jr. 1979. *The End of Liberalism*. rev. ed., New York: W. W. Norton.

Lowi, Theodore M., Jr. 1993. Two Roads to Serfdom: Liberalism, Conservatism, and Administrative Power. In eds. S. L. Elkins and K. E. Soltan. *A New Constitutionalism: Designing Political Institutions for a Good Society*. Chicago: University of Chicago Press, 149–73.

Lyman, Francesca 1990. The Gassing of America. *Washington Post*. (April 13), C5.

Lynn, Laurence E. 1987. *Managing Public Policy*. Boston, Mass.: Little, Brown and Company.

Maass, Arthur 1951. *Muddy Waters: The Army Engineers and Our Nation's Rivers*. Cambridge: Harvard University Press.

MacKenzie, James J., and Michael Walsh 1990. *Driving Forces: Motor Vehicle Trends and Their Implications for Global Warming, Energy Strategies, and Transportation Planning*. Washington, D.C.: World Resources Institute.

Mahoney, Laura 1992. Emission Trading Program for Southern California Promises Air Quality Improvements, Big Savings for Industry, *Environment Reporter*, 22 (February 21), 2423–24.

Main, Jeremy 1988. Here Comes the Big New Cleanup. *Fortune* (Nov. 21).

Management Institute for Environment and Business 1993. The Amoco/EPA Yorktown Refinery Pollution Prevention Initiative, ms, 14pp.

Mann, Charles C., and Mark L. Plummer 1994. *Noah's Choice: The Future of Endangered Species*. New York: Knopf.

Maraniss, David, and Michael Weisskopf 1996. GOP Lost Control of Members and Public Perception. *Washington Post*. (January 19), A1+.

Marcus, Alfred A. 1980. *Promise and Performance: Choosing and Implementing an Environmental Policy*. Westport, Conn.: Greenwood Press.

Marcus, Ruth 1992. Justices Make It Harder to Press Environmental Enforcement Cases. *Washington Post*. (June 13), A4.

Martin, Karen M., Harvey M. Richmond, and Willis Beal 1993. Economic Incentive Programs Under Title I of the Clean Air Act, presented at the 86th Annual Meeting of the Air and Waste Management Association, Denver, Colorado (June 13–18).

Mashaw, Jerry L., and David L. Harfst 1990. *The Struggle for Auto Safety*. Cambridge, Mass.: Harvard University Press.

Massachusetts Department of Environmental Protection. 1992. Air Pollution Control Regulations. Boston, MA: State of Massachusetts Printing Office.

Matthews, Donald R. 1960. *U.S. Senators and their world*. Chapel Hill, NC: University of North Carolina Press.

Mazmanian, Daniel A., and David L. Morell 1991. EPA: Coping with the New Political Economic Order. *Environmental Law*. 21 (Part 2), 1477–91.

Mazmanian, Daniel, and David Morell 1992. *Beyond Superfailure: America's Toxics Policy for the 1990s*. Boulder: Westview Press.

Mazmanian, Daniel, and David Morell 1994. The NIMBY Syndrome: Facility Siting and the Failure of Democratic Discourse. In eds. N. J. Vig and M. E. Kraft. *Environmental Policy in the 1990s: Toward a New Agenda*. 2nd ed., Washington, D.C.: Congressional Quarterly Press, 233–50.

Mazmanian, Daniel, and Daniel Press 1994. The Greening of Industry as a Problem of Collective Action, presented at the Annual Meeting of the American Political Science Association, (September 1–4).

McClellan, Michelle 1996. A Sampling of the West's Collaborative Efforts. *High*

Country News. 28 (May 13), 3 (http://www.hcn.org/1996/may13/dir/ Feature_A_sampling.html).

McCloskey, Michael 1990. Twenty Years of Change in the Environmental Movement: An Insider's View. In eds. Riley Dunlap and Ann Mertig. *American Environmentalism*. Philadelphia, PA: Taylor and Francis, 77–88.

McCloskey, Michael 1996. The Skeptic: Collaboration has Its Limits. *High Country News*. 28 (May 13), 1–3 (http://www.hcn.org/1996/may13/dir/Opinion_The_skepti.html).

McConnell, Grant 1966. *Private Power and American Democracy*. New York: Knopf.

McCoy, Charles 1995a. Catron County, N. M., Leads a Nasty Revolt Over Eco-Protection. *Wall Street Journal*. (January 3), A1+.

McCoy, Charles 1995b. The Push to Expand Property Rights Stirs Both Hopes and Fears. *Wall Street Journal*. (April 4), A1+.

McCubbins, Matthew, and Thomas Schwartz 1984. Congressional Oversight Overlooked: Police Patrols versus Fire Alarms. *American Journal of Political Science*. 28: 165–79.

McCubbins, Matthew, and Terry Sullivan. 1987. Introduction: Institutional aspects of decision processes. In eds. M. D. McCubbins and T. Sullivan *Congress: Structure and policy*. Cambridge: Cambridge University Press, 1–11.

McFarland, Andrew S. 1990. Interest Groups and Political Time: Cycles in America, ms, 35.

McFarland, Andrew S. 1993. *Cooperative Pluralism: The National Coal Policy Experiment*. Lawrence, KS: University Press of Kansas.

McGarity, Thomas O. 1992. Some Thoughts on 'Deossifying' the Rulemaking Process, *Duke Law Journal*. 41, 1385–1462.

McIntosh, David M., and Murray Weidenbaum 1995. Will Clinton Let Republicans Help Him? *Wall Street Journal*. (February 23), A14.

Meidinger, Errol 1985. On Explaining the Development of 'Emissions Trading' in U.S. Air Pollution Regulation. *Law and Policy*, 7 (October), 447–79.

Meidinger, Errol 1987. Regulatory Culture: A Theoretical Outline. *Law and Policy*, 9 (October), 355–86.

Melloan, George 1995. 'Waterworld,' Bootleg Freon and a Berlin Plot. *Wall Street Journal*. (April 3), A19.

Melnick, R. Shep 1983. *Regulation and the Courts*. Washington, D.C.: The Brookings Institution.

Milgrom, Paul, and John Roberts 1992. Bargaining Costs, Influence Costs, and the Organization of Economic Activity. In eds. J. A. Alt and K. A. Shepsle. *Perspectives on Positive Political Economy*. Cambridge: Cambridge University Press, 57–89.

Miller, Gary J. 1992. *Managerial Dilemmas: The Political Economy of Hierarchy*. Cambridge: Cambridge University Press.

Miller, Gary, and Terry Moe 1986. The Positive Theory of Hierarchies. ed. Wiesberg. *Political Science: The Science of Politics*. New York: Agathon Press, 167–98.

Mintz, Bill 1994. Yorktown: A Revolution in Regulation? *Houston Chronicle*. (March 13), F1+.

Mitchell, Robert C. 1991. From Conservation to Environmental Movement: The Development of the Modern Environmental Lobbies. In ed. M. J. Lacey. *Government and Environmental Politics.* Baltimore and London: The Johns Hopkins University Press, 81–114.

Moe, Ronald 1994. The Reinventing Government Exercise: Misinterpreting the Problem, Misjudging the Consequences. *Public Administration Review.* 54 (March–April), 111–122.

Moe, Terry M. 1984. The New Economics of Organization. *American Journal of Political Science.* 28 (November), 739–77.

Moe, Terry M. 1985. The Politicized Presidency. In eds. J. E. Chubb and E. Peterson. *New Directions in American Politics.* Washington, D.C.: Congressional Quarterly Press, 235–71.

Moe, Terry M. 1987a. An Assessment of the Positive Theory of Congressional Dominance, *Legislative Studies Quarterly,* 12 (November), 475–519.

Moe, Terry M. 1987b. Political Control and Professional Autonomy: The Institutional Politics of the NLRB, ms.

Moe, Terry M. 1989. The Politics of Bureaucratic Structure. In eds. J. E. Chubb and E. Peterson. *Can the Government Govern?* Washington, D.C.: The Brookings Institution, 267–329.

Moe, Terry M. 1990. The Politics of Structural Choice: Toward a Theory of Public Bureaucracy. In ed. O. E. Williamson. *Organization Theory.* New York: Oxford University Press, 116–53.

Moore, Richard, and Louis Head 1993. Acknowledging the Past, Confronting the Present: Environmental Justice in the 1990s. In ed. R. Hofrichter. *Toxic Struggles.* 118–127.

Mosher, Lawrence 1981. Tough Issues, Tough Style Could Lead to a Backlash Against Watt. *National Journal.* 13 (December 5), 2144–48.

Moynihan, Patrick Daniel 1993. A Legislative Proposal: Why Not Enact a Law that Would Help Us Set Sensible Priorities? *EPA Journal.* 19 (January–March), 46–7.

Municipality of Anchorage 1992. *Paying for Federal Environmental Mandates: A Looming Crisis for Cities and Counties.* Anchorage, Alaska (September).

Nader, Ralph 1965. *Unsafe at Any Speed.* New York: Grossman Publishers.

Nagel, Jack H. 1987. *Participation.* Englewood Cliffs, N. J.: Prentice-Hall.

National Academy of Public Administration 1984. *Steps Toward a Stable Future.* Washington, D.C.

National Academy of Public Administration 1988. *Congressional Oversight of Regulatory Agencies: The Need to Strike a Balance and Focus on Performance.* Washington, D.C.

National Academy of Public Administration 1994. *The Environment Goes to Market: The Implementation of Economic Incentives in Pollution Control.* Washington, D.C.

National Academy of Public Administration 1995. *Setting Priorities, Getting Results: A New Direction for EPA.* Washington, D.C.

National Acid Precipitation Assessment Program 1991. *1990 Integrated Assessment Report.* Washington, D.C.: NAPAP.

National Advisory Council for Environmental Policy and Technology (NACEPT) 1991. *Permitting and Compliance Policy: Barriers to U.S. Environ-*

mental Technology Innovation. Report and Recommendations of the Technology Innovation and Economics Committee, Washington, D.C.: U.S. Environmental Protection Agency, Office of the Administrator (January).

National Governor's Association 1989. *Funding Environmental Programs: An Examination of Alternatives*. Natural Resources Policy Studies Unit. Washington, D.C.

National Performance Review 1993. *From Red Tape to Results: Creating a Government that Works Better and Costs Less*. Washington, D.C.: U.S. Government Printing Office.

National Research Council, National Academy of Sciences 1981. *Atmosphere-Biosphere Interactions: Toward a Better Understanding of the Consequences of Fossil Fuel Combustion*. Washington, D.C.: National Academy Press.

National Research Council, National Academy of Sciences 1986. *Acid Rain: Long Term Trends*. Washington, D.C.: National Academy Press.

Natural Resources Defense Council 1995. *Trouble on Tap: Arsenic, Radioactive Radon, and Trihalomethanes in Our Drinking Water*. (with Clean Water Action and U.S. Public Interest Research group) (October), 1–62.

Neustadt, Richard E. 1960. *Presidential Power*. New York: John Wiley and Sons.

New York Times 1984. Environmental Protection Paralyzed [editorial], (November 30), A30.

New York Times 1989. Pollution-Control Business Hindered, (August 29), 1.

New York Times 1990. Cows, Bulls, and Clean Air [Mobil Oil op-ed advertisement], (December 13), A31.

New York Times 1991a. Customers and Industry to Pay Clean Air Cost [letter to the editor by executive vice president of Mobil Oil, J. L. Cooper], (January 26), 24.

New York Times 1991b. Everyone But Oil Companies is for Cleaner Gas [letter to the editor by Representative Henry Waxman], (February 6), A20.

New York Times 1991c. Cleaner Air, By Consensus [editorial], (August 27), A22.

New York Times 1992. Editorial [on Browner nomination at EPA], (December 12), A22.

Niskanen, William A. 1971. *Bureaucracy and Representative Government*. Chicago: Aldine-Atherton.

Niskanen, William A. 1991. A Reflection on Bureaucracy and Representative Government. In eds. Andre Blaise and Stephane Dion. *The Budget Maximizing Bureaucrat: Evidence and Appraisal*. Pittsburgh: University of Pittsburgh Press, 13–31.

Noah, Timothy 1993. EPA's New Smog-Control Plan to Emphasize Ethanol Mix in Gas. *Wall Street Journal*. (December 15), A3.

Noah, Timothy 1994. Environmentalists Hope 'Greener' Senate GOP Can Counter Antiregulatory Onslaught in House. *Wall Street Journal*. (December 22), A24.

Noah, Timothy 1995a. GOP Pushes Bill that Lets Regulated Industries Review Regulations, to the Chagrin of Critics. *Wall Street Journal*. (February 9), A16.

Noah, Timothy 1995b. GOP's Rep. DeLay Is Working in Every Corner to Exterminate Regulations that Bug Business. *Wall Street Journal*. (March 6), A16.

Noah, Timothy 1995c. GOP's Rollback of the Green Agenda is Stalled By a

Public Seeing Red Over Proposed Changes. *Wall Street Journal*. (December 26), A8.

Noah, Timothy 1996. Both Parties Paint Themselves Green, but Trend of Looser Environmental Rules is Seen Continuing. *Wall Street Journal*. (September 9), A20.

Noah, Timothy, and Scott Kilman 1995. Ethanol Industry Dealt a Blow as Court Blocks EPA Gasoline Order. *Wall Street Journal*. (May 1), B8.

Noah, Timothy, and Phil Kuntz 1995. Gingrich Blasts Environmental Policies of the Past. *Wall Street Journal*. (February 17), B5.

Noll, Roger G., and Bruce M. Owen. eds. 1983. *The Political Economy of Deregulation: Interest Groups in the Regulatory Process*. Washington, D.C.: American Enterprise Institute.

North, Douglass C. 1990. *Institutions, Institutional Change, and Economic Performance*. Cambridge: Cambridge University Press.

North, Douglass C., and Barry R. Weingast 1989. Constitutions and Commitment: The Evolution of Institutions Governing Public Choice in 17th Century England, St. Louis: Washington University Political Economy Working Paper 29.

O'Toole, Laurence J., Jr. 1994. Implementing Public Innovations in Network Settings, paper presented at the conference on Network Analysis and Innovation in Public Programs, University of Wisconsin-Madison (September 30–October 1).

Office of Technology Assessment 1989a. *Catching Our Breath, Next Steps for Reducing Urban Ozone*. Washington, D.C.: Government Printing Office.

Office of Technology Assessment 1989b. *An Analysis of Selected Mobile Source Provisions in H. R. 3030 and H. R. 2323*. Washington, D.C.: Government Printing Office (September 21).

Oleszek, Walter J. 1989. *Congressional Procedures and the Policy Process*. 3rd ed., Washington, D.C.: Congressional Quarterly Press.

Oliphant, Thomas 1994. A New Approach to the Environment, *Boston Globe*, (July 26), 13.

Olson, Mancur 1965. *The Logic of Collective Action*. Cambridge, Mass.: Harvard University Press.

Oren, Craig N. 1991. The Clean Air Act of 1990: A Bridge to the Future? *Environmental Law*, 21 (Pt. II), 1817–1841.

Osborne, David, and Ted Gaebler 1993. *Reinventing Government*. New York: Penguin Books.

Pashigian, Peter B. 1984. The Effect of Environmental Regulation on Optimal Plant Size and Factor Shares. *Journal of Law and Economics*, 27 (April), 1–24.

Pashigian, Peter B. 1985. Environmental Regulation: Whose Self Interests Are Being Protected, *Economic Inquiry*, (October), 551–84.

Pasztor, Andrew 1983. Reagan Goal of Easing Environmental Laws is Largely Unattained. *Wall Street Journal*. (February 18), 1, 15.

Pederson, William F., Jr. 1981. Why the Clean Air Act Works Badly, *University of Pennsylvania Law Review*. 129 (May), 1059–1109.

Peltzman, Samuel 1976. Toward a More General Theory of Regulation. *Journal of Law and Economics*. 19, 211–40.

Percival, Robert V. 1991. Checks Without Balance: Executive Office Oversight of the Environmental Protection Agency. *Law and Contemporary Problems.* 54 (Autumn), 127–204.

Perritt, Henry H., Jr., 1986. Negotiated Rulemaking in Practice. *Journal of Policy Analysis and Management,* 5: 482–495.

Phillips, Howard K. 1994. *The Death of Common Sense.* New York: Random House.

Piore, Michael J., and Charles F. Sabel 1984. *The Second Industrial Divide.* New York: Basic Books.

Polkinghorn, Brian. 1995. The influence of regulatory negotiations on the U.S. Environmental Protection Agency as an Institution. Presented at the Annual Meeting of the Midwest Political Science Association. Chicago, Illinois (April 6–8).

Pollution Prevention Partnership, A Colorado Private-Public Partnership 1993. Progress Report, (February), 20.

Polsby, Nelson W. 1968. The Institutionalization of the U.S. House of Representatives. *American Political Science Review.* 62, 148–68.

Porter, Michael E. 1993. Keynote Address: The Clean Air Marketplace 1993. In *The Clean Air Marketplace 1993: Conference Proceedings.* Washington, D.C.: U.S. Environmental Protection Agency (September 8–9), 31–47.

Portney, Paul R. 1990. Air Pollution Policy. In ed. R. Portney. *Public Policies for Environmental Protection.* Washington, D.C.: Resources for the Future, 27–96.

Pritzker, David M. 1990. Working Together for Better Regulations. *Natural Resources and Environment.* 5: 29–31.

Pritzker, David M., and Deborah Dalton. eds. 1990. *Negotiated Rulemaking Sourcebook.* Administrative Conference of the United States. Washington, D.C.: Government Printing Office.

Project Summary 1994. Pollution Prevention Pilot Project [4-P Project]. (November 15), 4.

Pytte, Alyson 1990a. Clean Air Conferees Agree on Motor Vehicles, Fuels. *Congressional Quarterly Weekly Report.* 48 (October 13), 3407–09.

Pytte, Alyson 1990b. A Decade's Acrimony Lifted in the Glow of Clean Air. *Congressional Quarterly Weekly Report.* 48 (October 27), 3587–92.

Rabe, Barry G. 1986. *Fragmentation and Integration in State Environmental Management.* Washington, D.C.: The Conservation Foundation.

Rabe, Barry G. 1988. The Politics of Environmental Dispute Resolution. *Policy Studies Journal.* 16 (Spring), 585–601.

Rabe, Barry G. 1994. *Beyond NIMBY: Hazardous Waste Siting in Canada and the United States.* Washington, D.C.: The Brookings Institution.

Ray, Dixy Lee (with Lou Guzzo) 1990. *Trashing the Planet: How Science Can Help Us Deal with Acid Rain, Depletion of the Ozone, and Nuclear Waste.* Washington, D.C.: Regnery Gateway.

Redford, Emmette S. 1969. *Democracy in the Administrative State.* New York: Oxford University Press.

Rees, Matthew 1993. The Mandate Millstone. *Wall Street Journal.* (August 18), A12.

Reich, Robert 1990. Policy Making in a Democracy. In ed. R. Reich. *The Power of Public Ideas,* Cambridge Mass.: Harvard University Press, 123–156.

Reinhold, Robert 1992. Environmental Truce Clears Smoke in Rice Fields. *The New York Times.* (Dec. 12), I8.

Reynolds, Ed 1990. The Acid Test on Acid Rain. *Environmental Protection.* (October), 36–41.

Ringquist, Evan J. 1993. *Environmental Protection at the State Level: Politics and Progress in Controlling Pollution.* Armonk, N.Y.: Sharpe.

Ringquist, Evan, Jeff Worsham and Marc Allen Eisner. 1994. Double agents—who is working for whom? Building a realistically grounded theory of political control of the bureaucracy. Presented at the 1994 meeting of the Midwest Political Science Association, Chicago, IL (April 14–16).

Ripley, Randall B., and Grace A. Franklin 1984. *Congress, the Bureaucracy, and Public Policy.* 3rd. ed., Homewood, Ill.: The Dorsey Press.

Rogers, David 1995a. Congress and White House Agree to Buy Time, But Gingrich Says Budget Pact Must Come Soon. *Wall Street Journal.* (October 2), A14.

Rogers, David 1995b. Waivers to House's EPA Funding Bill are Dropped in Rebuff to GOP Leaders. *Wall Street Journal.* (November 3), A16.

Rogers, David, and Christopher Georges 1995. House Derails Spending Bill in Blow to GOP. *Wall Street Journal.* (November 30), A3.

Rohde, David W. 1991. *Parties and Leaders in the Postreform House.* Chicago and London: The University of Chicago Press.

Rosenbaum, David E. 1995. Defying Odds, New Yorker Saves Milk Subsidies. *New York Times.* (December 6), A1+.

Rosenbaum, Walter 1976. The Paradoxes of Public Participation, *Administration and Society,* 8 (November), 335–83.

Rosenbaum, Walter A. 1989. The Bureaucracy and Environmental Policy. In ed. J. Lester. *Environmental Politics and Policy: Theory and Evidence.* Durham and London: Duke University Press, 212–37.

Rothschild, Edwin S. 1990. The Knock on High Octane Gasoline. *Washington Post.* (February 18), B3.

Rourke, Francis E. 1984. *Bureaucracy, Politics, and Public Policy.* 3rd ed., New York: Harper Collins Publishers.

Rubin, Alissa J. 1995. GOP Leaders Ready to Deal on Troubled Tax-Cuts Bill. *Congressional Quarterly Weekly Report.* 53 (April 1), 915–16.

Ruckelshaus, William 1985. Environmental Protection: A Brief History of the Environmental Movement in America and the Implications Abroad, *Environmental Law,* 15, 455–63.

Salamon, Lester M. ed. 1989. *Beyond Privatization: The Tools of Government Action.* Washington, D.C.: The Urban Institute Press.

Salant, Jonathan D. 1995. Senate Altering Its Course in Favor of Contract [With] America. *Congressional Quarterly Weekly Report.* 53 (April 29), 1151–54.

Sale, Kirkpatrick 1986. The Forest for the Trees: Can Today's Environmentalists Tell the Difference? *Mother Jones.* (November), 25–33.

Salisbury, Robert H., and Kenneth A. Shepsle 1981. U.S. Congressmen as Enterprise. *Legislative Studies Quarterly,* 6 (November), 559–76.

Schattschneider, Elmer E. 1960. The semisovereign people: A realist's view of democracy in America. New York: Holt, Rinehart and Winston.

Schelling, Thomas 1960. *The Strategy of Conflict*. Cambridge, Mass.: Harvard University Press.

Schlozman, Kay Lehman, and John Tierney 1986. *Organized Interests and American Democracy*. New York: Harper and Row.

Schmitt, Ronald E. 1994. The Amoco/EPA Yorktown Experience and Regulating the Right Thing. *Natural Resources and the Environment*. (Summer), 11–13+.

Schneider, Keith 1992a. New Breed of Ecologist to Lead EPA, *The New York Times*. (December 17), B20.

Schneider, Keith 1992b. Bush Offers Plan for Wider Use of Ethanol in Fuel. *New York Times*. (October 2), A15.

Schneider, Keith 1992c. Courthouse is a Citadel No Longer: U.S. Judges Curb Environmentalists. *New York Times*. (March 23), B7.

Schneider, Keith 1993a. Clinton is Seeking to Increase Role for Ethanol in Gasoline. *New York Times*. (December 15), A25.

Schneider, Keith 1993b. How a Rebellion Over Environmental Rules Grew from a Patch of Weeds. *New York Times*. (March 24), A1.

Schneider, Stephen H. 1989. *Global Warming: Are We Entering the Greenhouse Century*? New York: Vintage Books.

Schoenbrod, David 1983. Goals Statutes or Rules Statutes: The Case of the Clean Air Act. *UCLA Law Review*. 30: 740–828.

Schoenbrod, David 1993. *Power Without Responsibility: How Congress Abuses the People Through Delegation*. New Haven, CT: Yale University Press.

Scholz, John T. 1984. Cooperation, Deterrence, and the Ecology of Regulatory Enforcement. *Law and Society Review*. 18, 601–46.

Scholz, John T. 1991. Cooperative Regulatory Enforcement and the Politics of Administrative Effectiveness. *American Political Science Review*. 85, 115–36.

Schwartz, Bernard 1994. Some Crucial Issues in Administrative Law. In eds. D. H. Rosenbloom and R. D. Schwartz. *Handbook of Regulation and Administrative Law*. New York: Marcel Dekker, 207–222.

Selznick, Philip 1957. *Leadership in Administration: A Sociological Interpretation*. New York: Harper and Row.

Sen, Amartya K. 1976. Liberty, Unanimity, and Rights. *Economica*. 43 (August), 217–45.

Shabecoff, Philip 1989. EPA Nominee Says He Will Urge Law to Cut Acid Rain, *The New York Times*. (Feb. 1), A1+.

Sheets, K. R., and R. A. Taylor 1983. The EPA: An Agency Under Siege, *U.S. News and World Report*, (February 18), 24–6.

Shepsle, Kenneth A. 1989. The Changing Textbook Congress. eds. J. E. Chubb and E. Peterson. *Can the Government Govern*? Washington, D.C.: The Brookings Institution, 238–66.

Sinclair, Barbara 1983. *Majority Leadership in the U.S. House*. Baltimore and London: The Johns Hopkins University Press.

Sinclair, Barbara 1992. The Emergence of Strong Leadership in the 1980s House of Representatives. *Journal of Politics*. 54 (August), 657–84.

Sirianni, Carmen, and Lewis Friedland 1995. Social Capital and Civic Innovation: Learning and Capacity Building from the 1960s to the 1990s, paper presented at the annual American Sociological Association Conference (August 20), Washington, D.C., 29

Sirianni, Carmen, and Lewis Friedland. Forthcoming. *Participatory Democracy in America*. Cambridge: Cambridge University Press.

Smart, Bruce. ed. 1992. *Beyond Compliance: A New Industry View of the Environment*. Washington, D.C.: World Resources Institute.

Smith, Lawrence R. 1993. *Reformulated Gasolines—How Do Their Emissions Measure Up?* (September), San Antonio, TX: Southwest Research Institute, 7.

Smith, Steven S. 1989. *Call to Order: Floor Politics in the House and Senate*. Washington, D.C.: The Brookings Institution.

Solomon, Caleb 1993. What Really Pollutes? Study of a Refinery Proves an Eye-Opener. *Wall Street Journal*. (March 29), 1.

South Coast Air Quality Management District 1990. *Draft Air Quality Management Plan*.

Sparrow, Malcolm K. 1994. *Imposing Duties: Government's Changing Approach to Compliance*. Westport, CT: Praeger Publishers.

Stanfield, Rochelle 1984. Ruckelshaus Casts EPA as 'Gorilla' in States' Enforcement Closet. *National Journal*. (May 25), 1034–38.

Starr, Kenneth W. 1986. Judicial Review in the Post-Chevron Era. *Yale Journal of Regulation*. 3, 283–99.

Stavins, Robert N. 1991. *Project 88—Round II: Incentives for Action: Designing Market-Based Environmental Strategies*. Washington, D.C.: Project 88.

Stevens, William K. 1992. Novel Strategy Puts People at Heart of Texas Preserve. *The New York Times*. (March 31), C1+.

Stevens, William K. 1995. GOP Seeks to Delay Ban on Chemical Harming Ozone. *The New York Times*. (September 21), A13.

Stewart, Michael. 1983. *The age of interdependence: Economic policy in a shrinking world*. Cambridge, Mass.: MIT Press.

Stewart, Richard B. 1981. Regulation, Administration, and Administrative Law: A Conceptual Framework. *California Law Review*. 69 (Sept.), 1259–1377.

Stewart, Richard B. 1988. Controlling Environmental Risks Through Economic Incentives. *Columbia Journal of Environmental Law*. 13: 153–70.

Stigler, George 1971. The Theory of Economic Regulation. *The Bell Journal of Economics*. 2, 3–21.

Strock, James M., Paul E. Helliker, and David W. Chan 1991. Integrated Pollution Prevention: Cal-EPA's Perspective. *Environmental Law*. 22 (Part 1), 311–31.

Suskind, Ron 1993. Health-Care Reform May Seem Like a Bitter Pill to Localities Sick of Unfunded Mandates. *Wall Street Journal*. (December 21), A16.

Susskind, Lawrence, and Gerald McMahon 1985. The Theory and Practice of Negotiated Rulemaking. *Yale Journal of Regulation*. 3, 133–165.

Susskind, Lawrence, and Jeffrey Cruickshank 1987. *Breaking the Impasse: Consensual Approaches to Resolving Public Disputes*. New York: Basic Books.

Symonds, William 1982. Washington in the Grip of the Green Giant. *Fortune*. (October 4), 137–42.

Terry, Larry D. 1995. *Leadership of Public Bureaucracies: The Administrator as Conservator*. Thousand Oaks, CA: SAGE Publications.

Thomas, Lee M. 1987. The Successful Use of Regulatory Negotiation by EPA. *Administrative Law News*. 13 (Fall), 1–4.

Thompson, Victor A. 1969. *Bureaucracy and innovation*. University, Ala.: University of Alabama Press.

Tietenberg, Thomas H. 1985. *Emissions Trading: An Exercise in Reforming Pollution Policy*. Washington, D.C.: Resources for the Future.

Toner, Robin 1995. Senate Approves Welfare Plan that Would End Aid Guarantee. *New York Times*. (September 20), A1.

Trojanowicz, Robert, and Bonnie Bucqueroux. 1994. What community policing is and is not. In R. Trojanowicz and Bonnie Bucqueroux. *Community policing: How to get started*. Cincinnati, Ohio: Anderson Publishing Co. 3–39.

Truman, David B. 1951. *The Governmental Process: Political Interests and Public Opinion*. New York: Alfred A. Knopf.

Tsebelis, George 1989. The Abuse of Probability in Political Analysis: The Robinson Crusoe Fallacy. *American Political Science Review*. 83, 77–92.

Tsebelis, George 1990. *Nested Games: Rational Choice in Comparative Politics*. Berkeley: University of California Press.

U.S. Bureau of the Census 1982–83a. 90. GNP in Current and Constant 1972 Dollars: 1960 to 1981, in *Statistical Abstract of the United States*. 103rd ed., Washington, D.C., 419.

U.S. Bureau of the Census 1982–83b. 71. U.S. International Transactions: 1960 to 1981, in *Statistical Abstract of the United States*. 103rd ed., Washington, D.C., 390.

U.S. Bureau of the Census 1995a. 373. Gross National Product, by Country: 1985 to 1993, in *Statistical Abstract of the United States*. 115th ed., Washington, D.C., 855.

U.S. Bureau of the Census 1995b. 319. U.S. International Transactions, by Type of Transaction: 1980 to 1994, in *Statistical Abstract of the United States*. 115th ed., Washington, D.C., 802.

U.S. Congress. House of Representatives 1989. Clean Air Act Amendments, Part I, Hearings Before the Subcommittee on Health and the Environment of the House Committee on Energy and Commerce, 101st Congress, 1st Session (May 23).

U.S. Congress. House of Representatives 1991. Clean Air Act Implementation, Part I, Hearings Before the Subcommittee on Health and the Environment of the Committee on Energy and Commerce, 102nd Congress, 1st Session (March–July).

U.S. Congress. House of Representatives 1991. Oversight of Implementation of the Clean Air Act Amendments of 1990, Hearings Before the Subcommittee on Oversight and Investigations of the Committee on Energy and Commerce, 102nd Congress, 1st Session (November 12 and 14).

U.S. Congress. House of Representatives 1991–1992. Clean Air Act Implementation, Part II, Hearings Before the Subcommittee on Health and the Environment of the Committee on Energy and Commerce, 102nd Congress, 1st and 2nd Session (November, 1991–February, 1992).

U.S. Congress. House of Representatives 1996. An Assessment of EPA's Reinvention, a report by the Majority Staff of the Committee on Transportation and Infrastructure (September).

U.S. Congress. Senate 1980. Regulatory Negotiation, Joint Hearings Before the Senate Select Committee on Small Business and the Subcommittee on Oversight of Government Management of the Senate Committee on Governmental Affairs, 96th Congress, 2nd Session.

U.S. Congress. Senate 1989. *Clean Air Act Amendments of 1990*. Senate Report 28, Committee on Environment and Public Works, 101st Congress, 1st Session (December 20).

U.S. Congress. Senate 1992. Issues Affecting the Refining Sector of the Petroleum Industry, Hearings Before the Committee on Energy and Natural Resources, 102nd Congress, 2nd Session (May 19 and 28, 1992).

U.S. Congress. Senate 1993. House Debate on H. R. 3030 [including text of H. R. 399], May 23, 1990, A Legislative History of the Clean Air Act Amendments of 1990, 103rd Congress, 1st Session, S. Report. 103–38, Volume II, 2667–89.

U.S. Congress. Senate 1993. Implementation of the Acid Rain Provisions of the Clean Air Act Amendments of 1990, Hearings Before the Subcommittee on Clean Air and Nuclear Regulation of the Committee on Environment and Public Works, 103rd Congress, 1st Session (October 21).

U.S. Congress. Senate 1993. Taking Stock of Environmental Problems, Part I, Hearings before the Committee on Environment and Public Works, 103rd Congress, 1st Session (March 24, 31, and July 16.

U.S. Congress. Senate 1993. *Three Years Later: Report Card on the 1990 Clean Air Act Amendments*. A Report prepared by the majority and minority staffs of the U.S. Senate Committee on Environment and Public Works (November 15).

U.S. Environmental Protection Agency 1987. An Assessment of EPA's Negotiated Rulemaking Activities, Program Evaluation Division, Office of Management Systems and Evaluation, Office of Policy, Planning, and Evaluation (December), 13.

U.S. Environmental Protection Agency 1987b. *Unfinished Business: A Comparative Assessment of Environmental Problems*. Office of Policy, Planning and Evaluation (February).

U.S. Environmental Protection Agency 1988. *Potential Effects of Global Climate Change on the United States: Draft Report to Congress, Vols. I and II*. Office of Policy, Planning and Evaluation (October).

U.S. Environmental Protection Agency 1989a. *Memorandum on Summary and Recommendations Resulting from the Analysis of EDF's Acid Rain Proposal*. Office of Policy, Planning and Evaluation (June 2).

U.S. Environmental Protection Agency 1989b. *Policy Options for Stabilizing Global Climate: Draft Report to Congress, Vols. I and II*. Office of Policy, Planning and Evaluation (February).

U.S. Environmental Protection Agency 1990a. *Ozone Nonattainment Analysis: A Comparison of Bills*. Washington, D.C.: Government Printing Office.

U.S. Environmental Protection Agency 1990b. *Memorandum on Cost and Cost-Effectiveness Analysis of Selected Mobile Source Controls in the Proposed South Coast Federal Implementation Plan.* (August 22).

U.S. Environmental Protection Agency 1990c. *Environmental Investments: The Cost of a Clean Environment.* Office of Regulatory Management and Evaluation, Office of Policy, Planning, and Evaluation (December).

U.S. Environmental Protection Agency 1990d. *Public-Private Partnership Case Studies: Profiles of Success in Providing Environmental Services.* Office of Administration and Resources Management (September).

U.S. Environmental Protection Agency 1990e. *Reducing Risk: Setting Priorities and Strategies for Environmental Protection.* Science Advisory Board (September).

U.S. Environmental Protection Agency 1991a. Economic Incentives in Pending Environmental Legislation: 102nd Congress, prepared by the Regulatory Innovations Staff, Office of Policy, Planning, and Evaluation (November 19).

U.S. Environmental Protection Agency 1991b. Agreement in Principle and Outline of Supplemental Proposed Rules and Guidances for Reformulated Gasoline, Antidumping and Oxygenated Gasoline, (August 16), 1–9.

U.S. Environmental Protection Agency 1991c. Proposed Regulations for Reformulated Gas and Oxygenated Fuels, Clean Fuels Public Hearing, (July 15), [Air Docket A-91-02, Part IV-F-1].

U.S. Environmental Protection Agency 1991d. *National Air Pollutant Emission Estimates, 1940–1990.* Washington, D.C.

U.S. Environmental Protection Agency 1991e. *National Air Quality and Emissions Trends Report, 1990.* Washington, D.C.

U.S. Environmental Protection Agency 1992. *Memorandum on Applicability of One-Psi Ethanol Waiver Under Section 211(h) of the Clean Air Act to Reformulated Gasoline.* Office of General Council (November 17), 1–16.

U.S. Environmental Protection Agency 1993a. Economic Incentives in Environmental Bills Introduced in the 102nd Congress, prepared by the Regulatory Innovations Staff, Office of Policy, Planning, and Evaluation (February).

U.S. Environmental Protection Agency 1993b. *The Clean Air Marketplace 1993: Conference Proceedings.* Washington, D.C. (September 8–9).

U.S. Environmental Protection Agency 1993c. *State Program Costs for Implementing the Federal Clean Water Act.* Prepared by the Office of Water (December 6).

U.S. Environmental Protection Agency 1994a. The Common Sense Initiative: A New Generation of Environmental Protection, *EPA Insight Policy Paper,* (August), 4 [EPA 175-N-94-003].

U.S. Environmental Protection Agency 1994b. *1994 Update: Implementing the Clean Air Act: EPA Speaks.* Washington, D.C.: American Bar Association (February 10).

Udall, Stewart 1963. *The Quiet Crisis.* New York: Holt, Rinehart and Winston.

Vig, Norman J., and Michael E. Kraft 1990. Environmental Policy from the Seventies to the Nineties: Continuity and Change. In eds. Norman J. Vig and Michael E. Kraft. *Environmental Policy in the 1990s: Toward a New Agenda*. Washington, D.C.: Congressional Quarterly Press, 3–32.

Vogel, David 1986. *National Styles of Regulation: Environmental Policy in Great Britain and the United States*. Ithaca and London: Cornell University Press.

Vogel, David 1989. *Fluctuating Fortunes: The Political Power of Business in America*. New York: Basic Books.

Wald, Matthew 1990. Gasohol May Cut Carbon Monoxide But Raise Smog, Study Asserts. *New York Times*. (May 9), A1.

Wald, Matthew 1991. U.S. Agencies Use Negotiations to Pre-Empt Lawsuits Over Rules. *New York Times*. (September 23), A1.

Wald, Matthew 1992. Reformulated Gasoline, Ethanol, and Smog. *New York Times*. (August 3), D3.

Waldo, Dwight 1948. *The Administrative State*. New York: Ronald Publishing.

Walker, Jack 1983. The Origin and Maintenance of Interest Groups in America. *American Political Science Review*. 77 (June), 390–406.

Walsh, Michael 1990. Global Trends in Motor Vehicle Use and Emissions, *Annual Review of Energy*, 15:210–223.

Waterman, Richard W. 1989. *Presidential Influence and the Administrative State*. Knoxville, TN: The University of Tennessee Press.

Waxman, Henry A. 1991. An Overview of the Clean Air Act Amendments of 1990. *Environmental Law*. 21 (Pt. II), 1721–1816.

Waxman, Henry, Gregory Wetstone, and Philip Barnett 1991. Cars, Fuels, and Clean Air: A Review of Title II of the Clean Air Act Amendments of 1990, *Environmental Law*, 21 (Part II), 1947–2019.

Weber, Edward 1993. From Conflict to Collaboration: The Transformation of American Pollution Control Politics, presented at the Annual Meeting of the American Political Science Association, Washington, D.C. (September 2–5).

Weidenbaum, Murray 1978. The Second Managerial Revolution: The Shift of Economic Decision-Making from Business to Government. In ed. Walter Goldstein. *Planning, Politics, and the Public Interest*. New York: Columbia University Press.

Weingast, Barry R. 1984. The Congressional-Bureaucratic System: A Principal Agent Perspective (with applications to the SEC), *Public Choice* 44, 147–91.

Weingast, Barry R., and William J. Marshall 1988. The Industrial Organization of Congress: or, Why Legislatures, Like Firms, Are Not Organized Like Markets. *Journal of Political Economy*, 96: 132–63.

Weisskopf, Michael 1988. Professional Environmentalist Known as 'the Great Includer.' *Washington Post*. (December 23), A4.

Weisskopf, Michael 1989a. Under EPA, A Regulatory Breakdown. *Washington Post*. (June 4), A1+.

Weisskopf, Michael 1989b. A Changed Equation on Pollution. *Washington Post*. (June 7), A1+.

Weisskopf, Michael 1989c. Key Provision of Bush Clean Air Bill Under Siege. *Washington Post*. (October 10), A4.

Weisskopf, Michael 1989d. House Panel Votes to Weaken Clean Air Bill. *Washington Post.* (October 12), A1+.

Weisskopf, Michael 1990a. Clean Air Power: EPA's Man With a Mission. *Washington Post.* (December 7), A21.

Weisskopf, Michael 1990b. From Fringe to Political Mainstream. *Washington Post.* (April 19), A1+.

Wenner, Lettie M. 1982. *The Environmental Decade in Court.* Bloomington, Ind.: University of Indiana Press.

Wenner, Lettie M. 1990. Environmental Policy in the Courts. In eds. N. J. Vig and M. E. Kraft. *Environmental Policy in the 1990s.* Washington, D.C.: Congressional Quarterly Press, 189–210.

Western, Samuel 1995. After 17 Years, Property Rights Finally Win in Wyoming. *Wall Street Journal.* (July 19), A13.

White, Joseph B. 1993. EPA Extends Olive Branches to Auto Makers. *Wall Street Journal.* (March 23), A3.

White, Robert M. 1990. The Great Climate Debate. *Scientific American.* 263, (July), 36–43.

Whiteman, Lily 1992. Trades to Remember: The Lead Phasedown. *EPA Journal.* 18 (May/June), 38–9.

Wildavsky, Aaron 1979. *Speaking Truth to Power: The Art and Craft of Policy Analysis.* Boston, Mass.: Little, Brown and Company.

Wildavsky, Aaron. ed. 1994. *But Is It True?* Cambridge, Mass.: Harvard University Press.

Wilkinson, Charles F. 1992. *Crossing the Next Meridian: Land, Water, and the Future of the West.* Washington, D.C.: Island Press.

Williams, Florence 1993. The Compensation Game. *Wilderness.* (Fall), 29–33.

Williamson, Oliver E. 1975. *Markets and Hierarchies: A Study in the Economics of Internal Organization.* New York: Free Press.

Williamson, Oliver E. 1985. *The Economic Institutions of Capitalism: Firms, Markets, Relational Contracting.* New York: Free Press.

Williamson, Oliver E., and William Ouchi 1981. The Markets and Hierarchies Perspective: Origins, Implications, Prospects. In eds. Vade Ven and Joyce. *Assessing Organization Design and Performance.* New York: Wiley.

Wilson, Graham K. 1981. *Interest Groups in the United States.* Oxford: Clarendon Press.

Wilson, Graham K. 1982. Why Is There No Corporatism in the United States? In eds. Gerhard Lehmbruch and Philippe Schmitter. *Patterns of Corporatist Policy-Making.* London: Sage Publications, 219–236.

Wilson, Graham K. 1985. *The Politics of Safety and Health.* Oxford: Clarendon Press.

Wilson, James Q. 1973. *Political Organizations.* New York: Basic Books.

Wilson, James Q. 1980. The Politics of Regulation. In ed. J. Q. Wilson. *The Politics of Regulation.* New York: Basic Books, 357–395.

Wilson, James Q. 1989. *Bureaucracy: What Government Agencies Do and Why They Do It.* New York: Basic Books.

Wilson, Woodrow 1887. The Study of Administration. Reprinted in eds. J. M.

Shafritz and A. C. Hyde. *Classics of Public Administration.* (1978) Oak Park, IL: Moore, 1–17.

Wood, B. Dan 1990. Does Politics Make a Difference at the EEOC? *American Journal of Political Science.* 34, 503–30.

Wood, B. Dan, and Richard W. Waterman 1991. The dynamics of political control of the bureaucracy. *American Political Science Review.* 85, 801–28.

Yandle, Bruce 1989. *The Political Limits of Environmental Regulation.* New York: Quorum Books.

Yandle, Bruce. ed. 1995. *Land Rights: The 1990s' Property Rights Rebellion.* Lanham, MD: Rowman and Littlefield.

Name/Organization Index

Subject Index